# THE GREEK ISLANDS

# ⊙ Walking Eye App

## YOUR FREE DESTINATION CONTENT AND EBOOK AVAILABLE THROUGH THE WALKING EYE APP

Your guide now includes a free eBook and destination content for your chosen destination, all for the same great price as before. Simply download the Walking Eye App from the App Store or Google Play to access your free eBook and destination content.

## HOW THE WALKING EYE APP WORKS

Through the Walking Eye App, you can purchase a range of eBooks and destination content. However, when you buy this book, you can download the corresponding eBook and destination content for free. Just see below in the grey panels where to find your free content and then scan the QR code at the bottom of this page.

**Destinations:** Download your corresponding essential destination content from here, featuring recommended sights and attractions, restaurants, hotels and an A–Z of practical information, all for free. Other destinations are available for purchase.

**Ships:** Interested in ship reviews? Find independent reviews of river and ocean ships in this section, all available for purchase.

**eBooks:** You can download your free accompanying digital version of this guide here. You will also find a whole range of other eBooks, all available for purchase.

**Free access to travel-related blog articles** about different destinations, updated on a daily basis.

## HOW THE DESTINATION CONTENT WORKS

Each destination includes a short introduction, an A–Z of practical information and recommended points of interest, split into 4 different categories:
• Highlights
• Accommodation
• Eating out
• What to do

You can view the location of every point of interest and save it by adding it to your Favourites. In the 'Around Me' section you can view all the points of interest within 5km.

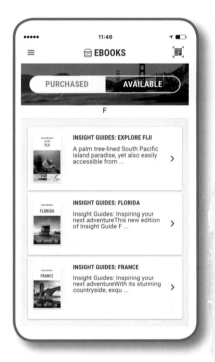

## HOW THE EBOOKS WORK

The eBooks are provided in EPUB file format. Please note that you will need an eBook reader installed on your device to open the file. Many devices come with this as standard, but you may still need to install one manually from Google Play.

The eBook content is identical to the content in the printed guide.

## HOW TO DOWNLOAD THE WALKING EYE APP

1. Download the Walking Eye App from the App Store or Google Play.
2. Open the app and select the scanning function from the main menu.
3. Scan the QR code on this page – you will then be asked a security question to verify ownership of the book.
4. Once this has been verified, you will see your eBook and destination content in the purchased ebook and destination sections, where you will be able to download them.

Other destination apps and eBooks are available for purchase separately or are free with the purchase of the Insight Guide book.

# CONTENTS

## Travel tips

### TRANSPORT

### A – Z

## Maps

### LEGEND
*P* Insight on
📷 Photo story

# THE BEST OF THE GREEK ISLANDS: TOP ATTRACTIONS

△ **Haniá Old Quarter.** An unusual combination of the Ottoman and Venetian distinguishes this port, a double bay with ample eating, drinking and people-watching opportunities. See page 304.

△ **Panagía Hozoviótissa Monastery.** Improbably wedged into a cliff above Amorgós's southeast coast, this monastery greatly impressed Le Corbusier on his 1911 visit. It is still the spiritual centre of the Cyclades, with a major festival held on 21 November. See page 189.

◁ **Corfu Old Town.** Eminently strollable, this town nestled between two giant fortresses is indisputably Greek – but Latinate in style with its slatted Venetian shutters, canal-tile roofs, intimate squares and celebrated arcades. See page 134.

▷ **Classical Temple of Aphaea.** The juxtaposed colonnades of this Doric temple on Aegina seem straight out of an M.C. Escher drawing; the piney hilltop site is everything you'd expect for an ancient sanctuary. See page 158.

△ **Santoríni.** Sailing into the bay of Santoríni is one of Greece's great experiences: broken pieces of an ancient volcano's rim – Santoríni and its attendant islets – trace a gigantic circle around the deeply submerged caldera, whitewashed villages clinging to the dark cliffs around. See page 195.

▽ **Agíou Ioánnou tou Theológou Monastery on Pátmos.** Founded in 1088, this labyrinthine monastery transcends the cruise-ship crowds besieging it with vivid frescoes, a rich treasury and unique architecture. See page 283.

△ **Evpalínio Órygma, Sámos.** Over 1,000 metres (1,100yds) long and now open to visit along its full length, this tunnel bored through a mountain as part of an advanced water-supply system is among the top engineering marvels of the ancient world. See page 236.

△ **Lésvos.** This island has more thermal springs than any other Greek island, thanks to its volcanic core; the Ottoman-era and domed Loutrá Géras on the eponymous gulf is the most user friendly. See page 227.

▽ **Skópelos Town.** Exquisitely preserved, it seems to exist in a 1980s time-warp, but in the best sense: old-fashioned shops, atmospheric arcades and a generous sprinkling of churches. See page 207.

△ **Ionian islands.** Flotilla-sailing between the islands is the best choice for novices; conditions are milder than in the open Aegean, but the scenery is every bit as gorgeous, and characterful anchorages are close together. See page 88.

# THE BEST OF THE GREEK ISLANDS: EDITOR'S CHOICE

*Potámi, one of Sámos's better beaches.*

## BEST MUSEUMS

**Museum of Modern Greek Art, Rhodes.** The most important collection of 20th-century Greek art outside of Athens. See page 247.

**Vathý Archaeological Museum, Sámos.** Exquisite small Archaic-era objects from the local Hera sanctuary, plus an enormous *kouros*. See page 236.

**Museum of Asian Art, Corfu.** World-class collection, embracing China, Afghanistan and all in between, assembled by three Greek diplomats. See page 135.

**Theophilos and Thériade Museums, Lésvos.** Over 50 works by 'primitive' local artist Theophilos, next door to Greece's finest modern art collection, amassed by his patron Thériade. See page 228.

**Iráklio Archaeological Museum.** Showcases the best Minoan frescoes and artefacts, impeccably reorganised and re-opened in 2016. See page 290.

**Archaeological Museum, Kálymnos.** State-of-the-art museum highlighting the island's Hellenistic and Roman past, featuring statues of Asklepios and a bronze matron in mint condition. See page 275.

*Minoan vase, Iráklio Archaeological Museum.*

## BEST FESTIVALS

See pages 60 and 58.

**Easter on Hydra.** Fishermen carry the *Epitáfios* (Bier of Christ) into the water to bless the boats and ensure calm seas, while Judas Iscariot is executed in effigy.

**15 August at Ólymbos, Kárpathos.** Exemplified by tables for communal feasting and music on *lýra*, *tsamboúna* and *laoúto*.

**St Spyridon Processions, Easter Saturday, Corfu.** The relics of the island's patron saint go walkabout in the Old Town to honour his past miracles.

**Carnival on Skýros.** Derived from pagan festivities, this features outrageously costumed revellers performing the "Goat Dance" over four weekends preceding Lent.

**Samos Young Artists Festival.** A week in August of jazz and chamber performances in the ancient amphitheatre near Pythagório.

*Easter celebrations at Kamíni, Hydra.*

## BEST LOCAL SPECIALITIES

*Marinated anchovy fillets (gávros marinátos).*

Astypálea and certain Cyclades produce the purest – dark and strongly aromatic. **Tzitzírafa, Alónissos.** Pickled wild pistachio shoots, gathered in spring – superb by themselves or in a salad. **Kalatháki féta, Límnos.** Small, drum-shaped sheep-milk cheese with telltale wire-mould marks; blissfully creamy. **Gávros marinátos, Léros.** Marinated anchovy fillets, headed and boned; an ideal oúzo or rakí partner. There's also koliós marinátos (mackerel), equally delicious. **Noúmboulo, Corfu.** Succulent smoked pork sirloin fillet. Expensive but addictive.

See pages 73 and 78. **Pickled caper greens, Nísyros.** The "national shrub" of this volcanic islet gets the vinegar treatment – leaves, thorns and all. **Genuine thyme honey.** Scrub-covered islands like Kálymnos, Foúrni,

## BEST BEACHES

**Egremní, Levkáda.** This west-coast paradise just pips two adjacent rivals for the Ionian crown. See page 144. **Pláka, Náxos.** Dune-backed and part naturist, this stretches for 5km (3 miles) towards other, wilder beaches. See page 193. **Soúda, Crete.** The most protected and scenic of many beaches near

Plakiás, fed by a palm-tree-lined stream. See page 305. **Evgátis, Límnos.** Stream-fed fine blonde sand framed by volcanic pinnacles, and with Agios Evstrátios islet to look at. See page 225. **Velanió, Skópelos.** A superb, long, pine-backed pebble stretch, the delight of naturists. See page 208.

*Idyllic Egremní beach, Levkáda.*

*Tables with a view, Hydra.*

## BEST HIKES

**Egiáli to Hóra, Amorgós.** This five-hour traverse takes in Hozoviótissa Monastery and sweeping sea views en route. See page 189. **Northwest coast, Sámos.** A path along this verdant coast links Potámi Bay and Drakéï village via the Seïtáni beaches, still home to monk seals. See page 237. **Samariá Gorge, Crete.** The Samariá Gorge slashes through the White Mountains and its descent is an

unmissable activity on Crete. See page 307. **Kálymnos.** Bare, craggy Kálymnos has some of the best walking in the Dodecanese, with old paths linking villages and remote chapels. See page 275. **Alónissos.** This island in the Sporades offers loop-walks through Kastanórema ravine from coastal Agios Dimítrios, or around Melegákia with its country chapels. See page 209.

*Hiking on the island of Amorgós, Cyclades.*

The Knights' castle overlooks the flat-roofed houses of Líndos, on the east coast of Rhodes.

Santoríni, famous for its clifftop villages and blue-domed churches.

*The exquisite natural harbour at Líndos, on the east coast of Rhodes.*

The blue balconies and multistoried houses of Mandráki, Nísyros.

# THE GREEK ARCHIPELAGO

The Greek islands have fascinated European travellers since the Grand Tourists first passed through during the 18th century.

*Páros windmill.*

The Greek islands rank among the most alluring realms in the Mediterranean – indeed the world. Clean, cobalt-hued seas, beaches of all sizes and consistencies, the availability of a range of sophisticated water sports and up to eight reliably sunny months a year ensure a winning combination. With recent infrastructure changes and a sharpening up of the tourism "product", the vivid, rough-and-ready country that first attracted large numbers of artists, writers and the generally bohemian during the 1960s has finally come of age.

Thankfully, even with development, the Greek islands will never become a type of Switzerland-on-Aegean. Despite inducements from the EU, of which Greece has been a member since 1981, and the most recent pressures to change owing to the severe economic crisis, the islanders stubbornly insist on their right to be Greek. Modernity, as manifested by proper espresso coffee machines and bank ATMs, is often only superficial. Pride in traditions is still evident to varying degrees. This goes hand in hand with an awareness of politics and history to put to shame that in most of jaded Northern Europe.

Indeed, a healthy historical consciousness comes with the territory due to all the islands having had a turbulent past. Never powerful enough – except, briefly, Crete – to rule themselves, but too strategically sited to be ignored by adventurers en route to richer pickings, the islands were fated to suffer a dizzying succession of invaders and foreign rulers, each of whom left an indelible legacy in terms of monuments, cuisine, language and culture in general.

*Tsambíka Bay, Rhodes.*

Perhaps the biggest surprise for new visitors to the archipelago – "chief sea", the age-old term for the Greek islands – is the sheer variety of what, from the map, looks like a homogeneous portion of the Mediterranean. Ranging from the small, arid islets of the central Aegean, with their poster-cliché Cubist houses, to the fertile, forested giants, whose high mountains even carry a frosting of snow in the right season, there is no such thing as a stereotypical Greek island.

# ISLAND MENTALITY

Greece has over 60 permanently inhabited islands.
Despite their superficial similarities, each has
a distinct identity and an often unique history.

It's one of those words that psychiatrists might use to trigger an automatic response from a patient stretched on the couch. Say "island" and childhood recollections of *Robinson Crusoe* may spring to mind. Often, islands are associated with escape from a complex universe into a private, more manageable world that offers individuals control over their own destiny. Crusoe becomes comfortable in his prelapsarian paradise, and it's a surprise, when rescue is at hand, that he doesn't tell his saviours to push off.

"Greek island" would probably add some specific touches to the imagery: a cluster of dazzlingly white buildings against a shimmering sea, donkeys bearing their burdens against a backdrop of olive groves, small circles of weather-beaten fishermen bent over their nets, jolly tavernas full of *retsína, moussakás*, shattered plates and background music from *Never on Sunday* and *Zorba the Greek*. Accurate in part until the 1980s, perhaps, but any generalisation about the Greek islands – anything more ambitious than the staringly obvious – would almost certainly be wrong.

## INTER-ISLAND RELATIONS

Although islands are classified as members of one group or another, each has a strong sense of separate identity and invariably an idiosyncratic history to back it up. Often, neighbouring islands exhibit mutual resentment bordering on loathing (though islands separated by two or three intervening ones are at least neutral about each other if not actively cordial). Visitors would seldom be aware of this unless they made a point of going down to the local café and chatting to the men

*Carrrying a heavy load on Skiáthos island.*

### ⊘ ILLEGAL SUBSTANCES

The apparently tolerant attitude towards tourist behaviour in Greece does not extend to recreational drug use, and islands like Íos, Ikaría or Crete with a youth clientele or counter-cultural reputation are subject to close undercover surveillance. Although customs searches of EU arrivals are very rare, on the whole, it's wise to err on the side of extreme caution. The legal system is largely based on a presumption of guilt, with up to 18 months in remand until charges are brought, and typical sentences for even small amounts of cannabis for personal use can be two to three years. That said, the use of medical cannabis products is being seriously discussed in Greece now.

ensconced there. Conditioned by long winter nights when nothing much happens, they have developed the knack of holding forth on any subject under the sun, and a new audience is welcome. Taxi drivers and landlords can be similarly garrulous.

The reasons for fraught inter-island sentiments may be current, as in smaller islands (eg Ikaría) perceiving the inhabitants of a larger, favoured provincial neighbour (Sámos, in the case of Ikaría) as overbearing. Or they may be of long-standing bad blood that has arisen from a variety of causes: rivalry in fishing or sponge-gathering (think Karpathians' views on the rapacious Kalymnian fleets); abductions and forced marriages generations back; or participation in a long-ago rebellion against the Ottomans, at their neighbour's behest, with disastrous consequences (as happened to the Hiots, goaded by the Samians). Even a proven historical incident will be given a different spin or even disputed by neighbours. Skiathots proudly describe the burning of much of their main port in August

*Greek smile.*

## ⊘ FOREIGN OCCUPIERS

Corfu's history is a saga of occupation by foreign powers, each of whom left a mark. From the 7th century AD, the island was ruled successively by Greeks (the Byzantine Empire), Normans, Greeks (the Despotate of Epirus), Sicilian Angevins and Venetians, the latter for over 400 years. Then it was the turn of France, then Russia, Britain and Greece. The Serbian army and government-in-exile stayed peacefully here during 1916, while Italy occupied Corfu briefly in 1923 and again during World War II. After Italy capitulated in September 1943, Germany became the last foreign occupier, until their evacuation in autumn 1944.

1944 as German reprisal for persistent, patriotic resistance activities; tell that to a Skopelot and the reply might be "They have to find some excuse for why their town is so ugly!"

Almost everywhere, you will be assured that "those people" (just on or over the horizon) are untrustworthy, inhospitable or worse, that the climate is unhealthy, the houses barely fit even for animals, the water undrinkable, the beaches uncomfortable. You shouldn't take such stories or opinions too seriously (often those propounding them don't): they are great fun, and the opportunity to move between neighbouring islands in order to compare notes should be savoured. It is almost axiomatic that if two islands were to strike the curious visitor as being practically identical, those islands would necessarily be at opposite ends of the Aegean.

Apart from the natural tendency for small island communities to be staunchly independent, there is a historical basis for their individualism – an outgrowth of centuries of self-sufficiency enforced by neglect or outright abuse by overlords. Since Neolithic times, the islands have been tossed around like loose pebbles in the cultural tides that have surged to and fro through the eastern

(see box). All of them have left some kind of legacy, even if finding traces today would require more diligent research than most visitors care to conduct while on holiday. Dedicated scholars could probably assemble a jigsaw, with pieces still extant on Corfu, that would reflect each and every one of these waves.

The evidence does not necessarily consist of archaeological ruins or excavated objects. Corfu extrapolated from one small chapter of its convoluted history an abiding passion for cricket, albeit played with local variations which would

*The Temple of Lindian Athena in Líndos, Rhodes.*

Mediterranean, and none has emerged from that experience quite like any other.

## INTRUDERS

Momentous events were taking place on some of the Cyclades as early as 6500 BC, and accelerated there some three millennia later with the advent of the Bronze Age. At about the same time, settlers from the Middle Eastern coast landed with the skills which developed into the Minoan civilisation.

To look at the history of Corfu, for instance, merely from the 7th century AD, is to pick up the chronicle of invasions a long way down the line. Nevertheless, the record from that date reveals an amazing cavalcade of intruders to the island

raise the eyebrows of traditionalists in England. The same epoch bequeathed to both Corfu and its tiny neighbour Paxí a taste for *tzíntzi býra* (ginger beer) – though again, scarcely recognisable as such to an Edwardian Englishman.

Other islands received almost as much unwanted outside attention as Corfu. Piracy was a perennial problem, hence the number of collective fortifications *(kástra)* to which the island population retreated when danger threatened. The defences did not always keep determined pirates like Khair-ed-din Barbarossa out, but they did mean that the pirates had to make an effort instead of lazily helping themselves to 10 years of stored harvests or all of the eligible virgins when they happened to be cruising by.

## STEPPING STONES

Crete, Náxos, Límnos, Samothráki, Thásos, Sámos, Kós and Rhodes have the richest and most thoroughly documented sites for historically minded visitors, but on any island there is bound to be something to pick over, even if it isn't mapped. A good tip for amateur archaeologists would be to consider where, taking into account security, prevailing winds, terrain, water supply etc, they themselves would have chosen to build something – and then start looking for evidence of past peoples.

*Playing boules in Corfu Town.*

The topographical differences among the islands are worth considering. If some islands look like mountain peaks, it is because, basically, they are – much of the area now covered by the Aegean was once a solid land bridge between the Balkan peninsula and Asia Minor, which became submerged completely only at the end of the last Ice Age, leaving just the summits exposed. The seabed around the islands can drop precipitously to 3,500 metres (11,600ft) in places, for example east of Crete. Closer to Asia Minor, the sea is generally much shallower, but even here the Aegean, quiet and bather-friendly one moment, can be transformed into a lethal cauldron within the space of an hour or two.

Anyone hiring a boat on holiday should never leave port without consulting the islanders. For thousands of years, lives have depended on accurate weather predictions, and local lore handed down is often more reliable than official forecasts on meteorological websites or via other electronic media.

## WAYS AND MEANS

If the purpose of a visit to the islands is nothing more than to settle on a stretch of agreeable beach and live (relatively) cheaply, visitors should be lucky on both counts. Greece has several thousand (mostly uninhabited) islands altogether, and these, plus the mainland shores, add up to technically the longest coastline of any country in Europe. The introduction of the euro in 2002 led to stiff price hikes well beyond inflation, while numerous new taxes plus the abolition of subsidies since 2010 have pushed hotel, travel tickets and meal prices higher still. That said, the Greek islands remain – just – competitive with other European Mediterranean destinations.

The most expensive locales are Spétses, Corfu Town, Kefaloniá, Rhodes, Mýkonos, Páros and Santoríni. Whatever local businesspeople may think in private of the antics of their visitors, they tend to be stoical about them in public and continue to pocket the money. Zákynthos, Kávos on Corfu, Íos and Mália on Crete (collectively ground zero for youth boozing) and Mýkonos (a gay mecca) in particular would not have been allowed to develop under the puritanical 1967–74 dictatorship, when even topless sunbathing was discouraged. However, since the 1980s if not earlier, what bathers choose to wear or discard has been a matter of personal choice, and there is usually at least one beach on every island where nudity is tolerated, if not officially so.

The best way to enjoy the islands is to arrive with a certain attitude. By all means, begin by uncritically enjoying the vistas seared into the senses by island holiday advertisements – the white buildings set against a shimmering sea, the donkeys on a backdrop of olive groves, and so on. But delve beneath the surface and you'll find a varied people who are proud of their home island's unique culture, history and traditions.

Fishing boat and crew in Mytilíni harbour, Lésvos.

# DECISIVE DATES

**c.3000 BC**
First Bronze Age cultures in Crete and the Cyclades.

**2600–1450 BC**
Minoan civilisation flourishes on Crete until tsunami from huge volcanic eruption on ancient Thera devastates north coast. Subsequently, many Cretan palaces destroyed by fire related to civil strife.

**c.1400 BC**
Mycenaeans occupy Crete and Rhodes, establish a trading empire, devise Linear B – the first written Greek.

**12th century BC**
"Sea Peoples" from beyond the Black Sea invade islands, destroying Mycenaean civilisation but bringing Iron Age technology with them.

**1150–800 BC**
"Dark Ages": cultural and economic stagnation. Refugee Mycenaeans (known as Ionians) settle on Aegean islands and in Attica.

**c.770 BC**
Contact with Phoenicians and Egyptians spurs a revival of Greek cultural life. Phoenician alphabet adopted and adapted.

**750 BC onward**
Rise of first city-states, foremost among them Athens, Sparta and Corinth.

**546–500 BC**
Persian Empire expands to control Ionian Greek cities on Asia Minor's west coast. Under

Darius the Great, Persians conquer many Aegean islands.

**490–479 BC**
Persian invasions of Greek mainland repulsed by united Greeks led by Spartan army and Athenian navy. Ionian cities freed from Persian rule.

## CLASSICAL AND HELLENISTIC AGES

**477–465 BC**
Athens establishes Delian League comprising islands and cities in Asia Minor. Islands attempting to secede are brutally suppressed.

**454 BC**
The League's treasury is moved from Delos to Athens; the islands are now part of an Athenian Empire. "Golden Age" of Classical Athens.

**431–404 BC**
Peloponnesian War leaves Athens defeated and weakened.

**338 BC**
Greek city-states defeated by Philip II of Macedon.

**336–323BC**
Philip's son Alexander extends a transient empire up to Persia.

**323 BC**
After Alexander's death, this empire is divided between his generals. Greek islands mostly run by Egyptian Ptolemies.

## ROMANS AND BYZANTINES

**197–146 BC**
Romans defeat Macedonian Antigonids and annex Greece.

**3rd/4th centuries AD**
Christianity spreads; barbarian raids from the north.

**330**
Co-emperor Constantine declares Constantinople his capital.

*The Prince of Lilies or Priest-king Relief in the Palace of Knossós, Crete.*

**391–5**
Theodosius I outlaws paganism and Olympic Games banned. Roman Empire splits into two, Latin West and Byzantine East.

**824–961**
Arabs occupy Crete until soon-to-be Emperor Nikephoros Phokas expels them.

**1080–1386**
Sicilian Normans raid, then occupy, Corfu.

**1204**
Constantinople temporarily taken by Latins in Fourth Crusade. Venetians seize Crete, Cyclades and Ionian isles.

**1309**
Knights Hospitallers of St John occupy and fortify the Dodecanese.

**1344–1478**
Genoese assume control of north Aegean islands.

**1453**
Ottoman Turks seize Constantinople, renamed Istanbul and made capital of their empire.

**1462–1523**
Aegean islands taken over in stages by Ottoman Turks.

**1649–69**
Ottoman conquest of Crete, which the Venetians lose.

**1797–1814**
Napoleonic French, then Russians, occupy Ionian islands.

**1814–64**
British rule in Ionian islands.

# INDEPENDENCE AND AFTER

**1821–9**
Revolt against Ottomans.

**1830–32**
At peace conferences, Ottomans cede Évvia to Greeks, but keep Dodecanese, northeast Aegean and north mainland.

**1834**
Athens becomes capital of Greece, replacing Návplio.

**1864**
Ionian islands ceded to Greece.

**1898–1912**
Crete becomes an independent principality within the Ottoman Empire.

**1909–10**
Army revolts in Athens allow Eleftherios Venizelos to form new government. Venizelos intermittently PM until 1935.

**1912–13**
Balkan Wars: Greece takes Crete, northeast Aegean islands and Macedonia. Italy occupies Dodecanese.

**1917**
Greece belatedly enters World War I on Entente side.

**1919–23**
Asia Minor campaign ends in catastrophic defeat. Expulsion of Greek civilians from Turkey. Greek possession of western Thrace confirmed.

*The aftermath of an Italian air raid on Corfu Town, April 1941.*

**1940–1**
Greece repels Italian invasion and fights with Allies until invaded by Nazi Germany.

**1944**
Greece is liberated by Allies.

**1946–9**
Civil War between Greek government and Communists opposed to restoring monarchy.

**1947**
Dodecanese joined to Greece.

**1967–74**
Greece ruled by junta of right-wing colonels; king in exile.

**1974**
Colonels fall; republic declared.

**1981**
Andreas Papandreou's PASOK party forms first leftist government. Greece becomes full member of EEC (now EU).

**2004**
Centre-right New Democracy takes power; Athens hosts Olympics.

**2009–11**
George Papandreou leads PASOK to victory in 2009 elections. Greece's finances revealed as insolvent after long mismanagement. Papandreou resigns in favour of unelected technocratic government. The first of several bailout packages offered by international lenders, including the EU, at the cost of harsh austerity measures and civil unrest.

**2012**
Two inconclusive elections yield a three-party coalition mandated to negotiate better terms from Greece's creditors. Neo-fascist Golden Dawn party emerges.

**2015–17**
Leftist, anti-austerity SYRIZA party, under Alexis Tsipras, finishes first in January 2015 poll but forced into coalition with anti-EU, far-right ANEL party. Despite the SYRIZA platform, and a "no to bailouts" vote in July 2015 referendum, more ensue. Second 2015 election returns the coalition and crushes anti-bailout hardliners. Tourism up, but the economy remains flat; next elections set for 2019.

*The famous Phaistos Disc, a highlight of Iráklio's Archaeological Museum.*

# WAVES OF INVADERS

The history of Greece, and especially its islands, is inextricably linked to the sea. It is largely a chronicle of foreign conquerors and occupiers.

What distinguishes the course of Greek history from that of her Balkan neighbours is the impact of the sea. The sea diffuses cultures, transfers peoples and encourages trade – and until our own times it was invariably a swifter means of transmission than overland. Nowhere in Greece is the sea as inescapable as on the islands.

The poverty of the thin island soil has forced inhabitants to venture far afield for their livelihood. At the same time, the islands have been vulnerable to foreign incursions, whether by Arab pirates, Italian colonists or modern tourists. All have played their part in transforming local conditions; some have had an even wider impact. Phoenician traders, for example, appear to have brought their alphabet, which the Greeks then adopted and changed, to the islands during the early Geometric period. At the same time, Egyptian influence was leading island sculptors to work in stone. It is no coincidence that the earliest examples of monumental Greek sculpture are all to be found on the islands.

On Crete, the Bronze Age produced the first urban civilisation in the Aegean: this was the age of the Knossos and Phaistos palaces, erected in the centuries after 2000 BC. Other islands such as Thera (today Thíra or Santoríni) also flourished at this time. Thucydides' account of how King Minos of Crete established his sons as governors in the Cyclades and cleared the sea of pirates certainly suggests considerable Cretan control of the Aegean. The Aegean was not to be dominated by a single sea power for another millennium until the rise of the Athenian Empire.

## ECONOMIC GROWTH

Before this, however, communities of Greeks had begun to flourish on most of the islands,

An inaccurate artist's view of the Colossus of Rhodes.

### ⊘ IMPERIALISM IN ACTION

The Italian occupation of the Dodecanese under Mussolini imposed the draconian prohibitions of an imperialist regime, intent on "Italianising" the islands and islanders. Secret police stamped out nationalist activity; the Orthodox religion had no official status from the late 1920s; the blue-and-white colours of the Greek flag were prohibited in public; and only Italian could be used in public from 1936 – slogans such as *Viva il Duce, viva la nuova Italia imperiale!* were daubed on the walls of recalcitrant shopkeepers. During the 1930s, many islanders emigrated to the Greek mainland, Egypt, southern Africa and America.

exploiting local quarries and mines, and developing indigenous political systems. Some communities achieved considerable wealth, notably on Siphnos (today Sífnos), whose gold and silver mines had made her inhabitants reputedly the richest citizens in the Cyclades by the 6th century BC. Some reflection of this wealth can be seen in the ruins of the marble treasury which Siphniots dedicated to Apollo at Delphi.

It was in the 6th century, too, that the inhabitants of Thera began to mint their own coinage, a physical manifestation of the island's power-

*Dionysios Solomos, the Ionian poet whose Hymn to Freedom was adopted as the national anthem after Independence.*

ful status in the Aegean. At one point Thera's influence was to extend not only to Crete, Melos (Mílos), Páros and Rhodes, but as far west as Corinth and as far east as Asia Minor.

During the 5th century BC, the islands' independence was curtailed as Athens used anti-Persian fears to manipulate the Delian League. This had been formed in 478 BC as an alliance between equal partners to form a strong naval power in the Aegean. But Athens soon controlled the League and used its resources in a series of wars against rivals such as the naval city-state of Aegina (Égina). It was Athenian intrigues with the Corinthian colony on Corfu, however, that led to the Peloponnesian War which was ultimately to cripple – and then break – Athens forever.

During the Hellenistic period the islands remained turbulent backwaters, prone to internecine struggles which made them easy prey for their more powerful neighbours. By the beginning of the 2nd century BC, Rome had established herself in the Aegean; Crete became the centre of a province, Cyrenaica, that included a part of North Africa.

Under Roman guidance roads were laid, aqueducts constructed, new towns and grand buildings erected. Despite this prosperity, the Aegean as a whole remained a Roman backwater. Little is known of conditions of life in the islands either then or after AD 395, when they passed under the control of the Eastern Roman Empire. Only with the onset of the Arab raids during the 7th century does the historical record become more complete.

With the decline of Roman power in the Mediterranean, the islands faced a long period of instability: for more than a millennium they were attacked by invaders from all points of the compass. From the north, briefly, came the Vandals and Goths; from the south, the Arabs, who established themselves on Crete in 824 and proceeded to plunder the rest of the Aegean for over a century. From the west came Normans in the 11th and 12th centuries, followed by the Genoese and Venetians; finally, from the east came the Ottoman Turks, who succeeded in dominating almost all of the islands in the Aegean between the 15th and 18th centuries.

Other groups, too, played minor roles – quite apart from powers such as the English, French and Russians, who all shared an interest in the Greek islands. The impact of these various peoples on the islands was complex and tangled, making it awkward to generalise about the historical experiences of the islands themselves. Only by considering the main island groups individually may things fall into place.

## THE IONIAN ISLANDS

On the eve of the 1821 Greek uprising, an English traveller to Corfu noted: "The natural weakness and position of the Ionian islands, and all their past history, demonstrate that they must ever be an appendage of some more powerful state; powerful at sea and able to protect them as well as to command." Situated close to the Greek mainland,

and vital staging-posts on the voyage from Western Europe to the Levant, the Ionian islands were perhaps inevitably a focus of constant conflict.

Corfu had suffered brief attacks during the 5th century from Vandals and Goths, the destroyers of the Roman Empire in the West, but it was not until the Eastern Empire lost its possessions in southern Italy that the Ionian islands again became vulnerable to invasion. This time the predators were the Normans. At the time when William the Conqueror was establishing Norman control over England, Robert Guiscard, Duke of Apulia and

under direct Venetian rule, which continued through a succession of Ottoman attacks (which intermittently captured Levkáda) down to 1797, when Napoleonic forces ousted the Venetians.

During these four centuries, the Ionian islands were ruled by local nobility and by administrators sent out from Venice. The influence of the Republic was felt in the introduction of cash crops such as olives and currants, in the repressive regime under which the peasants worked and in the Italian language which the nobility affected to speak. At first Venetian rule was energetic – so that, for

*A watercolour of Itháki harbour.*

Calabria, defeated a Byzantine army in Calabria during 1060–61. He vanquished another Byzantine force in 1071, and the Emperor Alexios I Komnenos himself in 1081 at Dyrrachium (in Albania), before dying of a fever on Kefaloniá in 1085. His nephew Roger I, King of Sicily, sent an expedition to besiege and occupy Corfu in 1147.

Although notional Byzantine allies, the Venetians soon proved to have territorial ambitions of their own. After the sack of Constantinople in 1204 during the Fourth Crusade, the Ionians were parcelled out among noble Venetian families, who in fact never took control of these islands, which swung between renewed Norman-Sicilian rule and that of the Despotate of Epirus. Not until 1386 did the Ionians come

## ⊘ "TURKS" ON CRETE

The Ottoman conquest of Crete was eased by the Venetian rulers having antagonised the islanders in various ways. Subsequently, few Anatolians actually settled on Crete; most of the local so-called Turks were Cretan converts to Islam, who did so to enjoy a higher civil status and who never even bothered to learn Turkish. These "Turks" made up as much at 40 percent of the population in the main north-coast towns. Mosques were limited in number, and many converts were adherents of the heterodox Bektashi dervish order. The Cretan origins of these "Turks" gave to the repeated Orthodox Christian uprisings the bitter nature of a civil war.

example, after Ottoman raids had left Zákynthos virtually uninhabited in the late 15th century, vigorous resettlement policies soon created the basis for new prosperity. Zákynthos (Zante to the Venetians) had only 36 families in 1485, but 752 families by 1516, and her revenues increased forty-fold in 30 years thanks to the introduction of these valuable crops.

By the 18th century Venice had lost her possessions in the Aegean and the Peloponnese; in the Ionian Sea, the Venetian-held islands were ravaged by pirates operating from Paxí and the Albanian coast; internally, blood feuds and political assassination made life precarious.

The end of Venetian rule was bloodless: when the French invaders arrived, they discovered the fortress guns rusting and the garrison without any gunpowder. Napoleon himself had written in 1797 that "the great maxim of the Republic ought henceforth to be never to abandon Corfu, Zante..." But within two years, the Napoleonic forces had antagonised the locals by suppressing the Orthodox Church, and a joint Ottoman-Russian force established the puppet, semi-autonomous Septinsular Republic, which lasted just eight years until the French retook the islands, introducing more constructive reforms until forced out by the British in 1814 after Waterloo.

Sir Thomas Maitland, the first Lord High Commissioner, in the words of a Victorian historian, "established a Constitution which, possessing every appearance of freedom, in reality left the whole power in his hands". But it could not satisfy the islanders' desire for freedom from

foreign rule, a desire that intensified after the creation of the Kingdom of Greece in 1832. In 1864 Britain ceded the Ionian islands to the modern Greek state, a condition stipulated by the new King George I for taking the throne.

## THE CYCLADES, SPORADES AND SARONIC GULF ISLANDS

The Cyclades, unlike the Ionian islands, were a commercial backwater: main trade routes passed via Crete and the eastern Aegean islands to Smyrna and Aleppo. While they remained a lure to

Detail of an embroidery from Skýros, probably from the 17th century.

pirates, they were never of comparable interest to major powers. Until the rise of the seafaring Italian city-states during the 11th century, most trade in the Aegean was in the hands of Greeks.

However, the weakness of the Byzantine navy was underlined by a series of Arab raids against the islands and the Greek mainland. By the 12th century a British chronicler noted that piracy had become the curse of the Aegean: many of the islands were abandoned, while others – Skýros in the Sporades, for example – became pirate lairs.

The sack of Constantinople in 1204 brought new masters to the Aegean. The unimportance of this group of islands to them meant that the Venetians were content to leave the task of occupying them to minor nobility. Of these, the most successful was Marco Sanudo, a nephew of the Doge Enrico Dandolo, who equipped eight galleys at his own expense and sailed to the Aegean where he founded the Duchy of Náxos in approximately 1207.

Náxos itself became the capital of a fiefdom of 10 surrounding islands, and on it Sanudo built a castle, erected a Catholic cathedral and provided solid fortifications for the town. Other adventurers helped themselves to islands such as Ándros and Thíra (Santoríni). The Ghisi family obtained Tínos and Mýkonos, as well as the Sporades islands, establishing a dynasty that clashed with the Sanudi until both were overwhelmed by the Ottoman navy during the 16th century. The Duchy of Náxos lasted over 350 years and only ended with the death of Joseph Nasi, the Sephardic Jewish favourite of Selim II, upon whom the sultan had bestowed the islands after their capture – though Nasi never actually visited.

But the exceptional longevity of the Duchy of Náxos should not obscure the turbulence of life in the Aegean in these centuries. Piracy had increased in the late 13th century, with Greek corsairs from Monemvasiá or Santoríni, Sicilians and Genoese – and had caused, for example, the inhabitants of the island of Amorgós to emigrate en masse to Náxos, whose fertile interior was relatively inaccessible.

In the 14th century, Catalan mercenaries, brought in for the conflict between Venice and Genoa, ravaged some of the islands, raided others and even occupied Aegina (Égina) for some decades. Ottoman troops landed on Náxos and took 6,000 captives. The Ottoman forces often consisted of recent converts to Islam, and were led by renegade Aegean Greeks such as the notorious 15th-to-16th-century brothers from Lésvos, Hayreddin and Oruç Barbarossa.

Local rulers began to complain of depopulation: Ándros had to be resettled by Albanian mainlanders; Íos, virtually uninhabited, was replenished by families from the Peloponnese. Astypálea was repopulated in 1413 by Cycladic colonists, abandoned in 1473 and only inhabited once more after 1570. During the 16th century, the islands suffered a series of attacks by the Ottoman navy and by mid-century Venetian influence was on the wane. Within 50 years, most of the islands had been brought under the sultan's rule, though Tínos only succumbed as late as 1715.

Conditions of life did not improve under Ottoman rule. Piracy, famine and fatal disease remained perennial problems. In the 18th century the plague decimated the islands on four separate occasions, continuing into the next century, well after this scourge had died out in most of Europe. Thus the Ottomans, like their predecessors, were forced to repopulate.

Often the new colonists were not Greeks. The Frenchman Joseph Pitton de Tournefort reported in the early 18th century that most of the inhabitants of Andíparos were descended

*A 1795 watercolour showing the unfinished Temple of Apollo, Náxos.*

from French and Maltese corsairs. He also noted that villages on Ándros were "peopled only by Albanians, dressed still in their traditional style and living their own way, that is to say with neither creed nor law".

It was the Albanians who were to play a major role in the struggle for Greek independence. Waves of Albanians had been colonising the islands of the Aegean since the 14th century. They were concentrated on the Saronic islands – the eminent Koundouriótis family, for example, moved from Epiros to Hydra around the year 1580. By the late 18th century, Hydra, with a largely Albanian population, possessed one of the largest and most powerful shipping fleets in the Aegean, which played a prominent role in the War of Independence.

The importance of these islands was underlined by the choice of Aegina (Égina), for a short time, as the first capital of the new Greek state. Refugees flocked here when it was the seat of government, only to leave again when it was replaced by Návplion, on the mainland. When Edouard About visited Égina town in 1839 he reported it "abandoned – the homes that had been built tumbled into ruins, the town once more became a village; its life and activity fled with the government".

*The sea battle of Sámos, one of the first clashes in the War of Independence; watercolour from 1824.*

## THE NORTHEAST AEGEAN ISLANDS

Although the east Aegean islands shared the experience of Arab raids with the Cyclades, the two areas developed differently as the rivalry between Venice and Genoa increased after the Fourth Crusade. As allies of the resurgent Byzantine Empire against her Latin enemies, the Genoese were given trading rights in the Black Sea and granted permission to colonise (and garrison) the northeastern Aegean.

A Genoese trading company controlled the mastic plantations of Híos from 1346, that year also seeing occupation of Ikaría and Sámos. In 1355 Lésvos passed into the hands of the Gattelusi family, who eventually extended their control

> *Italianate family names provide linguistic evidence of Venetian rule in the Cyclades, while Catholic communities have also survived on Tínos and Sýros: those on Náxos and Santoríni only died out in recent decades.*

to Thásos, Límnos and Samothráki. However, as in the west Aegean, the power of the Ottoman navies simply overwhelmed these local potentates, and with the fall of Híos in 1566 all the islands of the northeast Aegean passed into Ottoman hands.

Lésvos had been conquered by the Ottoman Turks as early as 1462, and most of the inhabitants emigrated. In 1476 the inhabitants of Sámos fled to Híos, but returned to the deserted island after 1562. Belon du Mans, who visited the island around 1546, wrote: "It is striking that an island like Sámos must remain deserted. The fear of pirates has rendered her uninhabited so that now there is not a single village there, nor any animals" (an exaggeration, as a few primitive hamlets persisted in the mountains). Despite these islands' proximity to the mainland, they attracted only a small number of Muslim colonisers, and the bulk of the population remained Greek, supplemented by immigrants from the Balkans and Anatolia. Only on Lésvos were Muslim settlers to be found farming the land; elsewhere they stayed close to the towns, and were totally absent on Sámos.

The 1821 insurrection had variable support in these islands. Sámos was the most fanatic supporter of the revolution. The Samians landed as agitators on Híos where, in 1822, the Ottomans brutally suppressed a rather half-hearted revolt. Numa Denis Fustel de Coulanges wrote in 1856: "Any person aged more than 32 years whom one meets today on Híos was enslaved and saw his father slaughtered."

It was little consolation to know that the massacre on Híos, melodramatically painted by Delacroix, had aroused the attention of European liberals, and strengthened philhellenic sentiment. Refugees fled westwards, transporting the island's traditional *loukoúmi* (Turkish delight) industry to Sýros in the Cyclades, whose port of Ermoúpoli became the busiest port in the new Greek state. Other refugees settled in Alexandria, Trieste, Marseilles and as far north as Amsterdam.

Elsewhere in the east Aegean, the changes were just as great. The Ottoman authorities were only able to suppress the uprising with the aid of Egyptian Ibrahim Pasha's army, who had as little respect for the local Muslim notables as they had for the Greeks: many Turkish land-owners sold up and emigrated to Anatolia, while their properties were bought by middle-class Greeks who became an increasingly powerful force in the aging Ottoman Empire.

By the end of the century the Ottoman hold had become tenuous: Sámos, for example, from 1832 onwards, had an autonomous regime under an appointed Christian "prince". And on Thásos the Oxford don Henry Tozer found in 1884 that there were no Muslims apart from the governor himself and a few soldiers. Since the islanders had to pay neither the "head tax" – universal elsewhere in the Ottoman Empire – nor Ottoman trade duties, it is not surprising that they appeared content with their system of government.

The Muslim islanders, on the other hand, continued to leave for the Anatolian mainland. Even before the Greco-Turkish population exchange in 1923, the Turkish communities on Híos, Lésvos and Límnos had dwindled considerably. Their place was taken by numerous Greek refugees from Anatolia.

## THE DODECANESE

These 18 islands, misleadingly known as the Dodecanese (*dódeka* means "12"), suffered as elsewhere from the collapse of Roman authority. They were repeatedly attacked and plundered. The Byzantine hold remained firmer here than it did in the West, but after 1204 many of the islands were ceded to Frankish adventurers in return for nominal acknowledgement of Byzantine sovereignty.

By the beginning of the 14th century, Venice had helped herself to those two crucial stepping stones to the East, Kásos and Kárpathos, and acquired Astypálea as well. At the same time, Rhodes was captured from the Genoese by the Knights of St John, a military order which, after the loss of Jerusalem in 1187, had been based in Cyprus since 1291. Foulques de Villaret, the first Grand Master of Rhodes, reconstructed the city.

Although the Knights of St John were able to withstand an Ottoman siege in 1480, they could not hold off the Ottoman threat indefinitely. During the summer of 1522 they were vastly outnumbered by a massive Ottoman force nearly 200,000 strong, and after a siege lasting five months the starving defenders were forced to

*When the Arabs occupied Rhodes from AD 653–8, they broke up the remains of the famous 3rd-century BC Colossus, which had collapsed in 227 BC, and sold the bronze for scrap to a Jewish merchant from Mesopotamian Edessa.*

*A 19th-century drawing of a Kásos woman.*

capitulate. Rhodes's Orthodox inhabitants were compelled to leave the Old Town and settle outside the walls. But because the Ottomans never made up more than a quarter of the Rhodian population, their overall influence was never that strong. With the fall of Rhodes, the position of neighbouring islands became untenable, and by 1541 they had all been incorporated into the formidable Ottoman Empire, Venetian-held Astypálea being the last to surrender.

Since the land on many islands was difficult to farm, the islanders looked elsewhere for their livelihoods. Many became seamen, while on Kálymnos, Hálki and Sými the sponge-diving trade prospered. In 1523, the islanders of Kálymnos paid homage to conquering Sultan Süleyman with sponges and white bread to demonstrate that "sponge-fishers do not cultivate corn, but buy flour – and only of the best quality". During the 19th century, the sponge-divers went international, opening agencies in London, Frankfurt and Basle.

But these developments, typical of the growing Greek middle class, did not lead to union with Greece until late in the day. These islands had been intended for the new Greek state in 1830, but were retained at the last minute by the Ottoman Empire in return for the central island of Euboea (Evvia). Liberation came unexpectedly

administrators to turn the islands into a Fascist colony. But the process was brought to an abrupt halt by World War II. Once Italy surrendered in 1943, the islands were taken over by the Germans who managed, in the course of their brief and very brutal occupation, to exterminate the ancient Jewish populations of Kos and Rhodes, against the evident wishes of the islanders and the Italians.

Of the 2,140 Jews deported from Kós and Rhodes in July 1944, only about 150 returned from Auschwitz. Just a few months after the Jews had been deported, the islands were occupied by the

*Oil painting of the 1866 Cretan Revolt.*

through the occupation of the islands by the Italians during their war with the Ottomans in 1912.

At first, the islanders welcomed the Italians. A congress on Pátmos passed a resolution thanking the Italian nation for delivering them from the Turkish yoke. However, another resolution at the same congress calling for unification of the islands with Greece was less satisfactory to the local Italian commander, who broke up the congress and forbade such public meetings.

The Italians initially did not intend to hold the islands permanently but, with the collapse of the Ottoman Empire, their dreams of establishing a foothold in Asia Minor led them to renege on a 1915 promise to return these islands (except Rhodes) to Greece. Mussolini sent groups of zealous

British, who finally handed them over to Greece in March 1947.

## STRATEGIC CRETE

The "Great Island" has had the most violent history of all, thanks to its strategic position, agricultural riches and, not least, the peculiar demographics of the Ottoman era (see page 31). Since before AD 824, when it was conquered by Arab freebooters from Andalucía, who made it the centre of the slave trade and a base for pirate raids throughout the Aegean, the strategic importance of Crete has been obvious.

From 2600 BC onwards, a prosperous civilisation spread its influence throughout the Aegean. The Minoans left proof of their architectural genius in the ruined palaces of Knossos and Phaistos. Although they were daring soldiers, they appear to have preferred commerce to agriculture. They established outposts in the Peloponnese and made contact with the Egyptians.

By 1550 BC, Minoan civilisation had reached its zenith. But Crete was vulnerable to natural disaster: a stupendous volcanic eruption on the island of Thera (Santoríni) in the preceding century unleashed tidal waves that damaged settlements along the north coast. Then, in around 1450 BC, most of the important sites in central and south-

Cretan artists such as Domenikos Theotokopoulos, otherwise known as El Greco, helped to enrich the Renaissance in Western Europe.

Though the Venetians developed the towns and fortresses on the north coast, they knew how little they were loved by the Cretans. In 1615 a certain Fra Paolo Serpi warned that "the Greek faith is never to be trusted", and he had recommended that the people "must be watched with more attention lest, like the wild beasts they are, they should find an occasion to use their teeth and claws. The surest way is to keep good garrisons to awe them".

*Iráklio at the turn of the 20th century.*

ern Crete were destroyed by fire. But the causes of the wider disintegration of Minoan control remain a mystery. Only Knossos continued to be inhabited as Cretan dominance in the Aegean ended.

In the early 13th century AD, Venice and Genoa tussled to wrest the island away from the waning Byzantine Empire. Although Venice ultimately turned Crete into a prize possession, Byzantine influence remained strong. The old Greek noble families survived, while ties with Constantinople were reflected everywhere in church art and secular literature.

This strong Byzantine tradition became crucial after 1453, when the island gave refuge to exiles fleeing the Turks, and briefly became the centre of a renaissance of Byzantine culture:

Under such a regime the peasants were probably worse off than under the Ottomans elsewhere.

Occasionally, as in 1263 and 1571, there were major uprisings which the Venetians harshly put down. After one such revolt, 300 people were executed and many exiled, their villages burnt and razed, their property confiscated and other severe penalties exacted. In 1538 the coasts were laid waste by the pirate-admiral Hayreddin Barbarossa. On top of all this, the inhabitants faced other, natural terrors, such as the famine of 1626 which reduced Crete's population by one-fifth. In these circumstances it is no surprise that the Venetian presence on the island remained small and that Roman Catholicism never became widespread.

Venice kept its hold on Crete long after most of her other Aegean possessions had been surrendered. But, in 1645–6, the towns of Haniá and Réthymno fell to the Turks and, in 1669, after a siege lasting 22 years, Iráklio fell too and the entire island – except three fortified islets – came under Ottoman rule. By this time, Ottoman administration had lost much of its early vigour: early in the 18th century one commentator described Megálo Kástro (later Iráklio) as "the carcass of a large city... little better than a desert".

*Watercolour of urban Cretan costume.*

In an effort to escape the burdens of Ottoman rule many Cretan families converted to Islam, especially during the 18th century, on a scale unknown elsewhere in the Aegean. But these converts continued to speak Greek, drink alcohol (as Bektashis were permitted to do) and had surnames such as Effendakis and Mehmedakis, which were linguistic hybrids of Greek and Turkish elements. Villages were still called by their Greek names even after all their inhabitants had converted.

From 1770, a series of revolts broke out against Ottoman rule. But it took more than a century to bring about autonomy; nevertheless, these insurrections altered the balance of power on Crete, as many Muslim farmers sold out to Christians before moving, first to the coastal towns – Réthymno became one-third Muslim – and then, after 1898, away from the island altogether. These revolts also had a catastrophic effect on the island's economy. Passing through the interior shortly after the 1866–9 insurrection, Henry Tozer noted: "Every village that we passed through [...] had been plundered, gutted and burnt."

In 1895, when the next major revolt broke out, the inadequacies of Ottoman rule were so evident that the European powers stepped in. For example, on the whole of the island there was just one short stretch of carriage road; William Miller reported, in 1897, that in Iráklio, the largest town on the island, there were no carriages at all, "for the two that used to exist were last employed for the conveyance of the admirals on the Queen's Jubilee last year, on which occasion the bottom of both vehicles fell out, and the distinguished officers had to walk inside the bottomless machines". In 1897, the troubles in Ottoman Crete provoked a wave of sympathy on the mainland. Greek naval forces were sent to the island while the army marched northwards – only to be crushed by Ottoman forces who pushed back down into Thessaly. This defeat was humiliating for the Greeks, but it proved only to delay the future enlargement of the kingdom for a while.

In 1898 Crete was made an independent principality under Ottoman sovereignty, but under French, British, Russian and Italian "protection". The new prince, George, was significantly the son of Greek King George I; after attempts to govern with an unruly local council, George resigned, and in 1913 union with Greece was finally achieved.

## A NEW REVOLT

In late 1909, junior army officers staged a revolt against the political establishment in Athens and, at their invitation, a new politician with a radical reputation, Eleftherios Venizelos, came to Athens from Crete, forming a new government early in 1910. A consummate diplomat and a man of great personal charm, Venizelos channelled the untapped energies of the Greek middle class into his own Liberal Party, which governed Greece for 13 of the next 25 years. It also marked the first time that leadership in Greece was held by someone from the islands, breaking the previous monopoly on power exercised by Peloponnesians and central mainlanders.

A Naïve-style painting of Elefthérios Venizélos.

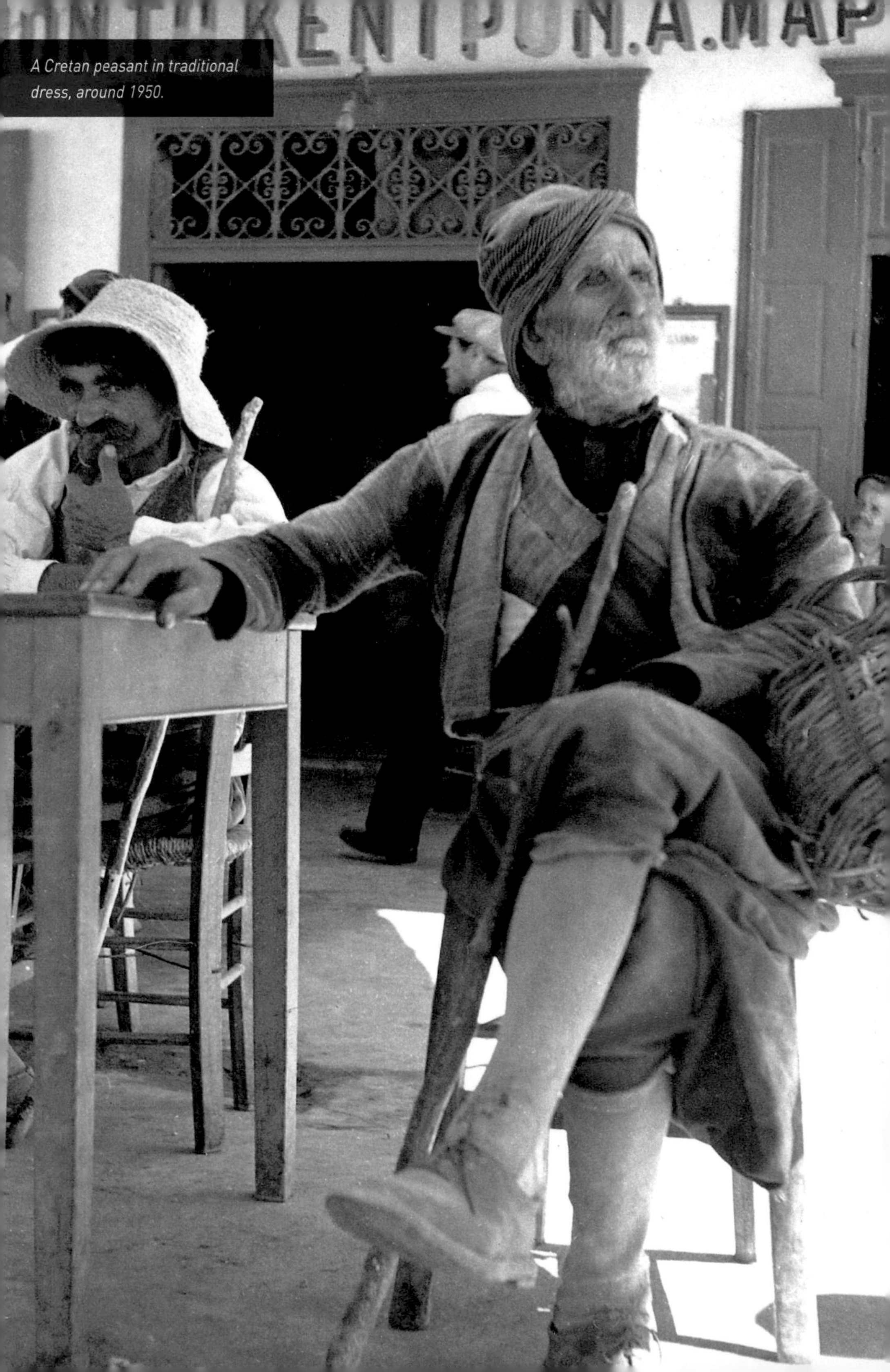


*A Cretan peasant in traditional dress, around 1950.*

# THE ISLANDS TODAY

The 20th century was a political roller-coaster for Greece and its islands, alternating between monarchy, military dictatorship and republicanism.

The islands did not all become part of independent Greece at the same time. Only the Cyclades, the Argo-Saronic group, the Sporades and Evvia (Euboea) formed part of the original state after the peace treaties of 1830–2. At the insistence of about-to-be King George I, a Danish prince (and – more to the point – because they were no longer considered of strategic value), the Ionian islands were ceded by Britain to Greece in 1864.

The other major additions resulted from war. Crete and the northeast Aegean islands became part of Greece in 1913 after the First Balkan War, except for Samothráki which was joined in 1922, along with mainland Thrace. The Dodecanese islands were freed from Italian occupation by World War II and formally incorporated into Greece in 1948 after a year of Greek military government. Since several of the islands were wealthy ports at a time when Athens was still a village, it is scarcely surprising that their influence on cultural developments in the new state was disproportionate to their size and overall population.

In politics, the Hydriot families of Voulgaris and Koundouriotis, the Metaxas clan in the Ionians, the Samian Themistoklis Sofoulis, not to mention the Cretan Eleftherios Venizelos – in many ways the founder of the modern Greek state – all typified the vigour which the islanders brought to the political scene. Greek literature and music were marked by the Ionian islands' close links with Italy – personified in Zakynthian poet Dionysios Solomos, whose *Hymn to Liberty* became the words of the national anthem; Corfiot Nikolaos Mantzaros actually wrote the tune – while many Aegean islands were the birthplace of musical stars in rebetic and folk genres (see page 65). Skiáthos bred the important fiction writers Alexandros Papadiamantis and

*A pelican once started an inter-island feud between Mýkonos and Tínos.*

his cousin Alexandros Moraïtis; Corfu-nurtured writer Iakovos Polylas; Lésvos has produced the Nobel Prize-winning poet Odysseas Elytis, the regional writer Stratis Myrivilis and the "primitive" painter Theóphilos; while Crete, not to be outdone, produced in literature and letters a figure to match Venizelos – Nikos Kazantzákis.

The islands' economic influence has also been profound, especially before the Balkan Wars of 1912–13 added the fertile regions of northern Greece to the impoverished state, and again in recent decades with the increasing traffic in tourists. The shipping fleets of the Aegean islands, exports of currants from Zákynthos and Kefaloniá, olive oil from Lésvos and Crete, salted fish from various east Aegean islands, and emigrant remittances from islanders scattered across the globe – from Canada to Australia to Florida – have all helped bolster the country's economy.

## ISLANDS FOR OUTCASTS

But islands have long had other uses, too. Límnos, under Ottoman rule, was used as a place of exile for political offenders. Henry Tozer, who visited the island in 1884, learnt that a former grand vizier had been living there for eight years and was "almost forgotten at the capital", while

Civil-war political prisoners await their fate.

### ⊘ JUNTA COLONELS

The military junta that ruled Greece from 1967 to 1974, under the leadership of Colonel George Papadopoulos, was driven by a mixture of self-interest and retrograde nationalism. The colonels – from peasant or lower middle-class backgrounds – largely recycled the ideology of the 1930s Metaxas regime, embodying provincial reaction to a new world of urban consumers. They wanted a return to traditional morality and religion, censored the press and suppressed intellectual debate, while closing the frontiers to bearded, long-haired or mini-skirted foreigners – at least until they realised the implications for Greece's tourist trade.

an extreme instance of isolation was Gávdos islet off Crete. According to Thomas Spratt, an English vice-admiral distinguished for his *Travels and Researches in Crete* who visited in 1865, its inhabitants did not see a boat for months on end, while

> The fortress islet of Spinalónga, off the northeast coast of Crete, after a long career as Venetian citadel and Muslim village, was used as a leper colony until the late 1950s.

he himself disembarked among naked swimmers who, to his Victorian eye, were "primitive in their habits and ideas... a mixed and degenerate race".

The Greek central government also found the islands useful as prisons, both for regular criminals in large compounds on Aegina (Égina) and Corfu and, more ominously, at certain times for political opponents. On Aegina, what was built as an orphanage under the new Kapodistrias government in the late 1820s soon became an important prison (now closed pending restoration as a potential museum), and the originally British-built jail on Corfu, now well short of humane requirements, is still used.

During the 1930s the Metaxas dictatorship sent its political opponents – as well as social misfits like the *rebétes* (see page 67) – to forbidding, isolated islands such as Folégandros, Síkinos and Amorgós. During the Civil War (1946–9), in which the left-wing forces which had strongly resisted the occupying Nazis and Fascists were suppressed, the uninhabited island of Makroníssos just off the southeastern coast of Attica was home to a vast, bleak prison camp for political detainees, while Ikaría, neighbouring Foúrni, Límnos and its tiny satellite Agios Evstrátios were used for house arrest of Communists.

The colonels, who ruled Greece with a heavy, sometimes brutal hand from 21 April 1967 until 24 July 1974, continued the tradition, incarcerating their political opponents in Makroníssos, Gyáros (a bare islet near Tínos), Léros and Amorgós, as well as the regular prisons on Aegina and Corfu. On occasions, particularly on Amorgós and Corfu, islanders managed to circumvent military security and give political prisoners some support.

## INCOMERS AND EMIGRANTS

Since the late 1950s most islands have experienced the erratic but inexorable growth of tourism, a trend initiated when Greek ship-owners began to acquire islands for their own private use. When Stavros Niarchos and Aristotle Onassis continued their competition by respectively buying the islands of Spetsopoúla just off Spétses in the Saronic Gulf and Skorpiós beside Levkáda in the Ionian Sea, they set an ideal which innumerable tourists have tried to follow in finding their own island paradise.

emigrants were from the mainland. For various reasons, large numbers of islanders did not follow until the 1950s: would-be island emigrants were constrained by the availability of transport and their own awareness of the wider world, and, in the case of islands like the northeast Aegean group and the Dodecanese, by citizenship status (Ottoman, Italian) which made obtaining passports and permission to enter countries such as the US awkward.

Moreover, several islands prospered after being incorporated into the Greek state. Sýros,

*Shipping magnate Aristotle Onassis and his first wife Tina.*

Mýkonos, Rhodes, Skiáthos and Corfu were the first to see large numbers of summer visitors, but the trend has spread to virtually all the inhabited islands. If a ship goes there, there will be tourists, and the luxury of what they will find varies more or less according to the island's accessibility. For both visitors and island residents, the biggest changes since the 1970s have been the increasing availability of hydrofoils, catamarans or "high-speed" ferries, more expensive but far faster vessels than traditional boats, as well as multiplied and/or improved airports and airlines.

The counter to this influx has been a steady flow of emigration from the islands. Between 1880 and 1920 or thereabouts, most Greek

for example, became the most important port and manufacturing centre in Greece in the first few decades after 1830. Even after the rise of Piraeus (Pireás) it remained an important centre, whose standing may be gauged by the fine 19th-century villas and warehouses of its capital Ermoúpolis. On other islands, such as Mílos, Thásos and Náxos, the late 19th century was a period of rapid exploitation of mineral resources.

By World War I, however, much of this activity had slowed down, and emigration both to Athens and abroad was increasing, taking advantage of improved transport and communications. In Athens and Piraeus, newcomers from islands formed closely knit communities, each with its own affinity clubs and cafés – recreated islands of familiarity in the urban sprawl. With the collapse of international trade between the world wars, the trend slowed for several decades, but gathered pace once more with the European "miracle" of the post-war years. Many islanders moved to Sweden, France, Belgium, Switzerland, Holland and West Germany, as well as to South Africa, Rhodesia, Australia and North America.

## IMPROVED COMMUNICATIONS

By the 1960s, road and rail links between Greece and Western Europe began to be modernised.

*Sokrátous, the main commercial artery in Rhodes' Old Town.*

So too were links between the islands and the mainland: the first seaplane connection with Rhodes had been established as early as 1927 by the Italians, but it was only in the 1960s that aerial links between Athens and the Aegean became significant; many airports on the border islands were built in the mid-1960s amidst the first major Cyprus Republic crises, and doubled as military airbases. At the same time, relatively modern, faster car ferries were introduced, replacing vintage rust-buckets which could take almost twice as long for the same trajectory. On the islands themselves, dirt – then paved – vehicle roads appeared, often for the first time, in some cases displacing local boat services (such

as, for instance, Haniá to villages of Crete's southwest coast).

Improved communications not only opened up the closed island societies, but also exposed their local economies – which had survived World War II mostly by subsistence farming – to a new world of export and import. Trucks could now be loaded with agricultural produce on Crete, say, and then be driven directly up from Piraeus to markets in northwestern Europe. The return flow was (and still is) consumer delights: household appliances, cars, motorbikes, clothes and technology.

A new balance has been established since about the 1970s. During the warm months at least, many islands appear to be thriving, what with the crowds disembarking from boats and clogging the village streets, and with their actual and official populations (compiled from voter registration rolls) more or less matching. With the advent of modern transport, weekend visits by internally emigrated islanders (or second-home owners) have become feasible almost year-round. But the bustle is often illusory.

## LIMITS TO FULL-TIME ISLAND LIFE

The stark reality is that keeping Greece's islands viable for year-round habitation – especially the smaller, remoter ones – is an uphill task, inevitably involving subsidies (EU or national) that are increasingly difficult to come by in the current political and economic climate. Financial assistance can mean everything from preferential VAT rates for border-zone islands (now abolished), state-of-the-art fibre-optic cables or offering intrinsically uneconomical ferry routes. Despite the optimistic picture of improved transport painted above, it's a constant battle to maintain links with the mainland; Olympic Airways and its successor Olympic Air steadily reduced flight frequencies to most islands, with competitors not always taking up the slack. Shipping companies also cherry-pick the most profitable routes to the largest islands, grudgingly providing often irrational schedules to other destinations while pocketing large subsidies for the privilege. Eastern border islands like Sámos and Lésvos once flourished as transshipment points within the Ottoman Empire, but in more recent times indeed languish literally and figuratively at the end of the line, a status only likely to be relieved in the improbable event that Turkey is accepted into the EU.

But this logistical summary can only hint at the everyday feeling of being marooned in the Aegean, so pleasant to short-term visitors but evidently irksome to islanders who have found it increasingly difficult to resist the black-hole-like gravitational pull of Athens (and to a lesser extent Thessaloníki, Pátra and Vólos). On a smaller scale, this proves true within large islands too – the five major coastal towns of

There are decent universities on Crete (Réthymno and Iráklio), Corfu and the east Aegean, where the University of the Aegean has its faculties deliberately scattered over Lésvos, Híos, Sámos, Léros and Rhodes to spread employment opportunities and inject life into communities during winter. But again they're competing with the higher-learning colossi of Athens, Thessaloníki, Pátra, Ioánnina and Vólos. Most mainland-bred doctors and public-school teachers consider island positions a short-term, hardship posting (paid extra as such) away from

*A café frequented by the locals of Plomári, Lésvos's second town.*

Crete have done a good job of emptying the villages of their hinterlands in recent decades.

The main three reasons for leaving can be summarised as employment opportunities (severely reduced outside of the tourist season), health care and educational facilities. With some sterling exceptions, state hospitals on the islands leave much to be desired – for instance, if they can manage it, Corfiots shun their own, brand-new but understaffed, hospital in favour of the vastly superior teaching hospital attached to Ioánnina University on the mainland. Before the advent of helipads suitable for medical evacuations on the smaller islands, those taken suddenly, severely ill were as good as doomed.

## ⊘ POST-JUNTA POLITICS

After the junta's 1974 collapse, a referendum abolished the monarchy. The new conservative PM Constantine Karamanlis secured Greece's entry into the EEC in 1981. That year, Andreas Papandreou's PASOK party won elections to form Greece's first "socialist" government. Scandals brought defeat in 1989, but when a centre-right Néa Dimokratía (ND) government fell in 1993, PASOK regained power until 2004 when ND again took office. Five years later PASOK returned, though Andreas' son George resigned in 2011 in favour of a technocratic interim government that preceded a three-party coalition, followed by today's SYRIZA-led coalition.

the bright lights – even if there are conscientious and/or eccentric exceptions, repeatedly signing up to staff a clinic on a *vrahonisída* (rocky outcrop). As for bright, ambitious islanders who have worked and studied abroad or on the mainland, they rarely return unless forced to by economic or family circumstances.

## LEFT-LEANING POLITICS

In politics, on average the islands poll slightly left of centre (in the case of Lésvos, Ikaría, Crete and certain Ionians, communist or nearly

*Compare and contrast the islands by hopping from one to the other.*

so), with somewhat less support for neo-fascist Golden Dawn than elsewhere. Besides his native Crete, Venizelos received staunch initial support from the northeast Aegean plus Corfu, this political affiliation still reverberating four generations on. The Cyclades and Dodecanese, as permanent net beneficiaries for every sort of subsidised programme, in the past generally plumped for PASOK as the party most likely to provide them, though since 2012 voting has been unpredictable. But despite their illustrious contributions to Greek leadership and territorial aggrandisement, today's islands are unlikely ever to swing a close election – these are typically decided in suburban

precincts of Athens or Thessaloníki – and their relative (un)importance was aptly symbolised by the late 2007 subsuming of the Ministry of the Aegean into that of the Mercantile Marine, prior to two more mergers and downgradings in 2009–10. Even during the late 2008/early

> On the larger forested islands, wildfires remain a constant fear – and temptation to unscrupulous developers and their hired arsonists.

2009 youth rioting, which convulsed Athens following the shooting of an unarmed 15-year-old boy by an Athens policeman, barely a ripple registered in most island towns other than some anti-establishment graffiti. Since then, austerity has prompted livelier island rallies and demos.

## TODAY AND THE FUTURE

One concern that most islands do share with the mainland – in fact to an enhanced degree owing to fragile ecosystems – is conservation and development policy. Limited water supplies are constantly outstripped, especially on the smaller islands, to such a degree that the tanker-boat is a routine sight in summer. Despite the economic downturn, purpose-built villa projects pitched at both Greeks and foreigners proliferate, the worst-planned ones amounting to visual pollution as well as putting pressure on water resources.

The future of the islands is, much as some Greeks might resent it, bound up with foreigners. Ignoring for the moment landed refugees (see page 56), settled immigrants – for the most part Albanians – make up an increasing proportion of the workforce, especially in the building trades (they also outnumber the native-born population in some neighbourhoods). Direct, non-charter, seven-months-of-the-year air links between Northern Europe and Corfu, Iráklio, Santoríni, Mýkonos and Rhodes attest to the burgeoning numbers of expats and holiday-home owners who also help keep local economies going. To these must be added numerous Turkish visitors who support tourism on many of the border islands.

Mule carrying a heavy load in Hydra Town.

*Locals dancing the traditional Ikaríotiko at the Feast of the Assumption of the Virgin Mary, Ikaría island.*

Waiting for custom in Parikiá, Páros.

# PEOPLE AND IDENTITIES

An attachment to the ancestral village, awareness of seasonal and diurnal rhythms dictated by climate and an assumed equivalence between Orthodoxy and Greekness typify the character of islanders.

Roughly 10 percent of Greece's population resides in the islands, nearly half in towns of over 5,000 inhabitants – which means that the stereotypical rural idyll, even (or especially) in the remotest spots, is fading fast.

Historically, Greeks rarely moved far from their *patrída*, or home province. But the mid-20th century saw a sort of seasonal transhumance established between one's native village and the big city, usually Athens, accordingly nicknamed *To Megálo Horió* (The Big Village). If the island in question is close enough to the town migrated to, weekend visits are feasible; otherwise, the *patrikó spíti* (ancestral family home) may only be occupied in high summer, typically from mid-July until the new school term starts on around 11 September. On arrival, dead bugs and dust are swept out, paint brushes and awnings deployed, repairs commissioned, barbecues lit, and positions taken on plastic terrace chairs, all with remarkable speed. Sadly, since 2010 the daunting costs of round-trip ferry transport for a car and four or five persons means that many island houses lie permanently vacant.

## WORK AND LEISURE

Until spiralling debt and expenses plus the current economic crisis dictated more nose-to-the-grindstone attitudes, most Greeks reckoned that they worked to live, not the other way around. Even in winter, when there is less need for a siesta, the midday *mikró ýpno* time is still sacred, to be spent over a long lunch with family, friends or business associates. The summer climate, meanwhile, dictates that people who work outdoors, in

*Taking refreshment at Iráklio's market, Crete.*

agriculture or the building trade, begin a single shift just after dawn and knock off by 3pm.

Nationwide and regional chains – specifically supermarkets, betting and lottery outlets, homewares, office furniture and technology – are widespread, but many island businesses are still small, family-owned and staffed. This helps disguise unemployment as underemployment, and permits various fiddles concerning pension contributions.

Sunday remains very much a day of rest, and at weekends warm weather prompts a mass exodus towards the beaches, which often have lively "all-day" bars complete with loud music. Despite recent laws dictating that nightspots should close by 2am, on weekends at any rate this is widely winked at: nights in island towns are long and loud, though with less motorcycle traffic than before owing to fuel costs, and with yet more noise (from car horns especially) when a favoured athletic team, or political faction, wins a contest. Earlier, at dusk, the local military band might march down the quay playing tunes not necessarily martial, and not necessarily in tune either, prior to lowering the flag.

Even in these pinched times, every sizeable island makes an effort to organise some sort

*Taking a wander in Skiáthos Town.*

of summer festival. This will include folk dancing, theatre and above all concerts with B- (or increasingly C-) list stars, pitched as much at seasonally returned islanders as at foreigners (or more so). But the most authentic entertainments arguably won't be experienced at organised events, but at tavernas. These can serve as informal showcases for Greek music and lyrics, the latter stemming from a rich mid-20th century tradition in poetry which spawned two Nobel laureates, Odysseas Elytis and George Seferis. A small group of men (or women), maybe a bit tipsy, will interpret well-loved songs accompanied by unamplified *bouzoúki*, guitar and accordion: the intimate *ta tragoúdia tis paréas* (songs with one's friends).

## CHILDREN, FAMILIES, GENDER ROLES

Children are adored – arguably spoilt, especially boys – and expected to behave like children; yet at the same time they are not allowed to determine adults' schedules, or kept segregated, as so often happens in Anglo-Saxon countries. Very early on, children are inculcated into the routine of late nights out at the taverna, either as toddlers asleep in a pram parked by the chairs, or as older kids playing tag around the tables. They are spoken to – and expected to converse up to their abilities – as adults, which accounts in part for the tremendous (over-)confidence of kids and teenagers. Not too many shrinking violets here: in an often rough-and-tumble culture like that of Greece, assertiveness is a survival skill.

> *Progonoplixía (ancestor fixation), crediting all and everything to the ancient Greeks – neatly embodied by dad Gus in My Big Fat Greek Wedding – is the flip side to xenomanía, a fetishisation of foreign consumer goods, music and foodstuffs.*

Individual families tend to be small. Like Spain and Italy, Greece has negative native population growth, with a birth rate well below replacement level at roughly 1.3 kids per couple. Much of this is a reaction to impoverished times before the 1960s when four or five siblings growing up in a single room was the norm. Now it's considered shameful to have more offspring than you can properly educate and set up with a house of their own (the D-word, "dowry", is used circumspectly since the practice of demanding it per se was outlawed in the 1980s). Abortion is widely resorted to, with surprisingly little comment from the Orthodox Church.

*Nipagogía* (crèches) certainly exist, a worthwhile legacy of the first PASOK government, but one suspects they are used to full capacity only in the biggest towns and cities and by the most harassed of working parents. Elsewhere, grandmothers are perennially available childminders, a role assumed with relish. Throughout the day there will be to-ing and fro-ing with foodstuffs and/or child in hand between the houses of the various generations.

The legal status of women was significantly upgraded by PASOK reforms, and many women (like former mayor of Athens, then foreign minister Dora Bakogianni, former Communist Party head Aléka Paparíga and current PASOK chief Fofi Gennimata) are now prominent in public life. Most, however, are still caught up in the bind of both having

forms an essential part of periodic memorial services for the departed, symbolically keeping the deceased linked to the living. Food-related terms are used as diagnostic, affectionate or insulting tags: an older relative will scoop up an adorable infant and exclaim *"Ná sé fáo!"* ("Good enough to eat!"); sleek, spoilt children (especially male), presumably overfed from infancy in the belief that a plump toddler is a healthy one, are dubbed *voutyrópeda* ("butter-kids"); coddled, 20-something offspring of either gender, still taking their

*Triangles of sticky baklavá are boxed up for a customer at this zaharoplastío (patisserie) in Levkáda Town.*

to work – if only in a family business – and fulfil traditional mother and wife roles. That said, men's attitudes have changed since the relatively recent, macho 1970s: happily seen in public pushing a pram or carrying children, they've even been rumoured to change a nappy or two.

## FOOD SYMBOLISM – AND CONSEQUENCES

Food and eating is not just a pretext for sociability, or proof of maternal virtue, but is highly symbolic and integral to a sense of identity. *Kólyva* (food for the dead, made up of varying proportions of grain, breadcrumbs, nuts, pomegranate seeds and raisins), for instance,

laundry to be done at the parental home, are deemed *mamóthrefti* ("mother-fed"). Since their attempted 1940 invasion, Italians are *makaronádes* ("macaroni-eaters" – though the Greeks eat just as much pasta), while Asia Minor refugees were long derided as *giaourtovaptisméni* ("yoghurt-baptised", after that Anatolian staple little known in Greece before the 1920s).

You'll notice that many people are, to put it diplomatically, stout. Despite some enforced slimming caused by austerity, Greece perennially ranks among the Top 10 in the European obesity sweepstakes. This is a consequence, in part, to uncomfortably close memories of hunger, especially during World War II and the Civil

War, as well as a diet enjoining the consumption of bread *and* potatoes/rice/pasta *and* oil with every meal.

> Bread is fraught with symbolism – chunks of leavened loaves comprise the andídoron, blessed and distributed to church congregations, while to refuse it at a taverna or shared table is considered deviant at best.

sappers on his reconquest of the island from the Arabs in AD 961 – the Catholics of the Cyclades (concentrated at Sýros and Tínos) and the Maltese-descended Catholics of Corfu.

In 1944, the numerous Jewish communities of the islands were wiped out with the exception of those on Zákynthos, though they elected to depart en masse for Israel after the war and subsequent 1953 earthquake. Refugees from Asia Minor were far less important than on the mainland – in the Ionian islands their settlement was actively resisted – although these commu-

*Baptismal font at Ekatondapylianí Church, Páros.*

Mortified by this ranking (especially in the run-up to hosting the 2004 Olympics), the islands are now well sown with gyms and rather more dubious slimming salons, while increasing numbers of Lycra-clad cyclists and joggers brave the hazardous road verges.

## ORTHODOXY, HELLENISM AND MINORITIES

Before the recent influx of immigrants (see page 56), Greece, the islands included, was remarkably homogeneous, not to say parochial, in being Greek Orthodox in religious affiliation. About the only exceptions were a significant community of Armenians in Iráklio, Crete – who have been there since they accompanied Nikephoros Phokas as

nities are noticeable on Thásos, Límnos, Lésvos, Híos, Sámos and especially Crete, where most north-coast towns had large Muslim populations before 1923.

Even for those who rarely set foot in a church, "Orthodox" is considered synonymous with "Greek", and vice versa; there seems little place in the national discourse for Jews, Catholics and Protestant sects such as the Jehovah's Witnesses, let alone Muslims, who are all considered at least faintly suspect. The 50,000 native Catholics (plus about 150,000 foreign resident ones) are particularly vociferous on the severe legal disadvantages of being a *xénon dógma* or foreign creed, unrecognised in contrast to the established Church.

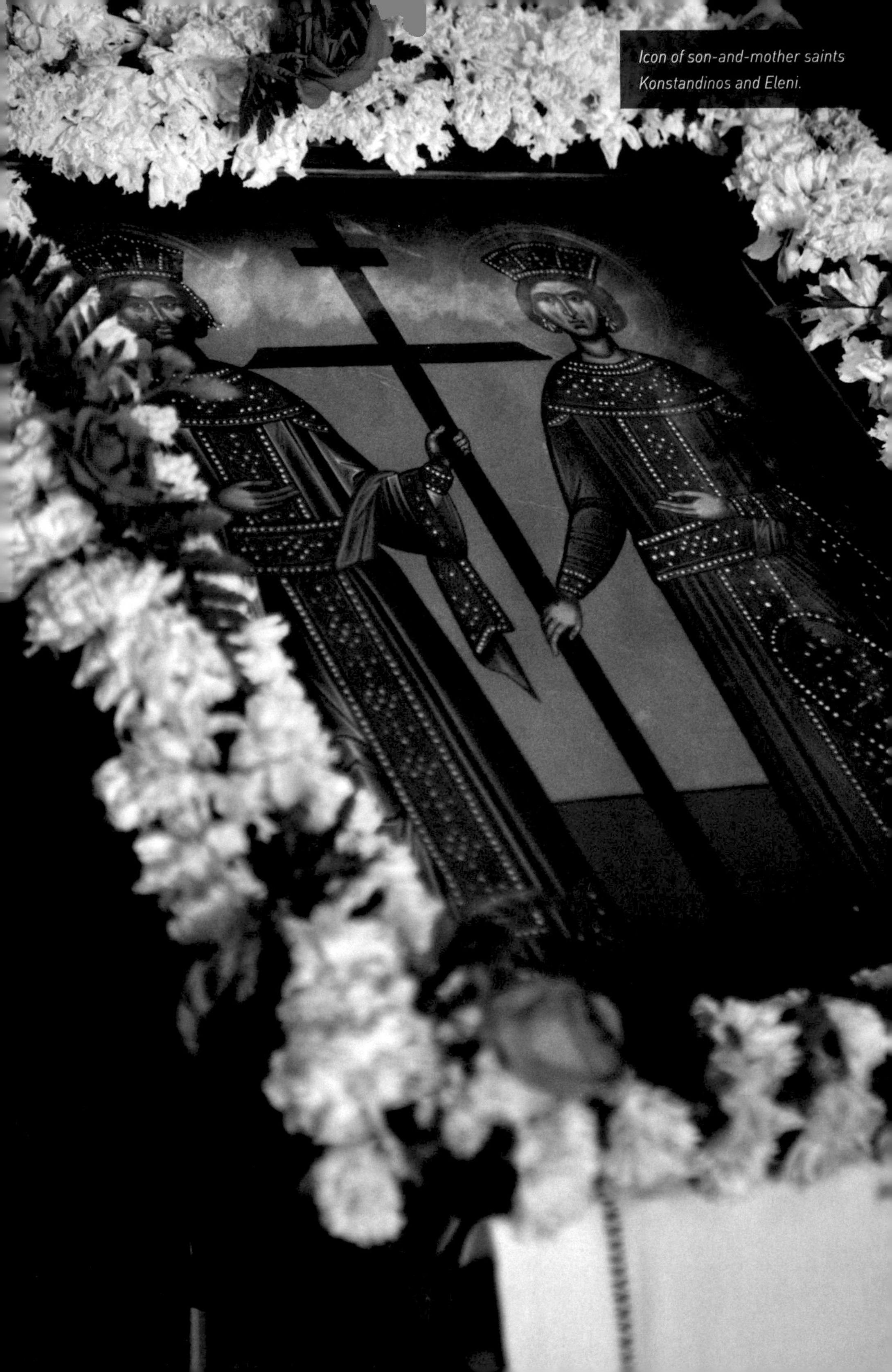

*Icon of son-and-mother saints Konstandinos and Eleni.*

**With its frontier islands doubling as a gateway to Europe, Greece faces an ongoing struggle to control illegal immigration.**

On a typical August evening on tiny Agathonísi, remotest of the Dodecanese, the quay might host 150 people preparing to bed down rough for the night – illegal immigrants landed over the previous three days following a clandestine sea-crossing from Turkey – mainly men, but also women and children, desperate to gain entry into Europe.

Despite appearances, these migrants are rarely completely destitute – money is usually concealed

*Refugees risk their lives to reach the Greek Islands.*

from the rapacious people-smugglers who demand thousands to get each individual to, through, and out of Turkey.

Every summer, the *akritiká nisiá* (frontier islands) off the Turkish coast act as an irresistible magnet for illegal immigration until winter storms halt the passage. Greece has demanded that Turkey stem the flow, and receive back illegal immigrants proved to have come via Turkey. But given the low pay of most Turkish port officials, bribes from captains for turning a blind eye to departing boats have the desired effect. Despite a 2012 re-admission protocol signed between the EU and

Turkey to repatriate them, and another one in 2016, Turkey typically accepts barely 10 percent of the annual Greek applications to return illegal migrants.

## SURVIVAL OF THE FITTEST

Walking across Agathonísi, you'll spot discarded life-vests – a few of them dangerous fakes – and synthetic drip-dry clothing inappropriate for summer, plus deflated rubber rafts on shore: unscrupulous captains, wary of being detained by the Greek coastguard, dump their human cargo in international or Greek waters, well shy of Agathonísi, and race back to Turkey. Alternatively, migrants are launched in overloaded rafts with just a compass and a baulky engine, leaving West Africans familiar with the sea in charge. Refugees know of these tactics, and are prepared to paddle or swim for land if close enough, or else wait to be fished out of the Aegean by the Greeks as required by law. Drownings occur regularly even in good weather, but it's amazing that there aren't more, considering that the coastguard is as likely to swamp the rafts or drive them back into Turkish waters. What you won't find amongst the debris, or on the migrants themselves, are any ID, SIM cards, clothing labels or bus tickets that would prove where they're from or where they have passed through – making it impossible for Greek authorities to repatriate them legally, and obliging them (as per the Dublin Regulations) to prevent them reaching other EU states.

The next afternoon the local ferryboat *Nísos Kálymnos* departs with all 150 refugees sitting quietly on the upper sun-deck, cordoned off from holiday-makers by marine rope. Upon arrival at Pátmos, they're kept at the police station until the midnight mainline ferry arrives from Rhodes to take them away to Athens and further processing. Many locals resent even this brief stopover – *"Dióhni ton tourismó"* ("It expels tourism"), they say – on their smart island more used to cruise-ship passengers than ragged refugees.

"Processing" means three days of shelter, meals and medical examinations at a score of Greek-mainland receiving centres – most established against strenuous local opposition – after which migrants are served with a deportation order giving them a month to leave Greece, something now impossible since land borders across the Balkans are sealed. Most disappear into the huge refugee underground, ripe for the attentions of Golden Dawn. A few apply for political asylum, giving them six to 24 months' residence while their case is reviewed. Less than 1 percent are accepted; Greece views asylum-seeking as economic migration by the back door.

## GREECE OVERWHELMED

Versus a total population of 10.9 million, Greece has almost 2 million settled immigrants and refugees, most of the latter having arrived since 2010 and comprising a significant eight percent of the population. While this isn't the highest proportion of refugees in the EU – Italy, Sweden and Spain top this – immigrants are now a major social and political issue in what previously had been a monochrome culture.

Most numerous are nearly 1 million Albanians, who arrived during the early 1990s; there are also Bengalis, Syrians, Afghans, Pakistanis, Chinese, Somalis, Lebanese, Iranians, Egyptians, Filipinos, Iraqis, North Africans, West Africans, Eritreans and nationals of various non-EU Central European states (to name the largest groups).

The ongoing economic crisis, plus illegal immigration, has fuelled the rise since 2011 of Golden Dawn (Hrysí Avgí), the most violent and brazen of Europe's neo-Nazi parties, with significant police toleration and even membership. Their platform can be summarised by their graffito "Work for Greeks only." Despite being severely cracked down on following their 2013 murder of a Greek public figure, vigilante actions against both legal and illegal immigrants, and breaches of parliamentary decorum, Golden Dawn might still finish third were elections held now. They have flourished in a society where racist or discriminatory attitudes and laws remain prevalent. In particular, non-EU immigrants hoping to be self-employed must prove investment of 60,000 euros, no matter how small the business – a ludicrous figure. So many refugees never escape being roving pedlars of fake designer bags, cheap jewellery and sunglasses. As one pro-immigrant NGO's leaflet ironically put it, "Our grandparents refugees, our parents emigrants, and we – xenophobes and racists?"

There were about 57,000 recorded illegal migrants in 2012, a quarter of these entering via the border islands. But following the escalation of the Syrian Civil War in 2014, a staggering 800,000 people arrived on the east Aegean islands from Turkey during 2015 – of whom 500,000 were Syrians. Poignant scenes of landings, drownings and rescues, especially on Lésvos, were broadcast worldwide. While 2016 and 2017 saw sharp reductions in crossings to the east Aegean islands, the main destinations – Lésvos, Híos, Sámos, Léros, Kastellórizo – between them at any moment still host up to 15,000 refugees in substandard holding facilities, with a thousand more on other islands – see current numbers at http://data2.unhcr.org/en/situations/mediterranean/location/5179. Arrivals on Sámos are kept in a designated holding centre, opened in 2008 at the behest of the UNHCR: a sun-baked, hillside camp – a former army firing range – that often holds five times its given capacity of 450. On Híos, Golden Dawn activists attacked and set alight a refugee camp in late 2016.

Overall, the official response to the illegal immigrants has been substandard, in breach of various UN and EU regulations, but Greece has received scant EU aid to cope with their unwanted guests since a 2009 grant strengthened its land borders and reinforced its coastguard. Little went to upgrade reception facilities,

*Athens Olympic Baseball Stadium has been transformed into a camp for refugees coming from Iraq, Afghanistan and Syria.*

since police claimed that this would just attract more migrants. Mid-crisis, local construction and agricultural industries have no need of cheap undocumented labour; as a result migrants gather near Pátra and Igoumenítsa ports, hoping to stow away on boats to Italy. "Greece is not really Europe," many say, their sights set firmly on Italy, Sweden, Germany or England, where they often already have relatives in residence. In September 2017, the European Court of Justice upheld a 2015 EU-wide refugee redistribution scheme, giving hope that migrants will finally be able to leave Greece.

# RELIGION

The degree of religious faith in the countryside, where many beliefs and acts of devotion are little changed since before the advent of Christianity, contrasts sharply with opinions on the all-too-human Church itself.

The Orthodox Church still exerts a noticeable influence over contemporary Greek life, especially on the smaller islands, and even the most worldly, sceptical families will arrange religious services for the critical rites of marriage, baptism and funerals. Yet there's a marked disconnect between private devotion and beliefs (some little changed since pagan times), and public disparagement of the Church, which has suffered a sharp loss in prestige since the 1960s.

## HISTORICAL BACKGROUND

In 1833, the Church in newly independent Greece was detached from the Constantinople Patriarchate and made autocephalous, but controlled by the Ministry of Education and Religion, which paid the salaries of priests and bishops (both ministry and this civil-servant status endure). As Greece expanded, territories incorporated after 1912 remained subject to the Ecumenical Patriarchate, which at times produced friction with the Athenian archbishop. Although the Church ran many charitable programmes for refugees and war orphans during the mid-20th century, its reputation suffered badly under the junta, which most clerics endorsed (with a few honourable exceptions). After the 1974 restoration of democracy, the Church was downgraded from state institution to just Greece's established religion; during PASOK's first term, civil marriage became mandatory.

Despite notional subordination to a secular ministry, however, no government ever managed to bring Orthodox institutions to heel. The most serious attempt, during 1987–8, saw incumbent Education/Religion Minister Andonis Tritsis make a stab at thorough reforms, specifically urging lay participation in elections for all Church offices and the expropriation of

*Colouring the everyday – devotional architecture in Firá, Santoríni.*

> Meeting a priest on the street is supposed to be exceedingly unlucky; many men dispelled the jinx by discreetly touching their testicles.

surplus ecclesiastical property. When thwarted by Andreas Papandreou himself, Tritsis resigned on principle – from the party as well – and was soon elected Mayor of Athens as an independent.

The next kerfuffle occurred in 2002 when, in accordance with EU directives, the government proposed to omit religious affiliation from identity cards. Led by combative, controversial then-Archbishop of Athens and All Greece, Khristodoulos, the faithful unavailingly marched in the streets against this godless innovation; a compromise bill to make declaration of creed optional foundered.

But this was as nothing compared to the consecutive scandals which erupted during 2004 and 2005, so lurid you couldn't make them up: monasteries as hotbeds of homosexual intrigue; embezzlement by the Archbishop of Attica (jailed for six years and defrocked); smuggling abroad of rare icons; bribing of judges (one of whom absconded). Greek media comics like Lakis Lazopoulos and Tzimis Panousis mercilessly satirised the clerical foibles – all of which made the attempted prosecution by a Church deacon (with Khristodoulos' connivance) of veteran musicologist and folk musician Domna Samiou, for singing bawdy carnival songs on state TV, that much more pathetic a diversion.

Still rumbling on are scandals emanating from two Mount Áthos monasteries: Esfigménou's refusal to recognise the current patriarch and a resultant long-running campaign by other Athonite monks and the Greek state to eject its tenants, and a rigged real-estate swap between Vatopedíou and the government, greatly to the latter's detriment, as well as undermining of the Cypriot banking system, with Vatopedíou's abbot briefly jailed for fraud and embezzlement. Some might say parishioners are getting poor value from their tax-paid clerics. Amidst the ongoing economic crisis, the first serious murmurings against the Church's tax-exempt status are finally being heard.

## A BEDROCK OF BELIEF

The old adage that organised religion need not have much to do with spirituality or belief is amply borne out by Greek everyday life, especially in rural areas. Out in the countryside, you will notice numerous hillside chapels and roadside shrines (proskynitária), many built by a family or by individuals in fulfilment of a vow of thanks (for supernatural assistance) to the patron saint. Inside are smaller votive offerings: the támmata, flat metal or 3D wax images representing the exact nature of the favour granted – a longed-for baby, healed body part or returned relative.

Saints are considered intercessors for the faithful: real, hovering personages in contrast with the remote deity. Icons, which form the core of Orthodox worship, are not just two-dimensional images hung with támmata but conduits to the "other side" which the saint inhabits. They are

emblems of the parish, village or island, paraded with honour in a perífora (procession) on feast days to bestow blessings and receive homage in return. The unseen world is contiguous in both its benevolent and menacing aspects: saints are occasionally still glimpsed in or near their chapels by the pure of heart, while priestly sermons advise the wearing of crucifixes around the neck, considered particularly vulnerable to demonic attack.

Though birthday parties for children are on the increase, traditionally Greeks only marked giortés (saints' namedays), which celebrate Orthodox

Mosaic of the Panagía on Hydra.

baptismal names. Even people named for pagan or mythological personalities have a "Christian" moniker, and a baby is usually christened after one of its grandparents. Someone will say "Giortázo símera" (I'm celebrating today) – which in the case of popular names can mean a quarter of the village holding open house for friends to drop by – to which the proper response is "Hrónia pollá" (Many years, or many happy returns).

Devotional fasting (nistía) may be on the wane in towns, but is still prevalent in rural areas, especially during "Great Lent" (before Easter), the first two weeks of August, and "Little Lent" (15 November to Christmas Eve). A whole range of foodstuffs is forbidden then, which has had a marked effect on Greek cuisine (see page 73).

# 📷 RELIGIOUS FESTIVALS

Greek religious festivals celebrate saints' days and other events in the religious calendar with devotion and high spirits.

Greek island life is punctuated year-round by saints' days and religious festivals, or *panigýria*. As there are about 150 major saints in the Orthodox calendar, there's an excuse for a party most weeks of the year.

Easter is the most important festival, and makes for a great time to visit. Colourful and noisy, traditional services mark the Resurrection everywhere, from humble chapels to sumptuous monasteries.

During *Megáli Evdomáda* (Holy Week), churches are festooned in purple velvet ribbons. On Maundy Thursday, Pátmos monks re-enact Christ's washing of his disciples' feet prior to Gethsemane. On Good Friday an *Epitáfios* (Bier of Christ) is decorated by women in each parish and paraded solemnly through the streets at dusk. On some islands an effigy of Judas is filled with fireworks and burnt or shot at, on Friday or Saturday.

On Easter Saturday, before the 9am Próti Anástasi service, church decoration changes to red and white ribbons. At midnight all is plunged in darkness as the priest lights the first candle from the holy flame representing the light of the world, and intones: *"Hristós anésti"* (Christ has risen) as the flame is transmitted to the entire congregation to light their candles. The moment is marked by deafening, potentially dangerous fireworks and more – on Kálymnos they throw dynamite from the cliffs, on Híos rival parishes rocket each other's steeples. Back at home, everyone plays a form of conkers with eggs dyed red on Maundy Thursday, then breaks the Lenten fast with *magirítsa* soup made from lamb's offal, lemon, rice and dill.

On Easter Sunday there's great rejoicing as meat is barbecued outdoors over coals (or baked in domed ovens on some islands), with the usual music and dancing.

*In the early hours of Easter Sunday after the midnight service, churchgoers, here on Aegina, head home in candlelit processions.*

*Icons are paraded during the celebrations for Lambrí Tríti (Easter Tuesday) in Ólymbos, the remote mountain village on Kárpathos, in the Southern Dodecanese.*

*Candles burning bright in the beautiful 6th-century Ekatondapyli" church (Our Lady of Hundred Doors) on Páros.*

*"Goat-clad" street performers adorned with pelts, kidskin masks and loops of metal goat bells, as they perform their annual goat dance, Skyros.*

## Celebrating all year round

Greeks mix piety and pleasure with gusto for all their festivals, from the most important to the smallest fair. The biggest religious event after Easter, the Dormition of the Virgin *(Kímisis tis Panagías)* on 15 August, draws Greeks home from across the globe. After a liturgy on 14 August evening, the icon of the Virgin is paraded – often with brass bands playing funeral dirges – prior to a communal feast which can last for days. Celebrations are especially spectacular in Ólymbos, Kárpathos, with dazzling costumes, special dances and traditional songs.

Seasonal festivals on the islands honour everything from sponges to sardines to snakes, and national holidays like *Óhi* ("No") Day (28 October) have patriotic parades marking Greece's reply to Mussolini's 1940 surrender ultimatum.

Celebrations usually occur the night before the actual feast day; everyone in the community attends, from babies to elders. The main liturgy is on the day, at churches hung with pennants and decked in cut foliage.

*Resplendent in their ceremonial garb, Greek Orthodox priests on Pátmos come together for the Easter ceremony.*

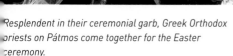

*Militínia, Cycladic Easter cakes with goat's cheese filling.*

*Hard-boiled eggs, dyed red on Easter Thursday to symbolise the blood of Christ, are cracked in a conkers-like game.*

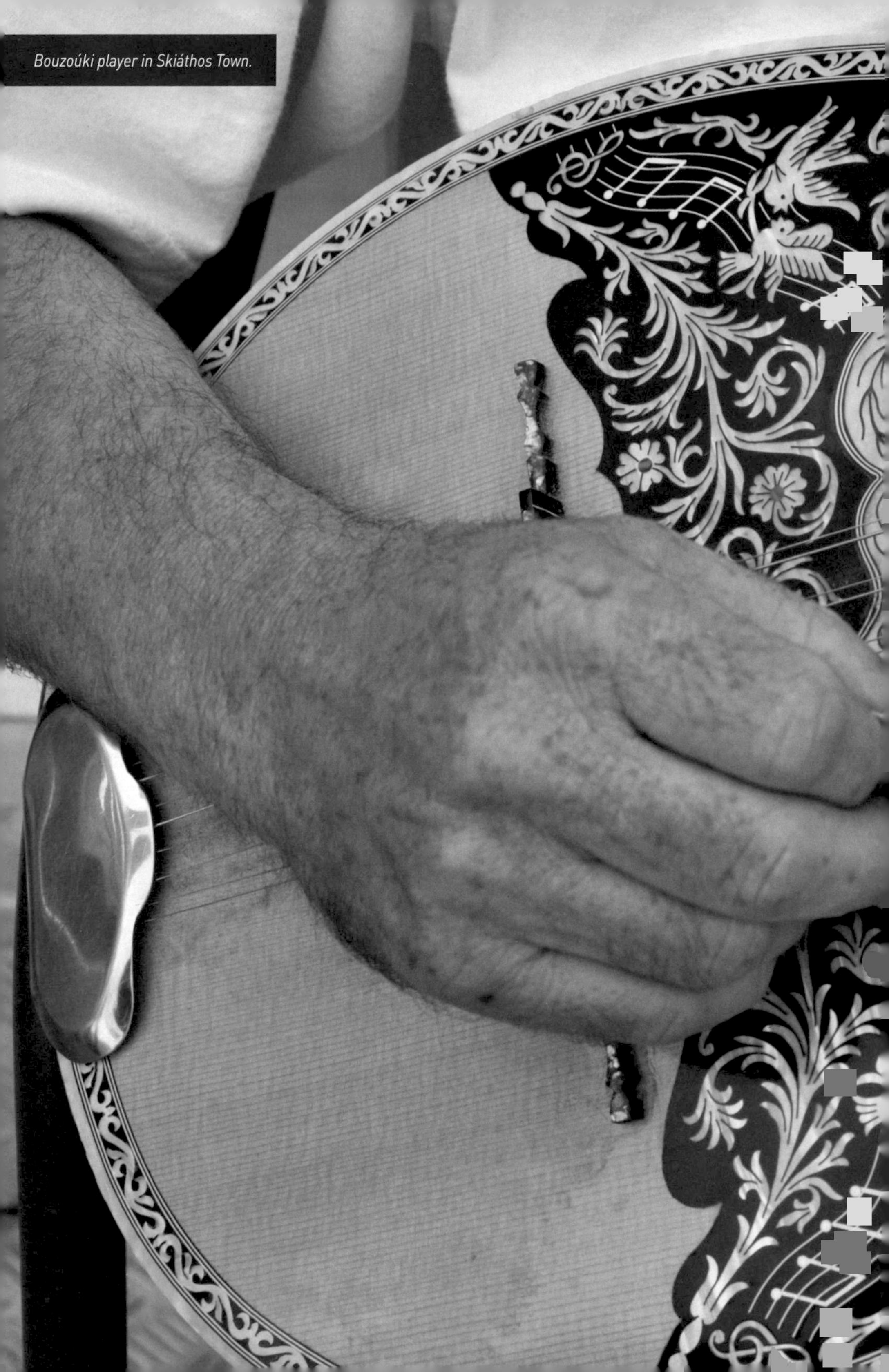

Bouzoúki player in Skiáthos Town.

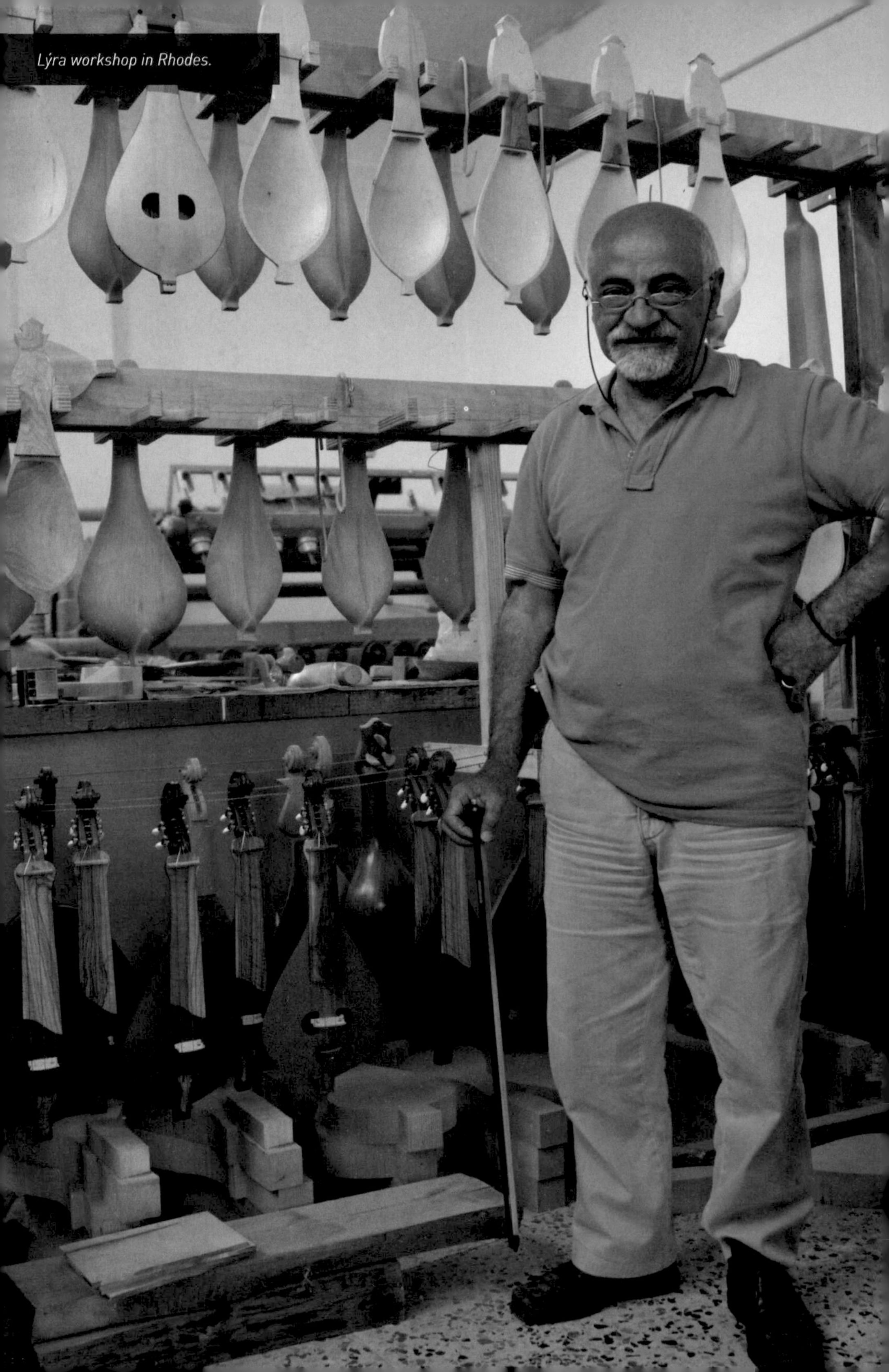

*Lýra workshop in Rhodes.*

# DEBUNKING THE *BOUZOÚKI*

Like the islands themselves, Greek music has been influenced by many neighbouring cultures, which gives it a richness and complexity far beyond the confines of stereotypical *bouzoúki* instrumentals.

The visitor is ambling along some photogenic island harbour at sunset, looking forwards to a meal of grilled octopus washed down with a little *oúzo*. What better way to complete the image than with some background music on the *bouzoúki*? After all, isn't *bouzoúki* music the quintessence of all things Greek?

Well, yes and no. Those familiar soundtracks for Manos Hatzidakis's *Never on Sunday* and Mikis Theodorákis's *Zorba the Greek*, sold ad nauseam in instrumental cover versions from resort souvenir stalls, have effectively closed foreign minds to anything else of value in Greek music.

What the big recording companies push on inexperienced foreigners, in catalogue sections cynically labelled *"Touristiká"*, is merely the tip of the iceberg, a snapshot of a brief period in the early 1960s which coincided with Greece's emergence as a mass-tourism destination. While the original compositions, arrangements and recordings skilfully distilled elements of Greek music into a cinema-friendly form, the offcut remixes adulterated for foreign tastes – with titles like *Disco Bouzouki My Love* (sic) – are another matter.

## DIVERSE INFLUENCES

Greece amply deserves the cliché image of a musical crossroads and collecting-basket, with a range of diverse influences inside a deceptively small country; even a small, random selection of popular songs will give some idea of Greece's rich musical traditions. The *bouzoúki* stereotype has obscured the Aegean music hidden away behind *skyládika* (roadhouse-type venues) with their heavy amplification. Acoustic *nisiótika* or island music has an altogether cleaner, gentler sound, and against the odds has mounted a modest comeback since the 1980s. In the Cyclades especially

*Folk musicians of times gone by.*

(of all Greek territories the least affected by the invaders – see page 32), it's very much *sui generis*, displaying only some Italian influence.

Rhythms, often in unconventional time signatures, are lilting and hypnotic; melodies, traditionally executed on violin, bagpipes and *laoúto*, the fretted folk lute, are exquisite. The lyrics, tokens of a more innocent time, grapple with eternal island concerns – the sea that claimed a loved one, the mother who wonders if her sons will ever return from exile, fishing or farming days interrupted by the festival of a beloved saint – but occasionally verge on the poetically surreal.

You're most likely to hear various members of the Naxian Konitopoulos clan, but a younger performer with better musicianship and new original compositions is fiddler Nikos Ikonomidis, a native of Skhinoússa, near Amorgós. Particularly prized are archival recordings of Anna and Emilia Hatzidaki, a mother-daughter team from Léros, and singing sisters from Kós, Anna Karabesini and Efi Sarri. On Crete, performers to watch out for include Vasilis Skoulas, the idiosyncratic Psarandonis, his gorgeous-voiced daughter Niki Xylouri, young *lýra* star Stelios Petrakis and – on old recordings – Stelios Foustalieris or Giannis Baxevanis. Neopolitan heritage is evident in *kantádes* of the Ionian isles sung in four-part har-

*Beautifully crafted bouzoúkis and baglamádes for sale.*

mony, accompanied by mandolin, violin and guitar tuned to Western scales.

Compositions and instrumentation (the *sandoúri* or hammer dulcimer, or brass bands) of Asia Minor enrich the repertoire of the northeast Aegean islands and the Dodecanese. Meanwhile, the long vocal introductions to Cretan songs bear traces of North African and Arab music.

## STRUCTURE AND SOCIAL CONTEXT

Most traditional Greek music is either pentatonic (five notes in the scale) or based on a modal system used in music of the Middle East. The *októehos* system at the basis of Byzantine ecclesiastical chant, however, was not (as many nationalist musicologists assert) descended from ancient Greek music,

> *Some modes do not start with do–re–mi (C–D–E), like the Western major scale, but do–do sharp–mi (C–C#–E). Violins on the islands are still sometimes tuned à la Toúrka, D–A–D–G.*

but from the modes of Jewish or secular melodies of ancient Palestine; its greatest composer was 5th-century Syria's Romanos O Melodos.

Greece's lyrics were never divorced from music as in the West, where for example opera librettos were commissioned separately. Since antiquity both have been inseparable, and in recent decades musical settings of poetry – or high-quality, purpose-written lyrics – have constituted some of Greece's most powerful music. Much-esteemed lyricists of poetic calibre include Kostas Virvos, Manolis Rasoulis, Nikos Gatsos and Manos Eleftheriou. The enthusiastic Greek website www.stixoi.info contains tens of thousands of song lyrics, including translations into foreign languages. Instrumental music remains a relative rarity, while unaccompanied voice still features in women's laments, *tis távlas* (table songs), *tis strátas* (road songs) and epics such as the medieval Cretan *Erotókritos*.

Like all folk music, *nisiótika* were not originally conceived as entertainment but were integral to religious festivals, weddings, funerals or work. Unfortunately, on the more touristed islands it's become almost impossible to hear genuine acoustic music – count yourself lucky if you're invited to a soirée with traditional instrumentation.

## GREEK RHYTHMS, AMERICAN BLUES?

Unlike Western metres in units or multiples of two, three or four beats, the Greeks seem to have matched their musical rhythms to the cadences of their poetry since the age of the Homeric hexameter; catchy 5/8, 7/8, 9/8 and even 11/8 time signatures are common in Greek traditional music. The composer Mimis Plessas (1924–), a jazzman also responsible for many Greek movie soundtracks, remembers a 1953 jam session with American jazz trumpeter Dizzy Gillespie. Plessas fingered a nimble 7/8 rhythm on the piano – and promptly lost Dizzy. "I can't do it, something's missing," said the great jazzman. Less convincingly, Plessas claimed:

"Imagine the field cry of the black man transported to Greece – that's what Greek music is."

Plessas was not the last to simplistically equate American blues and Greek song – especially *rebétika*, the genre most foreigners gravitate towards. Originally, this was the underground music of a particular segment of the Anatolian refugee population which appeared in Athens, Piraeus and Thessaloníki after the disastrous 1919–22 Greco-Turkish War, and the exchange of religious minorities between the two nations. A better analogy would be with Portuguese *fado* or Andalucían flamenco, styles particular to certain classes, neighbourhoods and venues.

Hardcore urban *rebétika* superficially resembles the blues in origins and preoccupations – poverty and social exclusion, disease, the allure of drugs and idleness, thwarted love – and its practitioners (the *rebétes*) and lyrics were persecuted and censored during the 1930s. Westernising Greeks despised its "oriental" roots, but one can safely say that *rebétika* existed in some form around the east Aegean coast and the Black Sea for decades before that. By the 1950s, however, *rebétika* became "domesticated" and incorporated into mainstream Greek music. In 1953 Manólis Hiótis killed off the original rebetic style by adding a fourth string to the *bouzoúki*, allowing it to be tuned tonally rather than modally – thus spawning *laïká* and *elafrolaïká*, the urban "popular" styles heard on the radio countrywide.

This was just one aspect of the ongoing postwar Westernisation of Greece, with the local musical scene arrayed in two opposing camps: adherents of traditionally derived styles versus those who forsook roots music for imported jazz/cabaret, symphonic and rock models.

## THE STATE OF THE ART

Mikis Theodorakis, after his 1964 *Zorba* outing, shunned Byzantine/rebetic/traditional sources completely in favour of Western quasi-symphonic works and film music. The political Left historically condemned apolitical, escapist *rebétika* and *laïkó*, attempting at one point to "raise mass consciousness" with recycled *andártika*, wartime resistance anthems – but Theodorakis, exiled to Ikaría in 1947, remembers everyone there singing *rebétika*.

More thoughtful musicians attempted to bridge the high–low culture gap with hybrid styles: the *éntekno* or "artifice" music of Crete-born Yannis Markopoulos, where traditional instruments and themes were used within large-scale compositions of great emotive power; a succession of guitarist singer-songwriters, led by Dionysis Savvopoulos and Nikos Papazoglou, who challenged the supremacy of the ubiquitous *bouzoúki* with modern lyrics too, giving rise to Greek folk-rock; and revivalists such as Cretans Haïnides and Loudovikos ton Anogion, who countered rock-drum-kit-and-electrification of live traditional performances with updated, rearranged

*A bouzoúki-playing busker in Athens.*

standards and original compositions.

*Rebétika* enjoyed a revival after the fall of the junta, which had tried to ban it like much else, although the fad – most pronounced among urban intellectuals – has long since waned. Subsequent re-issue recordings mainly targetted a foreign audience, many first exposed to the genre by Stavros Xarhakos' soundtrack to the 1983 film *Rebétiko*.

But "pure" *laïkó* and *nisiótika*, despite being looked down on by educated Greeks (especially overseas students), refuses to die. It's a perennial scenario in Greece, where a Westernised cultural elite keep busy attempting unsuccessfully to banish "low-class" habits. Unruly cosmopolitanism continues to be the nemesis of nationalists and reformers in search of an illusory "purity".

# AEGEAN ARCHITECTURE

Traditional architecture and town planning on the Aegean islands is a response both to the environment and local history between the 13th and 19th centuries; today islanders much prefer the qualities of more modern homes.

The development of both architecture and town profiles across the Aegean was spurred by several factors. By the late 12th century, Byzantine power had declined considerably, and the Venetians took advantage of this to divert the Fourth Crusade to Constantinople in 1204, smashing the central authority which until then had ruled all the islands. The Cyclades and Sporades in particular were parcelled out to Venetian nobles and adventurers, while in the course of the following centuries the crusading Knights of St John and the Genoese established themselves in the Dodecanese and northeast Aegean respectively. After various attempts, the Venetian Republic acquired sovereignty of the Ionian islands in 1386, and the main towns that evolved on Zákynthos, Corfu and Kefaloniá conformed very much to the example of Venice itself, with high, tottering, louvre-shuttered townhouses as well as Baroque churches giving onto vast piazzas.

Ermoúpoli balconies, Sýros.

## ANTI-PIRACY MEASURES

Piracy became rife in the Aegean, and most coastal settlements were abandoned in favour of inland or at least elevated towns known as the *hóra* ("the place"), from which hostile ships could be sighted from a distance and appropriate measures taken. Cycladic and Sporadic villages featured zigzagging lanes and cul-de-sacs, with the purpose not only of acting as wind baffles, but to confuse intruders, who (not knowing the maze-like street plan) could more easily be trapped and dispatched.

The ultimate anti-raider defence was the *kástro*, a usually rectangular compound with gated access, the backs of the contiguous houses substituting for conventional curtain walls. Some, but not all, *kástra* are originally Venetian-planned and built; others are adapted

> Rhodes Old Town is an instance of Western military engineering and a grid street-plan based strongly on the ancient city, and doesn't really count as vernacular architecture.

from Byzantine or even ancient sites. The best examples, still inhabited, are located on Páros, Andíparos, Sífnos, Náxos, Folégandros and Síkinos. The *kástra* at Kímolos (which was founded by a Greek Orthodox trader under Ottoman rule) and Astypálea were effectively abandoned after World War II, while Skáros on Santoríni and Kástro on Skiáthos were both deserted by the mid-19th century, after the Barbary corsairs had been suppressed by the French in 1833.

The Dodecanese and northeast Aegean had no *kástra* per se – except arguably the mastic villages on Híos – but towns grew up at the base of proper Genoese or Knights' castles, or on Pátmos around a fortified monastery.

## MATERIALS, STYLES, STRUCTURES

Construction of houses both humble and grand was drystone (without mortar), using local rock, though recycling ancient masonry was common,

perpendicular series of canes and finally a layer of *pateliá*, special earth tamped down with a roller.

Wooden balconies and railings are typical of many ports in the Cyclades and Dodecanese; during former times they were often made of

> *The doorways of kástra houses all faced inwards, with upper storey entrances reached by arpeggios of parallel staircases.*

*Panagía tou Pýrgou church, a diminutive landmark on Skópelos.*

and plaster rendering the rule on village-centre dwellings. On small islands, walls were (and still are) whitewashed regularly for hygienic reasons, to impart texture with built-up coats and to enhance heat reflectivity. Steps and walkways were also outlined in whitewash to aid night-time travel – invaluable before the era of streetlamps. Flat roofs served both for drying crops like figs or grapes, and to collect rainwater for cisterns; in the *kástra* they served a military purpose, as defenders could move rapidly on them from one threatened side of the settlement to another. Given a lack of deciduous hardwood, these flat roofs (and any upper floors) were supported by intertwined *fíthes*, gnarled but extremely strong trunks of a local juniper species, covered with a

katráni, a durable cedar imported from Asia Minor – now it is probably tropical hardwood. Ornate, wrought-iron fanlights and railings are a feature of many islands, particularly Kálymnos, Léros and the northeast Aegean.

Houses on the larger Dodecanese, and most of the northeast Aegean, tended to eschew whitewashing, opting either for bright colour (especially on Kálymnos), pointed bare masonry (Lésvos and Límnos) or painted lath-and-plaster upper storeys – notably on Sámos and Thásos – identical to that found across the mainland Balkans and Turkey.

### BUILDING FOR ALL PURPOSES

Multi-roomed houses around a courtyard emerged in the 19th century, replacing the one- or two-room modular houses typical of *kástra*; Cretan townhouses with courtyards date from the Venetian occupation. Neoclassical ornamentations and methods – including pitched roofs with canal- or pan-tiles, as well as the ironwork noted previously (see page 69) – became common after Greek independence.

Churches, many of them diminutive and incorporated seamlessly into the fabric of a village, were built in a similar style to secular buildings (though usually with vaulted roofs). Monasteries, especially isolated rural ones, had similar

offend Muslim sensibilities, though this proved less true in homogeneously Christian islands like the Cyclades.

Certain communal constructions were vital to a largely self-sufficient rural economy: domed ovens suitable for bread and roast meat alike, windmills to process the summer grain harvest (when the *meltémi* wind was conveniently at its height) and watermills – found on Kéa, Andros, Skiáthos, Skýros, Náxos and Kýthnos, as well as islands with more obvious, strong streams like Sámos, Lésvos, Ikaría and Crete.

*Windmill on Páros.*

*The benefits of whitewashing include heat reflectivity.*

> *Rarely are there any subsidies available to support those islanders who do wish to employ the invariably more expensive, labour-intensive traditional techniques.*

architecture but were always walled – both in accordance with Orthodox doctrine, in other words to mark them apart from "the world", and as a practical measure to deter piracy. Belfries and bell-walls, the star of many a postcard, are relatively recent, Western-influenced introductions: during Ottoman times there were restrictions on the ringing of church bells lest they

Some watermills have ended up outlasting windmills in terms of usage, working right up until the 1980s. Their profile, usually with a sluice preceding a staged descent tower, is unmistakable. Windmill construction and repair was a special trade, and hardwood tree trunks suitable for the main shaft had to be imported from mainland forests; walls might be over one metre (3ft) thick to support the tremendous stresses imparted through the masts.

Rectangular dovecotes, introduced by the Venetians as a feudal privilege, are restricted to Tínos (which has almost 1,200 of them), Ándros, Mýkonos and Sífnos. Stone-slab niches and vents in geometric designs adorn a leeward side of the structure.

Improved conditions within the Ottoman Empire from the late 18th century onwards fostered the growth of a Christian bourgeoisie, something evident in the opulent shipowners' mansions on Hydra and Spétses, plus others on a less grand scale at Límni, Evvia and on Andros. The same era saw the appearance of multi-storey, semi-fortified tower mansions around Mytilíni (Lésvos), structures with few parallels on other islands, though plenty on the mainland.

The 19th-century industrial warehouses of the larger east Aegean islands like Lésvos, Híos and

village-centre houses – deemed cramped, dark and insanitary – are left to those nostalgic Athenians and foreigners foolish enough to purchase them for renovation. When locals deign to remain in an old house, they typically deface it with mass-

> *Churches often owed their existence to a private vow, and they remained – and still remain – in the same family for generations.*

*Striking holiday apartment decked out in Greece's blue and white, Imerovígli, Santoríni.*

Sámos, typically devoted to the olive-milling, leather-tanning or distilling trades, constitute a special case in both style – derived from similar structures in Asia Minor, just across the water – and size, with typically 80cm (2.5ft) thick walls rather than the 50cm (1.5ft) thickness almost universal for dwellings across the Aegean.

## MODERN ADULTERATIONS

Sadly, none of the foregoing seems to interest many of today's islanders, especially those on the larger islands. Like most Greeks, their dream is of a modern rural villa or at least free-standing house amidst gardens or fields, with wraparound balconies, fireplaces doubling as space heaters and, above all, easy car access and parking. Traditional

produced aluminium windows and doors, and flanged, so-called *romaïká* tiles which arguably make many communities look like a slum when seen from above (unless the settlement has been declared *diatiritéo* – under a conservation order).

A stab at checking the spread of incongruous styles and materials was made in 2001 when then-Minister of the Aegean, Nikos Sifounakis, promulgated rules for building on the smaller, more picturesque islands – but not on any of the larger ones, where too many voters would have been antagonised. These restrictions, even where still in force, have been complemented or even substituted by those of the very powerful state archaeological service, which effectively controls areas like the Cycladic *kástra*, Sými and Rhodes Old Town.

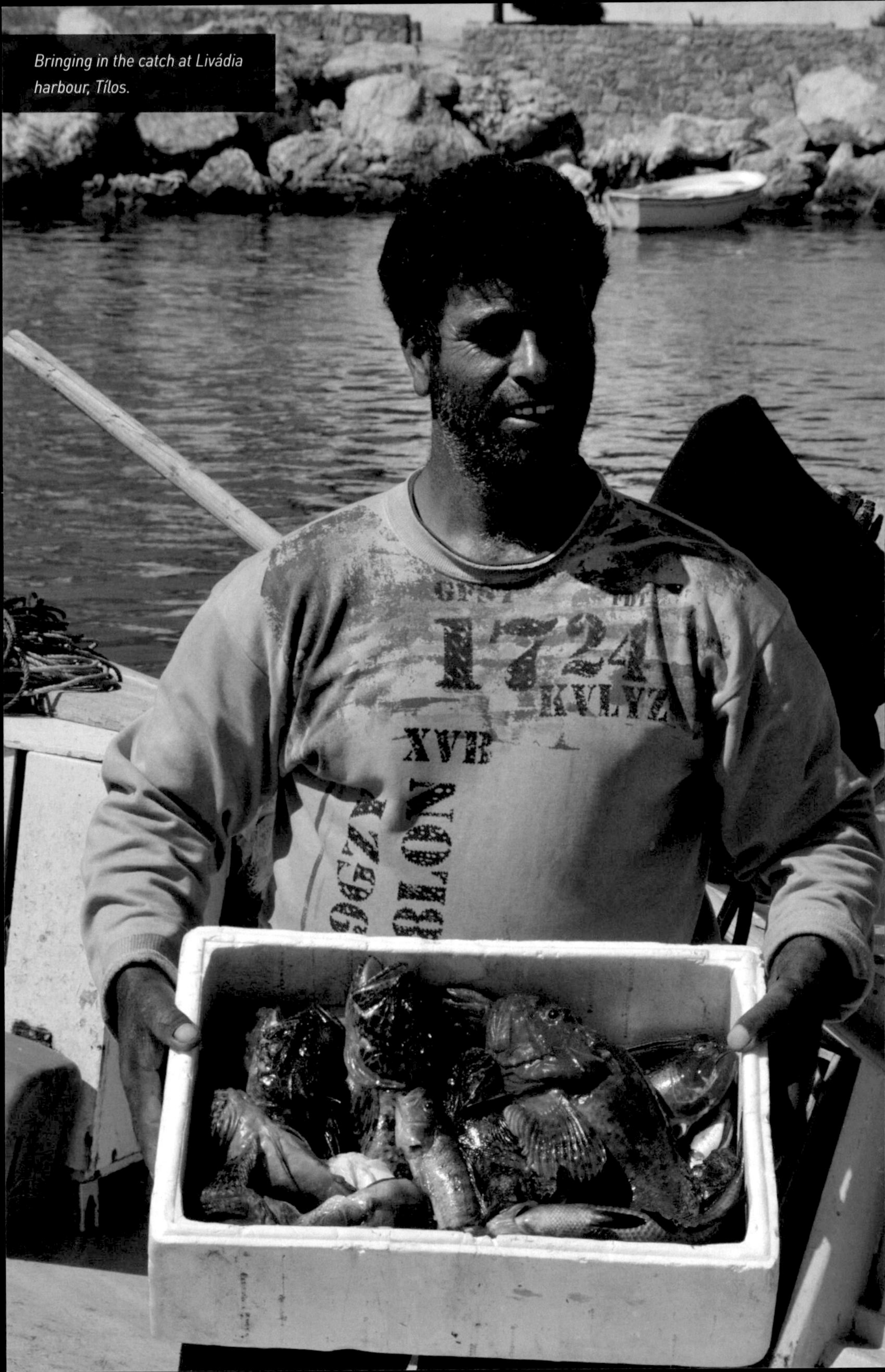


*Bringing in the catch at Livádia harbour, Tílos.*

# FOOD AND DRINK

Renewed pride in traditional regional recipes, a change in restaurant cooking habits and the advent of a quality wine industry have all done wonders for Greek cuisine.

Greek restaurant fare long had a poor reputation amongst foreign visitors. Casserole dishes (*magirevtá*) were saturated in oil, overcooked and served lukewarm; resinated wine was likened to paint stripper; leafy greens and seafood were severely limited in summer. Unless they travelled off-season, or were invited to eat by a family, visitors were apt to form a frankly libellous impression of local cuisine.

Eating in Greece at the dawn of tourism was constrained by the interrelated factors of poverty, religious strictures and the unforgiving Mediterranean environment, not to mention feelings of shame about "peasant" culture. Until the 1960s, most people ate meat just a few times a month and at major holidays – not just for financial reasons, but because of Church-mandated abstention from meat and cheese which, for the devout, could total several months of the year. A range of *nistísima* or fasting foods had evolved, many of them the so-called *laderá* or "oily" dishes comprising stewed or rice-stuffed fresh vegetables, and pulses; those ladles of olive oil, along with chunks of bread, also conveniently quelled hunger pangs. Piping-hot food was fervently believed to be bad for you. Bread was made partly or wholly from barley, easy to grow on the more barren islands, and equally easy to turn into long-keeping *paximádia* (rusks).

Snails emerging from hibernation after the first rains, *volví* (bitter wild hyacinth bulbs), various kinds of *hórta* (radicchio, amaranth and chicory) gathered from a hillside, *ftéres* (fern sprouts), *glystrída* (purslane) sprigs weeded from the summer garden: such were the wild foods much sought after by resourceful country-dwellers. But this kind of "granny" fare

*A simple aubergine dish in Santoríni.*

collided head-on with returning Greek emigrants and their Western, fast-food tastes, and a simultaneous tendency to give tourists what they seemed to want, not threatening "ethnic" food. Thus souvláki and chips ruled unchallenged for decades.

## SLOW FOOD REDUX

The late 1980s saw a rehabilitation and upgrading of traditional Greek cooking. Increased prosperity and travel or study overseas had broadened culinary horizons, while under the post-junta PASOK governments there was certainly an anti-Western backlash and increased pride in Greekness. But growing nostalgia for the *patrída* (rural homeland),

and the loosening of country cooking's association with grinding poverty, were more powerful forces. Crete, with its long growing season and rich wild flora, became a main focus for this renaissance. Cookbooks multiplied – Myrsini Lambraki's *Horta*, telling one what to do with every variety of edible wild plant, went through dozens of printings – while celebrity TV chefs emerged. Restaurants and *mezedopolía* began to update home-style recipes, emphasising fresh, locally sourced, seasonal ingredients, sensible cooking times and minimised use of

*A mouth-watering seafood platter.*

## Ø THE IDEAL VS THE REAL

While researching *Heirs to the Greek Catastrophe*, her classic 1970s study of an Asia Minor refugee community near Piraeus, anthropologist Renée Hirschon learned that a "good" housewife's worth was demonstrated by her reliable presence in the kitchen, slaving over labour-intensive dishes involving lots of rolling out of filo dough, canning, stuffing and baking – slow food *avant la lettre*. Quick fried or grilled dishes were dismissed by her informant as *tis poutánas to faï* or "whore's food", the sort of skillet-snacks that a prostitute might whip up between clients. Ironically, perhaps, such recipes are the staples of many contemporary *mezedopolío* menus.

oil, allowing intrinsic food flavours to emerge. The most *nouvelle* restaurants were (and are) dubbed *koultouriárika* – "highbrow" – often a bit precious in their menus, slimline portions and prices. But those survivors that succeeded in providing value left a lasting mark on the eating-out scene.

## THE BASICS

Despite the waning of strict fasting and more disposable income, vegetables remain the backbone of island cuisine. Tasty *nistísima*-compliant favourites include all manner of *hórta* drizzled with oil and lemon juice, fresh *koukiá* (broad beans – abundant during Lent), *angináres alá políta* (artichoke hearts, carrots, dill and potatoes), *briám* or *tourloú* (ratatouille) of courgettes, aubergine, tomatoes, garlic and onion, and stewed lentils or chickpeas. Potatoes, hand-cut daily into chips or medallions, are still the hallmark of a good restaurant; Belgian or Brit pre-pack chips are considered fit for tourists only. Minced meat appears in such *magirevtá* as *lahanodolmádes* (stuffed cabbage leaves), *giouvarlákia* (rice-and-mince-balls in egg-lemon sauce) and *giaprákia* (stuffed vine leaves) – the latter most commonly found as its vegetarian version, *gialantzí* ("liar's") *dolmádes*. *Píttes* (turnovers) can similarly be stuffed with *nistísima* or a meat/cheese filling.

Mezédes or orektiká (starters) are frequently meat-free: *fáva* (claimed best from Santoríni) is yellow split peas puréed, then served with chopped onions, lemon wedges and olive oil, while *mavromátika* (black-eyed peas) are boiled and then served chilled, garnished with onion and parsley. *Taramosaláta*, *tzatzíki* and *melitzanosaláta* will be familiar from a thousand overseas kebab houses, but in the islands no outfit with an eye to its reputation will decline to make these in-house to a notably chunky consistency; pre-purchased catering packs are for tourist tavernas or "snack bars" only.

Although *horiátiki*, or peasant's salad, is the summer mainstay, between October and April salads are more diverse – cabbage with grated carrot early in winter, followed by medleys of lettuces, rocket, radishes, spring onions and dill.

Perhaps surprisingly, Greeks are Europe's top per capita cheese-eaters. *Féta* – for which Greece has secured European court rulings protecting its "registered trademark" status – is the most famous of numerous varieties, which range from soft to hard, sweet to sharp. Cow, goat or sheep milk are used alone or in variable combinations. Hard cheeses (like *kefalograviéra*) are for grating, grilling or frying, crumbly (like *dermatísio*) for stuffing, soft (like the sweet *myzíthra*) for spreading or spooning. *Saganáki* is any suitable cheese, fried, or alternatively any cheese-based sauce.

or pork. Lamb and goat are more common from April to autumn.

Non-farmed scaly fish is as expensive in Greece as elsewhere in the Mediterranean. You're usually better off setting your sights on humbler, seasonally available species than on the bream and sea bass familiar from Northern European supermarket counters. East Aegean and Dodecanese islands near the nutrient-rich river mouths of Anatolia and Dardanelles outflow have the best choice. The profile changes from spring, with the last of

*Starters of féta cheese and fáva, which is made from puréed yellow peas and similar to pease pudding.*

## MEAT AND FISH

In terms of meat, pig is big, coming in budget form as *apáki* (Cretan cured pork, leanest from a piglet), *sýnglino* (chunky, fattier bacon) or *loukánika* (sausages); every island has their own, from the long, skinny ones of Cretan Sfakiá to the chunky, coarse-grained ones of Ándros. Cold piggy snacks mean *pikhtí* (brawn), air-dried salami (especially from Levkáda) or succulent *noúmboulo* from Corfu. More ubiquitous are *souvláki*, *gýros* (pork slices cut from a dense-packed, side-cooked cylinder) *brizóles* (pork chops) and *panséttes* (spare ribs, not belly bacon as elsewhere). On bigger islands with extensive flocks, there may be local *soúvla* or *exohikó*, various spit-roasted cuts of lamb, goat

*Certain shellfish must be eaten alive to avoid food poisoning: petalídes (limpets), gyalisterés (smooth Venus), kydónia (cockles), kténia (scallops) and petrosolínes (razor clams). If they twitch when drizzled with lemon juice, they're alive.*

the shrimp and sole, to early summer's swordfish and *marídes* (pickarel), to the deliciously flash-fried *atherína* (sand smelt) and *gávros* (anchovy), plus grillable *sardélles* (sardines) and *koliós* (mackerel) later in summer. The last two also make excellent marinated *mezédes*. Other affordable seafood includes grilled or stewed octopus and cuttlefish prepared with rice and greens. Once poor people's food, now trendy and expensive, are sea urchin roe and *foúskes*, a bizarre Dodecanesian invertebrate which tastes much like oysters.

## ISLAND DRINKS

Another motor for the makeover of Greek cuisine was the emergence from the late 1980s onwards of a quality wine industry, overseen by foreign-educated Greek oenologists. Owing to limited bottling capacity – many microwineries don't exceed 20,000 bottles annually – most premium wines are unknown outside of Greece, but they can be as good (and expensive) as French, Italian or southern hemisphere rivals. The best island wines are reckoned to hail from Límnos, Rhodes, Sámos, Santoríni, Híos, Kefaloniá and Crete. There's been keen interest in reviving heirloom grape varieties, some known since antiquity. Conversely, the Greek culinary renaissance included new-

*Try the humbler, seasonally available species of fish.*

*Do try the local wines.*

found esteem for bulk wines, which had nearly disappeared. Some are barely quaffable, some are great but even these will rarely break the bank. *Retsína* (wine flavoured with pine resin) is offered nationwide, but it travels poorly and bottled (as opposed to barrelled) *retsína* for many is an oxymoron; the best, genuine stuff comes from Attikí, around Athens.

*Oúzo*, the national aperitif, is distilled from grape-mash residue left over from winemaking, and then flavoured with aniseed or fennel; strength is typically 40–46 percent alcohol. The best island labels come from Lésvos, Híos and Sámos. Unflavoured variants of *oúzo* include *tsípouro* (Thássos and Sporades), *soúma* (Rhodes, Sámos) and *rakí* or *tsikoudiá* (Crete).

Al-fresco lunch in Skiáthos Town.

# 📷 EATING YOUR WAY ROUND THE ISLANDS

Traditional Greek food is better than its reputation, especially if you ignore what's offered to tourists and seek out traditional local dishes.

Anyone who has experienced tourist menus of chicken and chips or microwaved *moussakás* can be excused for believing that Greece isn't the place for culinary delights. So for a taste of real Greek cooking, follow the locals to backstreet tavernas. The food at such traditional places, geared for a lunch-hour clientele, more than compensates for any lack of fancy decor. If communication is a problem, take a look at what's cooking and point at what you want. Ordering this way is accepted practice.

You'll soon find there's more to Greek cuisine than *souvláki* and *taramosaláta*. Vegetables like fresh runner beans, okra or butter beans, cooked in olive oil and tomato; hearty fish soups; cheese, leek or spinach pies with a feather-light filo pastry; cuttlefish with spinach or fennel-root; rabbit stew; courgette flowers stuffed with herby rice and fried in batter – the islands offer dishes for all tastes. There are plenty of vegetarian options because of the many fast days in the Orthodox calendar.

Regional variations reflect island history and foreign occupations, and many dishes have strong Italian and Turkish influences. You'll find pastas and pilafs, plus vegetable recipes like *briám* and *imám baïldí*, their foreign names absorbed into Greek menus.

From the *krasotýri* of Kós, the *sofríto* (veal casserole) of Corfu to the *fourtália* omelettes of Andros, every island has its speciality. Some may seem strange – *foúskes* (a marine invertebrate) or *kokorétsi* (spit-roasted offal) are not for the fainthearted – but prove to be delicious. If all else fails, *horiátiki*, the classic Greek village salad, with feta, olives, peppers, cucumber and tomato, takes some beating.

*Pasta and wine on the beach in Levkáda.*

*Fresh fish and roasted vegetables in Santoríni. The fish and seafood in the Aegean is delicious but scarce, so prices can be high.*

*Lamb wrapped in vine leaves.*

*Many islands make their own oúzo.*

## And something to drink?

You can drink anything in Greece from cocktails to local firewater. *Oúzo*, the national aperitif, turns harmlessly milky when ice or water is added. It's usually drunk with olives or other starters *(mezédes)*. If you prefer wine, *retsína* (white wine flavoured with pine resin) is an acquired taste, ranging from lightly to heavily scented. The best bottled labels are Georgiadi and Malamatina from Thessaloníki.

Popular inexpensive bottled wines include Tsantali and Boutari, available nationwide in reds, whites and rosés, or Zítsa bulk wine from Ípiros. For something better, go for Tsantali Agioritiko in white and red, Papaïoannou reds or any white or rosé from Límnos. Try also premium island wines like Gentilini Robola white from Kefaloniá, Voultsos on Zákynthos, Economou or Lyrarakis from Crete, Methymneos from Lésvos, Hatziemmanouil or Hatzinikolaou from Kós, Ariousos from Híos or Ktima Argyrou, Venetsanos, Vasaltis or Sigalas from Santoríni.

*Grilled octopus is often an affordable seafood meal.*

*Kataífi is made from a vermicelli-like pastry of shredded filo dough, filled with chopped nuts and drenched in syrup.*

After dinner try Greek brandy, Metaxa, which comes in three starred grades (five is best). Any *kafenío* (coffee bar) will serve up Greek coffee – *skéto* (without sugar), *glykó* (sweet), *varýglyko* (cloying) or *métrio* (medium). Decent espressos/cappuccinos or filter coffees are steadily displacing a prior fixation with bad instant formulas.

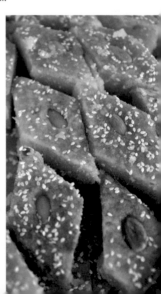

*Save space for dessert, they are usually very rich...*

# CRUISING ROUND THE ISLANDS

Greeks have sailed between the islands for thousands of years. Today it is possible to follow in their wake, on anything from day-trips to all-inclusive luxury cruises.

Having over 60 inhabited islands means having ships to serve them, and Greece has a long shipping tradition. Anyone who has sailed the Aegean, where white cruise-ship superstructures rival the dazzling sun itself, knows the affinity Greeks have for their boats.

The giants of the past, such as Aristotle Onassis and Stavros Niarchos, are no longer with us, and their successors keep a much lower profile. They are there, however: dozens of Greek shipping companies operating out of 1 sq km (0.4 sq miles) of office blocks in the port city of Piraeus overlooking the Aktí Miaoúli seafront, where suited office-workers rub shoulders with burly crewmen headed for the NAT (seamen's social fund) building.

Despite economic turmoil, owners remain emotionally committed to their businesses. In terms of satisfaction, little can equal gazing out of one's air-conditioned headquarters and watching one's ship come in. The same feeling prompted the great 18th-century captains of Hydra and Spétses to build their arhondiká (mansions) facing out to sea.

The transportation of goods to and from the Greek islands is fundamental to their economies. Visitors to the country, however, enjoy being human cargo on a cruise.

## WHICH CRUISE TO CHOOSE?

The most frequent voyages in Greece are one-day cruises. A typical one-day cruise from Piraeus is an excellent introduction to the Argo-Saronic islands. You will visit the 5th-century BC Temple of Aphaea (Aféa) on Aegina, one of the finest in all Greece; at Póros you will pass through the narrow straits with the town's tile-roofed houses towering

*Boat trip around Skiáthos, including Lalálaria cove.*

above the ship on one side and extensive lemon groves on the other, mainland side; in Hydra you will stroll through the beautiful little town arrayed around the harbour. From Corfu, one-day cruises visit its small, scenic neighbours – Andípaxi, with swimming in superb bays, and then Paxí for lunch. From Kos or Rhodes in the Dodecanese, day excursions visit many nearby, smaller islands.

There are also three-to ten-day cruises, most of them operating out of Piraeus, though some worthwhile eight-day cruises operate out of Rhodes or Crete. Two of the best outfits for this are Seafarer (www.seafarercruises.com) and Variety (www.varietycruises.com), which both market seven-to-eight-day itineraries on small-to-medium-sized motor or sail-assisted yachts like the *Galileo* or *Harmony*, both capable of anchoring in smaller, less visited ports of the Cyclades. The *Windstar*, a striking, four-masted small ship, is another excellent craft to book for a seven-to-ten-day odyssey (www.windstarcruises.com).

For longer, international cruises, it's wise to opt for a surviving company using medium-capacity craft (under 1,000 passengers) which – while perhaps not up to the luxury stand-ards of transatlantic or Caribbean cruises –

> *Examine itineraries carefully before you book. You want to cover long stretches of open sea after dark, with overnights or late-night stays only in interesting ports like Corfu, Návplio, Mýkonos or Pátmos. Many cruises are just too rushed.*

are usually small enough to manoeuvre into most chosen harbours, and do not dwarf their destinations like the towering new generation of gin palaces. They constitute the best way to see the most interesting ports in the south-eastern Mediterranean, in reasonable comfort and with good food.

A typical three-day cruise starts from Piraeus, taking in Mýkonos, Kuşadası (for Ephesus) in Turkey, Pátmos and either Rho-des or Crete; four-day cruises will definitely include all of the ports just noted, plus Santo-ríni, whereas a one-week cruise might stretch up to Istanbul too. Ten-to-14-day cruises for-sake Turkey in favour of add-ons to Katákolon (for ancient Olympia), Corfu, Dubrovnik and Split in Croatia, Malta and assorted Italian ports before finishing in Marseille or Bar-celona. Alternatively, longer cruises head southeast from select Greek islands, taking in Cyprus and Israel.

## POLITICS AT SEA

As with all things Greek, there is a political dimension, hingeing on the word *cabotage*. Cabotage is an international legal term mean-ing, as far as Greek shipping companies are

concerned, a monopoly on all lines connecting Greek domestic ports. Many foreign ships have historically cruised Greek waters with passen-gers they brought from outside, and returned to some port outside Greece, but cabotage long protected Greek cruise companies from foreign competition in Greek waters.

By European Union decree, this nautical monopoly was supposed to cease, for EU-reg-istered ships at least, in 2004. Since then, in theory, the market was incrementally opened, with many existing Greek ships improved and

*The Dodecanese islands make a dramatic backdrop to a cruise.*

brand-new ships brought into service to stave off competition. It certainly brought about a number of mergers to enable survival in try-ing times, although several companies also went bankrupt.

Greek governments are fond of impos-ing regulations, often impenetrable, usually expensive, upon every aspect of life imagi-nable, including Greek shipping. Many Greek shipowners long responded by registering their ships under a cheaper flag of conveni-ence (usually Malta, Liberia or the Caymans). Finally, with the lifting of cabotage in 2012, such foreign-registered ships could at last cruise between the Greek islands.

Sun, clean seas and sand (or shingle) have made for a winning tourist formula.

# MANAGING THE TOURISTS

Mass tourism has not brought many destination islands what they wanted. Diverse remedies have been attempted, but there is still quite some way to go.

Greece supports a permanent population of nearly 11 million. Yet every year – even in a very bad one – at least 16 million foreign tourists descend on the country, while over 25 million appear in good seasons. Tourism has been the second-largest or largest foreign-exchange earner for Greece since the early 1970s, and currently accounts for almost 20 percent of gross domestic product.

Accordingly, Greece's first Ministry of Tourism was put in charge of EOT (the Greek National Tourism Organisation) in 1987 to address long-neglected crises in the industry. After being subsumed by different governments into the ministries of Development and Economy, or of Culture, on various occasions, it was only revived as in independent entity in 2012. But over the years ambitious ministry initiatives have had little effect, not least because most ministers have no experience in tourism and are anyway rotated in cabinet shuffles every 18 months. EOT, devoting most of its energies to dubious marketing slogans like "Live your myth in Greece", or "5,000 years of history you can afford", has arguably outlived its usefulness and might be better off divided into lean, mean regional entities, as has been done in Spain.

## GROWING PAINS, THEORETICAL REMEDIES

Touristic Greece had, by the mid-1980s, become a victim of its own success – and of unplanned growth, beginning under the junta, when easy credit was extended to build hotels and *domátia* (private rented rooms). Popular islands teemed with thousands of summer visitors; streets designed for a donkey and its two panniers became rivers of slow-moving gawpers; hotels were booked far in advance, disappointing foolhardy travellers who arrived on spec. Arid,

*Easy riders.*

### ⊘ THE NEW BARBARIANS

Louts, usually British, thronged Faliráki (Rhodes), Mália (Crete), Laganás (Zákynthos) and Kávos (Corfu) from the 1980s onwards, drawn by a pub-crawl culture where tour reps got kickbacks from bars and clubs. In 2003, an English lad was fatally stabbed in Faliráki and others were charged with public lewdness. Rhodian authorities reacted sternly and Faliráki's scene collapsed. The party just moved on to other resorts, where islanders who thought they'd seen everything with nude beachgoers were scandalised by public sex. Two more murders at Laganás (2011, 2017) were the last straw for the Ionians; 2017 saw Kávos announce a 2am club curfew and begin rebranding as a family resort.

smaller islands, supplied by tanker, had to ration water for showers.

Beaches were jam packed with sun-worshippers, including nude sunbathers inimical to the sensibilities of conservative native islanders. Still less popular were thousands of penniless backpackers arriving without accommodation, often indulging in petty crime and sleeping rough on rooftops or beaches.

Ferryboats were consistently overcrowded at high season, and the craft themselves – retired from more demanding North Sea or Baltic ser-

*After its beaches, the largely tasteful nightlife of Skiáthos is its big draw.*

vices, pending relegation to Southeast Asia, or the wrecker's yard – were nothing to write home about either. Seats on island-hopping aeroplanes had to be booked two months in advance, transiting cramped 1960s-vintage airports.

The ministry's late-1980s response was to promote quality clientele over quantity. Impecunious backpackers were to be discouraged in favour of specialist, high-spending tourism, and the necessary infrastructure built. An initial measure forbade admission to charter-flight passengers with no accompanying room reservation, so as to quash "hooliganism" among young tourists. Athens also put a theoretical halt to licensing low-end hotels and rooms on

islands over-supplied with them, while granting more permits for luxury hotels, with generous incentives for facilities such as golf courses, tennis courts and convention halls.

But with the connivance of seat-only operators, the accommodation requirement was easily circumvented. Required vouchers soon became dummies, or were only for one night, and anyway could not be enforced for EU nationals after 1993. Local bribes frequently neutralised controls on hotel-building permits.

## REALITY BITES

Restored spas on Lésvos, a new marina on Híos where few yachters go – a more useful one on Sámos took 17 years to finish – and proposed golf courses in a perennially water-short environment: such "solutions" seemed like shuffling deckchairs on the *Titanic,* so inadequate was Greece's chaotic infrastructure.

Uneven accommodation distribution was a major bugbear. By 1998 there were almost 1 million licensed beds in hotels and *domátia* – up to 1.4 million in 2008, but little changed by 2015 – with several provinces (like Sámos and Iráklio) suffering from vast excess capacity, while other spots remain under-supplied; 1970s-vintage room quality embodied a cheap-and-cheerful mentality, ignoring the fact that travellers now had better-value choices elsewhere in the Mediterranean – though necessary renovations accelerated from the 1990s onwards.

The ferryboat scandals of 1996, when boats were loaded to double safe capacity, were confronted by theoretically mandatory computerised booking and ticketing. Numerous exceptions were finally winkled out by the September 2000 wreck of the *Express Samina,* which starkly exposed the ongoing shortcomings of Aegean shipping. Some rust-buckets were subsequently junked, but by no means all – shipowners repeatedly wangled exceptions to the EU law ordering disposal of 30-year-old craft. When NEL went bust in 2016, its ancient boats blocked docks for months before being towed away to wrecking yards. Reputable companies now order new, state-of-the-art boats rather than relying on north European cast-offs; but high-speed boats, with their enormous fuel consumption, only break even financially when three-quarters booked – which happens at mid-summer only.

Private competitors to state-owned Olympic Airways emerged – and survived –once domestic aviation was deregulated, and Olympic Air (as it is now) itself liquidated and reformed as a private entity in 2009, prior to becoming a subsidiary of Aegean Airlines in 2013. At present, six airlines (including Ryanair) operate domestically, still too many for the size of the market and economic conditions. Popular peripheral flights such as Rhodes–Sámos or Thessaloníki–Sýros – the subsidised PSO (Public Service Obligation) routes – have to be served by law; they are periodically auctioned, with winners often using aircraft flatly unsuitable in terms of seat or baggage capacity. Even on profitable main routes, frequencies and seat availability remain inadequate in high season.

## HOPES AND PROSPECTS

A budget, studio-based package in Greece compares in price to one in competing Mediterranean destinations such as Spain, Croatia or Malta. A higher-quality Greek holiday costs nearly the same as the exotic delights of Cuba, Goa or Florida. Individuals who love Greece, have a connection with a particular place and speak a bit of the language continue to return regularly; but the country overall (with, admittedly, exceptional pockets) hasn't been trendy since the 1970s and stacks up poorly against Spain and Italy in terms of food, wine, service and overall value. While Greece does have resorts as exclusive and slick as any in the world, for the most part professionalism and a service ethic are lacking, especially on the agricultural islands – an ingrained peasant mentality doesn't easily assimilate notions like training and investment.

The mountain to climb in terms of attracting new visitors and keeping old customers is a huge one, but it can be done through addressing weaknesses and playing to the islands' strengths: clean seas, a high degree of personal safety, characterful inland villages, affordable low-impact sports (see page 86). No headway has been made in extending the tourist season – in fact, more and more places are making their living only from mid-July to late August – and Greece is also vulnerable to forces beyond its control: the value of the euro, the economies and school terms of other European countries, Schengen Zone rules, bad press about refugees and uproar in the aviation industry. Nonetheless, there are green shoots; weekend visits by

Turks to border islands like Híos, Sámos, Léros and Rhodes have rocketed thanks to issuance of Greek consulates in Turkey of short-length visas in seeming contravention of Schengen norms, with direct flights between Istanbul and Rhodes or Iráklion now a feature. On many islands the tourist "crop" has drastically changed character, with nationalities unseen during the 1990s now prevalent: Spaniards, Slovenians, Czechs, Poles, Russians. The Russians in particular are most visible on Corfu, Crete, Kos, Rhodes – plus even in second-rank destinations like Skiáthos and Sámos.

*The islands are the setting for a range of wallet-friendly, low-impact sports.*

A worrisome development belying a supposed commitment to upscale tourism is the spread of all-inclusive resorts. These are paid a risible per-passenger sum by the contracting overseas companies, and the often mediocre full board they offer has devastated nearby tavernas – a far cry from when taverna outings were a quintessential part of the island experience. Potentially more positive is the upswing in residential tourism, repeat visitors who have bought island property and help keep shops and businesses going. And much more can still be done with Greece's abundant medieval ruins and historic buildings: boutique-restoration-hotel proprietors report nearly 100 percent occupancy even in lean years.

# OUTDOOR PURSUITS

With over seven months of clement weather annually, the Greek islands are an obvious venue for all manner of sporting activities, from leisurely rambles to the adrenalin-rush-inducing thrills of newer sports.

It was not so long ago that all an island had to offer was a few patches of beach (whether sandy or pebbly), some bars or cafés as meeting points and a reasonable choice of food and accommodation, and it was likely to have met the expectations of its prospective clientele. More energetic pastimes meant hiking inland and uphill from the beach onto the network of trails which still existed, largely intact, until the 1990s. No longer: visitors, especially younger ones, now expect to be tempted by a range of often high-tech options which have pretty well eclipsed walking and the modest commitment of those who remembered to tuck a mask and snorkel into their luggage.

## ON LAND

Despite destructive nibblings by bulldozers since the 1970s, a considerable portion of historic paths and exquisitely engineered *kalderímia* (cobbled lanes) – many centuries old and the only link between villages in pre-vehicle days – survives. Perhaps counter-intuitively, the biggest, greenest islands are not always the best choices for hiking; ongoing agriculture means that many old paths have been widened into muddy, tractor-width lanes. Reliable islands for quality trail-walking (best during the cooler months) include Nísyros, Sými, Kálymnos and Tílos in the Dodecanese; Anáfi, Andros, Kéa, Tínos, Sífnos, Sérifos and Amorgós in the Cyclades; Alónnisos in the Sporades and Hydra in the Argo-Saronic. The granddaddy of small-island walks is the five-hour lengthwise traverse from Hóra to Egiáli on Amorgós, an island – with its protected network of *kalderímia* and profuse documentation – that has done more than most others to promote walking.

Honourable exceptions to the big-island rule are western Sámos around mounts Kérkis and

*Windsurfing in Levkáda.*

Karvoúnis, Corfu, with its marked and maintained 200km (125-mile) Corfu Trail, and Crete, with two mountain ranges rising to over 2,400 metres (7,874ft); the westerly range, the White Mountains, cradles the Samariá Gorge.

Besides a surprisingly extensive trail network, Kálymnos has some of the best big-wall climbing in the Mediterranean on its limestone cliffs, especially in the north – again, an off-season activity unless you fancy baking against the sheer faces.

## ON THE SEA

With medallists at the 2000, 2004 and 2008 Olympics (though none since), windsurfing has the cachet in Greece that cycling has in France. While it might seem windy almost everywhere, only certain resorts have the right combination of exposure and onshore topography to be world-class. Indeed, sites like southern Kárpathos, Prassonísi on Rhodes and Vassilikí on Levkáda host annual European tournaments, although Kamári (Kós), Agios Geórgios or Mikrí Vígla on Náxos, Kokkári (Sámos) and Kouremános (Crete) will be more than enough for beginners and intermediates. Kitesurfing, where devotees standing on a small board are propelled very quickly by a parabolic kite controlled with four lines, is like windsurfing

the Sporades) by SwimTrek (www.swimtrek.com). Sea kayaking is a less strenuous way of covering much the same territory and visiting otherwise inaccessible coastal formations. The rewards are subtle but tangible, like glimpsing brightly hued kingfishers perching on sea-level rocks in autumn.

## UNDER THE SEA

Scuba-diving has been slow to take off in Greece, owing to historical restrictions on the practice: so much archaeological wealth is assumed still to be submerged that the gov-

*Hiking trail near Kástro on Skiáthos.*

> *The best topographical hiking maps, covering most islands listed, are published by Anávasi (www.anavasi.gr) in Athens; otherwise variably good local maps and guide booklets exist.*

on steroids. Frequently launched into the air, kitesurfers are the skateboarders of the sea.

Just about every island visitor gets into the Aegean, though perhaps not quite to the extent of inter-island swimmers, who think nothing of an afternoon's crawl back and forth amongst the smaller Cyclades lying between Náxos and Amorgós; tours are organised here (plus Crete and

ernment has generally denied applications to authorise new dive zones for fear of antiquity theft. In 2008, after years of lobbying, existing schools managed to have the list of allowable venues greatly expanded, especially around Rhodes, Skiáthos and Alónnisos, and more venues should be opened once the painfully slow process of archaeological surveying is completed. The most reputable schools are on Skiáthos, Alónnisos, Léros, Kálymnos, Mýkonos, Náxos, Mílos, Corfu, Kefaloniá, Sámos and Rhodes. Don't expect a tropical profusion of fish – the Aegean is far too exploited for that. The attraction lies rather in caves, tunnels and other formations, as well as in sedentary marine life. Léros, with its World War II wrecks and debris from the battle of autumn 1943, is arguably the most interesting spot.

## THE SAILING SCENE

Sailing is a rewarding way of exploring this country of islands, whether in your own yacht, in a chartered boat or as part of a flotilla.

While the package holidaymaker and the independent island-hopper are forced to rely on ferries and their often idiosyncratic timetables in order to travel among the islands, yachties enjoy a remarkable degree of independence – except,

*The clear waters of Skiáthos.*

of course, from the winds. Sailing around Greece is not over-complicated by bureaucracy, but some paperwork, unfortunately, is unavoidable – namely transit logs for the boat, and a crew list with full names and passport numbers.

Chartering, now a fundamental part of the sailing scene in Greece, began throughout the islands in the mid-1970s; it was the idea of an enterprising group of British boat-owners who decided that they had had enough of miserable English summers and wanted holidays in the sun. This type of sailing is increasingly prevalent and has done much to encourage the development of marinas and improved facilities. Increasing numbers in recent years have seen a spread of poorer-quality boats, but most reputable charter companies supply yachts that are renewed every five years or so. They are designed for holidays in the sun and equipped to a luxurious standard with deep freezes, deck showers, snorkelling equipment and even a pair of thick gloves to handle the anchor chain.

## MAKING THE RIGHT CHOICE

It's important to match experience with the correct type of charter. Inexperienced sailors should select a flotilla holiday where a group of yachts cruise as a fleet, under the instructive eye of a lead boat crew. If you are an experienced sailor, you may want to arrange a "bareboat" charter, in which you act as your own skipper. If you can afford a crewed charter, you can simply relax on deck and leave all the sailing, boat maintenance, cooking and bureaucracy to paid hands.

Whether you're taking your own yacht to Greece or chartering, the range of sailing areas is large and your choice should take account of varying local weather conditions.

The recognised sailing season is from April to October, when the skies are mostly clear; temperatures vary between 23° and 38°C (70s and 90s degrees Fahrenheit) in July and August. Winds throughout the Aegean Sea tend to be from the north. The most talked-about weather phenomenon is the *meltémi*, a steady north wind which can affect the entire Aegean, and can reach Force 7 to 8, even 9, on the Beaufort scale in midsummer. It's a capricious wind, typically appearing around mid-June and dying down in late September. Usually the *meltémi* arises just before or after midday and calms with sunset, but can arrive without warning and blow for as little as one hour or for as long as one week. Yachtsmen must take care not to be caught on a lee shore, and should be aware that the *meltémi* can cause an extremely uncomfortable steep, short sea.

In the northern Aegean the *meltémi* blows from just east of north and, further south towards the Cyclades and Crete, predominantly from true north. By the time it reaches Kárpa-

translate for you (though the graphics are obvious), and port authorities will be well informed. If you have a laptop or tablet and Wi-fi (almost universal in marina cafés), log on to www.meteo.gr

> Occasionally the hot, damp, southeasterly *sirókos* wind, often carrying reddish dust from North Africa, will blow hard across the southern Aegean and Ionian seas – but it rarely lasts long.

When choosing a sailing area, bear in mind the varying local weather conditions.

thos, Rhodes and other southerly Dodecanese, this wind has gathered even more strength and is from the northwest. Its local violence has persuaded some charter companies to classify the Dodecanese as the most difficult waters in which to sail.

Sailing in the Dodecanese has the additional problem of the nearby Turkish maritime border. The Turks insist that anyone sailing in their waters must clear customs at one of their ports of entry. The border is policed at sea and it is therefore unwise to sail in Turkish waters unless you intend to enter Turkey officially.

Weather reporting in Greece is generally good. Virtually every Greek evening TV newscast is followed by a weather report which someone can

or http://poseidon.hcmr.gr/weather_forecast.php?area_id=gr, the latter with vital wind-and-waves graphic profilers; www.sailingissues.com is another useful site.

The Argo-Saronic Gulf and the Ionian Sea offer the gentlest sailing conditions, mainly because the islands are relatively close to each other (and to the mainland) and because the *maístros*, the more northwesterly variant of the *meltémi* in the Ionian, is usually weaker. The *maístros* tends to blow mainly in the afternoon, when the heat of the Greek mainland accelerates the wind off the sea.

Despite this variety of local breezes, Greek seas are often quite windless, so yachtsmen should be prepared to motor. Whatever the conditions, you should always protect yourself against the sun and the increased glare off the water – which can produce temporary blindness.

The greatest appeal of the Greek islands is the solitude offered by their remoteness. The green islands of the Ionian – especially a half-dozen islets southeast of Levkáda – are a first-choice venue for several reasons. The shelter among the many islands offers safe cruising, but if you want more lively conditions, a trip in the open waters west of Levkáda (Léfkas) and Kefaloniá will provide marvellous sailing. Easy anchorages and safe village moorings are within a few hours' sail of each other throughout these islands. The best season here is definitely during spring and autumn: August sees Italian yachtsmen pouring over from Italy, clogging up the numerous but small harbours.

The Saronic Gulf is a favourite haunt of yachtsmen, being so close to Piraeus. The little island of Angístri, off Égina, has some lovely coves; Égina, Póros, Hydra and Spétses have attractive town harbours as well as quieter anchorages; and the east coast of the Pelo-

Yachts moored in Mandráki harbour, Rhodes Old Town.

## ⊙ ISLAND MARINAS

The biggest concentration of marinas lies near Athens and Piraeus, though these are not particularly attractive. Other major marinas among or near Greek islands are at Gouviá, north from Corfu Town; Mathráki islet, northeast of Corfu; and at Corfu Town itself. The marina at Levkáda abuts the town, as does the one at Argo-Saronic Póros. In the Dodecanese, there are marinas at Mandráki (Rhodes – best suited to longer yachts), Kálymnos and (the largest) Léros. The large marina at Pythagório (Sámos) is ideal as an end point for a one-way itinerary. All these marinas make excellent staging posts/charter bases.

ponnese is unjustly underrated. In mid-season it will be difficult to find a berth at the town quays where, almost without exception, mooring is stern to the quay.

Moving east from the Saronic Gulf, the influence of the *meltémi* becomes stronger, and it is not until you travel north of Évvia to the Sporades that you find dependable shelter in any weather – each island here has a protected, south- or southeast-facing harbour. Beyond Skýros to the northeast lies the open, and generally wild, Aegean, with little casual sailing owing to the great distances involved. From the Sporades, most skippers make for the inlets and peninsulas of the Halkidikí peninsula, east of Thessaloníki.

# 🔍 ISLAND HOPPING

The pleasures of travelling from one island to another using Greece's interlinking ferry routes are numerous, but it pays to be prepared.

First there's the never-ceasing view – a bas-relief pattern on a blue base of low, mysterious summits. Plus, there are unique opportunities to "visit" other islands besides your destination – 15 minutes observing a port from top deck can reveal much about a place and its people. Reunions, farewells and the redistribution of a warehouse's worth of goods take place just below the rear railing. Is that a piano or an ice-cream freezer being offloaded? Is that cheeping coming from an embarking truck with a battery farm's quota of chickens?

Without thorough advance checking, however, it's easy to experience the worst aspects of island-hopping in the form of missed connections, being stranded, or even sailing straight past the intended island with no way back for two days. Even ferry journeys that go according to plan can be lengthy, not to mention nerve-racking rather than restful: if the boat reaches your small, remote destination at 2am, it's your responsibility to wake up – set your alarm! – and get off.

The *meltémi* is a fact of Greek summer life, unaffected thus far by global climate change. When winds are too strong, ships are delayed or kept in port. If you are depending upon ferries to take you back to Athens for your flight home, leave at least one full day's leeway.

Hydrofoils and larger catamarans which may or may not carry cars figure largely in inter-island travel. They are twice as fast as conventional ferries – ideal if time is limited – but also twice as expensive, and not without other disadvantages. Neither "cats" nor hydrofoils provide much of a view, and both are far more sensitive to bad weather than conventional boats. A good compromise are *tahyplía* or "high speed" ferries (especially Blue Star's), which cost somewhat more than the old tubs but sail a good deal more quickly. *Symvatiká plía*

(conventional ferries) are an endangered species, restricted to just a few routes.

## ROUTES AND SCHEDULES

Classic ferry itineraries include the central Cyclades circuit (Mýkonos, Páros, Náxos, Íos and Santoríni), the Argo-Saronic line (Póros, Hydra, Spétses) and major Dodecanese route (Pátmos, Léros, Kálymnos, Kós and Rhodes). Less popular are the western Cyclades arc (Kýthnos, Sérifos, Sífnos and Mílos), the main Sporades islands (Skiáthos, Skópelos, Alónnisos), and the link between Rhodes and Crete via Hálki, Kárpathos and Kásos. In the Ionian islands, travel is easy between Levkáda, Itháki and Kefaloniá. Another useful line joins

*Safety prevails.*

Ikaría and Sámos with Kavála, via Híos, Lésvos and Límnos. Besides Piraeus, the primary mainland ports are Lávrio, Rafína, Kavála, Vólos, Igoumenítsa and Pátra; on the islands, Páros, Sámos, Rhodes and Kós are useful regional hubs. The most comprehensive, updated sources of ferry schedules is the website of the Greek travel agents' manual, Greek Travel Pages (www.gtp.gr), or alternatively www.openseas.gr. Peripheral, subsidised lines – the *agonés grammés* – often have user-hostile schedules, either with uncivilised departure/arrival times, unhelpful frequencies (departing on two consecutive days, then not for five), or both. The ministry which pays shipowners handsome subsidies does not seem to stipulate in exchange the provision of tourist-friendly timetables.

The domesticated goat.

# ISLAND WILDLIFE

The diverse island landscapes support a varied collection of flora and fauna. Birds in particular, both resident and migrant, bring delight to ornithologists.

Arrive at a mid-Aegean island in the heat of summer and you may feel you've inadvertently stumbled upon a remote outpost of the Sahara. Arid brown countryside sheds clouds of dust each time the hairdryer wind blows, and the only surviving plant life grows in carefully nurtured pots on village terraces.

Visit in spring, however, and the picture is an entirely different one. Lush greenery and brightly coloured flowers cover the plains and hillsides, and even waste ground becomes garden.

The first seedlings and bulbs sprout shortly after the first autumn rains. Growth gathers pace through the cool but partly sunny winters; a few weeks into the new year, flowers start to bloom in the far southeast. Rhodes, Kárpathos and eastern Crete are followed in succession by western Crete, then the Cyclades and the eastern Aegean. Spring arrives in the Ionian islands and the north Aegean as summer appears in Rhodes.

As plants lead, so other wildlife follows. The number of insects increase, and the insect-eaters flourish; food chains gear up for a spring and early summer of proliferation.

## LOCAL FAUNA

Before mankind first settled in the region, the Greek islands had a mixture of forest, some tall, impenetrably dense *maquis* vegetation, and much *garrigue*. The latter (*phrýgana* in Greek) consists of low shrubby bushes which are often spiny, resisting both the grazing of animals and the bare legs of walkers. Mixed together with the shrubs are fragrant herbs, colourful annuals and, enjoying protection under those spines, fragile orchids.

It's a myth that man and his flocks destroyed a verdant Greek Eden of continuous woodland:

*Butterflies are conspicuous from spring to autumn.*

some larger islands had populations of wild plant-munching animals – such as deer – long before any human arrivals. Native grazers led to the flora's evolution of discouraging defences – spines, foul tastes – which armed it well for the comparatively recent introduction of domesticated sheep and goats. (See also page 96.)

## RECLUSIVE MAMMALS

Wild mammals occur on the islands, but most are secretive. Crete has its ibex-like wild goat or *agrími* (also called the *krí-krí*), a shy inhabitant of the White Mountains. Amid fears of its demise from over-hunting, some animals were transferred to the island of Día, near Iráklio, where they flourished and multiplied – ironically eliminating the rare native plants.

Elsewhere, the largest mammals are the badger, and the jackal of the eastern Aegean

> On Skýros there is a very small wild horse, a unique breed thought to be that depicted on the frieze of the Parthenon; less than 150 pure-bred specimens survive.

population of less than 400 live here, with perhaps 200 more elsewhere in Greek waters. Between islands, look out for common dolphins shadowing ferries.

## A BIRDWATCHER'S PARADISE

While mammal-watchers may find themselves underemployed, the birdwatcher should not be. The spring migration brings a variety of species from Africa. Their final destination will probably be much further north, but the Greek islands may be their first landfall after the Mediter-

The white pelican, or Pelecanus onocrotulus.

and Corfu, but the one you are more likely to see is the stone marten. This resembles a dark-brown ferret, long, slim, agile and fast-moving, sighted both during the day and in headlights crossing roads at night. They are frequent victims of the taxidermist's art, and many tavernas have one stuffed on display.

Most other mammals are small: field rats (common on Corfu and Sámos), rabbits or hares, wild mice and a half-dozen species of bats, most commonly the pipistrelles seen above many island villages.

The National Marine Park northeast of Alónissos is an important haven for the Mediterranean monk seal – the most endangered of all the world's seals. About 60 of a worldwide

ranean crossing. Both black and white storks migrate through Greece, nesting on the way. Individual flamingos may turn up anywhere there is a salty coastal pool, but you should visit Kos, Lésvos, Sámos and Límnos to see them roosting in quantity between December and May (though since 2007 their flight patterns have favoured touchdown in western Greek wetlands instead).

Much smaller, but most colourful, are the crested pink, white and black hoopoe, the bright blue-and-brown roller and the multicoloured bee-eater – the latter two highly visible in May. For many ornithologists, raptors – hawks, vultures, Bonelli's eagles and Eleonora's falcons – prompt the biggest thrill, although numbers of the latter two species are down on Tílos, owing to decline in the populations of rock partridges and passerines, respectively their favourite prey.

Larger species inhabit mountain areas, especially on Crete, where gorges and cliffs provide secure nesting and the requisite isolation. Spectacular griffon vultures, sometimes in large flocks, patrol the skies in search of dead livestock, soaring effortlessly on broad wings the size of a door. The much scarcer lammergeier has narrow wings, the ultimate flying machine in its search for bones – or tortoises – to drop onto rocks and break open.

## REPTILES, AMPHIBIANS AND INSECTS

The most abundant reptiles are lizards, some 21 species, of which the Balkan green lizard is perhaps the most conspicuous. Bolder and more stockily built is the iguana-like agama, sometimes called the Rhodes dragon, though it's also found on Corfu and several Aegean islands. Unlike others, this greyish rough-skinned lizard, when disturbed, will often stay around for a few minutes to check out the danger. Worth special note are very vocal, chirping geckos (three species, the most common the so-called "Turkish"), which cling harmlessly to your hotel-room wall or ceiling.

Tortoises occur on many islands, though surprisingly not on Crete. Once gathered in tens of thousands for the pet trade, they now lead safer lives wandering noisily through the underbrush, especially during spring migration. Their freshwater aquatic relatives, the Caspian terrapins, favour streams with bare muddy banks for sunbathing.

Marine loggerhead turtles are decreasing in numbers as their nesting beaches are lost to tourism. They used to breed widely on Crete, Kós and Rhodes – now they are restricted to a few beaches on Kefaloniá, Zákynthos and possibly corners of Crete and southeastern Rhodes.

European green toads are easiest seen migrating in May, and can overwinter in partly drained swimming pools. Loud marsh frog croaking belies their small size, and tree-frogs cluster on leaf undersides.

Snakes often cause alarm, but most are harmless, and all prefer to be left alone. Locals tend to overreact and attack any snake they see, though this actually increases the chance of being bitten. Poisonous vipers do occur on some of the Ionian, Cycladic and east Aegean islands – they have a zigzag or diamond pattern down the spine, and move rather lazily.

Mosquitoes may seem the commonest insects at night, but Corfu is noted for its springtime fireflies, little flashing beacons that drift over damp fields and hedges after dark. Paler lights in hedgerows are wingless glow-worms. Butterflies are obvious by day, often in great quantity and variety. Some of the large hawkmoths are diurnal – the hummingbird

*A stone marten clambers atop a fallen branch.*

hawkmoth, like its namesake, relies on super-fast wingbeats to hover at flowers as it feeds.

Noisier are the huge, glossy blue-black carpenter bees which spend much of their time looking for suitable nesting sites, usually a hollow cane or utility pole. Noisiest of all are cicadas, basically overgrown aphids, which perch on trees and keep up a deafening racket. Despite their size and volume, they are well camouflaged, so surprisingly hard to see.

Praying mantids keep their barbed forearms in a position of supplication until an unwary insect moves nearby – then the mantid becomes a hungry atheist. Even the male of the species is devoured as he romances the female, his substance helping to nourish the next generation.

# 📷 THE ISLANDS IN BLOOM

The Greek islands are at their most colourful in spring and autumn, when every hillside and valley is bedecked with glorious flowers.

Greece in spring is a botanist's (and photographer's) dream. Some 6,000 species of wild plant grow in mainland Greece and the islands, and in the spring (February to May) visitors may enjoy a magnificent cornucopia of flowers and fragrances.

Hillsides resemble giant rock gardens, while brilliantly coloured patches of untended waste ground outdo Northern Europe's carefully tended herbaceous borders with ease. Winter rains, followed by a bright, warm, frost-free spring, produce a season's blooming compressed into a few spectacular weeks before the summer's scorching heat and drought become too much. By late May or early June the flowers are done, the seeds for next year's show are ripening and greens are fading to brown to match the tourists on the beaches.

Except in the cooler, higher mountains, most plants go into semi-dormancy to survive the arid summer. The first rains of autumn, as early as September but usually mid-October, tempt autumn cylamens and crocuses into flower but also initiate the germination of seed plants that will grow and gather strength during the winter in preparation for the following spring when their flowers will again colour in the waiting canvas of the hills and valleys.

The richness and diversity of the flora are due in part to the islands' location between three continents – Europe, Asia and Africa – partly to the Ice Age survival in temperate Greece of pre-glacial species, and partly to the wonderful variety of habitats. Limestone, the foundation of much of Greece, is a favoured home for plants, providing stability, minerals, water supply and protection.

*Pretty horned poppies on the beach.*

*A typical Santoríni church awash with colour.*

*Wild artichokes are painfully spiny to prepare for the pot, but their delicate flavour is much prized by Greek country folk over the spineless cultivated variety, and accordingly they command a price premium.*

*A busy bee.*

## Beetles, bees and butterflies

The profusion of flowers and plants provides food for an equal profusion of insects. Conspicuous from spring to autumn are butterflies, including the swallowtail, whose equally colourful caterpillars feed on the leaves of common fennel. Its larger, paler and more angular relative, the scarce swallowtail, despite its name, is even more abundant.

Look for clouded yellows and paler cleopatras, reddish-brown painted ladies and southern commas, white admirals and a myriad of smaller blue butterflies.

Butterflies, bees and day-flying hawkmoths tend to go for flowers with nectar, while beetles and flies go for the pollen. Some bugs even take advantage of the heat accumulated in the solar cup of many flowers in order to warm up their sex lives.

The leaves of plants feed armies of insect herbivores, which themselves are eaten by more aggressive insects. Some of the omnivorous Greek grasshoppers and crickets are as happy munching through a caterpillar, or even another grasshopper, as the grass it was sitting on.

*The hills are alive – sunshine, colour and quantity mark the spring flowering of the islands, as here on Lésvos in mid-April.*

*Spanish broom (Spartium junceum) splashes low hillsides with yellow blooms in May.*

*Bougainvillea decorates a wall in Kefaloniá.*

# ISLANDS OUT OF SEASON

The onset of winter and the disappearance of tourists bring sudden, dramatic changes to Greek islands small and large.

It is only when the charter flights have ceased for the year that the real character of many islands staggers out of its unseasonable estivation. Larger islands can absorb a deluge of visitors without having to adopt an entirely different identity. A visitor arriving in Crete in October would not discover, as may happen on a tiny Cyclade, that the post office was working a nine-hour week, matching boat arrivals, with daily operation not set to resume until the following spring. It is difficult to overstate the distorting impact of an island population measured in hundreds being swamped by four or five times as many people simultaneously.

## QUICK CHANGE

Superficially, the change into hibernal uniform is swift. Migrant waiters, kitchen staff and scooter-hire personnel depart to look for winter jobs elsewhere. Awnings over beachside cafés are rolled up and stowed, chairs and tables dragged away, tourist-geared shops boarded up; beaches are suddenly bereft of their loungers and umbrellas.

A good sign that the islanders have literally found their feet again, after grinding summer schedules, is the resumption of the evening promenade or *vólta*, a quasi-formal ritual stroll in which small groups file from one end of a locally prescribed route to the other, and back again. Among them are the elderly and disabled people, seldom seen in public during the season. However, in a few large, untouristed towns, such as Híos port, the *vólta* continues year-round.

The *vólta* makes visible all kinds of island machinery in motion. Orthodox priests, symbols of a notional propriety largely eclipsed by the summer heathens, reassert their magisterial

*Warming up in a traditional coffee shop, Crete.*

presence among the faithful. Office-holders and petitioners in island politics fall into step beside the mayor for a peripatetic conference.

A high-decibel motorcycle cavalcade by the groom's dozen best mates, followed by gunshots and be-ribboned cars, tips you off that a wedding is about to take place. October, while the weather is still fine enough for milling around outside a small village church, is a popular month for marriages, especially amongst young people working in tourism enterprises who are far too busy to celebrate nuptials during the preceding months.

The locals have to buy food and other supplies, so corresponding shops remain stocked (if not always with the same products lines as in summer). But no island is completely self-sufficient, and storms can play havoc with already reduced ferry services. Consequently, shelves go temporarily bare, and butane canisters for stoves and heaters may run out because the gas tanker-boat can't safely anchor opposite the fuel depot.

In calm seas, the fishermen sail at dusk and return at dawn but, for the rest of the male population, the longer nights are the cue to bring out the playing cards (or occupy themselves in other ways… Kastellórizo in particular has a huge quota of children, around 40 for its small adult population of about 230). Officially, no money changes

*Restaurants empty out during winter.*

hands, but substantial fractions of the summer takings surge back and forth. That said, the days when islanders in the seasonal tourism trade could spend all winter gambling away the proceeds in the *kafenío* are long gone: living costs have rocketed, pensions have been savagely cut and now everybody has to have a second (and maybe third) enterprise to tide them over until spring.

## WINTER RESIDENCE

Landlords don't expect to earn rent in winter, so out-of-season visitors will find prices negotiable. Prime accommodation near the sea may be worth a slight premium while the water is still at a tolerable temperature – for the hardy, until December, and then again from April on. It's worth asking about vacant farm-houses; these have the simultaneous advantages of privacy, as well as neighbours popping around with eggs, greens and a bottle of local wine.

If outdoor conditions are an important criterion, southerly islands like Crete and Rhodes are marginally warmer and brighter. All across the Aegean, however, winter winds can cut to the bone, and houses not built specifically for the summer trade are more likely to have some form of heating. On more vegetated islands, the shriek of chainsaws in autumn heralds the stockpiling of firewood, the best being olive prunings. A basic, cast-iron wood stove is affordable; energy-efficient or pellet-burning models a worthwhile step up. Even assuming a cosy interior, when rain runs in ankle-deep torrents down village lanes for hours on end, many expats discover the limits of their love for Greece.

## AN INSIDER'S VIEW

English novelist Simon Raven spent the winter of 1960 on Hydra looking into "what goes on when winter comes, when the last epicene giggle has hovered and died in the October air". He decided he was among a bunch of atavistic pirates who, happily engaged in making money during the summer, reverted in winter to the old distrust of strangers who used to come only to spy on their illicit booty.

Hydra has since acquired a considerable number of full-time expats and, assuming the Hydriots never read what Raven wrote, he would probably feel more comfortable among them now. But one of his conclusions stands the test of time: only in winter can one discern what an island is really like.

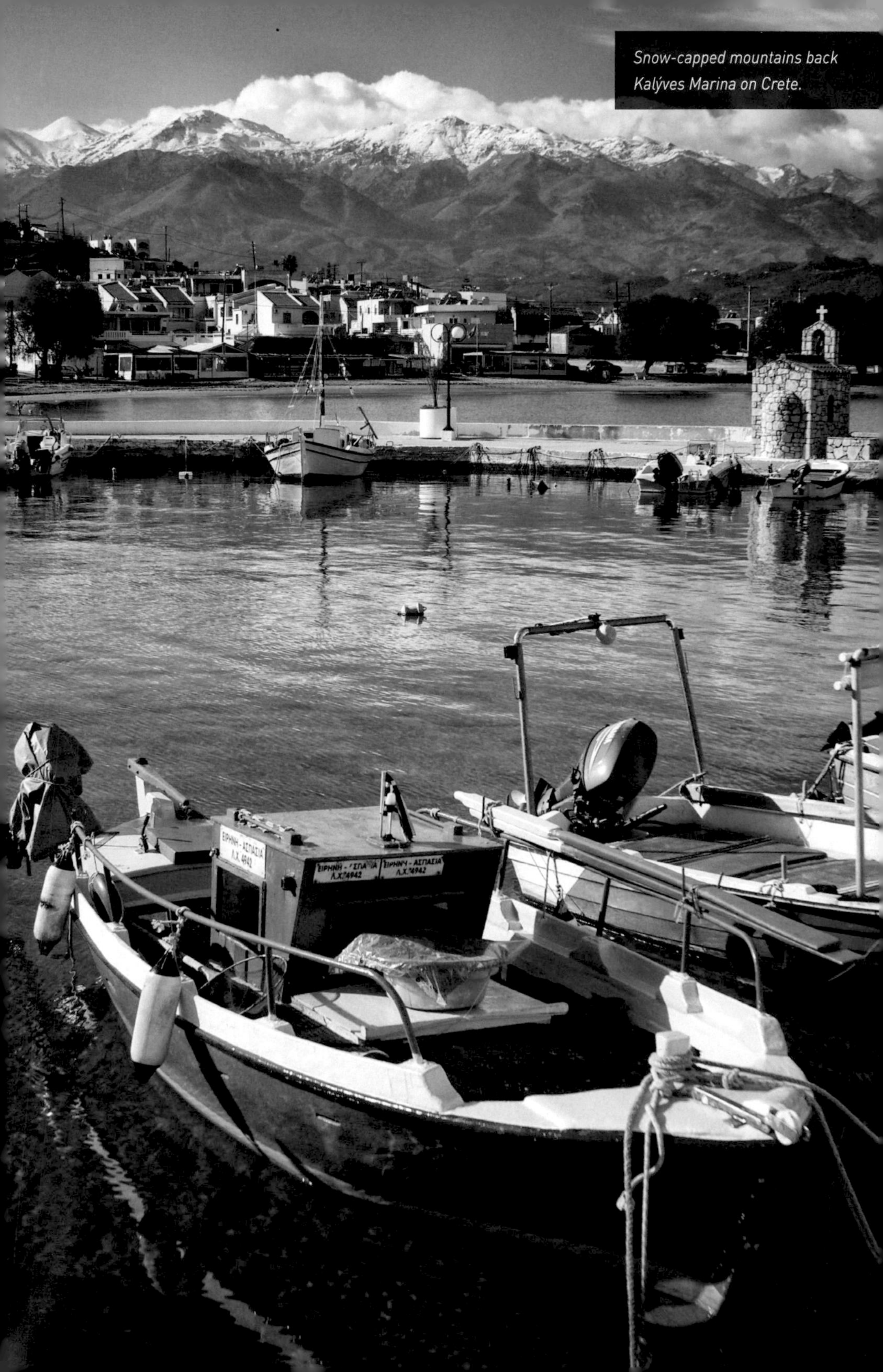


*Snow-capped mountains back Kalýves Marina on Crete.*

*Romantic evening drinks at a tavern on Páros.*

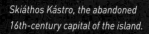
*Skiáthos Kástro, the abandoned 16th-century capital of the island.*

*Kitesurfing on Levkáda.*

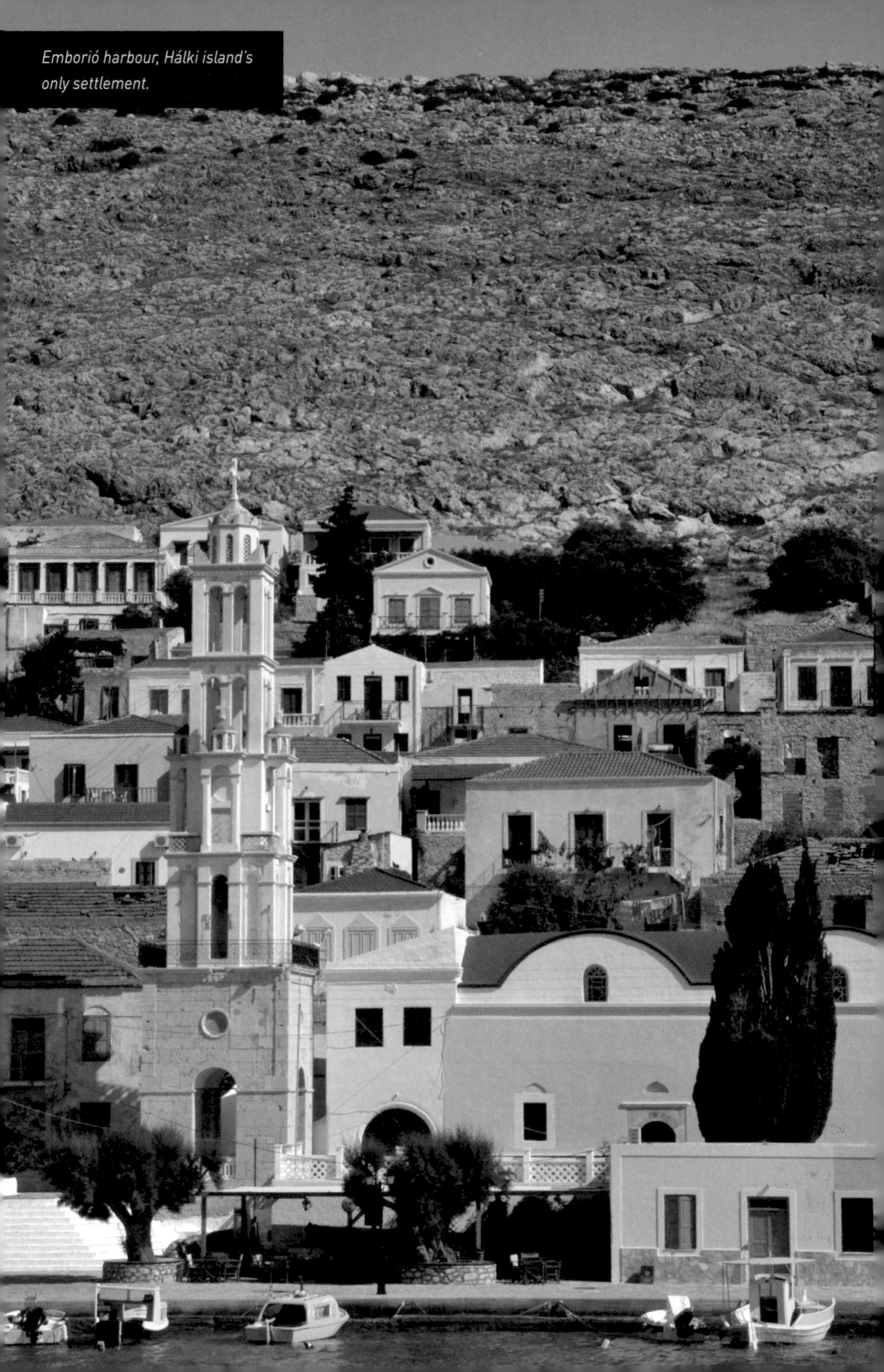

*Emborió harbour, Hálki island's only settlement.*

# INTRODUCTION

A detailed guide to all the island groups, with their principal sights clearly cross-referenced by number to the maps.

*The cove of Lalária, Skiáthos.*

The poet Odysseas Elytis once said: "Greece rests on the sea." It's an observation that few countries could claim with such authority. Some 25,000 sq km (10,000 sq miles) of the Aegean and the Ionian seas are covered by islands, the exact number of which has, in characteristic Greek fashion, been subject to dispute. There may be 3,000 islands and islets, of which 167 are inhabited; a more realistic total is 2,000, with fewer than 70 inhabited.

The definition of "inhabited" is open to interpretation, too. Does a tiny *vrahonisída* (rocky islet), bare save for one shepherd and 20 goats, count as uninhabited? Can an island that is totally deserted except for pilgrimages made annually to a small chapel at its summit claim to be inhabited?

The truth is perhaps immaterial; both visitors and inhabitants are more interested in sea and sky than in facts and figures. What is indisputable, however, is the sheer variety of landscape and experience behind the familiar images.

*Day-trippers departing.*

This is what we attempt to show here; islands with an ancient past and a modern outlook, the complex choices and the pure, simple pleasures. To accommodate everything implied in the phrase "a Greek island", we explore islets such as Ágios Evstrátios and Télendos, as well as well-known giants like Crete and Rhodes and holiday favourites such as Corfu and Mýkonos. Unearth the hidden gems and meet the people of the familiar, popular islands and you'll begin to grasp the true heart of the place behind the tourist clichés. So welcome aboard the ferry – and discover the varied delights that the Greek islands have to offer.

BULGARIA

BLACK SEA

Kárdžali • Edirne

TURKEY

Xánthi Komotiní

ráma

avála

Keşan

İstanbul

Marmara Denizi

Liménas Alexandroúpoli

Thásos

Kavakköy

Bandırma

Bursa

onikós
lpos

Samothráki

sós
Athos

Fengári ▲
1611 Therná
(Loutrá)

Çanakkale

Athos
2033 ▲

Thrakikón Pélagos

Gökçeada

Abíde

thonía

Mýrina

Ayvacık

Edremit

Balıkesir

Límnos

E

C

E

Ágios
Evstrátios

Mólyvos

Akhisar

TURKEY

Giourá
Pipéri

Sporádes

Lésvos

Mytilíni

Plomári

Skýros

Skyros

Paralía Kými s

Psará

AEGEAN

SEA

İzmir

Híos

Híos

Urla

Pyrgí

Çeşme

Káystos

Ándros

Sámos

Vathý
(Sámos)

Aydın

Denizli

Ándros

Karlóvassi

Ikaría

Kéa

Tínos

Gyáros

Ag.
Kírykos

Foúrni

Agathonísi

Ermoúpoli
Sýros

Tínos

Mýkonos

Arkí

Lipsí

Milás

Muğla

Kýthnos

Cycládes

Pátmos

Sérifos

Páros

Náxos

Léros

Sífnos

Andíparos

Náxos

Kálymnos

Bodrum

Kímolos

Síkinos

Íos

Amorgós

Kós

Kós

Fethiye

Sílos

Folégandros

Kéfalos

Nísyros

Sými

Astypálea

Dodecanese

Tílos

Ródos

Kaş

Santoríni
(Thíra)

Anáfi

Sýrna

Hálki

Atháyros
1215

Megísti
(Kastellórizo)

Kritikó Pélagos

Líndos

Ródos
(Rhodes)

Kárpathos

Réthymno

Iráklio
(Heráklion)

Kríti (Crete)

Kásos

Arkádi

Ida
(Psilorítis)

Ágios
Nikólaos

Horá
Sfakíon

Plakiás

2456

Knossós

Sitía

Zákros

Ag.
Galíni

Ierápetra

Gávdos

**The Greek Islands**

0        50 km

0        50 miles

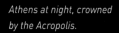
*Athens at night, crowned by the Acropolis.*

# ATHENS STOPOVER

Large and hectic, sometimes spectacular, always exhilarating, Athens can be simply exhausting. But if you have a day or two to look around, there's plenty to see.

Athens was suddenly designated capital of the new Greek state after the War of Independence, and despite diligent Bavarian attempts at town planning – largely disregarded – it never mellowed into a venerable old age. Since the post-1923 influx of Greek refugees from Asia Minor, Athens has grown haphazardly and rapidly, with incongruent juxtapositions of old and new: a faded neoclassical mansion, still with a garden, sits between modern office blocks, its windows hermetically closed against the traffic roar; a medieval chapel huddles under an overhanging high-rise. A whole raft of infrastructure projects completed before the 2004 Olympics – most notably the efficient metro system – have made this brash, sometimes plain ugly capital much more liveable.

Branching off from frenzied central arteries are the less congested minor veins of the city; most apartment blocks have balconies or full-sized verandas, where you glimpse half-clad Athenians emerging from their siesta to read the paper, water their plants, or eat their evening meal. The hot weather makes open-air life a necessity, or at least open-window life, once evening television draws folk indoors.

*The Tomb of the Unknown Warrior, by Sýndagma Square, is guarded by Evzónes, elite soldiers in traditional mountain costume.*

## ANCIENT ATHENS

If your time in Athens is limited, it makes sense to start with the premier monuments dating from Ancient Athens's "Golden Age", the 5th century BC. Seen from the right angle, driving or walking along below, the **Acropolis** ❶ (summer daily 8am–7pm, closed 1–5pm when temperatures exceed 39°C, winter shorter hours) can still make the grimy concrete fade into insignificance. Climb up in the early morning, when crowds are thinnest, and a

**⊙ Main Attractions**

Parthenon
Temple of Olympian Zeus
Pláka quarter
Acropolis Museum
Benaki Museum
Byzantine and Christian
   Museum
National Archaeological
   Museum
Museum of Popular
   Musical Instruments

Map on page 116

*Supporting the porch of the Erechtheion, the Caryatids' faces still bear the pigments of ancient "make-up".*

*The Parthenon, viewed from the west.*

strip of blue sea edged with grey hills marks the southwestern horizon.

The **Propylaia**, the official entrance to the Acropolis built by Mnesikles around 430 BC, was cleverly designed with imposing columns to impress people coming up the hill. Parts of its coffered stone ceiling, once painted and gilded, are still visible. On what was once the citadel's southern bastion, from which King Aegeus legendarily threw himself off when his son Theseus forgot to change his signal-sail from black to white, is the small, square temple of **Athena Nike**, finished in 421 BC, and recently completely rebuilt.

Still-scaffolded parts of the **Parthenon** look like a stonemason's workshop, just as it must have done in the 440s BC when it was under construction as the centrepiece of Perikles' giant public works programme. Some of his contemporaries thought it extravagant, accusing Perikles of dressing his city up like a harlot. In fact, the Parthenon celebrates Athena as a virgin goddess

and the city's protector. Her statue, 12 metres (39.5ft) tall, made of ivory and gold plate to Phidias' design, once gleamed in the dim interior. In late antiquity it was taken to Constantinople, where it disappeared.

The **Erechtheion**, an elegant, architecturally complex repository of ancient cults going back to the Bronze Age, was restored around the millennium. Completed in 395 BC, a generation after the Parthenon, it once contained the supposed tomb of King Kekrops, mythical founder of the ancient Athenian royal family. The Caryatids now supporting the porch are modern copies; four surviving originals (one is missing, one is in the British Museum) are prize exhibits in the **Acropolis Museum** (see page 117). In Ottoman times, the Erechtheion was used by the city's Ottoman military commander as a billet for his harem.

On the south side of the Acropolis lies the **Theatre of Dionysos ❷** (same hours as Acropolis). Surviving marble seating tiers date from around 320 BC

## ⊘ RESTORING THE PAST

Hundreds of blocks of marble have been levered down from the Parthenon, to replace the rusting iron clamps inserted in the 1920s with non-corrosive titanium ones (rust made the iron clamps expand, cracking the stone). The restorers have also collected and identified some 1,600 chunks of Parthenon marble scattered all over the hilltop. Many of these were blown off in the 1687 blast caused by a Venetian artillery shell igniting Ottoman munitions stored inside the temple. Once they have been painstakingly replaced, about 15 percent more of the building will be on view. New blocks cut from near the ancient quarries on Mount Pendéli, the source of the original 5th-century BC stone, will be used to fill the gaps, and fade within years to more closely match the original masonry. For now, scaffolding cloaks the west facade.

and later, but scholars generally agree that plays by Aiskhylos, Sophokles, Euripides and Aristophanes were first staged here at 5th-century BC religious festivals. A state subsidy for theatregoers meant that every Athenian citizen could attend these events.

Herodes Atticus, a wealthy Greek landowner and Roman senator, built the steeply raked **Herodes Atticus Theatre** ❸ (better known as the Iródio; usually shut) on the south slope of the Acropolis in the 2nd century AD, now used during the Hellenic Festival for performances of popular or classical music and ballet.

Earlier in the 2nd century AD, Roman Emperor Hadrian, a fervent admirer of classical Greece, erected an ornate **arch** marking the spot where the classical city ended and the provincial Roman university town began. Little of this Roman city can be seen beneath the **National Gardens**, or the archaeological area behind the towering columns of the **Temple of Olympian Zeus** ❹ (Stíles Olymbíou Dioú; daily, summer 8am–7pm, winter 8am–3pm), but excavations indicate that numerous Roman buildings stood in this area, at least as far as the **Kallimármaro** (Panathenaic Stadium), refurbished by Herodes Atticus. Work on the temple had been abandoned in around 520 BC when funds ran out, but Hadrian finished the construction and donated a statue of Zeus as well as one of himself.

While the Acropolis was mainly used for religious purposes, the ancient Greek **Agora** ❺ (daily 8am–7pm) was employed for most other public activities – commercial, political, civic and educational. Today it looks like a cluttered field of ruins, but the reconstructed **Stoa of Attalos**, a 2nd-century BC shopping mall, is a refreshingly cool place to linger and houses a worthwhile museum of Agora finds. The completely intact **Hephaestion**, the Doric temple opposite (alias the Thisseion), is rather clunky compared to the Parthenon.

A 1st-century BC astronomer, Andronikos Kyrrhestes, designed the picturesque **Tower of the Winds** ❻

*The Féthiye Tzamí, an Ottoman mosque on the edge of the Roman Forum.*

(Aérides; daily summer 8am–7pm, winter until 3pm), a well-preserved marble octagon within the scanty remains of the **Roman Agora** (same hours). The tower is decorated with eight relief figures, each depicting a different breeze, and once contained a water-clock, whose intricate drainage system is clearly evident inside, grooved into the marble flooring.

One block north of the tower stand the remains of **Hadrian's Library** (daily, 8.30am–3pm), actually an enormous multi-purpose Roman cultural centre built around a colonnaded courtyard.

## CITY STREETS

The heart of the modern city lies within a triangle defined by **Platía Omónias** (Omónia Square) in the north, **Platía Syndágmatos** ❼ (Sýndagma Square) to the southeast and **Monastiráki** to the south. Except for a few narrow cross-streets, this is a car-free area, which has taken on a new lease of life. **Ermoú** is now a long pedestrian walkway with reinvigorated shops (albeit some vacant with the crisis) and refurbished

facades, enlivened by pavement buskers and push-carts. Except when a rally or riot is taking place at nearby Sýndagma, this is an attractive area to wander in the evening. Be prepared for some extravagantly coloured, witty and often polemic graffiti – Athens is perhaps the most heavily "decorated" city in Europe.

Monastiráki has a tourist-pitched market selling a weird assortment of objects, where collectors of kitsch will find much to interest them. Across Ermoú, Psyrrí district has more workshops and more practical items on sale. The old, covered **Central Market** ❽ (Varvákios Agorá), a 19th-century gem roughly halfway between Monastiráki and Omónia, is the city's main meat and fish market, crowded with shoppers milling between open stands displaying fish, seafood and every variety of poultry and meat you could imagine.

**Pláka**, the city's oldest quarter clustering at the foot of the Acropolis, has been restored to its former condition (or rather, to a fairly good reproduction of it), with motor vehicles

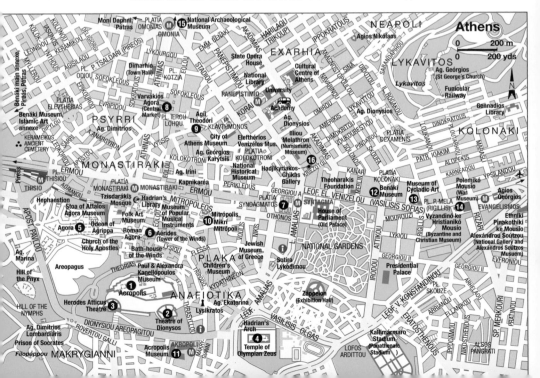

prohibited (for the most part), 19th-century houses refurbished and streets tidied up. It is now a delightful, sheltered place in which to meander, full of small beauties: look out for half a dozen Byzantine churches, a visitable Ottoman **hamam**, several museums and the 4th-century BC **monument of Lysikratos**.

Byzantine Athens is fairly well represented with mostly 11th-century churches – besides a dozen in Pláka, there are several others huddling below street level in the shadow of taller, modern buildings. They are still in constant use: passers-by slip in to light a yellow beeswax candle, cross themselves and kiss an icon in near-darkness before returning to the noise outside. One of the most handsome is **Agii Theodóri** ❾ just off Klavthmónos Square, built on the site of an earlier church, in characteristic cruciform shape with a tiled dome and a terracotta frieze of animals and plants. **Kapnikaréa** in the middle of Ermoú has an apsidal fresco of the Virgin Platytéra by the distinguished neo-Byzantine painter Photis Kontoglou, while the 12th-century **Mikrí Mitrópoli** ❿ (Small Cathedral) next to its garish successor features extensive external bas-relief masonry recycled from all previous eras. The huge, domed **Church of Sotíra Lykodímou** on Filellínon Street was bought by the Tsar of Russia in 1847 and completely rebuilt by 1856 to serve the city's growing Russian Orthodox community.

## ATHENS'S MUSEUMS

Top of the agenda for rushed visitors is likely to be the **Acropolis Museum** ⓫ (summer Tue–Sun 8am–8pm, winter Tue–Thur 9am–5pm, Sat–Sun 9am–8pm, Fri all year until 10pm), 500 metres (0.3 miles) south of and below the Acropolis rock. While decidedly retrograde-modern when seen from the outside, inside the building is arrayed to duplicate the experience of ascending the Parthenon's various levels. A ramp – reproducing the approach to the Propylaia – leads up from the ground floor to

*The Greek Parliament in Sýndagma Square.*

an intermediate one, home to all the free-standing statuary (and much more) displayed in the cramped old museum, including the four original Caryatids still in Greece, revealing an Archaic ideal of femininity in their earrings, tresses and crinkled, close-fitting dresses. The top floor has been built to mirror exactly the arrangement of the friezes on the Parthenon, clearly visible through windows – those originals that Greece retains pointedly abut plaster casts of the roughly 60 percent residing in the British Museum, with the clear implication that they ought to be returned.

The **Benáki Museum**  (www.benaki.gr; Wed & Fri 9am–5pm, Thur & Sat 9am–midnight, Sun 9am–3pm, winter Sun to 4pm, Wed & Fri to 6pm), at the National Gardens' northeast corner, houses an eclectic collection of treasures from all periods of Greek history – including jewellery, costumes, the recreated interiors of two rooms from a Kozáni mansion and two icons attributed to El Greco in the days when he was a Cretan painter called Doméniko Theotokópoulos. Beautifully laid-out galleries make this one of the most attractive museums in the city. There are always worthwhile temporary exhibits in a special room.

The privately endowed **Museum of Cycladic Art** ⑬ (www.cycladic.gr; Mon, Wed, Fri & Sat 10am–5pm, Thur 10am–8pm, Sun 11am–5pm) nearby features the beautiful prehistoric white marble figurines dismissed as barbaric by Belle Epoque art critics but numbering Picasso and Modigliani among their admirers. They come from graves in the Cycladic islands, but scholars are still uncertain of their purpose (see also page 184). There are also numerous worthwhile temporary exhibits, some held in the adjoining neoclassical Elena Stathatou mansion-annexe.

The **Byzantine and Christian Museum** ⑭ (www.byzantinemuseum.gr; summer daily 8am–8pm, winter 9am–4pm), across busy Vassilísis Sofías, originally occupied a mock-Florentine mansion built by the eccentric philhellene Duchess de Plaisance. Exhibits,

*Admiring excavations under the Acropolis Museum.*

dating from the early Christian period to 13th-century Attica frescoes, now reside in an impressive modern wing, subterranean yet bright and spacious, and include the 7th-century AD Hoard of Mytilene, well-displayed and informatively labelled.

The **National Archaeological Museum** ⓯ (www.namuseum.gr; Mon 3–8pm, Tue–Sun 8am–8pm) holds the city's most important collection of ancient artefacts. Highlights include the stunning gold work of the Mycenaean trove, more prehistoric Cycladic art, the Andikythera mechanism (an intricate astronomical computer 15 centuries ahead of its time), the Akrotiri frescoes (see page 196) and major bronze sculptures, including the wonderful Poseidon found off the coast of Évvia.

Of the many small Pláka galleries, two of the best are the **Folk Art Museum** – set to re-open during 2019 in purpose-built quarters in the block formed by Áreos, Adrianoú, Vrysakíou and Kládou streets (see www.melt.gr for current status) – and the **Museum of Popular Musical Instruments** (Tue–Sun 8am–3pm; free), in a fine neoclassical mansion at Diogénous 1–3. The collection here, curated by Greek ethnomusicologist Phivos Anogiannakis, features just about every traditional instrument ever played in Greece, with archival photos and listening posts to round out the experience. The museum shop sells folk recordings, particularly of island music.

With extra time available, you should take in some of the city's excellent private art galleries, which have multiplied since the millennium despite dire economic straits. The main **Benáki Museum annexe** just off our map at Pireós 138 (Thur & Sun 10am–10pm, Fri–Sat 10am–6pm) has consistently good temporary exhibits (often photographic), as does the **Theoharakis Foundation** just off Sýndagma at Vasillísis Sofiás 9 (www.thf.gr; daily 10am–6pm, until 8pm Thur Oct–May). Just a block or so behind, at Kriezótou 3, is perhaps the best Athens art museum for the uninitiated: the

**Hadjikyriakos-Ghikas Gallery**  (Fri–Sat 10am–6pm), technically yet another annexe of the Benáki. It's somewhat misnamed – while indeed installed in the former home of the great painter, with his top-floor residence and atelier preserved as at his death in 1994, most of the many galleries honour (with intelligent labelling) just about everybody who was anybody in 20th-century Greek cultural life, including architects, cartoonists and photographers as well as painters.

## ATHENS BY NIGHT

Not least because of roasting summer temperatures, Athenians are decidedly nocturnal. Even during the small hours the main streets are never entirely deserted, which makes Athens one of the safer cities in which to walk at night, although metro pickpocketing (especially at Monastiráki), muggings and car break-ins are on the rise. Lost night-time sleep is made up for with an afternoon siesta (*never* telephone an Athenian – or

any Greek for that matter – between 2.30pm and 5.30pm).

Both informal (bar-based) and organised nightlife is still fairly lively and long despite the economic pinch. The original central district for this was Psyrrí, just beyond Monastiráki (with which it shares a metro station). Accounts of hip Psyrrí's demise in popular lore are greatly exaggerated, but it is true that the margin of trendiness and gentrification spreads steadily outward and further northwest, encompassing the formerly dismal, rust-belt neighbourhoods of Gázi, Rouf, Keramikós, Metaxourgío and Votanikós. Hot venues, for cutting-edge arts events as well as music, change regularly – consult a listings website or a local friend. But durable examples include Pireós 260, a converted factory behind the School of Fine Arts that's a principal Hellenic Festival venue, or Gazarte (gazarte.gr), a multi-stage cultural hub for musical and theatrical events. There are also a half-dozen well-loved summer cinemas to be found in the central districts of Thisío, Petrálona, Kolonáki and Exárhia.

*Stunning displays at the Byzantine and Christian Museum.*

# COPING WITH PIRAEUS

**Most visitors only go to Piraeus to catch a ferry, but this bustling port offers some points of interest.**

Piraeus is a city in its own right. Although unabashedly industrial/commercial, with few concessions to the numerous tourists who pass through, it's worth allowing some extra time for it before or after a seagoing journey, even if there are few echoes of *Never on Sunday* these days. (The underworld moved to Athens during the puritanical colonels' dictatorship. Since then, successive mayors have been elected on a "smarten up Piraeus" platform.)

Get there well before sailing time so that you have half an hour or so to arrive at your departure quay – often very remote, although a shuttle bus does run – in good time: ships do leave promptly. You also need to allow time to buy a ticket; if you have a car or want a sleeping berth, this should be organised days (in season, a week or more) in advance.

The easiest way to get to Piraeus from central Athens is on the metro (line 1; allow around 45 minutes' journey time from Sýndagma). From Athens Airport, express bus X96 takes at least 90 minutes to the main quay at Piraeus – best allow two hours at peak times.

## TO THE RIGHT QUAY

Your ticket agent will tell you which is your departure quay; these are numbered E1 to E10 going clockwise around the main basin. As a general guide, most boats to the Cyclades depart from quays E6–E7 opposite the metro station; direct boats to Crete leave from E3 and E4, along Aktí Kondýli on the northern side of the port; catamarans and hydrofoils to the Argo-Saronic islands depart from E9, along Aktí Miaoúli, while slow car ferries to the same destinations go from E8 next to Karaïskáki Square; some Cyclades are served by E10, at the far end of Aktí Miaoúli. Dodecanese ferries leave from E1, at the bus-route terminus across the port, with northeast Aegean sailings from either E5 or E2.

The radical cosmopolitanism for which Piraeus was famous 2,500 years ago still exists – immigrants are conspicuous, and leftist deputies are regularly returned to parliament – but few remains survive. A stretch of elegant 4th-century BC wall runs beside the coast road beyond Zéa Marína, and an ancient amphitheatre backs onto the **Archaeological Museum** (Tue–Sun 8am–3pm) at Hariláou Trikoúpi 31, well worth visiting if you have time, although it is a very long walk from Quay E10. Its prize exhibits are two bronze statues found in 1959; a magnificent 6th-century BC *kouros* (idealised figure of a young man), known as the Piraeus Apollo; and a 4th-century helmeted Athena, looking oddly soulful for a warrior goddess, plus two more Classsical-era bronzes of Artemis, one large and one small.

*Statuary at the Piraeus Archaeological Museum.*

# THESSALONÍKI STOPOVER

With three airlines serving the city from three points in the UK, and numerous onward domestic flights, Thessaloníki has become a feasible gateway to the islands.

**Main Attractions**
Archaeological Museum
Agios Dimítrios church
Agía Sofía church
Kástra district
Modiáno market

**Map on page 123**

Modern apartment blocks characteristic of many Mediterranean seaside cities predominate. But 120 years ago, the skyline consisted of minarets rising above a tile-roofed town picturesquely climbing between medieval ramparts to an upper quarter. When more than half of this was destroyed by the Great Fire of August 1917, British and French architects accompanying the Allied expeditionary forces were commissioned to produce a new city plan; surviving Art Deco buildings enhance the wide boulevards they designed, although their advice to ban high-rises was disregarded. But the fire spared much. Roman ruins, Byzantine churches, Ottoman public and domestic buildings, and displaced Jewish tombstones lie encircled by Roman and Byzantine walls, or scattered alongside asphalt boulevards and pedestrian lanes. And after years of neglect, this great architectural heritage has been signposted and selectively renovated.

## A BRIEF HISTORY

Thessaloníki was founded in 315 BC by Macedonian king Kassander; it became an important halt on the Roman **Via Egnatia** between the Adriatic and the Hellespont. Saint Paul visited, and wrote two Epistles to the Thessalonians; Christianity (and the city) got further boosts from the Byzantine emperors Theodosius I (who issued here his edict banning paganism ) and Justinian, who began new churches to supplement those adapted from Roman structures. Despite hostile raids, earthquakes, fires and adjacent malarial swamps, Thessaloníki prospered.

After 1500, many Sephardic Jewish refugees from Iberia settled here at Ottoman invitation, lending Salonika – as they called it – its defining trait

*The White Tower was added to the Roman-Byzantine walls by the Venetians.*

until 1912, when they still constituted over half the population of 140,000, making it the largest Jewish city of that era. In 1943, 70,000 remained to be deported by the Nazis; fewer than 1,000 remain today.

After 1923, Thessaloníki epitomised a Greek refugee town: in absolute numbers, Athens had more, but by proportion of population, Thessaloníki contains more citizens with Anatolian ancestry than anywhere else in Greece.

After years in Athens' shadow, Thessaloníki has come into its own, with innovative venues occupying historic buildings, its native musicians (such as Nikos Papazoglou or Sokratis Malamas) frequently at the forefront of Greek song. The early November International Film Festival is a major event on the European cultural calendar.

## DOWNTOWN THESSALONÍKI

**Platía Aristotélous Ⓐ** is the hub of the downtown city, extending inland towards the ancient Agora and church of Agios Dimítrios. There are plenty of cafés and *mezedopolía*, both outdoors and tucked into nearby buildings.

On the easterly seafront, behind the landmark White Tower, the **Archaeological Museum Ⓑ** (www.amth.gr; daily 8am–8pm), displays sumptuous Macedonian, Hellenistic and Roman finds from the entire region. Just beyond, the splendidly laid out **Museum of Byzantine Culture Ⓒ** (www.mbp.gr; summer daily 8am–8pm, winter 9am–4pm; joint tickets available) displays artefacts from the Early Christian period (4th–7th century) through to the Middle Byzantine period (8th–12th century).

At **Platía Navarínou Ⓓ**, Roman Thessaloníki is exposed as the excavated **Palace of Emperor Galerius**, who martyred the city's patron saint, Demetrius, in AD 306. Nearby survives part of Galerius's triumphal **arch**, squirming with intricate reliefs, erected over the Vía Egnatía in AD 298 to celebrate his victory over the Persians.

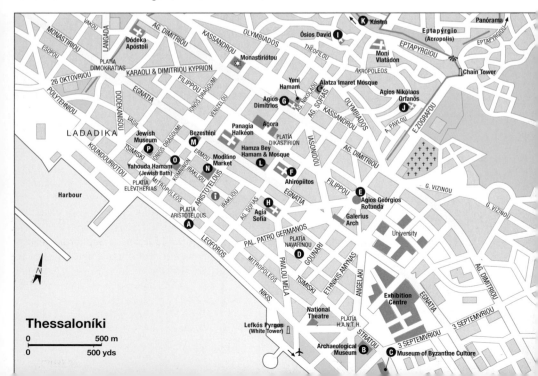

Thessaloníki

The other significant Roman relic is the **Agios Geórgios Rotunda** (summer daily 8am–7pm, winter until 5pm), northwest of the arch. Intended as Galerius's mausoleum, this is a rare circular Roman structure, later serving as a church, then a mosque. Glorious if hard-to-see 4th-century wall mosaics hide high up inside; a truncated minaret is the city's last standing one.

## BYZANTINE THESSALONÍKI

More Byzantine churches survive in Thessaloníki than in any other Greek city. The earliest examples are clear adaptations of the colonnaded Roman basilica. Near the Agora stand 5th-century **Ahiropíitos** (with fine mosaic patches under the arches between ornate columns) and its contemporary, **Agios Dimítrios** (daily 8am–10pm, crypt variable hours but not Mon), the largest church in Greece.

Agios Dimítrios is the city's main church, founded on the site of his martyrdom, and almost entirely rebuilt after the 1917 fire. Six small mosaics of the 5th to 7th century, featuring the saint, appear near the altar. The fire revealed a crypt thought to be adapted from the Roman baths where Demetrius was imprisoned.

South of Ahiropíitos is 8th-century **Agía Sofía** (Holy Wisdom; daily 8 30am–1pm, 5.30–8pm), built in conscious imitation of its namesake in Constantinople. Its dome contains a vivid Ascension mosaic.

Tiny 5th- or 6th-century **Ósios Davíd** church (Mon–Sat 9am–12 noon and 4–6pm) is hidden up here. Its western end has vanished, but not so an outstanding apsidal mosaic depicting the vision of the Prophet Ezekiel of Christ Emmanuel, shown as a beardless youth seated on the arc of heaven, surrounded by Evangelical symbols.

Other churches uphill from the Vía Egnatía date from the 13th and 14th centuries. Financial constraints meant that frescoes, rather than mosaics, were their preferred

*Inside the vaulted Bey Hamam.*

ornamentation. By far the best of these is **Agios Nikólaos Orfanós** ❶ (Tue–Sun 8.30am–3pm).

The steep alleys of **Kástra** ❻ lie about a 20-minute walk from the seafront. Since the 1980s, this once poor and despised neighbourhood has been renovated and now teems with trendy tavernas and cafés.

## OTTOMAN AND JEWISH THESSALONÍKI

The Ottomans, after their 1430 conquest, converted most churches for worship; thus there are as many civic buildings as purpose-built Ottoman mosques. Worthy 15th-century specimens include the graceful **Alatza Imaret Mosque** at the base of Kástra – around the corner from the **Yeni Hamam**, restored as an events venue – and the dilapidated **Hamza Bey Mosque** ❶ on Via Egnatia. It has yet to get the same treatment as the nearby **Bezesténi** ⓜ, a refurbished six-domed covered market now tenanted by luxury shops. The **Hamza Bey Hamam** (Tue–Sat 8am–3pm),

dating from 1444, has intact stalactite vaulting over the entrance and inside.

By contrast, few traces of Thessaloníki's Jewish past remain, owing to the 1917 fire and Nazi destruction of cemeteries and synagogues in 1943–44. Centrepiece of the vast central bazaar, selling everything from wooden furniture to live poultry – is the **Modiáno Market** ⓝ, a fish, meat and produce hall named for the Jewish family that established it. While barely half-occupied today, and spared "redevelopment' proposals", the Modiáno still supports authentic, atmospheric *mezedopolía*.

Close by, the Louloudádika Hamam or Flower-Market Bath was also known as the **Yahouda Hamam** ⓞ or Jewish Bath; the Jewish clientele is gone, but the flowers are still outside. On nearby Agíou Miná, the **Jewish Museum of Thessaloníki** ⓟ (www.jmth.gr; Mon–Fri 10am–3pm, also Wed 5–8pm, Sun 10am–2pm) presents the history of the Jewish community in Thessaloníki.

**⊙ Tip**

For atmospheric bars and clubs, head for Ladádika, the former red-light district and port quarter behind the passenger ferry terminal.

## ⊙ THE CITY WALLS

Thessaloníki's seafront **Lefkós Pýrgos** (White Tower; www.lpth.gr;summer daily 8am–8pm, winter 9am–4pm), the city's logo, was a Venetian addition to the Roman-Byzantine walls. An 1826 massacre of unruly Janissaries here earned it the epithet "Bloody Tower". The Greeks whitewashed it from 1912 to 1985 – thus the new alias. It houses a small, worthwhile museum; a spiral staircase emerges at the crenellated roof terrace, for fine views.

A vanished curtain wall leading inland from here linked the White Tower with the **Chain Tower**, the southeastern corner of the fortifications; beyond it lies **Eptapýrgio** (Yedi Küle in Turkish), the Seven Towers Fortress, a jail until 1989, on the northeastern corner of the walled **acropolis**.

The mostly abandoned Venetian-era village of Paleá Períthia.

# THE IONIAN ISLANDS

Corfu, Paxí, Levkáda, Itháki, Kefaloniá, Zákynthos, Kýthira.

*Family transport.*

The islands of the Ionian Sea just west of Greece are dubbed the Eptánisa – "seven isles". However, the seventh, Kýthira, lies south of the Peloponnese and, while sharing history, culture and architecture, remains isolated from the other six islands.

During the 8th and 7th centuries BC, colonists from Corinth occupied the most northerly Ionian islands; two centuries later Corfu's rebellion against Corinth helped start the Peloponnesian War. The Ionians have since had many overlords, but the Venetian period left the most indelible mark. Artists, craftsmen and poets were sent to Venice to be educated, returning home with a cosmopolitan perspective; others came from Crete after its Ottoman conquest. Today, thanks to regular links with Italy, the islands still have a distinctly Italian flavour in their cuisine and music.

*Northern Itháki.*

Heavy rainfall makes the Ionians among the greenest of Greek archipelagos. Olive groves, market gardens and vineyards are reminders that agriculture still plays a role in the economy. This same unsettled weather has ruined many a holiday: from mid-September until early June, storms can wash out beach outings without warning. But these fierce squalls rarely last more than a few hours, and there's usually a museum or taverna interior nearby to take shelter in. In extreme situations, you might escape to a sunnier neighbouring island; Paxí has regular links with Corfu (via mainland Igoumenítsa), while Levkáda, Itháki, Kefaloniá and Zákynthos are connected at least daily in season.

Today the Ionians are beset not by invaders (other than tour companies) but by earthquakes, the most recent serious one in 1953. Casualties were high and the beautiful Venetian-built capitals of Kefaloniá and Zákynthos were flattened. Reconstruction began almost immediately, though with different emphases. The Zakynthians recreated their Venetian town plan, albeit in reinforced concrete, while Ithacans rebuilt houses faithfully in the old style. Except in the central business district, the pragmatic residents of Argostóli in Kefaloniá put up makeshift buildings; a few unmodernised ones still remain.

The streets of Corfu Town.

# CORFU

Few places have been exploited for tourism as much as Corfu. Yet away from the package-tour resorts there is much to savour in this beautiful and verdant island.

Strategically poised where the Ionian Sea becomes the Adriatic, just off the mainland, Corfu (Kérkyra) has always been coveted, with a turbulent history of invaders and rulers. There's evidence of habitation dating back 50,000 years, but Corfu enters history as "Korkyra" in 734 BC, when it was colonised by ancient Corinth. By the mid-7th century BC, Korkyra was a major, independent naval power, siding in 433 BC with Athens against Sparta (and Corinth), thus triggering the Peloponnesian War. After 229 BC, the island fell under relatively uneventful Roman dominion.

Nearly eight centuries of Byzantine rule from AD 395 brought stability and prosperity, but latter years saw incursions and periods of domination by various groups: "barbarians", the Norman-Angevin Kingdom of the Two Sicilies, the Despotate of Epirus and the Venetians. Weary of misrule and pirate raids, the Corfiots themselves asked to be put definitively under the protection of Venice, which obliged in 1386 – and stayed for 411 years, successfully outlasting two Ottoman sieges and leaving a rich legacy of olive groves. Napoleon dissolved what remained of the Venetian Empire in 1797, and the French held the island until 1814 (except for the eight-year interregnum of the Ottoman/Russian-controlled "Septinsular Republic"). The

British took over in 1814, staying for 50 years until all the Ionian islands were ceded to Greece as a sweetener for George I's ascent of the Greek throne.

During World War I, Corfu and Vídos islet was the final destination of a retreating, defeated Serbian army; a museum and cenotaphs from that era remain. During the next world war, the city suffered extensive damage in September 1943 under a German bombardment to displace the Italian occupiers, who had surrendered to the Allies; during their brief but brutal stay,

### ⊘ Main Attractions
Listón
Néo Froúrio
Andivouniótissa Museum
Paleá Períthia
Eríkoussa islet
Angelókastro
Íssos beach

Map on page 134

*Corfu signs.*

the Nazis rounded up and deported Corfu's significant Jewish community, resident here since Venetian times.

## A MULTICULTURAL CAPITAL

Corfu Town, known as **Kérkyra ❶**, occupies a peninsula on the east coast. "Corfu" is a corruption of *koryfo*, or "peak", there being two such on a Byzantine/Norman-fortified outcrop much altered as the **Paleó Froúrio** (daily summer 8am–7.30pm, winter 8am–3pm) by the Venetians during the 15th and 16th centuries, when they cut a canal to make the citadel an island. The more complete **Néo Froúrio** to the west

(9am–3.30pm; free) is strictly Venetian, and offers superb views over the town, cradled between the two forts.

With its tottering, multi-storeyed Venetian-style apartments, and maze-like lanes ending in quiet plazas, the Old Town constitutes a *flâneur*'s paradise; it was tidied up prior to hosting a 1994 EU meeting, but you wouldn't know it. Vacant bomb sites still yawn near the Néo Froúrio, and many main thoroughfares are blighted by touristic tat, but the backstreets remain surprisingly unspoilt, festooned with washing-lines and echoing to pigeon coos. The elegant counterpoint to this is the

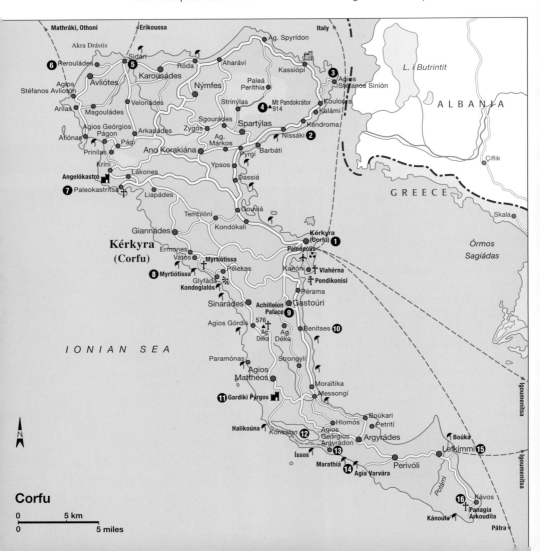

Corfu

0    5 km

0    5 miles

**Listón**, built by the French as a replica of the Rue de Rivoli in Paris. The name refers to local aristocrats listed in the Venetian *Libro d'Oro*, with sufficient social standing to frequent the arcades.

The Listón faces the Spianáda (Esplanade), a large and grassy open space cleared by the Venetians to deprive attackers of cover. At pricey Listón cafés you can order *tsintsibira* (ginger beer), an enduring British legacy; other legacies include cricket, played idiosyncratically on the Spianáda, and the Victorian cemetery at the edge of town, still used by the 7,000-strong UK expat community.

The Spianáda is also the focus for Orthodox Easter celebrations, among the best in Greece. On Good Friday eve, each parish parades its *Epitáfios* (Christ's Funeral Bier) accompanied by uniformed brass bands, playing funeral dirges. On Saturday morning the relics of local patron saint Spyridon go walkabout, and then the tunes get jollier around 11am as townspeople shower special pots and crockery from their balconies to banish misfortune. The Saturday midnight Resurrection Mass finishes with fireworks launched from the Paleó Froúrio.

Both music and Saint Spyridon are integral parts of Corfiot life. Until destroyed by Nazi incendiary bombs, Corfu had the world's largest opera house after Milan's La Scala, and premières of major works took place here; there are still regular classical music performances and thriving conservatories. Spyridon, after whom seemingly half the male population is named "Spyros", was actually an early Cypriot bishop whose relics ended up here after the fall of Constantinople. Credited with saving Corfu from several disasters, his casket is processed four times yearly from his 16th-century shrine a block back from the Listón.

## UNMISSABLE SIGHTS

The town's three must-see indoor sights are the **Museum of Asian Art** (daily summer 8am–8pm, winter 9am–4pm), a collection housed (together with excellent changing exhibits) in the British-built Palace of Saints George

*Beach fun.*

*The Achilleion Palace is stuffed with over-the-top statuary.*

*The 13th-century Angelókastro.*

**Archaeological Museum** (re-opening 2018), whose star exhibit is the massive Gorgon pediment from an Artemis temple at Paleopoli. The more detailed pediment of a Dionysiac symposium, complete with the god, acolyte and lion, however, equals it. Both came from excavations in **Mon Repos estate** (daily 8am––7.30pm; free), where there are not only other ruined temples and an early Christian basilica, but also the **Paleópolis Museum** (daily 8.30am–3pm), which holds worthwhile exhibits. Just south of this at **Kanóni** are the photogenic islets of **Vlahérna**, with a little monastery and causeway to it, and **Pondikonísi**, said to be a local ship petrified by Poseidon in revenge for the ancient Phaiakians helping Odysseus. North of Corfu town, served by launches from the old port, forested **Vídos** island was the final destination of many members of a retreating, defeated Serbian army; deaths overwhelmed small burial grounds so most casualties were buried at sea, just offshore. Vídos offers several good beaches plus a taverna.

and Michael; the **Andivouniótissa (Byzantine) Museum** in Mourágia district (Tues–Sun 8am–3pm), a medieval church crammed full of unusual icons of the 15th to the 18th centuries, many of them painted by refugee Cretan artists who came here after the fall of Venetian Crete in 1669; and the

## THE NORTH OF THE ISLAND

Northwest of town are busy resorts such as **Kondókali**, Komméno, Dassiá and Ypsos, used by both Greek and foreign visitors, though **Barbáti** is probably the first beach you would stop for. The coast between **Nissáki** ❷ and **Agios Stéfanos Sinión** ❸ fancies itself a mini-Riviera, with smart villas – there are hardly any hotels – and secluded pebble coves. But mass tourism takes over again at **Kassiópi**, important in antiquity but now with only a restored Angevin castle. Up the slopes of 914-metre (2,300ft) **Mount Pandokrátor** ❹ nestles **Paleá Períthia**, an almost abandoned Venetian-era village in the process of being slowly restored. Back on the coast, quiet beaches between Kassiópi and **Aharávi** are pleasant alternatives to overdeveloped **Róda** and **Sidári** ❺. From Sidári ply the most reliable boats to **Eríkoussa**, smallest of the three inhabited Diapóndia islets – and the most visited, thanks to its sandy beaches and close proximity.

Northwest-coast beaches beyond Sidári are superior, beginning at quieter **Perouládes** ❻, continuing through **Agios Stéfanos Avliotón** – start of day-trips to the other Diapóndians Mathráki and Othoní – Arílas and **Agios Geórgios Págon**, the latter being the best of this series. Beyond **Kríni** looms the shattered but superbly set Byzantine-Angevin **Angelókastro**, guarding the approach to the beautiful double bay of **Paleokastrítsa** ❼, now oversubscribed; best admire it from above, at Theotókou monastery, or from the cafés in **Lákones** village.

Beyond here, beaches resume at **Ermones**, but either **Myrtiótissa** ❽, small but beloved of naturists, or bigger **Kondogialós**, with lots of amenities, are better, while **Agios Górdis** is a backpackers' paradise. Inland, **Pélekas** has famous coastal panoramas and sunsets, which prompted Kaiser Wilhelm II to build a special viewing platform.

## THE SOUTH OF THE ISLAND

Inland and south of Kérkyra, near Gastoúri, stands the pretentious

**Achilleion Palace**  (daily Apr–Oct 8am–8pm, Nov–March 8am–4pm), built in 1890–91 for Empress Elisabeth of Austria, then acquired by Kaiser Wilhelm II after her death in 1898, at the hands of an assassin in Geneva. It once housed a casino, has hosted EU meetings and is now a museum of kitsch. **Benítses** ⑩ has seen its heyday come and go, though the village itself is quite attractive and is getting a new lease of life thanks to a 2012-completed marina; **Moraïtika** and **Messongí** are by contrast busier, but local beaches are better.

Inland, roads visit what is seemingly another island, winding around **Agii Déka** hill (576 metres /1,890ft), with the uninhabited monastery of Pandokratóra near the summit. Due west of Messongí is the **Gardíki Pýrgos** ⑪, a crumbling octagonal Angevin castle (always open) in a curious lowland setting. The castle road continues to the fine **Halikoúna** beach at the northwest end of the **Korissíon lagoon** ⑫, a protected nature reserve and a magnet for birdwatchers.

*The photogenic islet of Vlahérna, with its little monastery.*

Back on the main trunk road, Argyrádes gives access to the north-coast villages of **Boúkari** and **Petrití**, which have low-key facilities owing to a lack of good beaches. In the opposite direction lies **Agios Geórgios Argyrádon** ⑬, developed during the 1990s for mass tourism, with only splendid **Íssos** beach, a mecca for windsurfers, to its credit. Further east, adjacent **Marathiá** and **Agía Varvára beaches** ⑭ have better facilities.

The Corfiots have deliberately quarantined the Club 18–30 set at **Kávos**. The underrated, second-largest town on Corfu, **Lefkímmi** ⑮, goes about its business just inland, seemingly oblivious to its raucous neighbour; locals visit the beach at **Boúka**, the mouth of the river picturesquely bisecting Lefkímmi.

The southern end of the Corfu Trail is found nearby at the romantically ruined monastery of **Panagía Arkoudíla** ⑯, poised near Cape Aspókavos above idyllic, little-visited **Kánoula** beach.

# WORKING THE LAND

Traditional farming methods are still used on many islands, with the economic crisis prompting a back-to-the-land movement after years of rural depopulation. The silver-leafed olive trees that grace the Aegean landscape are an integral part of island life. Olive oil has long been a staple not only of the Greek diet, but the local economy. Even urban families have olive groves, gathering their own olives to take to a local mill. Depending on variety and locale, harvesting – either raking off the trees or collecting from black mesh nets that also mark the scenery – occurs between October and January, with pruning (the wood is a highly prized fuel) soon after.

For most full-time island farmers, agricultural produce is for local use only, with non-mechanised techniques enforced by hilly terrain, though roto-tillers have now replaced ploughing teams. The striking patterns of irregular fields result from the division of land to form inheritances and marriage dowries. A typical farming community consists of 10 to 100 close-packed houses, their small yards containing chickens and the occasional pig. Most villages now have at least dirt-road access, power lines (or solar panels) and perhaps some fixed phones, but water supply can be a problem.

A large-scale goat- or sheep-herder may have 100 to 500 animals, concentrating on producing kids or lambs for the peak Easter and summer periods. During the cooler months, most herders collect wild foliage for both bedding and fodder. By contrast, there might be the elderly widow with a few goats and fields, working them on her own. In spring, animals are taken to graze in fairly remote upland pastures.

## CROPS AND METHODS

Small-scale farmers supplement the family diet with lentils, broad beans and chickpeas, fruit and vegetables. During spring and summer, ubiquitous vegetable patches produce (in this order) potatoes, beans, tomatoes, courgettes, peppers, melons, okra and aubergines – in return for considerable investment in time and effort, but not always pesticides or fertilisers. Subsistence farmers unable to spend on these products make a virtue of necessity by producing de facto organic crops.

During early summer, grain – especially barley – is still often reaped by hand with a sickle, laid out in situ to dry, and then threshed. This is usually done by machine, especially on larger islands such as Rhodes, Kós and Límnos, but on a few remote, rugged islands, a team of mules or donkeys is still walked over the crop strewn on the threshing cirques (alónia) to smash the husks with their hoofs, prior to winnowing and sieving.

Traditional farming methods are disappearing however, sporadic EU subsidies notwithstanding. The youth exodus from the villages to towns or the mainland to find work, plus competition with other EU farmers, have spelt doom for labour-intensive methods, as numerous overgrown fields and crumbled terraces attest. One positive outcome of the ongoing economic crisis is a reversal in this migration: many younger people, unable to survive in the city, are returning to live rent-free in their ancestral village homes, in some cases to take up farming. The main hope for the agricultural sector is to increase value through official organic certification – difficult when your olive groves are aerially sprayed without your consent against the destructive dákos fly – or the marketing of speciality cash-crops such as almonds, pine-nuts and kumquats.

*The oil-producing olive grove, at the heart of both the local economy and of the Greek diet.*

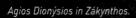

# SOUTHERN IONIAN ISLANDS

Everything here, from architecture to food, has been influenced by the Italians, who continue to arrive in large numbers each August. Yet in recent years Brits, and central Europeans, are as or even more numerous.

**Paxí** (Páxos), the smallest of the seven main islands of the Ionian archipelago, is 90 minutes by conventional excursion boat from Corfu (Kérkyra) – half that time by hydrofoil. Hilly and green, it has rugged west-coast cliffs, several sea-caves and various pebble beaches. Paxí figures little in ancient history and mythology, when it was uninhabited, though Tim Severin's *The Ulysses Voyage* identifies the Homeric spring and dell of Circe as the modern one beside the late Byzantine church of Ypapandí, in the far north. Paxí acquired extensive olive groves and served as a hunting reserve for the Corfiot Venetian aristocracy, but was only systematically populated during the 15th century. The gnarled olive trunks, their shimmering leaves like coins tossed in the breeze, are emblems of the island, and provided the main livelihood before tourism – Paxiot oil ranks among the best in Greece, and has won many international medals. Dwellings, from humble cottages to baronial mansions, are tucked into hollows out of sight, and out of reach of the *maïstros*, the prevailing northwest wind; only during modern times have villas with sea and coast views appeared.

All boats dock at the small capital, **Gáïos ❶**, arrayed fan-like around its main square and sheltered by the two islets of **Agios Nikólaos** and **Panagía**, sporting, respectively, a Venetian

*Fishermen on Levkáda.*

castle and small monastery. Gáïos preserves narrow streets and a few grand 19th-century buildings with Venetian-style balconies and shutters, plus most island shops, though tavernas are undistinguished.

Paxí's single main road meanders northwest, through the olive groves and tiny hamlets consisting of a few houses, and perhaps a *kafenío* at main junctions. Locally sold walking maps point you along a maze of old walled paths, dirt tracks and paved lanes, which provide the best way to see the

**⊘ Main Attractions**

Andípaxi beaches
Roniés Waterfalls
Pórto Katsíki beach
Odysseus trail
Assos
Melissáni cave
Vasilikós peninsula
Shipwreck Bay

**Map on page 142**

**Southern Ionian Islands**

```
0        10 km
0          10 miles
```

island. Reached by a side road, **Longós** on the northwest coast is the most exclusive resort, flanked by the popular beaches of **Levréhio** and **Monodéndri**, the latter with road access. The "motorway" ends at **Lákka ②**, beloved of yachts and the majority of landbound tourists, with a better choice of food and lodging; a signposted path leads to **Orkós** beach.

The northeast coast of **Andípaxi** (Andípaxos) islet shelters the two excellent beaches of **Vatoúmi** and **Vríka**, well known to day-trippers in summer but idyllic off-season. Only in summer, when several tavernas operate, do a dozen people live here; Andípaxi's vineyards produce a heavy red wine favoured for local festivals, and a lighter tawny white.

## LEVKÁDA (LÉFKAS)

Like Évvia, Levkáda is joined to the mainland by a swing bridge over a canal, opening on the hour to let yachts pass. Greeks seasonally crowd the place, glad to find an island exempt from the prices and weather-whims of a ferry crossing. Yet Levkáda feels like the Ionian, with standard Venetian influences on speech and cuisine, the imposing fort of Santa Maura by the bridge, plus spear-like cypress and bright yellow broom in May carpeting the steep hillsides. Kefaloniá may be higher, but Levkáda has a more rugged landscape, which has preserved rural lifestyles in the hill villages; older women still wear traditional dress, while local crafts and foodstuffs are avidly promoted.

**Levkáda Town ③** faces the canal and the lagoon enclosed by the Gýra sandspit; local topography provides safe mooring for numerous yachts on the southeast quay. Of all Ionian capitals, it's the most pedestrian-friendly; much of the central area is off-limits to cars. The municipal axis is Ioánnou Melá, which beyond lively Platía Agíou Spyrídonos becomes Odós Wilhelm Dörpfeld, in honour of the early

20th-century German archaeologist who attempted to prove that Levkáda was in fact Homeric Ithaca. He is again duly revered in the excellent **Archaeological Museum** (Tue–Sun 8.30am–3pm), with well-labelled exhibits on ancient religion and daily life. Also notable are several ornate Italianate churches dating from the late 17th or early 18th century, where arched windows, artwork of the Ionian School and Baroque relief work sit oddly beside post-earthquake belfries modelled on oil derricks.

Levkáda is the homeland of 20th-century poet Angelos Sikelianos, and Lafcadio Hearn, a 19th-century short-story writer who immortalised supernatural Japan, born here to Greek and Irish parents. There are cultural links between the island and Japan, and streets commemorate both men.

Heading down Levkáda's east coast, the little port-resorts of **Lygiá** and **Nikiána**, with pebble coves and fish tavernas, are the first places to prompt a stop. They are calmer and quieter than **Nydrí** ❹, 20km (12 miles) south of Levkáda opposite a mini-archipelago of four islets. The view out to them is the reason Nydrí has been earmarked for package-tourist development, since local beaches are frankly mediocre. Until the 1970s it was a tiny fishing village, where Aristotle Onassis used to pop over for dinner from Skorpiós, his private island; there's a statue of the man on the quay now named for him, but no trace of exclusivity lingers, and his granddaughter finally sold Skorpiós in 2013.

The one conventionally inhabited satellite island, **Meganísi**, accessible by at least four daily ferries, is an ill-kept secret; yachters already appreciate its quiet bays and attractive villages. The best escape for landlubbers lies 3km (2 miles) inland, where the **Roniés Waterfalls** prove surprisingly impressive, and indicative of abundant water at the heart of Levkáda.

Beyond Nydrí, Dörpfeld excavated extensively at Stenó, and is buried on the far side of **Vlyhó** bay. The island ring road curls past Mikrós Gialós pebble bay and Sývota yacht harbour before descending to **Vassilikí** ❺, 40km (25 miles) from town, one of Europe's

*Levkáda balcony.*

*Lunch by the lagoon in Levkáda Town.*

ΕΥΧΗΝ
ΟΔΥCCEI

*Stavrós is one of several places in Itháki claiming to be the site of Odysseus' castle, and marks its claim with this bust of the Homeric hero.*

*Vathý has retained a traditional style.*

premier windsurfing resorts. Boat tours are offered around Cape Levkátas – where Sappho legendarily leaped to her death – to spectacular west-coast beaches, also accessible by roads of varying steepness. Southernmost **Pórto Katsíki** ❻ stars on every third postcard of Levkáda; **Egremní** and **Gialós** are less frequented, while panoramic **Atháni** village has the closest tourist facilities. Further on, **Drymónas** is the most architecturally preserved settlement on the island, while **Kalamítsi** has an eponymous beach and "shares" **Káthisma**, Levkáda's longest strand, with **Aï Nikítas**. The only port actually on the west coast has become a relatively upmarket resort, though worth avoiding in peak season. Beyond Aï Nikítas's own little beach, **Pefkoúlia** stretches north to the headland dividing it from **Agios Ioánnis**, the nicest section of Gýra beach, with its abandoned windmills.

Journeys inland thread through the half-dozen **Sfakiótes** hamlets occupying a fertile upland, where churches with Venetian-style belfries may be seen. The usual destination is **Karyá**,

even higher and cooler, with a thriving crafts tradition and a vast central *platía* shaded by several giant plane trees.

## ITHACA (ITHÁKI)

Evidence that Itháki actually was the ancient home of Odysseus, wandering hero of Homer's *Odyssey*, is hardly conclusive, but this hasn't discouraged a local Homeric "heritage industry", with numerous streets and businesses named for characters in the epic, and modest archaeological sites assiduously signposted as putative locales for various episodes.

Most ferries dock at the cheerful capital, **Vathý** ❼, occupying the head of a long bay. Though badly damaged by the 1953 earthquake, many buildings survived, while others were tastefully rebuilt with traditional architectural elements. There are more tavernas and *kafenía*, especially along the quay, than in any other port town of this size. Several pebble beaches – pleasant, if not Itháki's best – lie close by; this is an island ideally sized for scooter exploration and walking.

Itháki is almost pinched in two by an isthmus barely wide enough for the main corniche road. The northern half has more lush vegetation and better beaches; below **Léfki** village the secluded pebble bays of **Agios Ioánnis** and **Koutoúpi** grace the west coast. **Stavrós** ❽, 16km (10 miles) from Vathý, is Itháki's second town, with another small museum devoted to finds from local sites with a better claim to being Odysseus' possible home. These are a citadel on **Pelikáta** hill and, more intriguing, an excavation marked as "**School of Homer**" off the road to Exogí. Walls and foundations, a few Mycenaean graves, steps carved into the rock and a vaulted cave-well lie exposed. In size and position, the place feels just right to be the base of a minor chieftain like Odysseus. **Exogí**, the highest village on the island, is seasonally occupied but offers superb views northeast. From Platrithiás village a paved drive goes to **Afáles** bay with excellent sand-and-pebble patches, while another road loops through Agii Saránda and Lahós, partly spared by the earthquake, en route to **Fríkes**. There are morning ferries here (to Levkáda) and many yachts, although most visitors continue, past attractive pebble coves, to **Kióni** ❾, Itháki's most upmarket resort, where again various houses survived the quake. At either port, accommodation is non-existent during high season.

From Kióni you can walk up the cleared and profusely waymarked old path to Anogí, a three-hour round trip; it's the best hike on the island, with only the last 20 minutes spoilt by the heliport and its access road. In half-deserted **Anogí**, there's a medieval church of **Kímisis tis Theotókou** (Dormition of the Virgin), with heavily retouched Byzantine frescoes and a Venetian belfry. Some 4km (2.5 miles) south, the **Monastery of Katharón** is by contrast a post-quake barracks-like structure, flanked by modern antennae, but the views are unsurpassed.

## KEFALONIÁ (KEFALLINÍA, CEPHALONIA)

Kefaloniá is the largest and second most mountainous Ionian island, its

⊙ **Eat**

Kefaloniá is noted for its honey (thyme-scented), quince jelly and a local speciality called riganáta – feta cheese mixed with bread, oil and oregano.

*Hiking Mount Énos, Kefaloniá.*

### ⊙ THE ODYSSEUS TRAIL

Odyssean sites near Vathý, Itháki include the **Bay of Phokrys** (now Fórkynos), the **Cave of the Nymphs**, the **Spring of Arethoúsa**, and ancient **Alalkomenae** (Alalkoméni). Having landed at Phokrys, it is said, Odysseus climbed up to the cave and hid various gifts given him by King Alkinoös of the Phaeakians. Next, Odysseus met his loyal swineherd Eumaeos and son Telemakhos at the Arethoúsa spring; the track-and-path walk from Vathý takes 90 minutes, challenging but with good views. Alalkomenae occupies a hillside 5km (3 miles) west of Vathý, above the road between Fórkynos and the secondary port (and a good pebble beach) of **Píso Aetós**; Heinrich Schliemann excavated here, but most of the finds (now in Vathý's museum) clearly do not date from the Homeric era.

*Kefaloniá blooms.*

*Peering down over the partly exposed lake of Melissáni cave.*

population famous for a studied (often creative) eccentricity. It has mixed feelings about being typecast as "Captain Corelli's Island", since political opinions expressed in Louis de Bernières's locally set blockbuster novel are not popular here.

The capital town of **Argostóli** , levelled by the 1953 earthquake, was rebuilt in utilitarian style and has a workaday feel, epitomised by meat and produce markets perched right on the commercial quay near the pedestrian-only, British-built **Drápano** stone bridge across the lagoon. The quay's names honour two islanders: Ioannis Metaxas, 1930s dictator and defier of the Italians, and Andonis Tritsis (1937–92), innovative architect, maverick politician and ultimately mayor of Athens. The heart of town is the 2016-revamped **Platía Vallianoú**, ringed by hotels, *kafenía* and pest-resistant palms; trendy cafés have sprouted on the pedestrianised, relatively elegant **Lithóstroto** beside smart shops. Specific sights are limited to three museums, of which the **Korgialenios Historical and Folkloric**

**Museum** (Ground floor of Korgialénios library; closed until further notice) is the most interesting. It offers, should it re-open, archival pictures of Argostóli pre- and post-quake, and thorough coverage of traditional life. Northwest of town, near the Doric rotunda of **Agios Theodóros lighthouse**, the "sea mills" at **Katavóthres** used to grind grain and generate electricity; salt water pouring down sinkholes here emerges three weeks later near Sámi, but the 1953 disaster reduced the flow to a trickle.

To the east looms **Mount Énos** (the ancient Ainos), at 1,628 metres (5,340ft) the highest peak in these islands and still partly covered with native firs *(Abies cephallonica)*; two small reserves protect the remaining trees, much reduced by fires and loggers. The inclined south coastal plain at the base of the mountain, **Livathó**, is punctuated by a conical hill bearing the Venetian capital of **Agios Geórgios**, inhabited from Byzantine times until the 17th century. The impressive summit **castle** (Tue–Sun 8.30am–3pm, may close off-season) has wonderful views. Aristocratic associations linger at certain Livathó villages: pre-quake stone walls enclose vast estates; Lord Byron lived at nearby Metaxáta in 1823; and Keramiés still harbours dilapidated pre-quake mansions and a huge olive mill. The largest beach in the area, with resort amenities, is **Lourdáta**.

On the west shore of Argostóli gulf, reached by frequent ferries used by drivers and pedestrians alike to avoid the tedious journey by road, **Lixoúri** has long been eclipsed by rival Argostóli, but it's a pleasantly sleepy town with views to Zákynthos. Beyond, southwest on the peninsula, lie the busy red-sand beaches of **Mégas Lákkos** and **Xí**; en route you'll see how the fertile, grain-and-grape-planted terrain was heaved and buckled by the force of the quake. Beyond Xí, **Kounópetra** (Rocking Stone) no longer does so since 1953. Northwest of Lixoúri is

the long, fine-pebble beach of **Petáni**, exposed but spectacular, although much the best beach near Lixoúri is the lonely, and facility-less, **Platiá Ammos**, reached by 300 steps from near Theotókou Kipouríon monastery.

Northern Kefaloniá was less damaged by the earthquake, and surviving medieval houses in various states of repair, especially at **Vassilikiádes** and **Mesovoúnia**, serve as poignant reminders of a lost architectural heritage. But the port resort of **Fiskárdo** ⑫ emerged almost unscathed, and ruthlessly exploits the fact despite a lack of beaches. The atmosphere is very pukka, if not precious, and yachts congregate in force, dodging the occasional ferry to Levkáda or Itháki. "Fiskárdo" is a corruption of the name of Norman-Sicilian adventurer Robert Guiscard, who made Kefaloniá his headquarters, but died near Lixoúri in 1085.

On the west coast, the perfect horseshoe harbour of **Assos** ⑬ sees only fishing boats and is the better for it; there's good swimming from the isthmus joining this partly preserved village to a pine-covered bluff, with its fine late 16th-century Venetian fort. A bit further south, **Mýrtos** is among the most famous – and overrated – beaches in the Ionians: coarse-pebbled and downright dangerous if a surf is up.

The water is calmer and the pebbles smaller at **Agía Evfimía**, a fishing village on the east coast; between here and the functional ferry port of **Sámi** lies the **Melissáni cave** ⑭ (daily May–Oct 8am–7pm, Nov–Apr Fri–Sun 10am–4pm), containing an underground lake with its roof partly open to the sky. Nearby, another cave, **Drogaráti** (Apr–Oct daily 9am–8pm) offers multicoloured stalactites and stalagmites, and is the occasional venue for concerts.

Beyond Sámi, a good road threads attractively through vegetated scenery to underrated **Póros**, another ferry/yacht port with a backdrop of green cliffs. From here you loop around the coast to busy **Skála**, with its superb sand-and-gravel beach fringed by pines, and extensive mosaic flooring in a Roman villa (unreliably open; free), and then around Cape Moúnda to the all-sand **Kamínia** beach, Kefaloniá's principal turtle-nesting venue.

## ZÁKYNTHOS (ZÁNTE)

*Zante, Fior di Levante* (flower of the East), said the Venetians, and its central plain – the most fertile in the Ionians – and eastern hills support luxuriant vegetation. The southeastern coasts shelter excellent beaches: some are almost undeveloped, others are home to notoriously unsavoury tourism.

At the once-elegant harbour town of **Zákynthos** ⑮, ferries dock by Platía Solomoú, named for native son Dionysios Solomos, a 19th-century poet who wrote the words to the Greek national anthem. At the rear of his *platía*, the **Zákynthos Museum of Post-Byzantine Art** (Tue–Sun 8.30am–3pm) features icons rescued from quake-blasted churches, as well as numerous 17th–19th-century religious paintings

*Looking out from the Agios Theodóros lighthouse.*

of the Ionian School, founded by Cretan artists fleeing the Ottoman conquest, who met local artists strongly influenced by the Italian Renaissance. At the southern end of the harbour is the cathedral of **Agios Dionýsios** (daily 8am–1pm and 5–10pm), the island's patron saint, designed in its latest incarnation by the archaeologist and Byzantinologist Athanasios Orlandos. The stained glass was donated after the 1953 earthquake by the island's small Jewish community in gratitude for being hidden from the Nazis by their fellow islanders.

In medieval times people lived above the present town in **Bóhali** district, inside the huge *kástro* (Tue–Sun July–Oct 8am–7pm, Nov–June 8.30am–3pm), which is mostly Venetian on Byzantine foundations. Nearby, several cafés provide superb views.

Unfortunately, most of the 700,000 annual visitors don't stray far from adjacent **Laganás/Kalamáki**  beach resorts, whose explosive growth since the late 1970s is endangering the survival of loggerhead turtles (see page

149), which have nested here for millennia. Luckily, the tourist tat is easily skirted, and Zákynthos shows its best side in the more remote corners. The **Vasilikós peninsula**, lying beyond forgettable Argási, has the island's best, most scenic beaches, culminating in **Agios Nikólaos** and **Gérakas**, nearest the easternmost cape.

Start a tour of the unspoilt western hill villages from **Kerí** at the far south cape, with its lighthouse; next stop would be **Kiloméno** ⓲, which survived 1953 largely intact. Tourists are coached to **Kambí** to watch the sunset, but **Éxo Hóra** and **Mariés** have more character, with pre-quake churches and wells, vital in this arid region. Still further north, **Anafonítria** village offers an eponymous 14th-century monastery with a daunting gate-keep; plaques recall the local legend that 1578–1622 abbot St Dionýsios forgave and sheltered his brother's murderer here. Nearby, the 16th-century monastery of **Agios Geórgios ton Krimnón** has a round lookout tower in its well-tended courtyard; just beyond is the overlook for **Shipwreck (Navágio) Bay** ⓲, the most photographed in the Ionians, where a rusty freighter – driven ashore in 1980 by the coastguard in the mistaken belief that it was a smugglers' ship – lies half-buried in sand. Boat trips, the only access, visit from **Pórto Vrómi**, below Mariés.

From "Shipwreck", head east through grain fields, and the two **Volímes** villages noted for their honey, textiles and cheese, to reach the east coast near **Makrýs Gialós** pebble beach and the bleak port of **Agios Nikólaos**, with daily summer morning ferries to Kefaloniá and excursion boats to the **Blue Caves** ⓳ – interconnecting grottoes with spectacular light effects at the right hour.

Back towards town, you wind through **Alykés** (the calmest beach resort), past secluded bays favoured by Greeks, before hitting mass tourism again at **Planós**.

*Shipwreck Bay, Zákynthos.*

# TURTLES VS. TOURISTS

## The survival of the loggerhead turtles of Zákynthos is under threat from some of the undesirable effects of mass tourism.

A loggerhead turtle crawls out of the sea onto the moonlit beach of her birthplace, the island of Zákynthos. She has crossed the Mediterranean to return, at last, to this spot. Summoning all her strength, the 90kg (200lb) reptile selects a place in the sand where she digs a nest with her rear flippers. In it she lays about 100 soft eggs, each the size of a ping-pong ball, covers them with sand and returns exhausted to the sea to rest in the shallows. However, the survival of the loggerhead (Caretta caretta) is endangered before she even reaches the beach. It has been estimated that nearly half the females basking in the shallows may be maimed or killed by the propellers of speedboats taking waterskiers and paragliders out to sea. Carelessly discarded litter creates another hazard, as turtles suffocate trying to swallow plastic bags that they mistake for jellyfish, a favourite food of theirs.

For the female turtle, hazards increase when she slips ashore. Disorientated by the glittering lights of hotels and the strange noises coming from the tourists and bars, she may scurry back to the surf-line, uncertain where to deposit her eggs. Those that try to continue their labours may suffer the indignity of ignorant spectators brandishing torches and flashing cameras, frightening the turtles back into the sea where the eggs may be released, never to hatch.

Eggs that are successfully laid are often crushed by thoughtless quad-bikers, horse-riders and motorists who drive across the sand, which also compacts it so that it is impossible for the hatchlings to emerge. Beach umbrellas are unwittingly driven into nests, piercing the eggs. Tamarisk trees, planted to shade sunbathers, pose another problem, as hatchlings become tangled up in the roots. Even sandcastles may create holes that become shallow graves for the young turtles.

Hatching takes place from early August to late September – precisely when most tourists arrive. The 6cm- (2.5in-) long hatchlings may emerge from their hazardous 50-day incubation and, instead of heading instinctively to starlight on the horizon line at sea, frequently wander confused up the beach to hotel and bar lights – an error that brings death from exhaustion or dehydration.

Zákynthos formerly had one of the greatest concentrations of nesting turtles in the Mediterranean. Laganás Bay was a particularly favourite spot but, confused by the combination of boats, lights and noise that tourism has brought, the turtles have abandoned these busy sands. The majority now nest in the more secluded beaches of Sekánia, Gérakas and Dáfni, where there is barely room for the activities of the bewildered reptiles. Fewer than 650 turtles now breed annually on Zákynthos, as against over 1,200 during the early 1980s.

The Greek Sea Turtle Protection Society (www.archelon.gr), locked in frequent, sometimes violent conflict with unscrupulous developers, midwifed the 1999 creation of the National Marine Park of Zákynthos (www.nmp-zak.org), encompassing the whole gulf between the capes of Gérakas and Kerí. Three levels of control restrict boating and land access; all affected beaches have dusk-to-dawn curfews. Volunteers are on hand during the season to help inform visitors, and monitor nests.

*The National Marine Park of Zákynthos was set up to protect nesting turtles.*

# KÝTHIRA

Geographically nearer to Crete than to the Ionian group, this is one of Greece's quietest islands. Most visitors are Greeks from Athens – or Greek-Australians returning home.

**⊙ Main Attractions**
Hóra
Mylopótamos
Agía Sofía
Paleohóra

**Map on page 151**

According to local legend, Kýthira, suspended off Cape Maléa in the Lakonian Gulf, was the birthplace of Aphrodite. (Others claim she was born off Cyprus.) A bleak, thyme-covered plateau slashed by vegetated ravines, the island forms part of a mostly sunken land bridge between the Peloponnese and Crete, from where many Venetian refugees arrived during the 17th century.

It has two names (Tsérigo was its Venetian alias); a history of Venetian and British rule, but today governed from Piraeus along with the Argo-Saronics;

an architecture that's a hybrid of Cycladic and Venetian; a pronounced Australian flavour, courtesy of remittances and personal visits from emigrants Down Under – and ubiquitous eucalyptus.

Kýthira (also spelt Kýthera and Kíthira) does not put itself out for outsiders. Accommodation is relatively expensive and hard to secure in summer; good tavernas are sparse. Rough seas, which can play havoc with ferries from Gýthio, Neápoli or Kastélli (Crete), prompted the construction of an all-weather harbour at Diakófti in 1997. Despite all that, Kýthira has become a popular haunt of trendy Greeks, thanks to its appearance in Theo Angelopoulos's 1984 film *Taxidi sta Kythira* and a more recent television series shot on the island.

**Hóra ❶** (also called Kýthira) is one of the finest Aegean island capitals. Imposing, flat-roofed mansions in the lower town date from the 17th to 19th centuries, though the Venetian *kástro* above is of earlier vintage. An elaborate domed cistern system is still intact, while a few rusty cannons guarding a church seem superfluous, given the incredibly steep drop to the sea at **Kapsáli** yacht harbour, where most tourists stay, though its beach is mediocre.

## AROUND THE ISLAND

Much better beaches lie east of Hóra at **Halkós**, south of **Kálamos** village, and at

*Kapsáli fortress.*

**Fyrí Ammos**, east of Kálamos, with sea-caves to explore. North of Fyrí Ammos, and easier to get to, more excellent beaches dot the east coast: **Kombonáda** and **Kaladí**, with a rock monolith in the surf at one end, and two – **Asprógas** and **Paleópoli** – to either side of Kastrí Point with its Minoan settlement, which was explored by Heinrich Schliemann in 1887.

The beachy strip ends at the fishing anchorage of **Avlémonas** ❷, where seemingly half the island's population comes for weekend lunches at three fish tavernas. The diminutive octagonal Venetian fort is scarcely more than a gun emplacement. There's a better, 16th-century castle, complete with a Lion of St Mark, at **Káto Hóra**, just outside the attractive village of **Mylopótamos** ❸, with a waterfall and abandoned mill in a wooded canyon. This fortress was not a military stronghold but a civilian pirate refuge; derelict houses remain inside.

Some 2.5km (1.5 miles) west of Káto Hóra, perched above the surf-lashed west coast, the black-limestone cavern of **Agía Sofía** ❹ (July–Sept daily 11am–6.30pm, not Mon Sept) is the best of several namesake caves on Kýthira. A 13th-century hermit adorned the entrance with frescoes of Holy Wisdom, and three attendant virtues, personified. (Locals insist that Aphrodite slept here, but today the only endemic life is a minute white spider.) About one-sixth of the cave, with marvellous stalactites and stalagmites, is open for visits.

The ghost village of **Paleohóra** ❺ in the northeast failed the pirate-proof test in 1537, when the notorious Barbarossa sacked it. The ruins, including six frescoed (but locked) churches, cover the summit of a high bluff plunging to the confluence of two gorges that unite as **Kakí Langáda**, reaching the sea at a small lake.

**Potamós** ❻, 2km (1.25 miles) north of the Paleohóra turning, is Kýthira's largest village, host to a Sunday farmers' market. **Agía Pelagía**, the former ferry port, has come down in the world since **Diakófti** started working. More rewarding is **Karavás** ❼, the northernmost and prettiest of the ravine oasis-villages, which meets the sea at **Platiá Ammos** beach; pebbly **Foúrni** cove lies adjacent.

*Sailing the waters around Kýthira, which legend links to Aphrodite.*

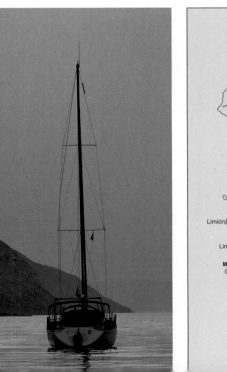

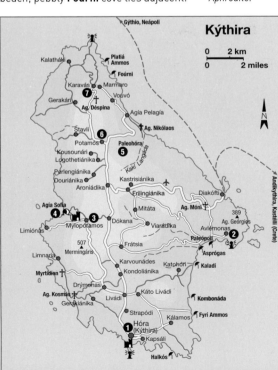

Kýthira

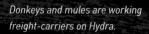
Donkeys and mules are working freight-carriers on Hydra.

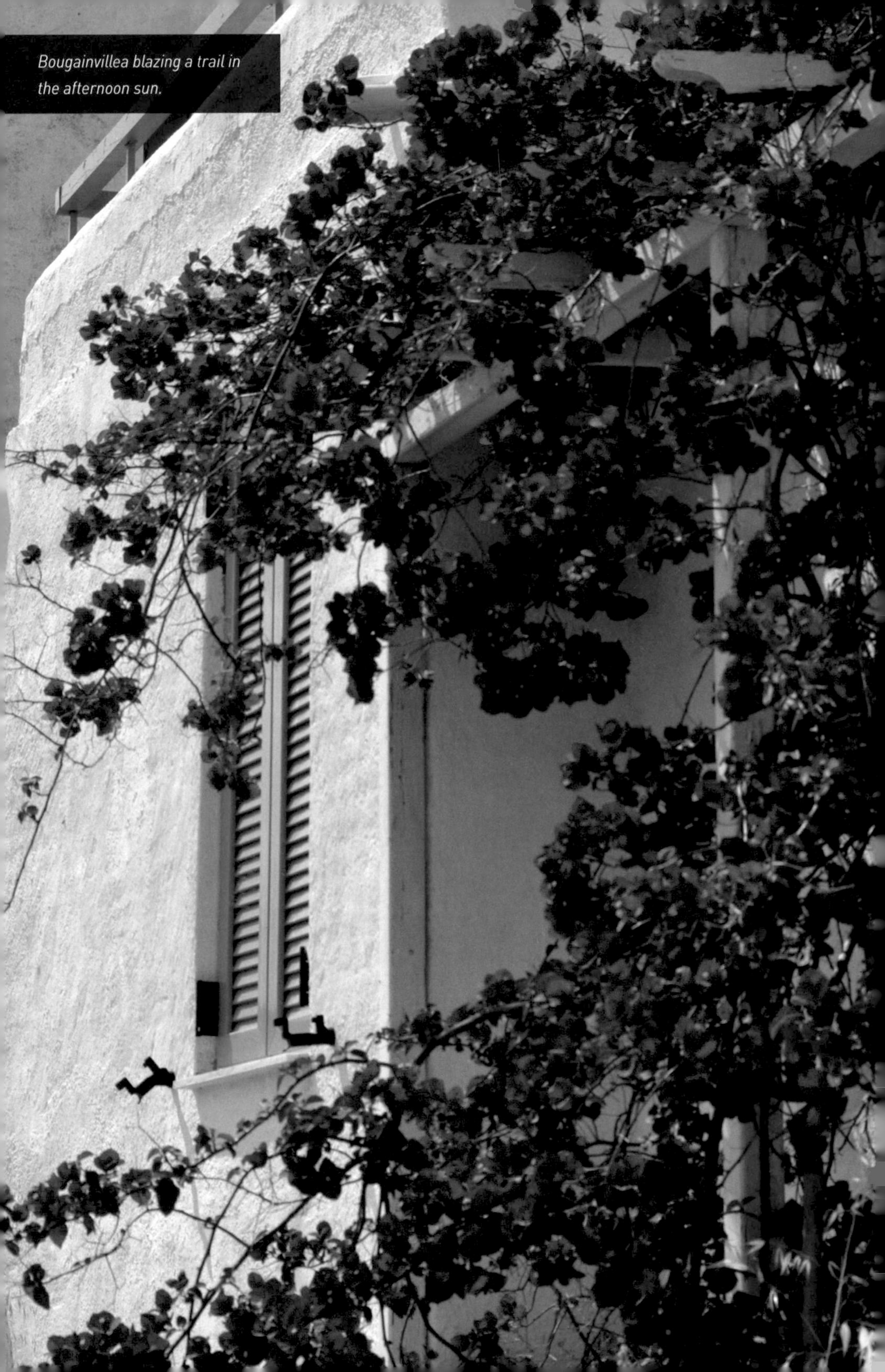

*Bougainvillea blazing a trail in the afternoon sun.*

# ISLANDS OF THE SARONIC GULF

Salamína, Aegina, Angístri, Póros, Hydra and Spétses.

*Mosaic at the Monastery of the Panagía, on Hydra.*

The six islands of the Saronic Gulf could be described as "commuter" islands – although that doesn't sound very romantic. As they lie within a short ferry ride (or an even shorter hydrofoil trip) from Piraeus, the temptation exists to treat the islands as an extension of the mainland or, more specifically, suburbs of Athens.

Entrepreneurs have been quick to exploit the islands' proximity. The one-day cruise from Piraeus calling at Aegina, Hydra and Póros remains a popular attraction for tourists visiting Athens, although numbers have been down of late. When the cruise ships mingle with the ferries, the hydrofoils and the catamarans, there is often what resembles a traffic jam on the waters, and foreign visitors temporarily out-number Greeks.

*Greek worry beads, or kombológia.*

In spite of all this, the Argo-Saronics are defi-nitely Greek islands, not Athens suburbs – dis-tinctive in character, rich in history and, behind the crowds and the chichi boutiques, remark-ably attractive places. Salamína (Salamis), the largest of these islands, is renowned for the epochal naval battle in 480 BC, which decided the outcome of the Persian Wars. Aegina (Égina) is home to the beautiful Doric Temple of Aphaea, which is one of the most important antiquities to be found on any Greek island; Angístri, situated opposite Aegina, is low key and veiled in pines.

Póros and its channel have been immortalised by American author Henry Miller (1891–1980) in *The Colossus of Maroussi*, and forested Spétses (thinly disguised as Phraxos) by John Fowles in his celebrated 1966 novel *The Magus*. Not to be outdone, since the late 1950s Hydra (Ýdra) has attracted artists, filmmakers, well-heeled Athenians, trendy Europeans, movie stars and other international celebrities.

# ARGO-SARONIC ISLANDS

These six islands all lie within easy reach of the mainland, and thus are popular destinations. Nevertheless, they are distinctive, rich in history and remarkably attractive.

Low, flat Salamína (ancient Salamis) is invariably overlooked by island-hoppers intent on more glamorous destinations. It's the largest Saronic Gulf island, but so close to Athens (and so frequently connected from Pérama port) that most Athenians regard it as a commuter dormitory.

## SALAMÍNA

Salamína is best known for the naval battle in 480 BC in which outnumbered Athenian ships routed Xerxes' Persian fleet, the Greek ships being the "wooden walls" that the Delphic Oracle had predicted would save Athens. Today the island is decidedly workaday, especially the port of Paloúkia, with its naval base; Selínia, 6km (4 miles) southwest, has tavernas and two hotels.

Most islanders live in the busy capital, **Salamína ❶** (or Kouloúri), which has an archaeological and a folk museum, and decent tavernas. The 13th-century **Faneroméni Convent ❷** overlooks the northwest coast, 6km (4 miles) from Salamína; it now houses nuns and has vivid 17th-century frescoes. **Eándio**, a pleasant village on the west coast, has a good hotel. From here you can reach the southeast coast resort of **Peráni** and the small but very pretty harbour of **Peristéria**.

*Aegina locals.*

## AEGINA AND ANGÍSTRI

An hour and a half by ferry from Piraeus, or 45 minutes by hydrofoil, Aegina (Aigina, Egina) has little trouble attracting visitors. Long a favourite Athenian weekend retreat, it remains more popular with them than among foreign tourists or other Greeks. Shaped like an upside-down triangle, Aegina's south is punctuated by the prominent cone of **Mount Oros**, the highest (532 metres/1,745ft) peak in the Argo-Saronic islands, visible on a pollution-free day from the Acropolis

**⊙ Main Attractions**
Faneroméni Convent
Hristos Kapralos Museum
Temple of Aphaea
Paleohóra churches
Zoödóhou Pigís monastery
Hydra Town
Bouboulína Mansion
Agía Paraskeví beach

Map on page 158

*Fishing boats in Aegina harbour.*

in Athens. The centre and eastern side of the island is mountainous; a gently sloping fertile plain runs down to the northwestern corner where Aegina Town (Egina) partly overlays the ancient capital.

From 1826 until 1828, Aegina served as the first capital of the modern Greek state. Elegant **Aegina Town ❸**, streaked purple with jacaranda-tree flower in late spring, has numerous 19th-century buildings constructed when the country's first president, Ioannis Kapodistrias (1776–1831), lived and worked here. In Livádi suburb, just north, a plaque marks the house where **Nikos Kazantzakis** lived during the 1940s and 1950s, and wrote his most celebrated book, *Vios ke Politia tou Alexi Zorba* (*Zorba the Greek* in English). The modern harbour, crowded with pleasure craft and fishing-boats, abuts the ancient harbour, now the shallow town beach north of the main quay. Aegina's main produce is pistachio nuts, sold all along the quay. The **Archaeological Museum** (Tue–Sun 8.30am–3pm), about 10 minutes' walk from the

ferry quay, features exquisite Middle Bronze Age pottery with squid or octopus motifs. It stands in the precinct of the ancient Temple of Apollo (built 520–500 BC), of which only a single column – **Kolóna** – remains, a landmark for approaching boats. Continuing 3km (2 miles) north from here brings you to the **Hristos Kapralos Museum** (June–Oct Tue–Sun 10am–2pm and 6–8pm, Nov–May excluding Dec Fri–Sun 10am–2pm), occupying the studio of this prominent sculptor and painter (1909–93), heavily influenced by Henry Moore. There's a replica of his famous *Monument of the Battle of the Pindos*, the original frieze adorning the Greek Parliament building.

Aegina's main attraction is the exceptionally beautiful **Temple of Aphaea ❹** (Aféa; daily May–Sept 8am–8pm, Nov–Apr 10am–5.30pm), in the northeast, on a pine-tufted hilltop commanding a splendid view of the gulf. Built around 490 BC in the Doric order, it is the only surviving Greek temple with a second row of small, superimposed columns in the interior of the sanctuary, and one of the

most completely preserved – wait for any crowds to disperse to enjoy it in solitude. A short distance below lies **Agía Marína** beach resort, now perking up after some very lean years, though there are much better tavernas – if not swimming – at quieter **Pórtes**, 8km (5 miles) south.

On the way to the temple you will pass the **Convent of Agios Nektários** (see margin page 158); a steady stream of pilgrims approaches his tomb in expectation of miracles. Across the ravine from Agios Nektários is the abandoned medieval **Paleohóra** (Old Town), established after the island was sacked by pirates in the late 9th century, and inhabited until 1827. Some 38 churches and little monasteries remain more or less intact, but only around six – Agios Geórgios Katholikós, Agii Anárgyri, Agía Kyriakí, Kímisi Theotókou and Metamórfosis are usually unlocked – retain frescoes of any merit or in recognisable condition; a helpful map near the site entrance (always open) helps locate them.

The west coast of the island is quite gentle, with a charming shelving beach

just south of **Marathónas**, another, much smaller one at shadier **Eginítissa**, and the best – Klíma – beyond Pérdika. **Pérdika ❺** itself is a picturesque inlet with popular tavernas; from its harbour several daily boats cross to uninhabited limestone **Moní** islet, a nature reserve with swimming in pristine waters.

**Angístri ❻** is the small, pine-covered, low-key island opposite Aegina Town. Like many of the Argo-Saronics, it was resettled by medieval Albanians, but since the 1960s has been colonised by Germans and Athenians, who bought up houses in the villages of hillside **Metóhi** and coastal **Mýlos**, which bracket the port, sandy beach and main resort of **Skála**. Car-ferries stop at Skála, while catamarans call at Mýlos. Tourism is mixed and increasing: young Greek trendies camp on the pebbly beaches (fuelling a lively nightlife), away from British and Scandinavian package-holiday-makers. A rough path heads south from Skála for pebbly **Halikiáda**, supposedly Greece's oldest naturist beach, while the paved road from Mýlos through the forest passes

*Bell tower.*

*The unique two-layered Temple of Aphaea.*

scenic **Dragonéra** cove en route to the southerly hamlet of **Limenária**.

## PÓROS

Volcanic Póros is separated from the Peloponnese by a narrow channel, which gives the island its name – *póros* means "ford". As you sail down the 350-metre/yd-wide passage from its northwest entrance, **Póros Town** ❼ comes into view, presiding over one of the most protected anchorages in the Aegean, with scores of yachts berthed in a row. From an approaching boat, the sight of the pyramidal, orange-roofed town culminating in a blue-and-white hilltop clock tower is one of the iconic images of the Argo-Saronics. **Galatás** village on the mainland opposite is comparatively dull, but sends constant passenger shuttles (and regular car barge-ferries) across. Póros Town, built on several hills, occupies most of the little sub-islet of **Sferiá**, attached to the bulk of Póros (called Kalávria) by a narrow isthmus cut by a disused canal. Whichever route you choose to climb to the clock tower, you'll probably lose yourself in narrow lanes overhung with vines and flowers. Down on the waterfront, pride of place is given to a busy meat and seafood market similar to Aegina's, and a small but worthwhile **Archaeological Museum** (Tue–Sun 8.30am–3pm) with finds from the island and mainland opposite.

Despite mediocre beaches on Kalávria (the best of these are **Monastiríou** in the east and **Megálo Neório** to the west), Póros sees far more (Scandanavian) package tourism than its neighbours, along with Athenian weekenders and second-home owners. The island has never been über-fashionable, but has had a naval connection since 1846 when a cadet-training station was established just beyond the isthmus bridge.

The main inland sights are both on Kalávria. The early 19th-century **monastery of Zoödóhou Pigís** ❽ (Virgin of the Life-Giving Spring), home to four monks, sits on a wooded hillside (20 minutes from town by bus), next to one of the Argo-Saronics' two natural springs (the other is on Hydra). From here, the paved road winds further inland through pines to the 6th-century BC **Sanctuary of Poseidon** (unrestricted but much roped off), near the island's summit. It's currently being re-excavated by the Swedish Archaeological School, though there isn't much to see yet beyond foundations – and a superb view.

## HYDRA

The island of Hydra (or Ydra, the ancient Ydrea, "the well watered") is today mostly a long, barren rock with a few unburnt stands of pine. But the postcard-perfect harbour bracketed by grey-stone mansions and Byzantine-tiled vernacular houses is incomparable, attracting the artistic and the fashionable since the 1950s, and many others ever since. It is one of the few islands declared an

*Fishing boats on Hydra.*

Architectural Heritage Reserve, which has helped Hydra retain its original beauty through strict building controls and the banning of most (but not all) motorised transport – the donkeys you see are working freight-carriers, not just photo opportunities.

The central port-town, also called **Hydra**  (Ydra), is a popular destination, packed out during summer and at weekends most of the year. The harbour, girded by a slender breakwater, forms a perfect crescent, its two ends flanked by 19th-century cannons. Overhead, white, tile-roofed houses climbing the slope are accented by massive grey *arhondiká*, mansions built by shipping families who made fortunes in the 18th and 19th centuries. Some of these imposing *arhondiká* are open for visits, for example the gorgeously restored **Lazaros Koundouriotis Museum** (Apr–Oct Tue–Sun 10am–2pm, also 5.30–8.30pm in summer), displaying many paintings associated with the nearby Fine Arts School, plus an extensive ethnographic section. Just back from the quay, with its multiple gift shops aimed at cruise passengers, is a wonderful marketplace and the belfry-studded, 18th-century cathedral-monastery of **Kímisi tis Theotókou**, built largely of stone removed from Póros's Poseidon temple.

The higher reaches of the town and the hills beyond, accessed by narrow alleys and steep stairways, remain surprisingly untouched, charming and full of Greek colour. The uniformity of white walls is broken again and again by a century-old doorway, a bright-blue window frame, a flight of striking scarlet steps or a dark-green garden fence. An hour's walk upwards and inland leads to **Agía Evpraxía Convent** and the **Profítis Ilías Monastery**, while **Zoúrvas Monastery** stands at the extreme eastern tip of Hydra. Island beaches, however, are less impressive. **Mandráki**, northeast of town, has the only all-sand beach. It's more interesting to follow a wide path tracing the coast southwest to the hamlets of **Kamíni** and **Vlyhós** , with its 19th-century stone bridge and pebble beach. There are good tavernas in both places, and

*View from the Póros rooftops across to the Argolid peninsula.*

## ⊘ NATIONAL HEROINE

The national heroine of the War of Independence, Laskarina Bouboulina was a wealthy Spetsiot who commanded eight of the local fleet's 22 ships after her seafaring husband was killed by corsairs. A colourful figure, she was said to have seduced her lovers at gunpoint (so plain was she reported to be), and ended up being murdered in 1825 by the father of a girl with whom her son had rashly eloped. The now defunct 50-drachma note showed her on her flagship *Agamemnon*, directing the gunnery crew; on land, she organised a successful ruse to deter an Ottoman landing by perching fezes atop asphodels on the shore, to simulate a massed army. Her mansion behind the Dápia (daily Mar–Oct 9.45am–8.15pm, guided tours only), still owned by her descendants, is now a museum dedicated to her life and works.

water-taxis to return to town. Better beaches are found in the far southwest at **Bísti**, with taxi-boat access, and **Agios Nikólaos**, with overland access only; the hardy can walk an hour and a quarter from town to **Limnióniza** bay on the southeast-facing shore.

## SPÉTSES

Spétses (or Spétsai) is the southwest-ernmost of the Argo-Saronic Gulf islands. In antiquity it was known as Pityoússa (Piney Island), and despite devastating fires in 1990 and 2001 it is still marginally the most wooded of this island group, and with the best beaches. Tourist development here is far more extensive than on Hydra but less than on Póros or Aegina; building in **Spétses Town** ⑪ is controlled, though not quite as strictly as on Hydra, and while private cars are banned within town limits, scooters and taxis are not. As with Hydra, though, no car ferries serve the island from Piraeus.

Like Hydra, Spétses was one of the main centres of activity during the Greek War of Independence, using its fleet for the Greek cause. It is distinguished for being the first in the archipelago to revolt against Ottoman rule in 1821, and the fortified **Dápia** harbour still bristles with cannons. Although Spétses's fleet declined after that war, with the emergence of Sýros, then Piraeus, as the main seaports, shipbuilding traditions continue, especially in the east end of town at **Baltíza** inlet, where a few boatyards continue to build caiques the old way. The local **museum** (Tue–Sun 8.30am–2pm) in the imposing *arhondikó* of Hatzigiannis Mexis, a late 18th-century shipowner, contains painted ship-prows of the revolutionary fleet, and an ossuary with the bones of heroine Laskarina Bouboulina (see box). Passed en route to Baltíza, the **Paleó Limáni** (Old Harbour) still radiates a gentle grace thanks to 18th-century mansions where wealthy Athenian families spend the summer. Above it, the courtyard of **Agios Nikólaos** church has a particularly outstanding pebble mosaic, a highly developed Spetsiot art.

Out of town in the opposite direction (west), in more modest **Kounoupítsa** district, stands the **Anargyríos and Korgialénios College**, a Greek version of an English public school, where John Fowles taught, memorialising institution and island in his 1966 novel *The Magus*. Like the Edwardian waterfront Hotel Poseidonion, it was founded by local benefactor Sotirios Anargyros; the school no longer operates, but is occasionally used for conferences and children's summer programmes.

A paved road circles the island, giving access to several fine beaches. Heading anticlockwise, the first tempting stop is sandy **Zogeriá**. Next is pine-backed **Agía Paraskeví** ⑫, the most scenic on Spétses, then **Agía Anargyrí**, the longest, sandiest and most developed. Solitude-seekers will prefer less crowded **Xylokériza** pebble cove to the west.

*In a port where all motor vehicles are banned, Hydra's mules and donkeys perform all haulage.*

Waiting for the water-taxi, Hydra.

Ía's windmill, Santoríni.

Agios Konstandínos, Parikiá, Páros.

# THE CYCLADES ISLANDS

Andros, Kéa, Tínos, Kýthnos, Sýros, Mýkonos, Sérifos, Sífnos, Andíparos, Páros, Náxos, Mílos, Kímolos, Folégandros, Síkinos, Íos, Amorgós, Santoríni, Anáfi.

*Firá, Santoríni.*

The 24 inhabited Cyclades evoke visions of sun-drenched hillsides and intimate little coves. The famous white Cubist houses have inspired many modern architects, Le Corbusier among them. The beaches are dazzling, the food fresh, fellow travellers companionable and seagoing connections allow you to take in more than one "small paradise" on a short holiday.

For many people the Cyclades *are* the Greek islands; other groups are mere distractions from this blue-and-white Aegean essence. The scenic high point is probably dramatic, southernmost Santoríni, created by a volcanic explosion about 3,600 years ago, and there is nothing like it. The spiritual centre remains Apollo's ancient Delos: "Cyclades" means a cycle around Delos.

There are three basic ferry routes from either Piraeus or Rafína ports: the easternmost takes in bucolic Ándros, religious Tínos and cosmopolitan Mýkonos, sometimes extending to metropolitan Sýros. The latter is also served on the "central" line from Piraeus, continuing to Páros, Náxos, Íos and Santoríni. Another route continues past Náxos to the "Back Islands" like Skhinoússa and Koufonísi before winding up at Amorgós and Anáfi. The western-most itinerary calls at Kýthnos, Sérifos, Sífnos and Mílos, usually extending to Folégandros and Síkinos. Especially in high season, links are possible between these basic routes. With scant connections to other Cyclades, Kéa attracts Athenian weekenders.

*Aegean bounty.*

The Cyclades were inhabited as early as 6500 BC. By the third millennium a flourishing culture had emerged, with beautiful crafts and lively commerce, as anyone who visits the Museum of Cycladic Greek Art in Athens will appreciate. This museum is the world's first devoted to Cycladic art, most famous for its marble female figurines. High culture continued through Roman-era decline, and while this may not be evident amid the hedonistic jet-setters of Mýkonos or youthful merrymakers of Íos, one sunset over the Vale of Klíma, the valley in Mílos where the Venus de Milo was discovered, will convince you.

As Greek Nobel laureate poet Odysseas Elytis wrote in Axion Esti: "Íos, Síkinos, Sérifos, Mílos – each word a swallow to bring you spring in the midst of summer."

# THE CYCLADES

From the hectic nightlife of Mýkonos and Íos to the rugged beauty of Mílos and Sérifos or the quiet seclusion of tiny Kímolos and Anáfi, there is something for all tastes on these islands.

Glorious beaches, Bronze Age art, oak groves, gleaming white villages and the archaeological marvels of ancient Delos are just some of the reasons visitors return to the Cyclades again and again.

## ANDROS

The reddish Andros soil makes everything glow sienna at sunset, especially on the heights of the north, settled centuries ago by Orthodox Albanians; their basic stone huts contrast with the whitewash and red tile of other, wealthier villages. Farmland is still divided by painstakingly built drystone walls, the *xirolithiés*, sporting a pattern of triangular slates incorporated into them.

The port town in the northwest, **Gávrio**, also doubles as a serviceable resort, though **Batsí ❶**, 6km (4 miles) south, is more conventionally picturesque, with more development and an attractive beach. On the east coast, **Andros Town ❷** (Hóra) has more upmarket tourism and a significant contingent of Athenians with weekend homes. The Goulandrís shipping family established the excellent **Museum of Contemporary Art**, a few steps north of the main square (July–Sept Wed–Mon 10am–2pm & (except Mon) 6–9pm, Oct–May 10am–2pm, with exceptions), featuring works by top-notch figures like Matisse and Kandinsky, as well as temporary exhibits

*In the olive grove.*

and an exquisite sculpture garden. The prize exhibit in the **Archaeological Museum** (Tue–Sun 8.30am–3pm) is the Hermes of Andros, a 1st-century BC copy of Praxiteles' statue.

Between Batsí and Andros Town extends a long, deep valley, with terraces all the way up its sides towards the island's highest mountain range, which rises to 994 metres (3,261ft). Plane, mulberry and walnut trees are nourished by a series of springs that flow from the heights, most notably at **Ménites**, with its church of **Panagía**

## ⊙ Main Attractions

Andros, Museum of Contemporary Art
Ermoúpoli townscape
Mýkonos nightlife
Ancient Delos
Andíparos cave
Folégandros Kástro
Hozoviótissa Monastery
Anáfi beaches

Map on page 170

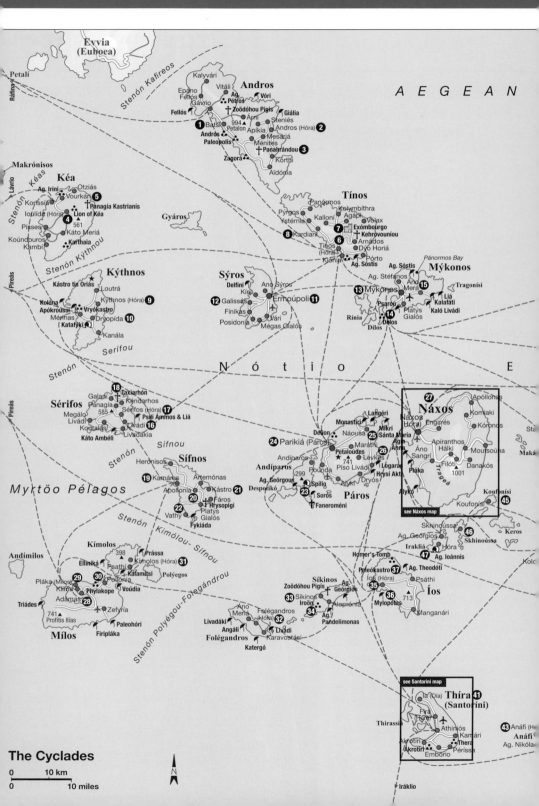

Evvia
(Euboea)

Petali

Rafína

*Stenón Kafíreos*

Kalyvári

Epáno
Fellós
Gávrio
Fellós

Vitáli
Ag.
Pétros
Zoödóhou Pigís

Batsí
Andrós
Paleopolis

**Andros**

994 ▲ Petalon

Vóri

Giália

Árni
Apíkia

Steniés
Mesariá
Ménites
Panahrándou
Kórthi
Aidónia

Vóri

Andros (Hóra) ②

③

Zagorá

A E G E A N

Makrónisos

Lávrio

**Kéa**

Ag. Iríni

Otziás
Vourkári
Panagía Kastriarís
Lion of Kéa

Korissía
Ioulída (Hóra)
Pisses

Koúndouros
Kambí

Kárthaia

561 ▲
Káto Meriá

*Stenón Kýthnou*

Gyáros

**Kýthnos**

Kástro tis Oriás
Kolóna
Apókroussi
Mérthas
Katafýki

Loutrá
Kýthnos (Hóra) ⑨
Vryókastro
Dryopída
Kanála

*Stenón Kéas*

*Stenón*

Pireás

**Tínos**

Pánormos
Pýrgos
Ystérnia
Kardianí

Kolymbíthra
Kalloní
Agápi

Exómbourgo
Kehrovouníou
Arnádos
Dýo Horiá
Pórto
Ag. Sóstis

Tínos
(Hóra)
Klónia

Vólax

⑦

⑥

⑧

Ag. Sóstis

Ag. Stéfanos

**Sýros**

Delfíni
Áno Sýros
Galissás
Fínikas
Posidonía
Vári
Mégas Gialós

Ermoúpoli ⑪

⑫

Áno
Merá

**Mýkonos**

Mýkonos ⑬
Psaroú
Plátys
Gialós

⑮
Liá
Kalafáti
Kaló Livádi

⑭

Dílos
Rínia

Tragonísi

Pánormos Bay

N ó t i o

E

Pireás

**Sérifos**

Galaní
Panagía
Megálo
Livádi
Koutalás
Káto Ambéli

Taxiárhon
Kendarhós
585 ▲
Sérifos (Hóra)
Psili Ámmos & Liá
Livádi
Livadákia

⑱

⑰

⑯

*Stenón Sérifou*

Herónisos

**Sífnos**

Kamáres
Apollonía
Vathy

Artemónas
Kástro
Hrysopigí
Platys
Gialós
Fykiáda

⑲

⑳

㉒

㉑

Myrtöo Pélagos

*Stenón Kimólou-Sífnou*

**Kímolos**

Ellinká
Psáthi
Kafamútsi
Prássa
Kímolos (Hóra)
Voúdia
Políegos

398 ▲

㉛

Andímilos

Pláka (Milos)
Klíma
Adámas
Triádes

Zefyría

Profítis Ilías
741 ▲

Firipláka

**Mílos**

Phylakope

Paleohóri

㉙

㉚

㉘

Delion
Monastíri
Náousa

**Paros**

Parikiá (Páros)
Petaloúdes
Pounda
Alykí
Spília
Sorós
Faneroméni

Langéri
Mikrí
Sánta María
Ambelás
Maráthi
Léfkes
Logarás
Hrysí Aktí
Dryós

Lángeri

㉔

㉕

㉖

㉓

**Andíparos**

Andíparos
Despotikó

299 ▲
741 ▲
Piso Livádi

Ag. Geórgous

**Náxos**

Náxos
(Hóra)
Engarés
Galíni
Sangrí
Áno
Filóti
Tragéa
1001 ▲

Apóllonas
Komiakí
Kóronos
Apíranthos
Háliki
Moutsoúna
Danakós

Alykó

see Náxos map

㉗

Koufonísi
Koufonísi

㊺

Keros

Makáda

Stá

Ag. Geórgios
Iráklia
Homer's Tomb

Skhinoússa
Hóra
Skhinoússa

㊻

Ag. Ioánnis

㊼

**Íos**

Paleókastro
Íos (Hóra)
Mylopótas
Manganári

Ag. Theodóti
Psáthi
713 ▲

㊲

㉟

㊱

**Síkinos**

Zoödóhou Pigís
Síkinos
(Hóra)
Iroón
Aleprónia

Ag.
Geórgios

㉝

㉞

**Folégandros**

Áno
Meriá
Livadáki
Angáli
Karavostási
Katergó

Folégandros
(Hóra)
Livádi
Ag.
Pandelímonas

㉜

see Santorini map

**Thíra**
(Santoríni)

Ia (Oía)
Fyrá
(Hóra)
Athiniós
Akrotíri
Akrotíri

Kamári
Théra
Emborió
Périssa

Thirassía

㊶

Anáfi (He
**Anáfi**
Ag. Nikóla

㊸

**The Cyclades**

| 0 | 10 km |
|---|---|
| 0 | 10 miles |

N

Irákli

**Koúmoulos**. Its multi-spouted spring is considered sacred; possibly there was once a big temple to Dionysos sited here. The centre of Andros is good walking country, with some of the 12 waymarked local trails.

The Convent of **Zoödóhou Pigís** (Life-Giving Spring) also claims a sacred site by its eponymous spring. Situated in the hills northeast of Batsí, it is today inhabited part-time by one elderly nun; the most vital and populated (by monks) monastery on the island is that of **Agía Marína**, near Apíkia north of Hóra. Three km (2 miles) east of Gávrio, the purpose of the remarkable, round Hellenistic tower of **Agios Pétros** remains a mystery.

South of the Paleópolis–Hóra road is the most spectacular of Andros's fortified Byzantine monasteries, unreliably open cliffside **Panahrándou** ❸ – more than 1,000 years old, it was founded in 961. The round trip on foot lasts about three hours from **Mesariá**, a green valley town with the Byzantine Taxiárhis (Archangel) church.

**Paleopolis**, the ancient capital, doesn't give much hint of its past, but the Hermes statue in the archaeological museum was discovered here. A bit further south, **Zagorá** promontory is the site of a walled town that flourished in the 8th century BC, Homer's time.

Andros has many fine beaches; the easiest to get to are **Nimborió** north of Hóra, the string of beaches either side of Batsí and **Giália** (near Steniés, north of Andros Town). **Kórthi** in the far southeast is popular with windsurfers.

## KÉA

During the 19th century there were a million oaks on Kéa, and many still survive. Since ancient times, the island has also been noted for its almonds, though olive trees are curiously lacking. Traces of four ancient cities – Koressia, Ioulis, Karthaia and Poiessa – testify to the island's one-time importance. Kéa (popularly Tziá,

*Intricately designed stone dovecotes are a feature of Tínos, where the Venetians were the first to embark on the systematic breeding of pigeons.*

*Easter Sunday mass on Andros.*

in ancient times Keos) has long been popular with Athenians. Regular Kéa-bound boats leave from Lávrio, some 50km (30 miles) from Athens, and land at **Korisía**; perhaps once a week there is a continuation to other Cyclades.

Kéa's main town, **Ioulída ❹** (Hóra), covers a rounded ridge overlooking the island's northern reach; home to most islanders, it was a spot chosen precisely because it was inaccessible for pirates. Unlike most Cycladic villages, its houses have pitched, tiled roofs. The **Archaeological Museum** (Tue–Sun 8.30am–3pm) contains abundant finds from the four towns of ancient Keos; the most interesting antiquity is the 6th-century BC **Lion of Kéa**, a 15-minute walk northeast of Hóra. Carved from granite, almost 6 metres (19ft) long, it represents a real lion brought in to eat malicious Nereids.

The scalloped coast has surprisingly few accessible beaches; **Písses**, at the mouth of a fertile valley, **Koúndouros** with Athenians' villas, and **Kambí** with a good taverna, are among the exceptions. Close to Korissía, the bayside village of **Vourkári ❺** is popular among

yachties, with a notable concentration of fish tavernas. Further around the same bay stands a ruined Minoan palace at **Agía Iríni**. Northeast of Agía Iríni, a paved road leads to **Otziás**, a sandy but exposed bay, and continues to **Panagía Kastrianí** monastery (open June–Sept), focus of a 14–15 August pilgrimage. Southeast of here, a dirt road leads to excellent **Spathí** beach.

Walkers are well served by a network of numbered trails, intelligently rehabilitated and marked with EU funds. The best are from Ioulída to Otziás, and from Ioulída to ancient Karthaia, where there are two ruined temples to see.

## TÍNOS

Tínos receives many thousands of visitors annually – but they are mostly Greek Orthodox pilgrims bound for the church of **Panagía Evangelístria** (Annunciation). In 1822, the nun Pelagia dreamt of an icon of the Virgin; it was duly unearthed and the church was built to house it. The icon's healing powers have made **Tínos Town ❻** (Hóra) the Lourdes of Greece.

Women fall to their knees upon arrival, and crawl painfully to the church (the marble steps are carpeted). Healing miracles are said to occur. On the Virgin's feast days – 25 March (Annunciation) and 15 August (Dormition) – thousands of Greeks pour off the boats for the procession of the little icon, which is carried downhill in an ornate baldachin over the kneeling supplicants. The church complex is full of marble, precious votive offerings (especially silver boats), and contains several museums. Like nearby Sýros, the island is, ironically, actually half Catholic in population.

The site of the Temple of Poseidon and Amphitrite at **Kiónia** beach, one of the few ancient sites, is neglected, though the town's **Archaeological Museum** is worth a look (Tue–Sun 8.30am–3pm). Among the exhibits are a Roman-era marble sundial from Kiónia that shows the time, the equinoxes and solstices, plus a large number of artefacts from excavations at Exómbourgo.

Tínos is renowned for marble work – especially fanlights and bas-relief plaques – and there is still a marble-sculpture school and many active workshops in the village of **Pýrgos**. Tínos's other speciality is Greece's most elaborate dovecotes. There are hundreds of them inland, a tradition started by the Venetians. Their pattern of triangular windows is mimicked over doorways, on fences and in window shapes. It is a versatile symbol, which seems to represent anything from the shape of a sail to the Holy Trinity.

For an insight into Catholicism on Tínos, visit the peak of **Exómbourgo** ❼, 643 metres (2,110ft) high, with a ruined Venetian fortress, and the surrounding villages, which are mostly Catholic. Xinára at its base is the seat of the local Catholic bishop, and there are Catholic monasteries and convents in nearby villages. Tínos was the last island to fall to the Turks, in 1715. **Vólax** (Vólakas) village, famous for its basket-weavers, is surrounded by weird, mushroom-shaped, wind-sculpted rocks, which attract boulderers; the climate up here is cool year-round, and potatoes flourish.

**Kardianí** ❽, on the Pýrgos-bound road, is exceptional among Orthodox Tiniot villages, a spectacularly set oasis settlement with views across to Sýros. From Ystérnia, a bit beyond, a mostly surviving marble-paved *kalderími* or cobbled path, among the finest of several on the island, leads down to Órmos Ysterníon. Southeast of Exómbourgo, the well-watered, arcaded villages of **Arnádos** and **Dýo Horiá** are equally handsome, and have attracted second-home buyers. Just above looms the Byzantine **Convent of Kehrovouníou**, where Pelagía had her vision of the icon.

**Kolymbíthra** in the north is Tínos's best beach, though **Agios Fokás, Agios Sóstis** and **Pórto** on the south coast, closer to the Hóra, are fine, if more commercialised.

## KÝTHNOS

Unfashionable with foreigners, and among the quietest of the Cyclades,

*Journey's end for pilgrims to Tínos – Panagía Evangelístria church.*

*Local colour.*

*Dryopída, the blue domes of its church stark among the red roofs.*

Kýthnos appeals mostly to Athenian weekenders of more modest means. Native Kythniots are mainly dairy and livestock farmers, belying the apparent infertility of the dun-coloured, undulating countryside. Elderly and/or unwell visitors frequent the thermal spa at **Loutrá** (the island's medieval name was Thermiá), on the northeast coast, whose 19th-century spa building was designed by Ernst Ziller – though the resort is now making conscious attempts to appeal to a broader spectrum of visitors. About 90 minutes' walk northwest is medieval Kástro tis Oriás, once home to thousands but abandoned by the 1700s.

**Mérihas** port on the west coast has most of the island's accommodation. In summer, taxi-boats run from Mérihas to **Episkopí**, **Apókroussi** and **Kolóna** beaches, the last a stunning sand-spit tethering **Agios Loukás** islet to the rest of Kýthnos. Near Apókroussi, **Vryókastro** is an ancient 10th-century BC town where a huge hoard of artefacts was uncovered in 2002.

Landlocked **Kýthnos** ❾ (Hóra), 6km (4 miles) northeast of Mérihas, is exquisite. Whereas most Cycladic towns crawl spider-like over local topography, Hóra adheres mostly to a rectangular plan. Wood-beamed arches span narrow streets to join two sides of one house; in the passages underneath, pavements are playfully decorated in whitewash with fish, stylised ships, or flowers. There is a small main square, around which are the better island tavernas (though not much lodging). Fields at the back of town rise gently from the ravine to the south, dotted with farmhouses and tile-roofed chapels.

A stream bed splits into two at **Dryopída** ❿, successor to Kástro as medieval capital; the chambered **Katafýki** cave here is linked in legend with the Nereids. The town itself presents, like Ioulída on Kéa, an appealing red-roofed spectacle, especially seen from above.

## SÝROS

When Sýros was overtaken as Greece's premier port by Piraeus in the late 1800s, it was left, as one writer put it, "a grand but old-fashioned lady who lives on her memories of the good old days and on her half-forgotten glories". This is a shame, for with its excellent inter-island ferry links and low-key but useful facilities, Sýros – still capital of the Cyclades – makes a pleasant and rewarding place to stay. Not so the exceedingly barren islet of Gyáros just northwest, used for the exceptionally cruel exile of political dissidents by the Romans, and again by modern Greece between 1946 and 1974.

Just one large shipyard barely survives at the port-capital, **Ermoúpoli** ⓫, which doesn't help its resort image, but hasn't prevented the elegant neoclassical town from being designated a Unesco Heritage Site. The congested quay with its scent of roasting octopus doesn't give much away, but head inland and you'll see why the honour was bestowed.

The marble-paved main square, **Platía Miaoúli**, is lined with imposing

buildings, some housing lively bars and cafés, and hosts a buzzing evening *vólta*. The Apollon Theatre, on nearby Platía Vardáka, is modelled after La Scala in Milan; its 1980s renovation is still a point of pride. Beyond the Apollon, the imposing dome and twin belfries of **Agios Nikólaos** mark the **Vapória** quarter, where the wealthiest 19th-century shipowners and merchants built sumptuous mansions with painted ceilings and the like.

Ermoúpoli is dominated by two hills, each capped by a church. On the lower, **Vrontádo**, stands the Greek Orthodox **Church of the Resurrection** (Anástasis). On the higher is **Ano Sýros**, the medieval Catholic quarter – like Tínos, Sýros is approximately half Catholic – dominated by **Agios Geórgios** cathedral and the 16th-century Capuchin monastery (adjacent is a British World War I cemetery). One of Greece's greatest *rebétika* musicians, Markos Vamvakaris, was born an Ano Sýros Catholic, and the **Vamvakaris Museum** (June-Sept daily 11am–2pm and 7–10pm) duly honours him. The worthwhile **Industrial Museum**, on the road to Kíni (Mon, Tue, Thu, Fri 9am–5pm, Sun 9am–2pm), commemorates the island's now vanished shipping and mining enterprises.

The south of Sýros is gentler and greener than the rugged, empty north and has good beaches, especially near **Galissás** ⑫, a sizeable resort. Further up the west coast, **Kíni** and lonelier **Delfíni** bay offer more good bathing. South of Galissás, **Fínikas** and **Posidonía** – the latter immortalised by Vamvakaris, along with other Syrian locales, by its alternative name, Dellagrázia, in his overplayed standard *"Frangosyriani"* – are more mainstream resorts. Pythagoras' teacher, Pherekydes, the inventor of the sundial, hailed from here, and several caves bear his name. The southerly loop road continues east through **Mégas Gialós** and **Ahládi** towards **Vári**, the most protected of the local coves.

## MÝKONOS

Mýkonos represents an emphatic victory of style (and energetic self-promotion) over intrinsic substance. This rocky, treeless, gale-force windy, dry island, with admittedly excellent, granite-sand beaches and a Cycladic-cliché port town of dazzling beauty, receives a million visitors in a good year. They are drawn by a deserved reputation for big-city-standard shopping, sexy nightlife for all orientations and some of the most luxurious accommodation in the islands – all of which makes Mýkonos the most expensive of the Cyclades, rivalled only by Santoríni.

**Mýkonos Town** ⑬, like the island overall, is one of the world's premier **gay** (male) **resorts**, with legendary clubs and quieter piano bars. Cruise ships are also very much part of the picture, especially during spring and autumn, with passengers packing out the town for some retail therapy, then horn-blasted back aboard, clutching purchased designer clothing and jewellery.

It is possible to eschew all this and still enjoy Mýkonos. The **Folklore**

*Galissás beach resort, Sýros.*

*Elegant facade on Platía Miaoúli, with the Anástasi church overhead.*

*One of Mýkonos Town's resident pelicans.*

**Museum** (Apr–Oct Mon–Fri 5.30–8pm; free) and the **Archaeological Museum** (Tue–Sun 9am–4pm), at different ends of the quay, are full of interesting objects, the latter mostly Geometric and Archaic pottery, intricately painted with scenes from the Iliad and assorted beasts. And the town is among the most photogenic and solicitously preserved in the Cyclades, graced by wooden balconies loaded with flowers, red-domed chapels and irregular whitewashed surfaces. The odd-shaped **Panagía Paraportianí** (Our Lady of the Postern Gate), four chapels lumped into one structure, is probably Greece's most photographed church – and a noted gay cruising area after dark.

The town mascot has long been a **pelican** called Petros. The original one settled on the island in 1955 after being blown off course by a storm. After various adventures, including an alleged kidnapping by a fisherman from Tínos, the original Petros was killed by a car in 1985. His replacement, who still inhabits the quayside, scattering his pink feathers, was donated in 1986 by a German zoo, although there are now actually three pelicans in residence.

Caiques depart from Mýkonos town for **ancient Delos** ⓮ (modern Dílos), the sacred island that is the hub of the Cyclades (see page 178). Or you could strike inland to **Ano Merá** ⓯ 7km (4 miles) east, the only real village on the island, which is less spoilt by tourism. Its main attraction is the 17th–18th-century **Tourlianí Monastery** (summer daily 10am–2pm & 5.30–8pm; earlier closure winter), with an atmospheric central church and intricate relief carving on the marble fountain outside. Mýkonos is famous, indeed notorious, for its all-night bars and all-day sandy south-coast beaches. For bars, enquire when you arrive; the scene changes constantly. For beaches, **Paradise** is half straight nude, **Super Paradise** partly gay nude, and both are beautiful; **Kaló Livádi**, **Kalafáti** and **Liá**, all reached via Ano Merá, are respectively very long, popular with windsurfers, and a relatively quiet retreat. **Platýs Gialós** and **Psaroú** in the west are more family-oriented, while nearby **Paránga** is more mainstream. With the exception of **Pánormos** and **Agios Sóstis** beaches on **Pánormos Bay**, the north coast is too exposed and windy for bathing.

## SÉRIFOS

Only at the last minute do approaching ferries round the long peninsula concealing the bay of **Livádi** ⓰, the harbour and main resort of Sérifos, along with its annexe **Livadákia** just south. Livádi makes a pleasant base, with most of Sérifos's tourist facilities and to either side good beaches such as **Karávi**, **Liá**, **Agios Sóstis** and **Psilí Ammos**, accessible by paved roads and/or paths.

**Sérifos Town** ⓱ (Hóra) spills precipitously like scattered dice from the mountain above, contrasting with higher, gaunter ridges behind. Buses ascend to Hóra regularly, but the long flights of old stone steps (a

40-minute climb) make a more satisfying approach.

Hóra has two parts: somewhat neglected Káto (Lower) and Ano (Upper). The upper, with arcaded passageways and an incongruous neoclassical town hall, is the more interesting; its ridge leads towards the east to an archaeologically protected *kástro*. The view of Livádi Bay and other islands is spectacular – and in the old days, eminently functional, as no pirate ship could approach without being seen long in advance.

A paved road system circles the heart of the island, but it's better to walk north on the remains of a wide *kalderími* (cobbled path), beginning from Ano Hóra's main square, designated "No.1" of half a dozen local paths. Numerous small bays with tiny, empty beaches lie below. Habitation is sparse, and there are just a few small farms along the way. After a good 90-minute walk, the village of **Kéndarhos** (Kállitsos) appears at the far side of a steep valley. Though there are no tavernas, a fresh-water fountain – despite appearances, Sérifos has abundant ground water – will refresh you. From here you must take the paved road west to the fortified medieval, uninhabited **Taxiarhón Monastery** ⑱ a half-hour distant. If the parish priest is inside he may show you the ornate icon-screen, vivid frescoes and such rare treasures as Egyptian and Russian lamps and an ivory-inlaid bishop's throne.

From the nearest village, **Galaní**, the numbered path system resumes, taking you either down to **Sykaminiá Bay** or straight over to **Panagía** village. Scattered, tiny vineyards in this region produce the tawny-pink, sherry-like wine Sérifos is famous for – ask for it at local tavernas. Panagía's original 10th-century church is infamous for its 16 August feast day *(Xylopanagía)*, when boys and girls used to rush in pairs to be the first to dance around the adjacent olive tree: the first couple to complete the dance would be allowed to marry during the year. Jealousy often prompted pitched battles, so nowadays the parish priest always goes first.

*Most of the Cyclades islands that grew their own grain have windmills, but the majority have fallen into disuse.*

## ⊘ UNDERGROUND TOURISM

The Cave or Spílio (summer daily 10am–6pm, spring/autumn 10am–4pm, closed Nov–March), the principal sight on Andíparos, was discovered during the 7th century BC, perhaps by the poet Arkhilokhos of Paros (the first recorded visitor), and has been attracting them ever since. Despite the depredations of souvenir-hunters, who have broken and removed stalactites and stalagmites for centuries, it is still a fantastically spooky chamber, even if the impact is reduced somewhat by concrete steps down and a constant bilingual narration soundtrack.

Almost as impressive as the formations are the inscriptions left by past visitors, including King Otto of Greece and Lord Byron. The oldest piece of graffiti has sadly been lost – a note from several individuals stating that they were hiding in the cave from Alexander the Great, who suspected them of plotting his assassination. Another inscription (in Latin) records the Christmas Mass celebrated here by the French Marquis de Nointel in 1673, for an audience of 500.

In summer, buses and boats run to the cave from Andíparos Town, or else it's a two-hour walk. Then you descend more than 70 metres (230ft) from the cave entrance to the vaulted main chamber. The entire cave is actually twice as deep as the part to which you are allowed access, but the rest has been closed for safety reasons.

# ANCIENT DELOS

## The archaeological wonders of Delos, first excavated in the late 19th century, make the boat trip well worthwhile.

Tiny Delos island (Dílos in modern Greek) is an archaeological mecca. Extensive Greco-Roman ruins covering much of Delos's 4 sq km (1.5 sq miles) make the site as extensive as Delphi or Olympia.

The mid-morning caique – a type of traditional boat – voyage southwest from Mýkonos takes only 25 minutes in calm seas, but twice as long in rough conditions, as the boat heaves and shudders. Dress appropriately for the likely breezes, and have a dry-biscuit breakfast – a classic seasickness preventative.

It was on ancient Delos that the nymph Leto, pregnant by Zeus and pursued jealously by Hera, supposedly gave birth to the divine twins Apollo and Artemis – although interestingly, an equally compelling legend (and elaborate sanctuary) places the momentous event in Lycia on the Asia Minor coast. Delos, until then just a floating rock, was honoured when four diamond pillars stretched up and anchored it in the heart of the Cyclades.

On arrival at Delos, orientate yourself with the aid of the helpful folding map available at the ticket

*One of the guardians of the Lion Terrace.*

booth, to avoid getting lost among the ruins (daily 9am–8pm summer, until 5pm winter). Most of these occupy the two arms of a right angle. On your right (south) are the theatre and mainly domestic buildings. To the left is the sanctuary to which pilgrims from all over the Mediterranean came with votive offerings and sacrificial animals.

For nearly 1,000 years, this sanctuary was the political and religious centre of the Aegean and host to the Delian Festival every four years. This, until the 4th century BC, was Greece's greatest festival. The Romans turned it into a grand trade fair and made Delos a free port. It also became Greece's main slave market, where as many as 10,000 slaves were sold on one day.

By the start of the Christian era, the power and glory of Delos was waning, with frequent raids for plunder; soon afterwards the island, once home to 25,000 people, lay deserted. During the next two millennia the stones were silent; then, with the arrival of French archaeologists in 1872, they began to speak.

Follow the pilgrim route to a ruined gateway leading into the Sanctuary of Apollo. Here are three temples dedicated to Apollo – there is also a temple of Artemis – and parts of a colossal marble statue of Apollo which was destroyed when a massive bronze votive palm tree fell on it during a storm. Close by is the Sanctuary of Dionysos with several phalli (now mutilated) on pedestals and Dionysiac friezes.

Continue to the stunning Lion Terrace, where scrawny, Archaic lions squat as if ready to pounce. They are replicas; five of the originals, carved from Naxian marble, stand in the inadequate, soon-to-be-replaced site museum, but one was taken to Venice in 1716, where it stands in front of the Arsenale. Below this is the Sacred Lake and the palm tree that marks the spot of the divine twins' birth.

Most visitors delight in that part of Delos which was occupied by artisans rather than gods. Their houses, close to the port, are a regular warren of narrow lanes lined by drains dating right back to 2,000 years ago, with niches for oil lamps which illuminated the streets. The main road leads to the theatre, which seated 5,500. It is unimpressive, but there are superb views from the uppermost of its 43 rows. Close to the theatre are grander houses with colonnaded courtyards and exquisite floor mosaics.

From Panagía, scenic – if rough – trails lead back to Hóra; those with vehicles can continue to southwestern Sérifos for isolated beaches. **Megálo Livádi** is the most developed, with two tavernas; once an iron- and copper-mining centre until the deposits became uneconomical in the 1960s, it has a monument to four workers killed during a 1916 strike. Other, south-facing beaches on the way back to Livádi – along a mostly paved road – include **Koutalás**, **Gánema** and **Káto Ambéli**.

## SÍFNOS

Noticeably greener than Sérifos or Kýthnos, and speckled with an improbable number (even by Cycladic standards) of churches and monasteries, Sífnos has long been a favourite of wealthier Athenians and French visitors, and at peak season can be nearly as crowded as Mýkonos, Páros or Santoríni. The harbour, **Kamáres** ⑲, at the base of two opposing dinosaur-back ridges, is relatively picturesque, and with ample facilities should you want to stay there.

The main road climbs a steep, deep valley from Kamáres 5.5km (3.5 miles) to **Apollonía** ⑳ the capital, the slopes on the right culminating in the peak of Profítis Ilías with its atmospheric monastery, the most worthy hiking target of several paths. Pick of Apollonía's many churches is **Agios Athanásios**, with frescoes and a carved wood icon screen. There are fine examples of local weaving in Apollonía's **Folklore Museum** (Apr–Oct daily 9.30am–2pm and 6–10pm). The other island crafts are jewellery, a legacy of ancient times when Sífnos was rich in gold and silver, and **pottery**, with an equally long tradition. In Kamáres, Fáros, Platýs Gialós and isolated Herónisos, potters still set out long racks of earthenware to dry in the sun prior to glazing.

Contiguous with Apollonía, **Artemónas** (the towns take their names from Apollo and Artemis, both of whom had temples in the vicinity) is Sífnos's wealthiest settlement, with mansions and more old churches, such as multi-domed **Kóhi** (Nook), in whose courtyard cultural events are sometimes held in summer. Down the block a plaque marks the house where mournful poet Ioannis Gryparis (1871–1942) was born.

Perched 100 metres (328ft) above the sea and 3km (2 miles) east of Apollonía is **Kástro** ㉑, the former capital originally established atop the ancient acropolis by a renegade Catalan Knight of St John in 1307. It soon passed by marriage of his heirs to the Venetians, who elaborated the elongated ground plan along the ridge top. A former Catholic church in the town centre shelters the **Archaeological Museum** (Tue, Fri, Sun 8am–3pm, Sat 2–9pm), mostly containing Hellenistic and Roman finds.

Sífnos's south-shore settlements make tranquil seaside bases, although beaches – as at **Fáros** and **Apókofto** – are not always the best the island has to offer. Just beyond the latter looms **Hrysopigí** (Golden Well) **Monastery**, built in 1653 on an islet reached by a footbridge. It is no longer in monastic

*Rich pickings for this butterfly on Sýros – not to be confused with the Jersey tiger moths of Páros.*

*Sérifos Town.*

*Inquisitive goat, Páros.*

*Hrysopigí Monastery, Sífnos.*

use, but its main festival, 40 days after Easter, is well attended.

Still further southwest, **Platýs Gialós** has the longest – if windiest – beach on the island, and ample (perhaps too ample) development. Just above it is the glorious rural monastery of **Panagía tou Vounoú**, while the old trail west short-cuts the paved road to the almost landlocked bay of **Vathý** ㉒, which can also be reached by a more adventurous and scenic marked path from **Katavatí** just south of Apollonía. Caiques make the trip from Kamáres to the little hamlet here in summer, and there are tavernas and modest rooms on the excellent beach that sit somewhat at odds with a luxury hotel. The visually arresting hallmark of Vathý is little **Taxiárhis** (Archangel) **Monastery**, poised with its feet in the sand as though ready to set sail. Misanthropes may take a track south to the tip of the island and a glorious beach, **Fykiáda**.

## ANDÍPAROS

Until the end of the last glacial period, 10,000 years ago, this small, pretty island was joined to Páros. A narrow channel now separates the two, plied by enthusiastic kite-boarders – and frequent car ferries from Poúnda on Páros bringing visitors to its famous cave, **Spílio** ㉓ (Cavern; see box page 177). Most day-trippers bypass characterful **Andíparos Town**, so it is relatively easy to find rooms here outside the month of August. Andíparos first appeared on people's radar by serving as location for the 1960 film *Mantalena*, which boosted Greek starlet Aliki Vougiouklaki's career – and subsequently the little island became an obligatory stop for alternative types transiting between Ibiza and India. Beyond a husk of modern hotels and Athenian second homes is the 1440s-vintage, barely inhabited *kástro*, one of the finest such in the Cyclades, of a type seen elsewhere only at Síkinos and Kímolos: a square compound with just a single arched entrance and a central cistern/chapel.

Andíparos measures only 11km by 5km (7 miles by 3 miles), so distances are not daunting, especially if you bring a scooter over from Páros (or hire one here). Approaching ferries pass two islets; on one, **Saliangós**, British excavators in 1964 revealed a Neolithic (pre-4000 BC) settlement, including a fat female figurine now in the Parikiá museum. The other islet belongs to the Goulandris family, they of the museums in Andros and Athens.

Beaches are surprisingly numerous, the better ones on the east and south coasts. **Glýfa** is the closest to the town, and tamarisk-shaded **Panagiá**, 2km (1.2 miles) away, is decent enough, but with your own transport (or the seasonal bus) **Sorós**, 9km/5.5miles away on the southeast coast, is Andíparos' best beach, with two tavernas just inland. **Agios Geórgios** in the far south faces the archaeologically important islet of Despotikó.

## PÁROS

**Parikiá** ㉔ (also called Páros) is the attractive capital of this heavily visited

island. In August, make sure you book ahead, as the cheaper rooms go fast – although in the evening they are empty as their tenants hit the town. Parikiá is as pretty as Mýkonos Town, but less labyrinthine; it has one of the better town beaches in the Cyclades just northeast at Livádia, where tiny children confidently learn to sail at the Nautical Club. The beautiful 6th-century **Ekatondapylianí Church** (Our Lady of a Hundred Doors; open 7am–9pm) retains its Byzantine form, including a side chapel adapted from a 4th-century BC building. By the church is a **Byzantine Museum** (same hours) full of icons, while the prize exhibit at the nearby **Archaeological Museum** (Tue–Sun 8am–3pm) is a chunk of the Parian Chronicle, embossed on a marble slab. The ancient **cemetery** abuts the seafront, while the 13th-century Venetian *kástro* southwest along the water incorporates a Classical watchtower and is otherwise largely built of masonry recycled from a 6th-century BC temple that stood here.

At beautiful **Náousa** ㉕ on the north coast, the little harbour's colourful fishing boats nudge right up against the quayside houses, and the old quarter forms a quasi-kástro. Though the village has become notably fashionable, with upmarket boutiques, accommodation and restaurants, the port still retains its traditional charm. There are several fine **beaches** around the larger bay, accessible on foot or by taxi-boat. To the east, protected **Mikrí Sánta María** has soft sand and juniper-stabilised dunes. Otherwise, head northwest to the lighthouse peninsula and monastery of **Ágios Ioánnis Détis**, giving its name to the natural reserve just behind, car-free and criss-crossed with marked hiking trails towards the lighthouse. Best of the southeast-coast beaches are **Logarás** and **Hrysí Aktí**, both with plenty of facilities and the latter a windsurfers' mecca, with three schools.

Unspoilt **Lévkes** ㉖, the Ottoman-era capital, is the largest inland village, with several 17th-century churches, and a lovely lower *platía* flanked by cafés. From Lévkes, walkers can follow a surviving portion of the old marble-paved *kalderími* that used to cross the

*Gloriously clear waters on Sífnos.*

An ice-cold frappé hits
the spot.

The snug little harbour
of Náousa.

entire island. Go east to Pródromos
and Mármara, with views en route to
**Náxos** looming across the straits
(see page 192), or north to Kóstos, then
west to **Maráthi**, whose ancient tunnel
quarries – still active until 1844, now
fenced off – supplied the world with
some of the finest marble.

Southeast of Parikiá lies the much-
visited **Valley of the Butterflies** (Petaloúdes), a walled garden with huge
trees. The black-and-yellow butterflies – actually Jersey tiger moths –
are colourful and countless in summer
(June–Sept daily 9am–8pm). En route,
stop in at **Hristoú stou Dássous**, a picturesque 18th-century convent whose
church, unusually, is off-limits to men
(in Greece it's usually the other way
around). South of Petaloúdes lies the
workaday fishing port (with beaches
and tavernas) of **Alykí**.

## MÍLOS

Volcanic Mílos is a geologist's paradise. Snaking streams of ancient lava
formed much of the island's coastline. The lava dripped into caves and
solidified as it hit the sea, thrusting
up weird rock formations that take on
animal shapes, shadowed purple in
the rays of the setting sun. Offshore
clusters like the Glaronísia are popular boat excursions. On the map, Mílos
resembles a bat in flight; almost all
the island's population of just under
5,000 inhabits the northeastern wing;
the southwestern wing is ruggedly
beautiful.

Modern Miliots have graciously
adapted to the growing stream of
tourism the island receives, concentrated in **Adámas** (Adámanda), the
main port, and Pollónia, a smaller
harbour in the northeast. The closest of several open-air hot springs
is at Kánava beach, 3km (2 miles)
east; the water wells up at 50°C
(120°F) in the cooler shallows, mix-
ing to a comfortable temperature.
Inside **Agía Triáda** church in Adámas,
Cretan-style icons dominate. Links
have always been strong between
Mílos and the "Great Island": Cretan refugees founded Adámas in
1853 (though ancient tombs have

### ⊘ MINERALS AND MINING

Mílos is, in reality, a far older, cooled-
down version of Santoríni – at some
point in the distant past a volcano collapsed, leaving a caldera, which became
today's huge central bay. Its volcanic
mineral wealth has always been extensively mined: in prehistory for obsidian,
nowadays for bentonite, perlite, pozzolana, kaolin and china clay. Gaping
quarries disfigure the landscape, especially in the east, and the local mining
companies still provide employment for
a quarter of the islanders. Kímolos has
quarries from which Fuller's earth and,
to a lesser extent, bentonite, are
extracted. The latter has various uses (it
even turns up as an ingredient in Nivea
cream). Ironically, the chalk (*kimoliá* in
Greek) that gave the island its name is
no longer extracted locally.

been found on the town site), and the island was colonised by Minoans who came to trade obsidian.

Pláka ㉙ (Mílos), the island's attractive capital, 4km (2.5 miles) northwest, has both an **Archaeological Museum** (Tue–Sun 9am–3pm), whose star is the Minoan "Lady of Phylakope" idol, and a **Folklore Museum** (Tue–Sun 10am–2pm). The latter, set in an old house, offers diverse exhibits including archival photographs, homeware and samples of local weaving. A climb up the old *kástro*, with its vast rain-collection system and churches of **Panagía Thalássitra** and Kímisis tis Panagías, provides splendid views of the well-protected bay and, weather permitting, over many other islands. The escutcheon on Panagía Thalássitra is of the Crispi family, who wrested Mílos from another Venetian clan, the Sanudi, in 1363.

About 1km (0.5 mile) southwest of Pláka lies the verdant **Vale of Klíma**, where the ancient Meliots – their "dialogue" with the Athenians immortalised by Thucydides prior to their annihilation in 416 BC – built their city. Excavations undertaken by the British School in Athens in the late 1800s uncovered a Dionysian altar, remains of an ancient gymnasium with a mosaic, and a well-preserved Roman-era theatre. Nearby, a marble plaque marks the spot where a farmer unearthed the Aphrodite of Mílos (Venus de Milo) in 1820. In a feat of robbery approaching that of the appropriation of the Parthenon friezes (though here the French were the villains rather than the British) she was whisked off to Paris, never to return. The statue was probably carved in the 1st century BC of Parian marble, since Mílos lacks suitable stone.

Below ancient Melos lurk the **Christian catacombs** (Tue–Sat 8.30am–6.30pm, Sun 8.30am–3pm). Carved into the hillside, they are the earliest evidence of Christian worship in Greece. Hundreds of tombs arranged along three subterranean corridors held as many as 5,000 bodies, all now vanished. Though cheerily lit by tiny electric lanterns, frescoes and religious

*The road to Maráthi's ancient tunnel quarries.*

# THE CYCLADIC BRONZE AGE

## Numerous artefacts illuminate the Bronze Age culture of the Cycladic islands, shedding light on the way their ancient people lived and died.

Bronze Age Cycladic peoples left behind many beautiful artefacts, most famously their stylised marble sculptures, evidence of an organised and flourishing culture. Settlements and cemeteries excavated on a number of Cycladic islands are generally considered to be the first complex, organised, settled communities in Europe.

The Early Cycladic Bronze Age is thought to have begun around 3200 BC, and to have lasted until about 2500 BC. The middle Bronze Age in the Cyclades (2500–2000 BC) falls into two general periods, referred to by scholars and archaeologists as Middle and Late Cycladic respectively. These periods increasingly display the influence of the Minoan culture of Crete and the move towards urban settlement. In general, the term "Cycladic culture" refers to the Early Cycladic era, and it is during this period that the individuality of the culture of the Cycladic islands is most evident.

*Cycladic figurine.*

Early Cycladic settlements were small, numbering around 50 people, comprising densely packed stone-built housing, usually of only one storey. Accompanying the settlements, outside the residential area, are cemeteries of small cist graves (rectangular graves lined with stone) and chamber-tombs, clustered in family groups; the dead were inhumed in a contracted (foetal) position, along with everyday objects. Much of the evidence we have of how Early Cycladic society functioned comes from these cemeteries.

The often stark differences in grave goods between tombs provide evidence of a stratified society. While some graves contain an extremely rich variety of artefacts, including gold and silver jewellery, others have very little, often only a single marble figure. How these differences between rich and poor were manifest in practice is a matter of conjecture, but many artefacts display a high degree of skill in their manufacture, indicating the presence of skilled craft workers.

Besides hunting, fishing, animal husbandry and agriculture, much trade was carried out from the Cycladic islands, pointing to the existence of a merchant class, presumably among the wealthier members of society. The Cycladic peoples were skilled sailors and had contact with the Greek mainland, Crete, Anatolia and even the distant Danube Basin.

### WHITE MARBLE FIGURINES

Of all the items left by these peoples, the marble figurines are perhaps both the most beautiful and enigmatic. Their different typologies are used by scholars to differentiate the various Cycladic eras. The predominantly female figures are generally around 20cm (8in) in length (a few near life-sized sculptures have been discovered) and are made of white marble. Almost two-dimensional in their execution, they have flattened oval heads and arms folded below schematically rendered breasts; many features would have been painted onto the marble (on the face, only the nose is rendered in relief). It is conjectured, from the position of the feet, that the figures were intended to lie horizontally, but there is no conclusive evidence for this, just as there is no firm consensus about their function. Explanations from scholars range from their being apotropaic (intended to ward off evil) to divinities, ancestors or symbolic companions for the deceased.

graffiti are hard to discern, and only one of the three colonnaded galleries is visitable. Steps from the catacomb area lead down to the shore and one of the island's most picturesque villages, **Klíma**, with brightly painted boathouses at sea level, carved into the volcanic cliff.

Mílos's best beaches are in the southwest "bat wing", starting with **Paleohóri** – its far end part-naturist, with steam vents in the sand near which eggs can be fried, and hot water bubbling up in the sea – and ending with isolated **Triádes**, facing the sunset. Others hereabouts are easiest (or only) accessible by boat.

Ten kilometres (6 miles) northeast from Adámas lies the rubble of the ancient city of **Phylakope** (Fylakopí; daily 8.30am–3pm; free), whose script and art resembled that of the Minoans. It flourished for 1,000 years after 2600 BC. The famous flying-fish fresco from here is now in Athens, but many objects are in the Pláka museum. All around Phylakope are strewn flakes of obsidian, used for sharp tools before bronze became common; visitors came to Mílos for it from 7000 BC onwards. Mílos's polychrome geology is especially impressive here. Next to the site glitters the **Papafrángas ravine**, where precipitous stone steps take you down for an atmospheric swim in a pool connected to the sea by an inlet running under a rock bridge. **Sarakíniko**, further west, is another inlet framed by wind-sculpted white rock formations.

**Pollónia** 🟥, 12km (7.5 miles) northeast of Adámas, is a wind-buffeted resort popular with boardsurfers and scuba-divers. Decent beaches are limited to **Voúdia** (Tría Pigádia), where the island's best hot springs erupt to an ideal temperature by a rock formation just offshore, at the far right as you face the sea. Pollónia is also the departure point for several small daily ferries across to Kímolos.

## KÍMOLOS

This tiny island – 41 sq km (16 sq miles), with a population of about 800 – is an alluring temptation when seen from Pollónia on Mílos, about a nautical mile across a strait. The boat takes only 20 minutes to cross to **Psathí**, Kímolos's little port. Some ferries between Sífnos and Adámas also stop here. **Kímolos** or **Hóra** 🟥, the single hilltop town, is a 15-minute walk up from the quay; at its core is a two-gated, 16th-century **kástro**, which, unlike the ones on Sífnos and Síkinos, is mostly uninhabited and derelict. Just outside the *kástro* precinct stands un-whitewashed, well-preserved **Agios Ioánnis Hrysóstomos** church, of the same era.

Kímolos, once a pirates' hideout, today provides a limited refuge from the more crowded islands – there are fewer than 500 tourist beds. Although blessedly undeveloped (the mining and lack of water sees to that), it has half a dozen beaches – going anticlockwise along the south and east shores – **Elliniká**, **Bonátsa**, **Kalamítsi**, **Alykí**,

*Detail of a ruined kástro doorway on Síkinos.*

*The cove at Alogómandra, Mílos.*

*In the village of Langáda, Amorgós, a boy in local costume performs a traditional dance.*

*Poppies and daisies carpet this field on Mílos.*

Skála and **Prássa**, all within easy walking distance, some with tavernas and a few rooms to let. The northern half of the island is abandoned and inaccessible except on foot; on the eastern shore between Klíma and Prássa, **thermal springs** of varying utility pour into the sea.

## FOLÉGANDROS

The sheer palisades of Folégandros's coast have deterred invaders over the centuries and so lent the islanders security. Despite its tiny size – 32 sq km (12 sq miles) populated by less than 700 people – its role in recent history has not been insignificant: many Greeks were exiled here during both the 1930s Metaxás dictatorship and the 1967–74 junta. Its ancient and early Christian ties with Crete were strong, and many icons of the Cretan School can be found in its churches today.

For such a small island, Folégandros has a fair number of beaches, especially on the less sheer eastern and southwestern coastlines. The easiest to reach are **Livádi** (with an organised campsite); **Várdia**, by the port; **Angáli**, at the narrow waist of the island on the west shore; naturist **Agios Nikólaos** just beyond; and **Livadáki** in the far southwest. From Livádi hamlet it is possible to walk (strenuously) south to the remote, scenic beach at **Katergó**.

A paved road (and bus service) links **Karavostási**, the port, to the capital, **Folégandros** or **Hóra** ㉜, a magnificently sited medieval town with an inner *kástro* perched above a sheer drop to the sea. The dazzling, wedding-cake church of Kímisi tis Theotókou presides over the town and marks the general direction of the **Hrysospiliá**, the "Golden Cave" in the cliff beyond, today accessible only to technical climbers. Folégandros is now decidedly trendy with both Greeks and foreigners, something reflected in the variety, prices and mixed clientele of the numerous bars, tavernas and lodgings in and around Hóra.

The island's second settlement, **Ano Meriá**, is actually a series of straggly hamlets strung out along the ridge road, comprising stone houses, a few

### ⊘ AMORGÓS WALKS

The best part of the well-marked and well-mapped Amorgian trail system links Egiáli in a triangular route with both **Tholária** and **Langáda**, handsome villages with excellent tavernas and seaward views. Hardy hikers can strike out beyond Langáda, first past the ancient **Theológos Monastery** with its frescoes of John the Evangelist, and then on a spectacular corniche trail to **Stavrós** church, at the base of **Mount Kríkelos**, the island's highest point, rising to 822 metres (2,696ft). In the week after Easter, the icon of Hozoviótissa goes walkabout (*la periforá*); devout pilgrims, some walking barefoot as a penance, follow it back from Egiáli to the monastery for five hours along the ancient trail that was the island's lifeline before the automobile age.

shops and cafés, farms and knoll-top chapels; the bus continues out here regularly to drop walkers at the start of trails to some of the beaches noted previously. Threshing cirques, for processing the barley that is still grown here, are conspicuous as well.

## SÍKINOS

Rocky Síkinos, despite the usual variety of harbour-side lodgings, couldn't be less like its larger neighbour, Íos. Although connected to Piraeus and other Cyclades (in particular Íos and Folégandros) regularly by conventional ferry and high-speed craft, Síkinos (with just over 200 permanent inhabitants) so far seems to have shrugged off tourism. It also escapes mention in the history books for long periods, but there are antiquities and venerable churches to be seen.

The main beaches, **Aloprónia** (also the port), **Dialiskári** and **Agios Geórgios** to the northeast, and **Agios Pandelímonas** to the southwest, face Íos. From Aloprónia harbour there's a high-season-only bus or an hour's hike to **Síkinos Town** ㉝ consisting of conjoined **Hóra** and **Kástro**, with yet another such Venetian defensive complex at its heart. There are few places to stay but several tavernas and *kafenía*, some serving limited-production local wine – Síkinos's former name, Oenoe, alludes to a long history of producing wine (*oinos* in ancient Greek). The half-ruined convent of **Zoödóhou Pigís** (church open in the evening) dominates Kástro to the northeast; nearby, the small chapel of **Panagía Pandohará** was dedicated in 2011 to poet Odysseas Elytis's memory by his lifelong companion Ioulita Iliopoulou.

Síkinos has few obvious diversions other than walking. One destination of note, the **Iroön** ㉞ at **Episkopí**, is an elaborate Roman family temple-tomb, incorporated into a 7th-century church. Hikers can continue down to the coast at Agios Pandelímonas and thence back to Aloprónia.

## ÍOS

A small island with few historic attractions, Íos has drawn the young and

**⊘ Fact**

Locals are convinced that Homer is buried on Íos: he either died here on a voyage from Sámos to Athens, or his mother was born on Íos and the poet chose to return here to die. Either way, he is celebrated by the so-called Omíria cultural events during early May.

*The steep, terraced slopes of Folégandros.*

footloose since the 1960s. The contemporary influx, who flock here to party by night and hit the beach by day, are a faint echo of their hippie forbears; "family" tourism is now actively promoted, holiday villas sprout north of the harbour and rough camping is a thing of the past.

The centre of Íos's nightlife shifts constantly among dozens of bars and dance clubs in the tiny capital town, **Hóra** (also called **Íos**). By 11pm, the last beach stragglers (a bus runs regularly between the beach and Gialós harbour, via Hóra, to bring them back) have arrived for the night-time revels; once ensconced inside a bar, they could be anywhere in the Mediterranean. Veteran Hellenophile travel writer Michael Haag less charitably deemed them "a plague of locusts who pack snack bars, boutiques and discotheques, appreciating nothing, giving nothing, taking everything."

The results of industrial-strength tourism have been twofold: Íos is no longer poor, and traditional life has disappeared, since there are no small,

remote villages where people maintain old traditions. Weddings were once four-day feasts for all comers; now, unless they are held in winter, they last an evening, as everyone is too busy tending tourist-related enterprises. However, with all the action concentrated in and around Hóra, it is still possible to find quiet corners and relatively empty beaches.

Íos is not devoid of natural beauty or charm; even the bleary-eyed can see it. **Gialós** port is one of the Aegean's prettiest. The hilltop **Hóra**, capped by a windmill and blue church domes, reached by a long marble stairway from Gialós, appears vaguely Levantine with its palm trees and kasbah-like layout.

The most famous beach is **Mylopótas** , with organised water sports and youth-oriented campsites. Alternatives include posher **Manganári Bay** in the south, served by both bus and caique; superior **Agía Theodóti** in the northeast; and **Psathí** in the east. Between them stand the remains of **Paleókastro** , a Venetian fortress containing

*One of the numerous tavernas in Hóra, Folégandros.*

the marble-clad ruins of what was the medieval capital. At a lonely spot towards the island's northern tip, beyond Plakotós Cove, is a series of ancient **graves**, one of which the islanders fervently believe is **Homer's**.

## AMORGÓS

Narrow, rugged and mountainous, Amorgós is a haven for walkers, bohemians and connoisseurs of still vibrant island culture, rather than for beachcombers. Before a road was opened between them in the late 1970s, the two port-resorts of Katápola and Egiáli were gateways to two effectively separate islands; ferry schedules still alternate in calling at them. **Katápola** ⑱ is bigger and more commercialised and with fewer beaches, but more convenient to the uphill **Hóra** ⑲ (or Amorgós Town), accessible by a regular bus service or a well-preserved *kalderími*. Its whitewashed houses and numerous domed and belfried churches cluster around a 13th-century Venetian castle.

Half an hour east of Hóra, clinging limpet-like to a 180-metre (590ft) cliff – French explorer and botanist Joseph Pitton de Tournefort likened it to a "chest of drawers" – the spectacular 11th-century Byzantine **Panagía Hozoviótissa Monastery** ⑳ (daily 8.30am–1pm and 5–7pm) is home to a revered icon of the Virgin from Palestine, as well as to three hospitable monks who treat visitors to a shot of *rakómelo* (spiced spirit) with *loukoúmi*, and a ground-floor treasury-museum. The 20–21 November festival, despite being subject to dodgy weather, is attended by pilgrims from Athens and across the Cyclades. Below the monastery, **Agía Anna** and **Kambí** beaches are the most famous of several protected south-coast coves.

Southwest from Hóra, **Agios Geórgios Valsamítis**, 4km (2 miles) away, is built atop a sacred spring that had served as an oracle since pagan times, and was only cemented over in the 1950s (though the flow still irrigates lush gardens). Vivid frescoes adorn a gazebo over the *agíasma* inside the church where the water is still audible, and (briefly) accessible for collection.

Because there were reasonable anchorages nearby, three ancient cities thrived here. **Minoa** (just above Katápola) is still being excavated; **Arkesíni**, in the far southwest, comprises a burial site and dwellings on Cape Kastrí, plus the well-preserved Hellenistic fortress at **Agía Triáda**, near modern Arkesíni village. Of ancient **Aigiale** (above modern **Egiáli** and its beaches), very little remains, but the nearby village of **Tholária** (Vaults) takes its name from Roman tombs in the vicinity.

## ANÁFI

In legend, Apollo conjured up Anéfi to shelter Jason and the Argonauts when the seas grew rough and they risked losing the Golden Fleece; an Apollo shrine was built here in thanksgiving. Divine intervention has never again been reliable. Earthquakes originating

*By ferry or by caique, any trip out to the "Back Islands" should include a quiet day on the beach.*

*Inside a Katápola kafeníon, Amorgós.*

*A sunny backstreet.*

*Amorgós, a magnet for walkers.*

on its volatile neighbour **Santoríni** ⓐ (see page 195) usually affected Anáfi with tidal waves and a rain of volcanic debris. Anáfi's appearance has probably not altered much since its conception: it still looks like a rough boulder heaved up out of the sea and kept in place only by divine benevolence.

However, a different god is involved now: **Zoödóhou Pigís Monastery** ⓑ (daily 11am–1pm & 4–6pm) was erected over the old Apollo temple in the island's southeast corner, and incorporates plenty of marble masonry fragments from its predecessor. Above the monastery, with festivities 11 days after Easter and on 7–8 September, perches the smaller **Monastery of Kalamiótissa**, atop a 450-metre (1,480ft) -high limestone monolith – claimed to be larger than Gibraltar – that is Anáfi's most distinctive feature. A swooping but well-engineered path takes you there in under an hour; some people stay overnight at the top to catch the sunrise.

About 270 people live on the island today, surviving mainly by fishing and subsistence farming. Since the 1980s, though, the economy has been boosted slightly by summer tourists, attracted by Anáfi's peace and quiet, and superb south-facing beaches. The island is no longer a traveller's dead end; there are main-line ferries from Piraeus, which for the foreseeable future will continue once or twice weekly to certain Dodecanese, then back again.

The south-facing harbour, **Agios Nikólaos**, has few facilities, but the main town, **Hóra** ⓒ (or Anáfi Town), a short bus ride or half-hour walk up, offers a wider choice and finer setting. It's a windy place, sharing anti-earthquake vaulted roofs with Santoríni.

The closest of the beaches is palm-tree-adorned **Klisídi**, walkable east from Agios Nikólaos, with reliable food and lodging. From near there, the old path (and a newer road, inland) heads further east to superb **Roúkounas** beach, with dunes, the **Katelímatsa** coves, **Katsoúni** and **Monastíri** beach – all clothing-optional except the last, owing to its proximity to Zoödóhou Pigís. Inland from Roúkounas looms

**Kastélli**, site of both ancient Anaphe and a Venetian castle.

## THE BACK ISLANDS OR MINOR CYCLADES

The so-called "**Back Islands**" between Náxos and Amorgós were far more inhabited in antiquity. Now Donoússa, Irakliá, Skhinoússa and Koufonísi have populations of 100 to 200 each, but appreciable summer tourism, especially Athenians. Mains power only arrived during the mid-1980s, and fresh water is scarce on all these islets. They're hardly secret (or cheap) destinations now, with ample facilities including bank ATMs on each one. Getting to them is fairly easy: the somewhat buckety, splashy but reliable small caique *Express Skopelitis* (nicknamed the *skylopníktis* or "dog-drowner" by the unkind) plies an almost daily schedule among them, leaving Amorgós at dawn and returning from Náxos around 3pm. Several times a week faster, more comfortable Blue Star ferries or smaller catamarans call from Piraeus as well.

Hilly **Donoússa** ❹, remote from the others due east of Náxos, has good south-facing beaches near **Stavrós** port at **Kédros** and **Livádi**, both with fluffy blonde sand, naturism and free camping. Livádi stretches below **Mersíni**, the only inland hamlet, with a gushing fountain under a plane tree. Ill-advised bulldozing has ruined what was until the 1990s a comprehensive network of cobbled paths.

**Koufonísi** ❹ (technically Áno Koufonísi) is the flattest of the quartet, and the busiest with a Páros-Mýkonos-type clientele, thanks to excellent south-east-facing beaches and a charming main village. The entire south coast looks across to **Káto Koufonísi** (day-trip accessible, with another beach and taverna) and hulking **Kéros** (off-limits), which was a third-millennium BC burial site and source of much of the Cycladic material in

Greek museums. Beyond appreciably developed seaside Hóra stretch the beaches: **Fínikas**, **Italída**, **Platiá Poúnda** with sheltering sea caves, and **Porí** with yachts at anchor, all linked by road or path.

**Skhinoússa** ❹ is far quieter, with most facilities in the hilltop Hóra 1km (0.5 mile) above the port; there are 16 beaches scattered around the island, of which only **Tsigoúri** has amenities. Solitude-seekers prefer nearby **Alygariá** and **Almyrós** in the south, less than half an hour's walk distant from Hóra.

**Irakliá** (or Iraklía) ❹ is the largest of the "Back Islands", and has two proper settlements: the northerly port of **Agios Geórgios**, with all tourist facilities; and smaller **Hóra** (aka Panagía after its main festival date). Compared to its neighbours, Iráklia's beaches are disappointing – Livádi is the best – but it does have an undeniable attraction in the huge **Cave of Agios Ioánnis** in the far south, reached by following one of the eight marked hiking routes prepared for walkers.

*Hozoviótissa Monastery clings to an Amorgós cliffside.*

# NÁXOS

Rugged, lofty Náxos offers green valleys, lush even in the height of summer, and sweeping sandy beaches along its southwest-facing coast, as well as superb medieval and ancient monuments, and good locally produced food.

**⊘ Main Attractions**
Náxos Kástro
Portára
Fotodótis Monastery
Panagía Drosianí
Temple of Demeter
Alykó coves

**Map on page 193**

**Hóra ❶** (Náxos Town) is a labyrinth of mansions, fortifications, post-Byzantine churches and ancient and medieval ruins. The **Orthodox Cathedral** to the northeast marks the Fondána district; the adjacent residential Boúrgo quarter is full of arched passageways and narrow lanes. Higher up, within the gated *kástro*, live Catholic descendants of the Venetians look for their coats of arms over doorways. The former French Commercial School, built into the ramparts, briefly educated Nikos Kazantzakis until his suspicious father came to rescue him from the Jesuits. Today it houses the **Archaeological Museum** (Tue–Sun 8.30am–3pm), with a huge and excellent collection (including many Cycladic figurines and a Hellenistic mosaic). Nearby, the Catholic Cathedral on the main Kástro plaza contains icons lending unusual takes on religious personalities.

On **Palátia** islet (connected by a causeway) to the north of Hóra's ferry dock, a colossal free-standing marble door frame, the **Portára**, marks the entrance to the **Temple of Delian Apollo** of 540–530 BC. It was never completed, despite the efforts of Lygdamis, Náxos's tyrant. Had it been finished, it would have been Archaic Greece's largest temple.

The rest of the island rewards exploration by hired car, bus or on foot. Hemmed in by the Cyclades' highest ridges, the interior recalls the wilder parts of the Peloponnese. **Mount Zas** (a corruption of Zeus) is 1,001 metres (3,284ft) high, but not hard to climb for superb views. In the central **Trageá** region, orchards conceal Byzantine churches and crumbling fortified manors.

On the northern shore of Náxos, at the end of a bus line, sits the little resort of **Apóllonas ❷**. A huge *kouros* (Archaic statue of an idealised youth) lies on the hillside above it, abandoned around 600 BC when the marble cracked. (Two other flawed *kouroi*, smaller but more elaborately worked, repose at Flério, 10km

*Laid-back sightseeing on the ferry to Náxos.*

[6 miles) east of Náxos, respectively in a walled garden at Melanés, and up a nearby hillside.)

On the road from Apóllonas to Hóra, handsome **Koronída** ❸ (Komiakí), the island's highest village, looks over terraced vineyards, and is home of the local *kítron* liqueur – and of emery miners until nearby deposits became unprofitable. Marble-paved **Apíranthos** ❹ (Aperáthou), 20km (12 miles) south, was settled by Cretan refugees in the 17th and 18th centuries, and is the natal village of Manolis Glezos, the leftist activist, later politician, who tore down the Nazi flag from the Parthenon on 30 May 1941. Southeast stands the buttressed tower-monastery of **Fotodótis** ❺ (summer Mon–Sat 10am–2pm, winter 9am–1pm), juxtaposed against Donoússa and star of many local posters.

**Filóti**, 8km (5 miles) below Apíranthos, is Náxos's second-largest settlement. The Trageá extends west from Filóti to **Halkí** ❻, with several fine churches, including 11th-century **Panagía Protóthronis**. Nearby rears up the 17th-century **Grazia-Barozzi Tower**, one of many defensive towers scattered across Náxos.

From Halkí a good road heads north to **Moní**; just before the village is the turning for **Panagía Drosianí** (The Dewy Virgin; daily 10am–4pm), built in stages between the 4th and 12th centuries and retaining some of the oldest, albeit battered, frescoes in Greece.

From Ano Sangrí just southwest of the Trageá, a paved road descends 5km (3 miles) through a beautiful valley to the well-reconstructed **Temple of Demeter** ❼ (grounds always unlocked), dating from circa 530 BC.

Some of the Cyclades' best beaches line the southwest coast. The merged resorts of **Agios Prokópios** and **Agía Anna** ❽ at the north end are the main bases for holidaymakers; the long white sands of **Pláka** ❾ just southeast have fewer facilities, and more scantily clad beachcombers, the further you go. **Kastráki** ❿ and Glyfáda, beyond Mikrí Vígla headland with its kite-boarders, offers more of the same. Once past scenic **Cape Kouroúpia**, with its pristine coves, lie bigger beaches at **Pyrgáki** and **Agiassós**.

*The Portára gateway of the unfinished temple of Delian Apollo.*

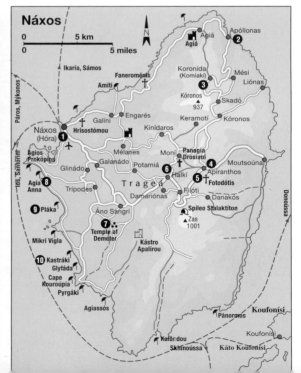

Santoríni's red cliffs plunge into the Aegean.

# SANTORÍNI

Santoríni's whitewashed villages sit atop volcanic cliffs above midnight-blue caldera waters. It is an island shaped by geological turmoil, and one of the most dramatic in all of Greece.

Sailing into the bay of Santoríni is one of Greece's great experiences. Broken pieces of a volcano's rim – Santoríni and its attendant islets – trace a multicoloured circle around a deep submerged caldera which, before the cataclysmic volcanic eruption in about 1625 BC, was a hummocky volcanic plateau. The earthquakes, tsunami and rains of pumice that followed the eruption devastated much of the Aegean, and contributed to the end of Minoan civilisation. The island's long crescent, formed of solidified lava, seems at sunset still to reflect fire from the dormant volcano.

The sensual lines of Cycladic architecture, augmented here with anti-earthquake barrel-vaulting cemented with pozzolana (sandy volcanic ash), are doubly disarming on Santoríni, set against the smoky purple or rusty orange striations of weathered lava in the background. Thera is the island's ancient name, and Thíra the official one in modern times. Both Greeks and foreigners, however, prefer the medieval Santoríni, after Saint Irene, one of three sisters martyred by Diocletian in AD 304.

Only excursion boats put in at **Skála Firás**, 580 steps below Firá (*skála* means both landing stage and staircase in Greek); most seacraft dock at ugly **Athiniós**, 10km (6 miles) further south. **Firá ❶** (Hóra), the capital, sits high on

*Norfolk pine.*

the rim, its white houses mostly rebuilt in concrete after a devastating earthquake in 1956. The town centre is mostly pedestrianised, its winding cobbled streets terraced into the volcanic cliffs.

Firá has an **Archaeological Museum** (Tue–Sun 8am–3pm) and the far better **Museum of Prehistoric Thera** (Apr–Oct Mon, Wed, Fri 8am–3pm, Tue noon–8pm, Thu, Sat, Sun 8am–8pm, winter Wed–Mon 8am–3pm), devoted to the Minoan Akrotiri site – star exhibits are original frescoes of cavorting blue monkeys, elegant women and Nilotic vegetation

## Ⓞ Main Attractions
Firá museums
Ancient Thera
Ia
Perívolos beach
Pýrgos

Map on page 197

*On the phone in Firá.*

proving seafaring contacts with Egypt. The **Megaro Gyzi Museum** (May–Sept Sun–Mon 10am–4pm, Tue–Sat 10am–9pm, Oct daily 10am–4pm) occupies the former Catholic archbishopric, spared by the 1956 earthquake, which is stuffed with antiquarian engravings, documents and maps as well as pre-earthquake photographs. The **Lignos Folklore Museum** in Kondohóri suburb (daily 10am–2pm) completely reproduces a 19th-century cave-house, along with mocked-up workshops for all the vanished rural crafts of the island.

Although packed with more jewellers and chichi boutiques than strictly necessary, Firá can still enchant, especially over a drink at sunset while contemplating the midnight-blue caldera waters with their volcanic islets. Traditionally, Santoríni was said to be the main Greek home of vampires – possibly because corpses failed to decompose completely in the lava soil.

## ANCIENT THERA AND AKROTIRI

East of Firá, the landscape drops into fertile, level, pumice-rich fields, though

*Remains at ancient Thera, on the Mésa Vounó headland.*

in the southeast some non-volcanic mountains shrug themselves up. On one of them, the non-volcanic Mésa Vounó headland, sits ancient **Thera 2** (Tue–Sun 8am–3pm), founded during the 9th century BC just uphill from the only freshwater spring on the island, still flowing, and remained inhabited (with a Hellenistic zenith) until medieval times. The best approaches are the fine, if twisting, cobbled paths up from either Kamári or Períssa (see page 197).

In the south, ancient **Akrotiri 3** (Apr–Oct daily 8am–8pm except Tue until 3pm, winter Tues–Sun 8am–3pm), a Minoan town preserved in volcanic ash like Pompeii, had comfortable two-storey houses, good plumbing and attractive little squares. Only about 30 percent has been excavated thus far and no bones have been found, which suggests that the inhabitants had some warning of the pending eruption, and fled with their valuables (though leaving other artefacts behind). The beautiful frescoes, pots and furniture found here are divided between the Museum of Prehistoric Thera, and the National Archaeological Museum in Athens (see page 119).

## IA AND THE CALDERA

Santoríni's population swells fivefold in summer from the permanent winter population of about 25,000; while Firá is the most developed tourist centre, many other places offer accommodation and places to eat, although bus services are hopelessly overcrowded. **Ia 4** (Oía), on the island's northernmost peninsula, is among Greece's most photographed villages, carefully restored since the 1956 earthquake destroyed most of its famous cave-houses. Today, these same cave-houses converted into exclusive accommodation are an Ia speciality. A steep walk down twisting stone steps from the western end of town leads to the tiny twin ports of **Arméni** and **Ammoúdi**. The gentle trail-hike along the caldera's edge from Ia to **Imerovígli**

(3km/2 miles north of Firá) allows you to experience the island's tempestuous geology from close up.

The volcano is only dormant, not extinct; besides regular earthquakes, it has produced the two cinder-cones of **Néa** and **Paleá Kaméni** (the Burnt Islets) out in the caldera. Regular boat tours from both Skála Firás and Ammoúdi take you to them, where you can swim to sulphurous hot springs off Paleá, and hike up to a crater on Néa which still emits gas and steam; the last actual eruption was in 1950. Tours and regular small ferries from Ammoúdi continue to **Thirasiá**, the only one of Santoríni's satellite islets which is inhabited, with a pace of life still stuck in pre-tourism once the day-trippers have gone – there are tavernas, and rooms to rent, though few beaches.

## COASTAL RESORTS AND THE CENTRAL PLAIN

After Firá and Ia, the next major resorts are **Kamári** ❺ and **Períssa** ❻ on the east coast. Both have roasting hot, black-sand beaches (the one at Périssa is 8km/5 miles long, called **Perívolos** ❼, at its superior southerly end). From ancient Thera (see page 196), between the two, another good path heads west to Santoríni's summit, Profítis Ilías (566 metres/1,860ft), home to multiple antennae and an eponymous 18th-century monastery (rarely open to the public) that is the focus of the island's major 19–20 July festival.

From here, a steep road descends to conical **Pýrgos** ❽ village above the central plain, its houses arrayed around a Venetian citadel with several bulbous churches. It contrasts with **Mesariá** ❾ further north, which seems to consist only of more church domes, until the approach reveals a warren of dwellings and alleys sunk below ground level. The farmland around and between features yellow grain sheaves, vines twisted into wreaths to protect grapes against the wind, and tiny thick-skinned tomatoes, grown without water for concentrated flavour, then dried. Small caves (*kánaves*), natural or dug out, are used as toolsheds, barns and (formerly) as homes.

## ⊘ SANTORÍNI WINERIES

Santoríni is now an AOC domaine and winemaking is the only flourishing traditional trade. For a few euros, winery tours allow generous sampling. Venetsanos (www.venetsanoswinery.com), near Megalohóri, is the oldest industrial winery (daily May–Aug 10am–10pm, Sept–Oct 10am–9pm, Nov–Apr Mon–Fri 10am–3pm). There are also microwineries like Art Space in Episkopí Goniás (www.artspace-santorini.com; May–Oct), with a museum inside a long subterranean gallery. Ktima Argyrou (www.estate-argyros.com), also in Episkopí Goniás, does excellent red Mavrotragano and distinctive Aidani white. Santoríni's north also supports a few wineries, the most interesting being Vassaltis near Vourvoúlos, opened in 2016 with industrial-chic tasting rooms. Most Santoríni wineries produce *vinsánto*, a fortified (14%) dessert wine.

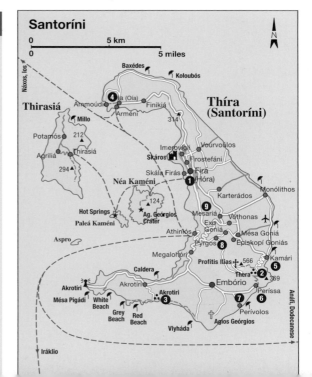

Santoríni

Lalária beach, Skiáthos.

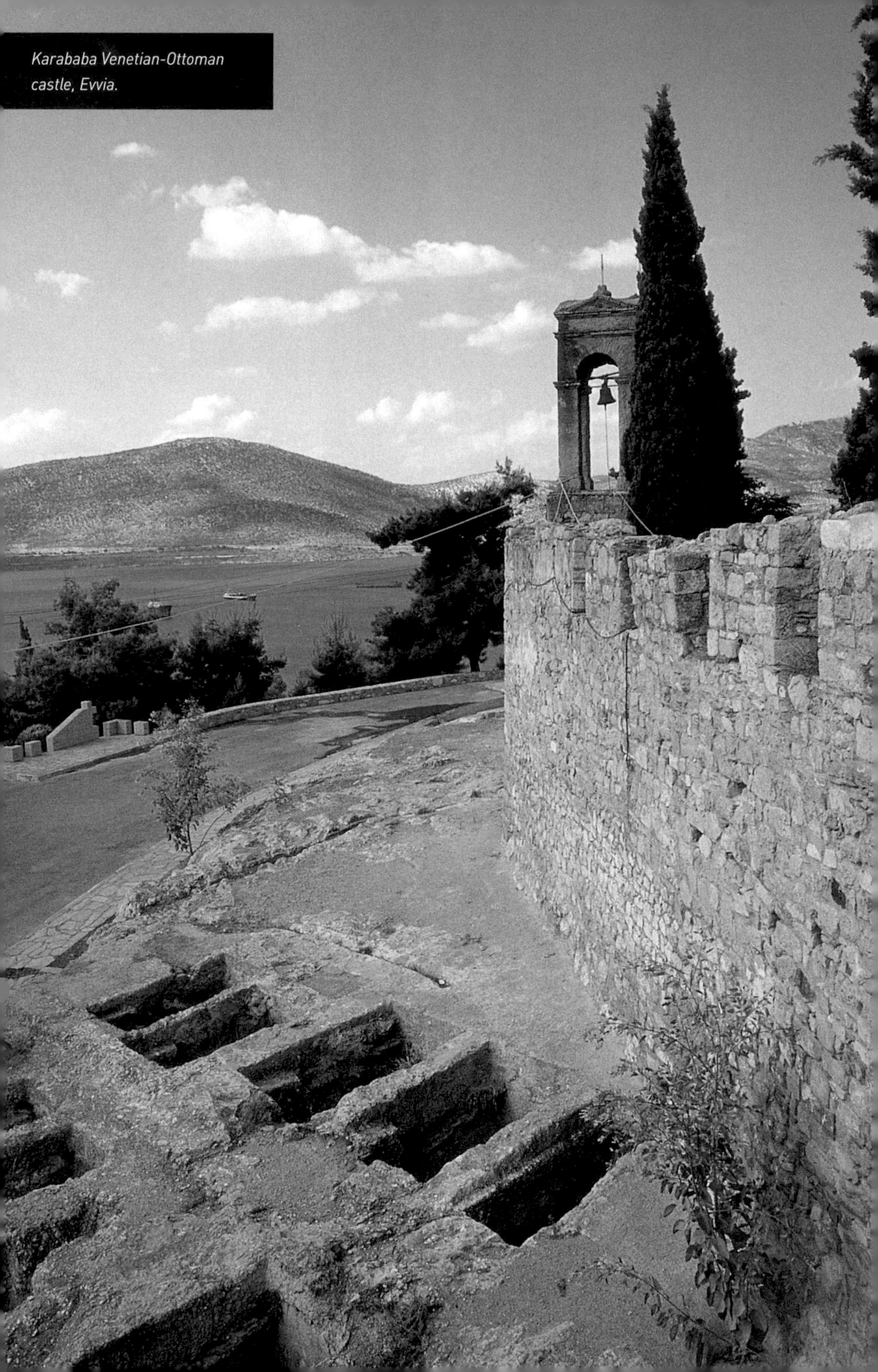

*Karababa Venetian-Ottoman castle, Evvia.*

# THE SPORADES AND EVVIA

Skiáthos, Skópelos, Alónissos, Skýros and Evvia.

*Watching the world go by on Skópelos.*

The Sporades – meaning "sporadic" or "scattered" – is a group of four islands in the northwest Aegean. Evvia, extending along the Greek mainland south of the Sporades, is Greece's second-largest island, after Crete.

Mainlanders have long appreciated Skiáthos's beaches and made annual pilgrimages, though they are now outnumbered by foreigners. In spite of a rich history, Alónissos is the least developed of the Sporades in terms of tourism, while Skópelos is slowly catching up to Skiáthos in terms of beaches and level of development. Skýros, the largest and in certain ways the most interesting of the group, is remote from the others, with a deeply entrenched local culture.

Evvia, despite easy access from the mainland, has been mostly unaffected by tourism. Its diverse landscape and rich history make it almost a microcosm of the whole country.

Hopping between Skiáthos, Skópelos and Alónissos is very easy, but reaching Skýros usually involves a longer trip via Evvia, with only mid-summer connections with its three northern neighbours. Skiáthos alone of the Sporades has an international airport with regular overseas arrivals, mainly from Britain, Italy and Scandinavia, and domestic flights to Athens and Thessaloníki. Skýros Airport also receives planes from Athens and Thessaloníki, scheduled to allow long weekends away. Conventional ferries and catamarans run to the three

*Skiáthos Town bathers.*

northerly Sporades from Vólos and Agios Konstandínos on the mainland.

The islands are what remain of a mountain range that detached itself from the mainland in a geological convulsion and "sank". Prevailing winds and other factors produce reliable winter rainfall and lush vegetation, notably pine forests. Summers can be humid, especially on south-facing shores, but the *meltémi* helps keep a lid on temperatures.

The traditional trade route between the Mediterranean and the Black Sea passed the Sporades. This strategic position has often brought unwanted callers, including invasion fleets and pirates, so medieval remains and major archaeological sites are few.

# THE SPORADES

Long beloved of the yachting fraternity and wealthy Greeks, the Sporades now attract foreigners in even greater numbers, whether for the nightlife of Skiáthos or the quieter charm of Alónissos.

The Sporades islands are popular destinations, known more for their lush vegetation, limpid seas and equable climate than their archaeological sites.

## SKIÁTHOS

The long sandy scythe of **Koukouariés** ❶ is used as evidence on thousands of local postcards that the Aegean can produce the kind of beach normally associated with the Caribbean. Propriety would prevent any postcards from featuring **Mikrós Krassás** (Small "Banana Beach") and its usual population of nudists. That, and the thumping all-day bars at several south-coast beaches, exemplifies the relaxed nature of tourism on Skiáthos, long nicknamed "the straight Mýkonos".

The island has beaches for all occasions, not least because some among the alleged 50 (plus more on surrounding islets) will always be sheltered, whatever the wind direction. Koukounariés and "Small Banana" are near neighbours at the west end of the twisting, busy 13km (8.5-mile) coast road from the town; there are half a dozen others along it and many better ones on Skiáthos's northwest coast. The best of these are adjacent **Mandráki** and **Eliá**; most have a taverna or at least a *kantína* selling drinks and snacks. A path leading

*Kástro beach in the north.*

down from a track's end usually indicates a beach below, few as crowded as Koukounariés.

Anticlockwise round-the-island boat trips pass the rocky and largely inaccessible northern shoreline, where the only construction is **Kástro** ❷, the abandoned 16th-century capital once connected to the rest of Skiáthos by a drawbridge. For 300 years the inhabitants huddled on this windy crag, hoping the pirates would overlook them. During World War II Allied stragglers and commandos hid out

### Main Attractions
Kástro of Skiáthos
Skópelos Town
Velanió beach, Skópelos
Paleá Alónissos
Walking on Alónissos
National Marine Park

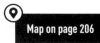

Map on page 206

here, waiting for evacuation to Turkey by a friendly submarine or British Special Operations Executive *kaïki*. Nowadays it is an obligatory stop for the excursion caiques, after they have dipped into three technicolour grottoes and anchored at **Lalária** cove, famous for its smooth, round stones and rock arch, and before proceeding to a beach taverna (usually at Megálos Asélinos) for lunch.

A tough scooter or hired jeep is necessary to follow mostly unpaved roads looping through the hills towards the north shore. They provide stunning views as well as the chance to pop into monasteries which, with the Kástro, are more or less the only buildings of historic interest. Of these, the grandest and closest to town is **Evangelistrías** (daily 10am–sunset; museum 10am–2pm), with frescoed **Panagía Kehreás** further west, set above a stream valley and **Lygariés** beach.

Fires started by the Nazis in August 1944 destroyed most of the pretty pre-war town; only the bluff-top old quarter in the southwest escaped. But

**Skiáthos Port** ❸ makes up in liveliness what it lacks in architectural merit. In fact, its nightlife is probably the most important consideration, after the beaches, for the numerous peak-season visitors – mostly young Italian and Spanish fashionistas, plus a few Central Europeans – that Skiáthos attracts. Their preferences change annually, but it's not difficult to spot which places are in vogue this season, whether one's taste is for beer and blues, wine and Vivaldi, *tsípouro* and trance, or caipirinhas and 1950s rock and roll. The two classiest and trendiest foci are the quay of the Old Port and a shoreline strip at the start of the airport road, just past the yacht marina. Skiáthos is a major sailing and chandlery centre, elaborating on a tradition of caique-building.

The main nod to culture in the town is the **Aléxandros Papadiamándis Museum** (Tue–Sun 9.30am–1.30pm and 5–8pm) on Mitropolítou Ananíou, lodged in the 19th-century home of one of Greece's pioneering short-story writers and novelists, who also

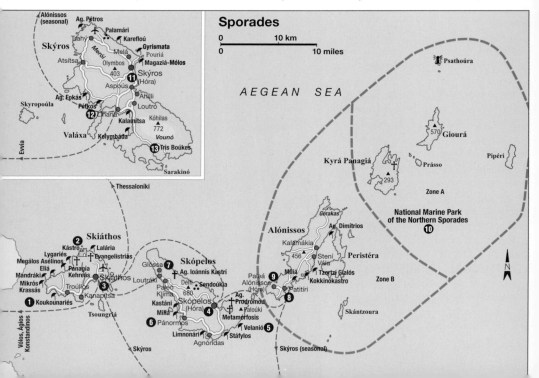

cfficiated as a priest. **Galeri Varsakis** above the Old Port stands in for a formal ethnographic museum, but prices for the admittedly rare antiques are triple what they would be elsewhere.

## SKÓPELOS

If Kefaloniá has become, somewhat reluctantly, "Captain Corelli's Island", lushly wooded Skópelos has enthusiastically embraced the sobriquet of "The Island of *Mamma Mia!*", partly shot here in 2007, with boat tours offered to filmic locales. Not that the island was any less photogenic or alluring before then; its beaches are consistently underrated, and unlike Skiáthos, it has not suffered so many forest fires.

Visitors waiting in **Vólos** rather than Agios Konstandínos for passage to Skópelos (the alternative is to fly to Skiáthos and catch a catamaran or ferry) may enjoy the excellent **Archaeological Museum** (Tue–Sun 8am–3pm). On display, among lots else, are the contents of a grave discovered in 1936; the gold crown and ornate weapons purportedly belonged to Staphylos, a semi-legendary Minoan who colonised Skópelos.

The island's distinguished past is demonstrated not so much by prominent sites – except for the three intriguing Hellenistic **Sendoúkia** tombs on Mount Délfi – as by the exceptionally fine vernacular houses in **Skópelos Town ❹** (Hóra), arrayed around a harbour lined with cafés and tavernas under mulberry trees. The town was only lightly damaged in a 1965 earthquake, and despite local participation in the resistance, escaped Nazi vindictiveness thanks to Alfons Hochhauser – an Austrian in the garrison who had lived here as a spy before the war – and is therefore the most "authentic" and traditional capital of the three northern Sporades. Slate roofs, wooden balconies, idiosyncratic local shops and flagstone streets give Hóra a serenity and dignity rarely found in Skiáthos. The only specific attractions are the 18th-century **Vrakatsa Mansion** (Tue–Sun 10am–2pm & 7–10pm), the mansion of a leading family donated to the

*Sunset over the Aegean.*

*Whiling away the afternoon in Skópelos Town.*

## ⊘ RIGÍNOS THE BORING

A legend tells of a rampaging dragon on Skópelos that proved resistant to all conventional attempts to get rid of it. The local priest (and later patron saint of the island), one Riginos, was implored to direct a sermon at the beast, the islanders having heard enough of his homilies to think that it might do the trick. Finding itself as bored as any human, the dragon reared up and fled. The pious Riginos, determined to save his flock, followed doggedly and, upon cornering his quarry on a seaside clifftop, prepared to deliver another lengthy homily. Despairing at the prospect, the dragon chose to dive to its death instead. The impact it made on landing created a deep ravine on the south coast that is today known as the *Drakondóskhisma* (Dragon's Rift).

*Skópelos Town can lay claim to some distinguished houses, which its inhabitants are proud to adorn.*

*Church with a view, Skópelos Town.*

community by the last of the line in 2001, kept much as it was when they lived there; and the **Folklore Museum** (June–Sept; by application to Vrakatsa Mansion), three floors detailing local costumes and crafts such as the vanished weaving tradition.

On the slopes of **Mount Paloúki**, east of the bay, perch three medieval **monasteries**, all inhabited to some degree; the most architecturally distinguished, its church dome supported by coral-rock columns, is **Metamórfosis**. These are just some of the reputed 40 monasteries on the island, plus 360 churches, 123 of them tucked among the houses of Hóra, crowned by a crumbled Venetian castle set on ancient foundations.

Mixed sand-and-pebble beaches speckle the south and west coasts. Closest to town are cramped **Stáfylos**, site of the Minoan tomb, and the far superior, long, fine-pebble **Velanió** **⑤** just beyond, with eyefuls of Évvia and a nudist zone. **Agnóndas** is the island's second port, with popular waterside tavernas; **Limonnári** nearby has a better, white-sand beach and another

taverna. **Pánormos** **⑥**, about halfway along the coast road, is a major resort and yacht anchorage, although beaches at nearby **Miliá** and **Kastáni** are far better and sandier than Pánormos's coarse-pebble shore.

The road continues past three hamlets: **Paleó Klíma**, declared uninhabitable after the 1965 quake, but its houses since mostly acquired and restored by outsiders, **Agii Anárgyri** (which suffered the same fate) and **Athéato** (Mahalás), the most architecturally distinguished of the three, still inhabited by a few local people. Just beyond sprawls hillside **Glóssa** **⑦**, Skópelos's second town, apparently settled by Thessalian mainlanders. It, too, is experiencing a minor housing boom, thanks not least to its sweeping views. At the bottom of a steep, twisty road lies the second, somewhat dozy port of **Loutráki**. There are a few more beaches beyond Glóssa, notably beside **Agios Ioánnis Kastrí**, a church perched in postcard-perfect style on a rock monolith and duly used as a locale by the *Mamma Mia!* film-makers.

# ALÓNISSOS

On a hill west of **Patitíri** ❽, the port of this rugged island and last call on ferry or catamaran routes, is **Paleá Alónissos** ❾ (Hóra), the former capital shattered by the earthquake of March 1965. This compounded the blow the islanders had already suffered when all their grapevines withered and died from phylloxera during the 1950s. Alónissos seems to have been always jinxed: the ancient capital, Ikos, literally disappeared when the ground on which it stood slumped into the sea.

In 1970, Palaeolithic-era evidence was found that could mean that Alónissos was inhabited before any other Aegean island, and it was considered a prize worth fighting over by Philip of Macedon and the Athenians. Its famous **wines** were once shipped all over ancient Greece in amphorae stamped "IKION"; today there is a modest revival of the industry based on phylloxera-resistant vines, though you're more likely to be offered the luscious local apricots or pickled *tzitzírafa* (terebinth) shoots.

A marked, cobbled path links Patitíri and Paleá Alónissos (45 minutes' walk); there is also a bus. By 1977, coercive government policies had forced the total abandonment of Hóra by locals; as at Paleó Klíma on Skópelos, Athenians and foreigners bought up the old ruins and restored them in variable taste. The effect is somewhat twee, and most food and drink is predictably overpriced, but the views west to Skópelos and north as far as Mount Athos are undeniably spectacular.

The way the island has adjusted to its unrealised potential and bad luck is something for which many visitors are grateful. Alónissos remains the least developed of the Sporades, with second-home ownership matching short-term tourism, which tends to be low-key and trendy, with art exhibitions, a yoga school and a home-opathy academy – although there are also two all-inclusive resorts. Walkers are admirably catered for with an accurate topographic map, numbered and maintained paths and a walking guide written by resident expat Chris Browne.

Usable, accessible beaches are concentrated on the more protected south and southeast coasts. Several are a short distance by path or track from Hóra, but superior ones lie northeast of functional Patitíri, Roussoúm Gialós and Vótsi ports at **Kokkinókastro** (site of ancient Ikos), **Tzortzí Gialós** and **Leftós Gialós**. Improved roads make wheeled access easy (and safer than on Skiáthos or Skópelos); overland journeys have largely replaced summer taxi-boats from Patitíri up the coast as far as **Agios Dimítrios**. **Kalamákia** is an authentic fishing port – nearby waters are rich in marine life – while yachts like to put in at **Stení Vála**.

## NATIONAL MARINE PARK

Alónissos, as well as half a dozen islets scattered to the east and north, fall within the **National Marine Park**

⊘ **Where**

The Manos Faltaïts Museum on Skýros (daily 10am–2pm and 5.30–8pm, summer 6–9pm), in a mansion north of the town, is a private collection presenting the life of the island through rare antiques, pottery, a traditional house mock-up, documents, costumes and photographs.

*A flock of sheep on Skýros.*

of the Northern Sporades , established in 1992 to conserve declining fish stocks and provide sanctuary to seabirds and marine mammals, in particular the severely endangered Mediterranean monk seal, of which fewer than 400 survive worldwide. The park is proving, however, a bane to traditional livelihoods; many local fishermen have been paid a stipend of a few tens of thousands of euros to cease work and smash up (under close supervision) their historic wooden *kaïkia*.

Two of the islets – **Pipéri** and **Giourá** – are off-limits to all but licensed scientists for conservation reasons. **Skántzoura**, with an empty monastery, is rather out of the way, but seasonal **caique excursions** from Patitíri visit others. The first stop is **Kyrá Panagiá**, which belongs to Megístis Lávras monastery on Mount Athos and itself has a restored 10th-century monastery inhabited by one farmer-monk. With enough passengers to defray fuel costs, peak-season tours extend to northerly **Psathoúra**, with the

*A goatman at Skýros Carnival.*

tallest (26 metres/81ft) lighthouse in the Aegean (built in 1895, now solar-powered) and a lovely white-sand beach. Olive-covered, only seasonally inhabited **Peristéra**, cradling Alónissos to the east, is the final afternoon swim-stop in low season. Passengers are most unlikely to spot seals, but will probably encounter dolphins.

## SKÝROS

The main character in the "goat dance" of **Skýros Carnival**, staged in the four weekends before Lent and with its roots in a pre-Christian pagan festival, is the *géros* (old man) who wears a goat pelt and kid-skin mask, plus tens of kilograms of sheep bells, which he shakes noisily with waist movements. The *géri* are accompanied by their "brides" the *korélles* (maidens), young men in drag. Foreign visitors enjoying the spectacle ought perhaps to know that the third type of figure (the *frángos*), a buffoon dressed in ridiculous clothes and blowing on a *bouroú* or conch shell, represents a foreigner.

Only recently has Skýros shed its near-complete economic dependence on the Greek navy and air force to court foreign tourism, mostly Italian, French, Dutch, German and British, although the island has been well known to Greeks for years. The effects of the summer season have not yet eclipsed a vigorous and idiosyncratic local culture, even if the older generation, which faithfully wore the elaborate island costume, has pretty much died off. Cubist white houses often contain amazing collections of copperware, embroidery and painted ceramics, the last acquired by trade or piracy and serving as a spur to the development of a local pottery industry based in several kiln-workshops at Magaziá beach. Carved wooden furniture passed down though the generations is often too small to be practical, so may be hung on the wall.

**Skýros Town ⓫** (Hóra) is on the northern half of the island, fanning out on the lee side of a rock plug overlooking the east coast. Life in the town is played out all along the meandering main commercial street or *agorá*, which begins near the downhill edge of what is a remarkably workaday place, albeit with picturesque archways and churches.

A left fork in this thoroughfare leads down towards a plaza at the northern edge of town, where a nude bronze male statue representing *Immortal Poetry* (in memory of Rupert Brooke) commands the view; it scandalised locals when first installed in 1931. Just below this is a worthwhile **Archaeological Museum** (Tue–Sun 8.30am–3pm), with fine Geometric-era pottery, and the Mános Faltaïts Museum (see page 209). The right-hand option wanders up to the *kástro*, the old Byzantine/Venetian castle built atop the ancient acropolis where, in legend, King Lykomedes raised Achilles and later threw Theseus to his death. A 2001 earthquake closed the *kástro* and the monastery inside for safety reasons, but plans are afoot to re-open them.

Long, sandy **Magaziá** beach below Hóra merges seamlessly with the one of **Mólos**, which terminates at **Pouriá** point with sea-weathered, squared-off rocks quarried by the Romans. There are better, if sometimes exposed, beaches in the north at Gyrísmata, **Kareflou** and **Agios Pétros**, bracketing the airport/air force base, and the site of Bronze Age **Palamári** (Mon–Fri 7.30am–2.30pm; free). The paved loop road continues through pines past other coves with mediocre beaches like Atsítsa, until reaching longer, sandier **Péfkos**. **Linariá ⓬**, the ferry port, also has accommodation and tavernas, but most visitors will continue on the circuit back towards Hóra, perhaps pausing at **Aspoús**, with a good beach.

At one time Skýros may have been two islands. Today's halves – **Merói** and **Vounó** – join in a noticeably flat valley connecting Kalamítsa Bay with Ahílli fishing port. In contrast to northerly Merói, Vounó (dominated by Mount Kóhilas) is relatively barren, though strong springs emerge on the northwest flank facing the "divide", and there is enough pasture on the heights for the island's wild ponies, which have been bred here since ancient times. Beaches, except for **Kolymbáda**, are few and compare poorly with those in the north. Most visitors are bound for **Trís Boúkes ⓭** and the **grave of Rupert Brooke**. Serving as a naval officer in the fleet bound for Gallipoli, the poet died of blood poisoning on a French hospital ship on 23 April 1915 and was buried in the olive grove here.

Roads beyond this point are minimal, and accordingly **boat excursions** from Linariá are popular. They visit **Sarakinó islet** with its sandy inlet and sea-caves in the sheer coastal cliffs extending all the way up to Ahílli, home to seemingly innumerable Eleonora's falcons.

*Fishing boats bobbing in Skýros harbour.*

*The Manos Faltaïts Museum above Skýros Town.*

# EVVIA

Greece's second-largest island is largely unspoilt by tourism, and little known to foreigners. Although barely separated from the mainland, Evvia has a distinctive character.

**⦿ Main Attractions**
Halkída Kástro
Erétria Museum
"Dragon Houses"
Kárystos
Dimosári Gorge
Límni

**Map on page 213**

Halkída, the capital of Evvia (Euboea) is close enough to the mainland for a draw-bridge and a newer suspension bridge to arc over. Aristotle is supposed to have been so frustrated by trying to under-stand the rapid, fluctuating tides in the Evripos channel here that he killed him-self by jumping into the roiling waters.

In antiquity Evvia's most prominent cities were Khalkis (modern Halkída) and nearby Eretria (Erétria), which both established colonies across the Mediterranean. Evvia then came under the control, over subsequent centuries, of the Athenians, Macedo-nians, Romans, Byzantines and Otto-mans, and became part of Greece in 1830, after the War of Independence.

**Halkída ❶** (Hálkis) is now an indus-trial town, but the **Kástro** district, with a 15th-century **mosque** and ornate **foun-tain**, plus the Crusader-modified **Church of Agía Paraskeví**, are worth visiting. In the newer district are an **Archaeologi-cal Museum** (Tue–Sun 8am–3pm) and, lodged in the old prison, a **Folklore Museum** (Wed–Sun 10am–1pm, Wed also 6–8pm), as well as a 19th-century **synagogue** still used by the remaining Jewish Romaniote community. **Erétria ❷** to the south is a crowded, grid-plan summer resort where ferries call from mainland Skála Oropoú. The **Archaeo-logical Museum** (Tue–Sun 8.30am–3pm) and adjacent archaeological site with its mosaics are worth a stop.

The road south hugs the coast past the attractive resort of **Amárynthos** until just before **Alivéri**, where it turns inland to a junction at **Lépoura**. The northerly option here goes through **Háni Avlonaríou**, with a large and unusual 13th-century **Basil-ica of Agios Dimítrios**, before continu-ing to **Stómio** beach. The road threads through **Platána** resort to the harbour at **Paralía Kými** and ferry to Skýros. **Kými** proper, up the hill, is a sizeable town, and start of a mountain road back to Halkída.

*The spa town of Loutrá Edipsoú.*

Southern Evvia, reached by the other option at Lépoura, is drier and less green. From the main road beyond Almyropótamos there are views down to the sea on either side. Near **Stýra** ❸ are the ruins of three mysterious stone buildings, known locally as "**Dragon Houses**" (drakóspita). The most convincing theory is that they are temples built by slaves or immigrants working nearby quarries in the Classical era.

The main town in the south is **Kárystos** ❹, stuck in a 1970s time-warp, with a long beach, scattered Roman ruins and a Venetian tower. On **Mount Ohi** (1,399 metres/4,617ft) just inland there's the medieval **Castello Rosso**, another drakóspito and the start of the three-hour traverse through the superb **Dimosári Gorge**.

Northeast of Halkída, **Stení** ❺, on the slopes of **Mount Dírfys** (1,743 metres/5,718ft), is a favourite goal for Athenians seeking clean air and grill restaurants. **Prokópi** ❻, on the main road north, sits on a broad upland purchased by Englishman Edward Noel in the 1830s. On Mount Kandíli to the west, the family estate of his descendants is available for holiday lets and hosts special-interest courses. Prokópi was settled after 1923 by refugees from Cappadocia who brought the relics of 18th-century Saint John the Russian (actually Ukrainian).

North of Prokópi lie some of Evvia's best beaches; most renowned is **Angáli**. Just uphill is **Agía Anna** ❼, with an excellent **Folklore Museum** (Wed–Sun 10am–1pm, 5–7pm). Continuing along this coast, you pass **Paralía Kotsikiás**, **Psaropoúli** and **Elliniká**, the last beach the smallest and prettiest.

**Límni** ❽ on the southwest coast is Evvia's beauty spot, a 19th-century port with an interesting **Ethnographic/ Archaeological Museum** (Mon–Fri 9am–1pm, Sat 10am–1pm, Sun 10.30am–1pm), and **Agíou Nikoláou Galatáki Convent** in the hills behind, its narthex vividly frescoed. Sadly, a summer 2016 forest fire devastated the entire area. The closest beaches are at **Spiáda** and **Hrónia**, on the way to **Loutrá Edipsoú** ❾, a spa town and ferry port with some imposing Belle Epoque and Art Deco hotels.

The Roman aqueduct on Lésvos.

Off Metallía beach, Thásos.

The view from the 18th-century
Panagía Glykofiloússa, Pétra.

# THE NORTHEAST AEGEAN

Thásos, Samothráki, Límnos, Ágios Evstrátios, Lésvos, Psará, Híos, Ikaría, Foúrni, Sámos.

*Lésvos pottery.*

The northeast Aegean islands have little in common other than a history of medieval Genoese rule. Thásos, Samothráki, Ágios Evstrátios and Límnos in the north have few connections with the south Aegean; indeed, Thásos belongs to the Macedonian province of Kavála, and Samothráki to Thracian Évros. Greeks' affection for these islands, so convenient for the mainland, exceeds that of foreign tourists. Except for marble-cored Thásos, these isles, as well as Lésvos, are volcanic in origin, with thermal springs, their slopes home to lava-loving oaks.

Lésvos, Híos and Sámos to the southeast were once prominent in antiquity, colonising across the Mediterranean and promoting the arts and sciences, though scant traces of ancient glory remain. All three served as bridges between Asia Minor and peninsular Greece and were joined to Asia Minor until Ice Age cataclysms isolated them. Turkey is still omnipresent on the horizon, less than 2km (1 mile) away across the Mykale Straits at Sámos. Híos, Sámos and Ikaría are rugged limestone and schist (with lots of granite, too, on Ikaría), forested with pine, olive, oak and cypress. Delicate wild flowers, especially on Sámos, heighten their appeal, and numerous small mammals and birds thrive, some (like Lésvos's red squirrel and Sámos's jackal) having migrated over from Anatolia before the rising, post-Ice Age sea marooned them. Beaches vary from long shores of fist-sized pebbles to sheltered, sandy crescents.

*Mykáli beach on Sámos.*

As ever, transport to, between and on these islands varies with population and level of tourism. Samothráki has a skeletal bus service and overpriced ferries or catamarans from Alexandroúpoli; Thásos has frequent buses and regular car ferries from Kavála and Keramotí. Límnos and Lésvos have regular flights and sailings from Piraeus, Lávrio and Thessaloníki, plus between each other; Híos is linked almost daily with Athens and Lésvos, less regularly with Lávrio, Sámos and Ikaría. Ikaría is connected to certain Cycladic islands. Sámos is best connected, with seasonal catamarans to all the isles from Pátmos to Kós, plus flights to Rhodes, and receives more international charters than the runner-up, Lésvos.

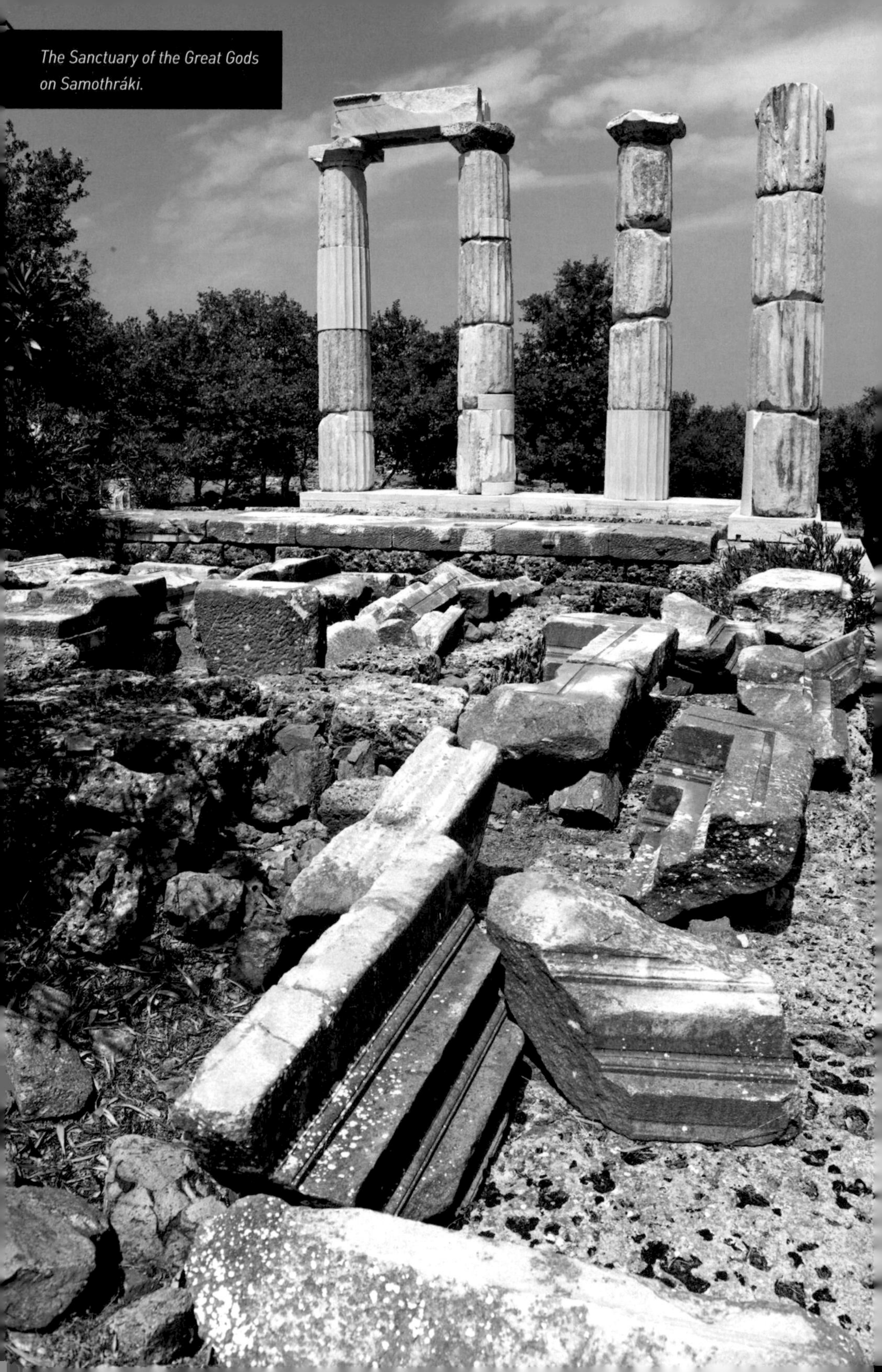

*The Sanctuary of the Great Gods on Samothráki.*

# THÁSOS, SAMOTHRÁKI AND LÍMNOS

Greece's most northerly islands see relatively few foreigners, but they offer more than enough by way of ancient ruins, empty beaches and picturesque villages.

Whether you want to wander through forest, laze on sandy beaches or take in some major archaeological sites, you will be happy on these northerly islands.

## THÁSOS

Just seven nautical miles from mainland Macedonia, Thásos – always a favourite retreat of northern Greeks – has, since the 1980s, welcomed a cosmopolitan assortment of foreigners. Yet the island seems relatively unspoilt, with package tourism well quarantined. Almost circular, mountainous Thásos is essentially a giant lump of marble, mixed with granite and schist, crumbling into white sand at the island's margins. Lower elevations, covered in olive plantations, remain attractive, but the "Diamond of the North" (Diamándis tou Vorrá) had its lustre severely dulled in 1981, 1985, 1989 and 1993 by forest fires, deliberately set by developers wanting cheap building land. Thásos is now three-quarters denuded of its original pine forest, which survives mainly in the northeast. Elsewhere, only the inland villages and a thin fringe of surrounding vegetation were saved, and while there is regrowth, it is painfully slow – it takes 50 years for a conifer forest to regenerate completely. The bus service around the coastal ring road is quite adequate, although most visitors hire motorbikes or cars (Thásos is small enough for a long day tour).

*Natural seawater pool on Thásos.*

The east and south coasts have better beaches; the west coast gives access to most inland villages.

Thásos's past glory, fuelled by local gold deposits, is evident at the harbour capital of **Liménas** ❶ (aka Limín, also just Thásos), where substantial remnants of the ancient town have been excavated; choice bits of the ruined **acropolis** are illuminated by night. Beginning at the Temple of Dionysos, a good path permits a rewarding walking tour of the ancient walls and acropolis, taking in the Hellenistic theatre,

⊘ **Main Attractions**

Acropolis and agora, Thásos
Alykí
Samothráki (Hóra)
Sanctuary of the Great Gods
Mýrina kástro
Evgátis beach
Allied World War I cemeteries

Map on page 222

medieval fortress, Temple of Athena and Shrine of Pan.

The biggest area of the Old City, behind the picturesque fishing harbour that traces the confines of the old commercial port, is the **agora**. In the nearby **Archaeological Museum** (Tue–Sun 8am–3pm), the prize exhibit is a 4-metre (13ft) -high Archaic *kouros* carrying a ram.

The first village clockwise from Liménas, slate-roofed **Panagía ❷**, is a large, busy place where life revolves around the *platía*, with its plane trees and four-spouted fountain. **Potamiá**, further down the valley, is less

architecturally distinguished: visitors come mainly for the sake of the **Polygnotos Vagis Museum** (May–Sept Tue–Sat 9.30am–12.30pm and 6–9pm, Sun 10am–12.30pm; free), featuring the work of the eponymous locally born sculptor. Beyond, the road drops to Potamiá Bay.

**Skála Potamiás**, at its south end, is all lodging and tavernas, with more of that to the north at **Hrysí Ammoudiá**. In between stretches a fine, blond-sand beach. There are even better strands at **Kínyra**, 24km (15 miles) from Liménas, but most tourists schedule a lunch stop at one of the several tavernas of

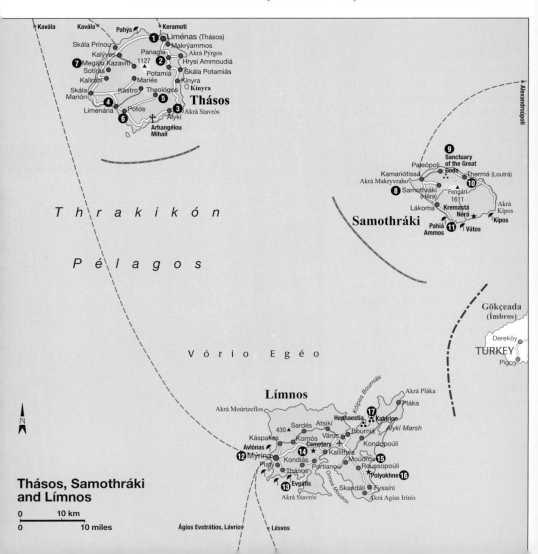

**Thásos, Samothráki and Límnos**

0    10 km

0    10 miles

**Alykí ③** hamlet, architecturally pre-served thanks to adjacent ruins: an ancient temple and two atmospheric Byzantine basilicas. The local topography of a low spit, sandy to the west, nearly pinching off a headland, is strikingly photogenic. So too is the **Convent of Arhangélou Mihaíl** 5km (3 miles) to the west, high above a barren coast – but mainly from a distance; it has been renovated hideously.

At **Limenária ④**, now the island's second town, Ottoman-era mansions of departed German mining executives survive. More intriguingly, it's the starting point for a safari to hilltop **Kástro**, the most naturally pirate-proof of the inland villages. Beyond Limenária, there's little to encourage a stop.

**Theológos ⑤**, actually reached from the overdeveloped resort of **Potós ⑥**, was the island's Ottoman capital, a linear place where most houses have walled gardens. **Mariés** sits piled up at the top of a wooded valley, just glimpsing the sea. By contrast, **Sotíras** enjoys phenomenal sunsets, best enjoyed from its central café under enormous plane trees. Of all the inland settlements, **Megálo Kazavíti ⑦** (Megálo Prínos) has the grandest *platía* and the best-preserved traditional houses, snapped up and restored by outsiders. Ground-floor windows still retain iron bars, reminders of pirate days.

## SAMOTHRÁKI

Samothráki (Samothrace) raises forbidding granite heights above stony shores and storm-lashed waters, both offering poor natural anchorage. Homer described Poseidon perching atop 1,611-metre (5,285ft) **Mount Fengári**, the Aegean's highest summit, to watch the action of the Trojan War just east. Fengári and its foothills occupy much of the island, with little level terrain except in the far west. Its southwest flank features scattered villages lost amid olive groves varied by the occasional poplar. North-facing slopes are damper, with chestnuts and oaks, plus plane trees along the numerous watercourses. Springs are abundant, and waterfalls even plunge directly to the sea at **Kremastá Nerá** in the south.

Only the northwest of the island has a rudimentary bus service. Tourism is barely developed, and the remaining islanders prefer it that way. In its absence the population has dipped below 3,000, as farming can only support so many. Boats and catamarans dock at **Kamariótissa**, the functional port where rental vehicles are in short supply.

**Hóra** or **Samothráki ⑧**, the official capital 5km (3 miles) east of Kamariótissa, is more rewarding, nestling almost invisibly in a circular hollow. A cobbled commercial street serpentines past basalt-built houses, many now uninhabited. From outdoor seating at the two tavernas on Hóra's large *platía*, you glimpse the sea beyond a crumbled Byzantine-Genoese fort at the edge of town.

Samothráki's other great sight lies 6km (4 miles) from Kamariótissa along the north coast road. From the late Bronze Age until the advent of

*Byzantine-era tower on Samothráki.*

Christianity, the **Sanctuary of the Great Gods**  was the major religious centre of the Aegean. Local deities of the original Thracian settlers were syncretised with the Olympian gods of later Aeolian colonists, in particular the *Kabiroi*, or divine twins Castor and Pollux, patrons of seafarers (who needed all the help they could get in the habitually rough seas hereabouts).

The sanctuary ruins (daily, 8.30am–3pm) visible today are mostly late Hellenistic, and eerily impressive, if half-overgrown. Obvious monuments include a partly re-erected Doric temple of the Second Initiation; the peculiar round Arsinoeion, used for sacrifices; a round theatre area; and the fountain niche where the celebrated Winged Victory of Samothrace, now in the Louvre, was found. This 4th-century BC statue of Victory (Athena Nike) was discovered in 1863 by the French diplomat Charles Champoiseau, who immediately sent it to Paris. The Greek government has long demanded its return, but so far has had to settle for a plaster copy. The site **museum** (same hours but closed Mon)

*Límnos windmill.*

contains finds from the Archaic to Byzantine eras.

Some 6km (4 miles) further east, hot springs, cool cascades and a dense canopy of plane trees make the spa hamlet of **Thermá**  (Loutrá) the most popular base on the island, patronised by an uneasy mix of the elderly infirm and young bohemian types, who used to flock to a late-summer psychedelic trance festival until it was shut down by the authorities. Hot baths come in three temperatures and styles – including outdoor pools under a wooden shelter – while cold-plunge fanatics make for **Gría Váthra** canyon to the east. Thermá is also the base camp for the climb up Mount Fengári, a six-hour round trip.

The villages south of Hóra see few visitors, though they lie astride the route to **Pahiá Ammos** , the island's only sandy beach. From **Lákoma** village, it's about 8km (5 miles) by road to the beach, where a single seasonal taverna operates. Beyond Pahiá Ammos, you can walk to smaller **Vátos** nudist beach, but you'll need a boat – or to drive clockwise completely around Samothráki – to reach the pebble beach of **Kípi** in the far southeast.

## LÍMNOS AND AGIOS EVSTRÁTIOS

Dominating the approaches to the Dardanelles, Límnos has been occupied since Neolithic times, and always prospered as a trading station and military outpost. The Greek military still controls much of the island's area, including half the airport, belying an otherwise peaceful atmosphere. The volcanic terrain subsides to excellent beaches, or produces excellent wine and other products. The surrounding seas yield plenty of fish, thanks to periodic migrations through the Dardanelles.

Most things of interest are found in the port-capital, **Mýrina** , or a short distance to either side – luckily, since the bus service is appalling and rental vehicles in short supply at peak season. Volcanic stone has been put to good

use in the older houses and street cobbles of Mýrina, while sumptuous Ottoman mansions face the northerly town beach of **Romeïkós Gialós**, with its popular cafés. The southerly beach of **Néa Máditos** abuts the fishing port with its seafood tavernas.

Mýrina's admirable **Archaeological Museum** (Tue–Sun 8am–3pm) holds finds from the island's several ancient sites. Public evidence of the town's Ottoman period is limited to an inscribed fountain and a dilapidated, octagonal dervish hall behind a supermarket, both near the harbour end of the long market street. Festooned over the headland above town, the ruined local *kástro* (always open) is worth climbing for sunset views.

The road north from Mýrina passes popular **Rihá Nerá** beach en route to an even better one at **Avlónas**. In the opposite direction lie decent beaches at **Platý** and **Thános**, with tiered namesake villages on the hillsides just above. Continuing southeast from Thános brings you to **Evgátis** ⓑ, acknowledged as the island's best beach. **Kondiás** ⓒ village just beyond is home to the **Balkan Art Gallery** (Sat–Thur 10am–2pm, 7.30–9.30pm), the result of a 2005 residential seminar organised by the Bulgarian painter Svetlin Russev.

Two Allied cemeteries maintained by the Commonwealth War Graves Commission flank the drab port town of **Moúdros** ⓓ. During World War I, Moúdros was the principal base for the disastrous Gallipoli campaign. Of roughly 36,000 casualties, 887 are buried outside Moúdros on the way to **Roussopoúli**, while 348 more lie behind the village church at **Portianoú**, across the bay.

Límnos's major archaeological sites all lie in the far east of the island. **Polyokhne** ⓔ (Polyóhni), southwest of Roussopoúli, was a fortified town even older than Troy, but was destroyed by an earthquake in 2100 BC and never rebuilt. **Hephaestia** (Ifestía) on the north coast was the island's ancient capital until the Byzantine period. The foundations of a temple of Hephaestos (the island's patron deity) and a Roman theatre are visible. Across the bay at **Kabirion** ⓕ (Kavírio) was a sanctuary to the *Kabiroi*. Not much remains except the stumps and bases of columns.

A sliver of land south of Límnos, **Ágios Evstrátios** (Aï Strátis) is the most desolate spot in the northeast Aegean, especially since a 1968 earthquake devastated the lone village. Owing to corruption, reparable dwellings were bulldozed and the surviving inhabitants (22 had died) given ugly, prefabricated replacement housing on a grid plan. This, plus 20 surviving old buildings on the left, is what you see when disembarking the mainline ferries stopping here on the Lávrio–Kavála route, or the Límnos-based *kaïki* – together Aï Strátis's lifelines.

Only fish abound here. There is little arable land aside from the valley behind the sad pre-fab settlement (population 200). A few taverna-cafés and pensions rely mostly on Greek summer tourists. You may just have company at one of the several beaches.

*Límnos' ruined kástro overlooks Mýrina town.*

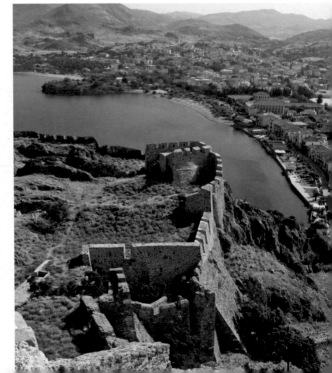

# LÉSVOS, HÍOS, IKARÍA, FOÚRNI AND SÁMOS

These were some of ancient Greece's wealthiest islands, although today there are more reminders of their dramatic recent history.

These islands, with their gentle wooded slopes, have long been popular with Greek visitors, who appreciate their relatively untouristed feel and natural advantages.

## LÉSVOS

Greece's third-largest island, measuring 70 by 40km (43 by 25 miles) at its widest, Lésvos is the antithesis of the *nisáki* (cute little islet). Between far-flung villages lie 11 million olive trees producing 45,000 tonnes of oil every year. Shipbuilding, fish-curing, *oúzo*-distilling and livestock-rearing remain important, but no enterprise rivals the olive, especially since it complements the second industry – tourism. Nets to catch this "black gold" are laid out in autumn, as soon as the tourists leave.

Lésvos was a preferred Roman holiday spot, what with its thick southern forests, idyllic orchards and hot springs– the island's thermal baths and spa facilities are still a considerable attraction. The Byzantines considered it a humane exile for deposed nobility, while the Genoese Gattilusi clan held court here from 1355 until 1462. To the Ottomans it was the "Garden of the Aegean", their most productive, strictly governed and heavily colonised Aegean island.

Following 18th-century reforms

*Taking the shade in Plomári.*

within the empire, a Christian land-owning aristocracy developed, served by a large population of labouring peasants. This quasi-feudal system made Lésvos fertile ground for post-1912 leftist movements, and its habit of returning Communist MPs since the junta fell has earned it the epithet "Red Island" among fellow Greeks. The years after 1912 also saw a vibrant local intelligentsia emerge, but since World War II Lésvos's socio-economic fabric has shrunk considerably with emigration to Athens, Australia and America. However, the

### Main Attractions

Theóphilos & Thériade Museums
Mólyvos
Sykiás Olýmbon Cave
Néa Moní
Armenistís beaches
Sámos Archaeological Museum
Evpalínio Órygma

Map on page 230

*Garlic for sale.*

*Mólyvos surmounted by its medieval castle.*

founding here in 1987 of the University of the Aegean has helped arrest decline.

**Mytilíni** , the capital (its name a popular alias for the entire island), has a revved-up, slightly gritty atmosphere, as befits a port town of almost 30,000. Behind the waterfront, assorted church domes and spires enliven the skyline, while Odós Ermoú one street inland threads through the heart of the bazaar, passing a mosque (ruined) and Turkish baths (well restored) en route. On the headland to the northeast sits the medieval *kástro* (Tue–Sun 8am–3pm), with internal structures from various eras.

Behind the ferry dock is the two-wing **Archaeological Museum** (Tue–Sun 8am–3pm); the new gallery a bit uphill features Hellenistic mosaics depicting scenes from Menander's comedies.

Even more noteworthy are two museums at **Variá**, 4km (2.5 miles) south of town. The **Theophilos Museum** (Tue–Sun 8.30am–3pm) contains more than 60 paintings by locally born Theophilos Hatzimihaïl, Greece's most celebrated Naïve painter. The adjacent **Thériade Museum** (Tue–Sun summer 9am–2pm, 5–8pm, winter 9am–5pm) was founded by another native son who, while an avant-garde art publisher in Paris, assembled this astonishing collection, with works by Chagall, Miró, Picasso, Matisse, Léger and others.

The road running northwest from Mytilíni follows the coast facing Turkey. **Mandamádos** ❷, 37km (23 miles) from Mytilíni, has a surviving pottery industry and, on the outskirts, the enormous **Monastery of the Taxiárhis**, with its much-revered black icon of the Archangel Michael. At **Kápi** the road divides; the northerly fork is wider, better paved and more scenic as it curls across the flanks of **Mount Lepétymnos**, passing by the handsome village of **Sykaminiá** ❸, the birthplace of novelist Stratis Myrivilis, and its photogenic, taverna-crammed port, Skála Sykaminiás.

You go back down to sea level at **Mólyvos** ❹ (officially Míthymna), linchpin of Lésvos tourism and understandably

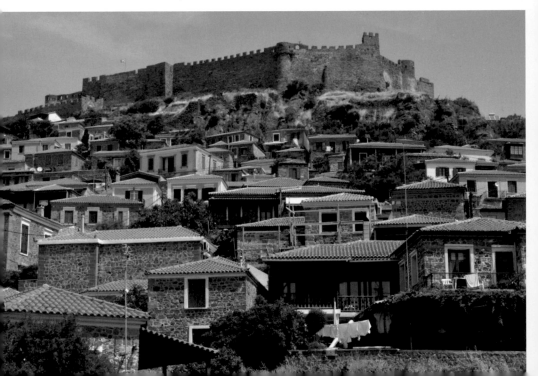

so: the ranks of sturdy tiled houses climbing to the medieval castle are an appealing sight, as is the stone-paved fishing harbour. But its days as a retreat for bohemian artists and alternative activities are over, with package tourism dominant since the late 1980s. **Pétra ❺**, 5km (3 miles) south, accommodates the overflow behind its long beach; inland looms a rock plug crowned with the **Panagía Glykofiloússa** church. At its foot the 18th-century **Vareltzídena Mansion** (Tue–Sun 8am–3pm; free) with its extensive murals is well worth a look, as is the frescoed, 16th-century church of **Agios Nikólaos**.

From Pétra, head 17km (11 miles) south to **Kalloní ❻** market town and the turning east for **Agía Paraskeví** with the excellent **Museum of the Olive-Pressing Industry** (March–15 Oct Wed–Mon 10am–6pm, closes 5pm winter), in the old communal olive mill.

Alternatively, head west towards more rugged **western Lésvos**, with its lunar volcanic terrain. Stream valleys foster little oases, such as the one around **Perivolís Monastery ❼** (daily 10am–1pm and 5–6pm), 30km (19 miles) from Limónos, decorated with wonderful frescoes. After 10km (6 miles), the **Monastery of Ypsiloú ❽** with its small museum, on top of an extinct volcano, contemplates the abomination of desolation – complete with scattered trunks of the "Petrified Forest", prehistoric sequoias mineralised by volcanic ash.

There are more fossilised trees in and around **Sígri ❾**, 90km (56 miles) from Mytilíni, a sleepy place flanked by good beaches, and very much the end of the line, though most years it's an alternative ferry port. Most people prefer livelier **Skála Eresoú ❿**, 14km (9 miles) south of Ypsiloú, for a beach experience on its 3km (2 miles) of sand. In particular, numerous lesbians come to honour Sappho, who was born here.

Southern Lésvos, between the two gulfs, is carpeted with olive groves and chestnut forests, rolling up to 968-metre (3,176ft) **Mount Olympos**. Back on the coast is **Plomári ⓫**, Lésvos's second town, famous for its *oúzo* industry; the Varvagiánni distillery lays on tours. Most tourists choose to stay at pebble-beach **Agios Isídoros** 3km (2 miles) east, although **Melínda** 6km (4 miles) west is more scenic. **Vaterá ⓬**, with its 7km (4.5-mile) sand beach, reckoned the best on the island, lies still further west, reached by a different road. En route, you can stop for a soak at the restored **medieval spa** – one of four on the island – outside **Polihnítos**, 45km (28 miles) from Mytilíni. Inland from Plomári, the remarkable hill village of **Agiásos ⓭** nestles in a wooded valley under Ólymbos. Its heart is the major pilgrimage church of **Panagía Vrefokratoússa**, focus of the 15 August festival, Lésvos's biggest.

## HÍOS, INOÚSSES, PSARÁ

Although Híos (alias Chíos) had been important and prosperous since antiquity, the Middle Ages made

*Lésvos claims to produce the finest olive oil in all Greece. The olives are harvested in November and December, and pressed within 24 hours of being picked.*

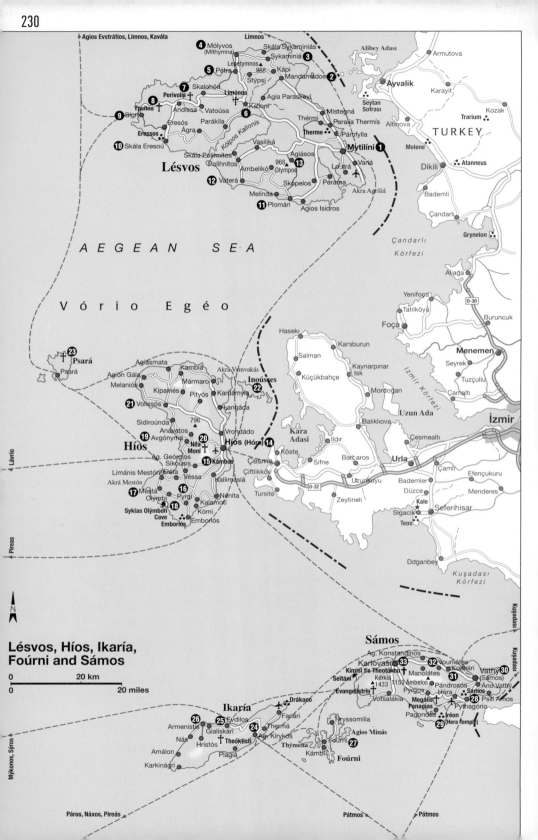

Lésvos, Híos, Ikaría,
Foúrni and Sámos

0        20 km
0        20 miles

the Híos of today. After the Geno-ese seized control here in 1346, the Giustiniani clan established a car-tel, the *maona*, which controlled the highly profitable trade in gum mas-tic. During their rule, which also saw the introduction of silk and citrus production, Híos became one of the wealthiest and most cultured islands in the Mediterranean.

In 1566 the Ottomans expelled the Genoese, but granted the islanders numerous privileges, so that Híos con-tinued to flourish until March 1822, when poorly armed agitators from Sámos convinced the reluctant Hiots to participate in the independence upris-ing. Sultan Mahmut II, enraged at this ingratitude, exacted a terrible revenge. A two-month rampage, commanded by Admiral Kara Ali, killed 30,000 island-ers, enslaved 45,000 more, and saw all the island's settlements razed, except the mastic-producing villages. Híos had only partly recovered from this out-rage when a March 1881 earthquake destroyed much of what remained and killed 4,000 people.

Today Híos and its satellite islet Inoússes are home to some of Greece's wealthiest shipping families. The cata-strophic 19th century ensured that **Híos Town** or **Hóra** ⓮ (population 32,000) seems offputtingly modern at first glance. But scratch the ferro-concrete surface and you will find traces of the Genoese and Ottoman years. The most obvious medieval feature is the *kástro*; moated on the landward side, it lacks a seaward rampart, destroyed after the 1881 earthquake.

Just inside the *kástro*'s impressive **Porta Maggiore** stands the **Giustiniani Museum** (Tue–Sun 8am–3pm), a con-tinually changing collection of frescoes and icons rescued from rural churches. On a small nearby square is the Mus-lim cemetery, with the tomb of Kara Ali – the admiral responsible for the 19th-century massacre, blown up along with his flagship by one of Admiral Kanaris's fire-boats in June 1822. The square itself is enlivened by a popular, trendy bar-ouzerí. Still further inside lies the old Muslim and Jewish quar-ter, with a derelict mosque, hamams

*Harvesting resin from mastic bushes, Híos.*

## ☉ THE MANY USES OF MASTIC

The mastic bushes (*Pistacia lentiscus; skhiniá* in Greek) of southern Híos are the unique source of gum mastic. In the past, it was used as a chewing gum to freshen the breath of the sultan's concubines; the Romans had toothpicks made from mastic since it kept their teeth white and prevented tooth decay; the "father of medicine", Hippocrates, praised its therapeutic value for coughs and colds; and lately some alternative medicine practi-tioners have made even more ambitious claims on its behalf.

The first stage of the mastic production process has remained unchanged since ancient times. In late summer, villagers make incisions in the bark of the trees, which weep resin "tears"; these are carefully scraped off and cleaned of leaves or twigs. Next, the raw "tears" are washed, then baked or sun-dried and re-formed at a processing plant. Up until 2012 when a devastating fire damaged the plantations, 150 tonnes of mastic were produced annually, most of it exported to Middle Eastern countries where it is a culinary spice; this level of production will dip for some time until the plantations recover.

It also appears in Greek *mastíha* liqueur, *tsouréki* bread and the chrism oil (*myron*) used in the Chrismation (confirmation) ritual of the Orthodox Church. Mastiha Shop (www.mastihashop.com) is a Greek chain retailing a range of mastic products, from shower gel to chocolate and nougat.

*Donkey taking shade under the olive trees.*

*An exquisite example of xystá decorations in Pyrgí.*

(one restored as an exhibit venue) and overhanging houses; Christians had to live outside the walls.

The lively bazaar extends south of central **Platía Vounakíou**, with Aplotariás as its backbone – fascinating alleys between this street and Venizélou culminate in a wonderful Belle Epoque meat-and-produce gazebo. Also on Platía Vounakíou, the former **Mecidiye Mosque** houses the **Byzantine Museum** (Tue–Sun 8am–3pm); the **Archaeological Museum** (Tue–Sun 8.30am–3pm), in the south of town, well lit and well laid out, is more rewarding.

South of Hóra lies **Kámbos** ⑮, a broad plain of high-walled citrus groves dotted with the imposing sandstone mansions of the medieval aristocracy, set back from narrow, unmarked lanes. Many were destroyed by the earthquake, while a few have been restored as accommodation or restaurants. Irrigation water was originally drawn up by a *manganós* or waterwheel; a few survive in the centre of ornately paved courtyards.

The onward road heads southwest towards southern Híos, with its 20 *mastihohoriá* (mastic villages), built as pirate-proof strongholds by the Genoese during the 14th and 15th centuries. Each village is laid out on a dense, rectangular plan, with narrow passages over-arched by earthquake buttresses, and the backs of the outer houses doubling as the perimeter wall.

**Pyrgí** ⑯, 21km (13 miles) from Hóra, is one of the best-preserved *mastihohoriá*. A passageway off its central square leads to Byzantine **Agii Apóstoli** church, decorated with later frescoes. In Pyrgí's back alleys, tomatoes are laboriously strung for drying in September by teams of local women. Some 11km (7 miles) west, **Mestá** ⑰ seems a more sombre, monochrome labyrinth, which retains defensive towers at its corners. Several houses have been restored as accommodation. Such quarters are typically claustrophobic, though, and guests will appreciate the nearby beaches of **Kómi** (sandy) and **Emboriós** (volcanic pebbles).

Southeast of Mestá is the mastic village of Olýmbi, after which the road south to the coast leads to the **Sykiás Olýmbon Cave** ⓲ (June–Aug Tue–Sun 10am–8pm, Sept 11am–6pm). Stumbled across as recently as 1985, this 150-million-year-old cavern, a riot of stunning rock formations, is fantastically floodlit.

From Mestá, if you have your own transport the beautiful, deserted west coast, with its many coves, is accessible via atmospheric **Véssa**, more open and less *kástro*-like than other *mastihohoriá*. Between **Kastélla** and **Elínda bays**, a good road snakes uphill to **Avgónyma** ⓳, a densely clustered village well restored by returned Greek-Americans. Just 4km (2.5 miles) north perches almost deserted, crumbling **Anávatos**, well camouflaged against its cliff. In 1822, 400 Hiots leapt from this to their deaths rather than be captured.

Some 5km (3 miles) to the east, **Néa Moní** ⓴ (daily summer 8am–1pm, 4–8pm, winter 8am–1pm, 4–6pm) constitutes one of the finest surviving examples of mid-Byzantine architecture, founded in 1049 by Emperor Constantine Monomahos IX. It suffered heavily in 1822 and 1881, first with the murder of its monks, plus the pillage of its treasures, and then with the collapse of its dome. Despite the damage, its mosaics of scenes from the life of Christ, which emerged in 2009 from a five-year restoration, are outstanding. The outbuildings have lain in ruins since the events of the 19th century. By the gate, an ossuary displays the bones of the 1822 martyrs, together with generations of monkish skulls. The onward road eventually takes you to castle-crowned **Volissós** ㉑ in the northwest. To either side of this half-empty village are the island's finest beaches – and visible scars from several fires since 1981, which have burnt two-thirds of Híos's forests.

Despite provincial appearances, the peaceful, green islet of **Inoússes** ㉒

(Oinoússes), some 16km (10 miles) north of Híos harbour by regular caique, is actually among the wealthiest territories in Greece, home to the Livanos, Lemos and Pateras shipping families. Appropriately, a marine academy training seamen for Greece's merchant fleet stands at the west end of the quay, with a small private maritime museum in the centre of the single town. Small but decent beaches lie to either side.

The tiny islet of **Psará** ㉓, about 30km (19 miles) offshore from Volissós, derives its name from the ancient Greek adjective *psarós* (grey) – and a grey place it is, especially since 1824, when 14,000 Ottoman troops landed here to avenge continued harassment of their shipping by Psaran Admiral Kanaris, who commanded the third-largest Greek fleet after those of Hydra and Spétses. Some 27,000 islanders died – many blowing themselves up in a ridge-top powder magazine rather than surrender – and only about 3,000 escaped. The Ottomans burnt any remaining buildings and vegetation.

*The Muslim cemetery in Híos kástro.*

**⊘ Fact**

Apparently impervious to the irony, the Greek air force has adopted the doomed aviator Ikaros as its patron.

Today about 400 inhabitants remain on melancholy Psará, its bleakness relieved only by occasional fig trees. Besides the lone port village, there's just a monastery in the far north, frequented once a year at its 5–6 August festival. Six beaches lie northeast of the port, each better than the one before. Just a few tourists trickle over from Híos on the local ferry from Híos town; long-haul ferries call rarely from Sígri on Lésvos, Límnos and Kavála.

## IKARÍA AND FOÚRNI

Narrow, wing-shaped Ikaría is named after the mythical Ikaros (Icarus), who supposedly fell into the sea nearby when his wax wings melted. One of the least developed large islands in the Aegean, Ikaría has little to offer anyone intent on ticking off four-star sights, but it appeals to those disposed to an eccentric, slightly Ruritanian environment. During both the 1930s Metaxas dictatorship and the 1946–9 Civil War, Ikaría served as a place of exile, first for opponents of Metaxas and then hundreds of Communists under house

arrest. Local people thought the latter were the most noble, humanitarian folk they had ever met, and still vote Communist in droves.

From 2012 on, Ikaría made the news with various articles entitled "The Island Where They Forgot to Die" or "Aegean Blue Zone", highlighting the unusual longevity of Ikarians and attributing this to a stress- and pollutant-free lifestyle, plus a healthy diet. Unfortunately for this thesis, since then many of the nonagenarians profiled have passed on, though this hasn't deterred eager "Blue Zone" tourists.

Although little more than a fishing village, **Agios Kírykos** ㉔ is the capital and main southerly port. Its tourist facilities are geared to the clientele at the neighbouring spa of **Thermá**. Beyond that, there is a long beach at **Fanári** and an impressive, 2011-restored Hellenistic tower at **Cape Drákano**.

Taxis are far more reliable than the bus for the spectacular 41km (25-mile) drive over the 1,000-metre (3,300ft) Atherás ridge to **Evdilos** ㉕, the north-facing second port and would-be resort. Another 16km (10 miles) takes you past **Kámbos**, with its sandy beach and ruined Byzantine palace, to **Armenistís** ㉖. Only here do foreign tourists congregate, for the sake of excellent beaches just east – **Livádi** and **Mesaktí** – though the surf can be deadly, with annual drownings.

**Nás**, 4km (2.5 miles) west, is named for the *náos* or temple of Artemis Tavropoleio, on the banks of the river, which drains to a popular pebble cove. **Gialiskári**, a fishing port 4km (2.5 miles) east of Armenistís, is distinguished by its photogenic jetty chapel.

There are few bona fide inland villages, as the proud Ikarians hate to live on top of each other, and like to keep plenty of room for orchards between their houses. Above Armenistís are four hamlets lost in pine forest, collectively known as **Ráhes**. At **Hristós**,

*Foúrni landscape.*

the largest of these, people cram the café-bars all night long, sleep until noon, and carry their belongings (or store potent local wine) in hairy goatskin bags. The surrounding countryside completes the hobbit-like image, with vertical natural monoliths and troglodytic cottages for livestock made entirely of gigantic granite or slate slabs. One of these formations, inland from Kámbos, shelters the **chapel of Theoskepastí**, just above frescoed **Theóktisti monastery**.

**Foúrni** ㉗, one of several islets southeast of Ikaría, makes a living from its thriving fishing fleet and boatyards. Seafood dinners figure high on the agendas of arriving tourists, who mostly stay in the main – and surprisingly large – port town. A road links this with Agios Ioánnis Hrysóstomos in the south – superior beaches like **Vlyháda**, **Kasídi** and **Vitsiliá** lie nearby – and Hryssomiliá in the far north, the only other habitations. Good beaches within walking distance south of the port include **Kámbi**, just over the ridge, with some tavernas, or the naturist beach of **Aspa** beyond.

# SÁMOS

Sámos, an almost subtropical island with vine terraces, cypress and olive groves, surviving forests of black and Calabrian pine, hillside villages, and beaches of every size and kind, appeals to numerous tourists. Half a dozen wildfires since 1986 – the worst in July 2000 – and development have blighted the eastern half of the island, but impassable gorges, the Aegean's second-highest mountain, and beaches accessible only on foot beckon in the far west.

Natural endowments take precedence here over man-made ones, and Sámos has an identity problem owing to a 15th-century depopulation and later recolonisation. First settled in the 13th century BC, by the 7th century Sámos was a major maritime power thanks

to its innovative triremes (warships), still shown on local wine labels. The island's zenith came under the rule (538–522 BC) of Polykrates, a brilliant but unscrupulous tyrant who dabbled in piracy. Wealth, however accumulated, supported a luxurious capital of 60,000, and a court attended by the likes of philosopher-mathematician Pythagoras, the astronomer Aristarhos and the bard Aesop. Decline ensued with Polykrates' death at the hands of the Persians, and the rise of Athens.

Heavily developed **Pythagório** ㉘ occupies the site of Polykrates' capital, three of whose monuments earned Herodotus' highest praise: "I have spoken at greater length of the Samians because of all the Greeks they have achieved the three greatest constructions." From the immense harbour mole constructed by ancient slaves (the first great construction), you can watch Mount Mykale in Turkey majestically change colour at dusk. The main in-town attraction is the **archaeological museum** (Tue–Sun 8am–3pm), where highlights include a huge hoard

*One column is all that remains of Polykrates' great temple to Hera. He planned it to be the largest temple in Greece, but it was never completed.*

*The remote chapel at Gialiskári port, Ikaría.*

*Giant kouros in the Archaeological Museum, Vathý.*

of Byzantine gold coins found in 1984, and monumental Roman statuary.

The 1,036-metre (3,400ft) **Evpalínio Órygma** (Eupalinian Tunnel), an aqueduct engineered by Eupalinos of Megara in the 6th century BC through the hillside northwest of town, is the second marvel, one of the technological wonders of antiquity. Surveying was so good that two work crews, digging from either end, met with no vertical error and a horizontal one of less than 1 percent. Re-opened in 2017 after long repair, you can trace its entire length (Tue–Sun 8.30am–3pm; no under-14s; book escorted visits on 22730 62813) along the catwalk used to remove spoil from the water channel far below. Most people choose the 30-minute "second itinerary", about halfway through the tunnel to the meeting point of two crews. Wearing supplied helmets is mandatory, as you *will* bang your head on the low ceiling.

The ruins of the third construction, the **Hera Temple ㉙** (ancient Heraion, Iréon in modern Greek; Tue–Sun summer 8am–8pm, winter 8.30am–3pm), stand 8km (5 miles) west of Pythagório, past coastal Roman baths. But Polykrates' grandiose commission was never completed, and Byzantine builders later pilfered most of the cut stone, save one column left as a navigation landmark.

**Vathý** or **Sámos Town ㉚**, built along a deep inlet on the north coast, has been the capital and main port since 1832. The **Archaeological Museum** (Tue–Sun 8am–3pm) is one of the best in the provinces, with a rich trove of finds from the Heraion. Given pride of place is a 5-metre (16ft) almost intact *kouros* (male votive statue), the largest ever found. The small-objects collection in a separate wing confirms the Middle Eastern slant of worship and clientele at the temple, with orientalised ivories and locally cast griffin's heads.

**Ano Vathý**, the large village clinging to the hillside 1.5km (1 mile) southeast, existed for almost two centuries before the harbour settlement. A pleasant stroll will take you through steep cobbled streets separating 18th- and 19th-century houses, their overhanging second storeys in lath and plaster more evocative of northern Greece and Anatolia than the central Aegean.

The first stop of note on the north-coast road is **Kokkári ㉛** after 12km (7.5 miles), a former fishing village now devoted to tourism. The original centre is cradled between twin headlands, and w ndsurfers zip along off a long, westerly pebble beach. Overhead loom the now much-denuded crags of **Mount Ambelos** (1,150 metres/3,773ft), formerly a favourite of hikers. Paths still go up directly from behind Kokkári, while cars climb a road just past sleepy **Avlákia** to **Vourliótes ㉜**, a thriving village with several tavernas. A trail (and a separate road from the pleasant coastal town of Agios Konstandínos) continue up to more dramatically set **Manolátes**, where some tavernas stay open in winter.

The coastal highway continues west to **Karlóvasi ㉝**, 29km (18 miles) from Vathý; just 3km/2 miles before, a side road leads up through Kondakéïka to the **Church of Kímisi tis Theotókou** at Petaloúda, the oldest (late 12th century) and most vividly frescoed of several painted chapels on Sámos.

Karlóvasi is a somewhat dishevelled place, sprawling over several districts. **Néo**, the biggest, has ornate mansions, and cavernous, derelict warehouses down by the water at **Ríva**, vestiges of the leather-tanning trade that thrived here before 1970. In one former warehouse, the excellent **Tanning Museum** (Mousío Vyrsodepsías; **unreliably** Tue–Sat 9am–2pm; free) gives a fascinating overview of the vanished industry, including massive machinery in situ. **Meséo** is more villagey, as is **Ano** (or Paleó), lining a vegetated valley behind the sentinel church of Agia Triáda. **Limín**, just below Ano, has most local tourist facilities, including the ferry port.

West of here beckon some of Sámos's best beaches, including **Potámi**, a sand-and-pebble stretch visited by most of Karlóvasi at weekends. Beyond Potámi, a pair of remote, scenic beaches at **Seïtáni** can only be reached on foot.

Karlóvasi lies roughly halfway round an anticlockwise loop of the island, threading an interior dotted with small villages of tiled, shuttered houses and churches with striped domes. At Agii Theodóri junction 5km (3 miles) south of Karlóvasi, the southwesterly turn takes you past **Ormos Marathókambos** port to **Votsalákia**, Sámos's largest beach resort. More secluded coves lie further west along the road curling around the base of **Mount Kérkis** (Kerketévs; 1,433 metres/4,700ft), which forms the west end of the island. The refuge of several hundred guerrillas, then Civil War fighters, from 1943 to 1948, it is usually climbed from uninhabited **Evangelístria Convent** on the south slopes – a full day's outing.

The southeasterly choice of route at Agii Theodóri heads for Pythagório. You could schedule stops in **Pýrgos** for a can of local honey, and at the **Monastery of Megális Panagías** (Mon–Sat 10am–1pm, 5.30–8pm), just below Mavratzéï, which has partly cleaned frescoes dating from around 1586, second in merit only to Petaloúda's.

*Lounging cat, Sámos.*

*Fishing boats in Pythagório harbour.*

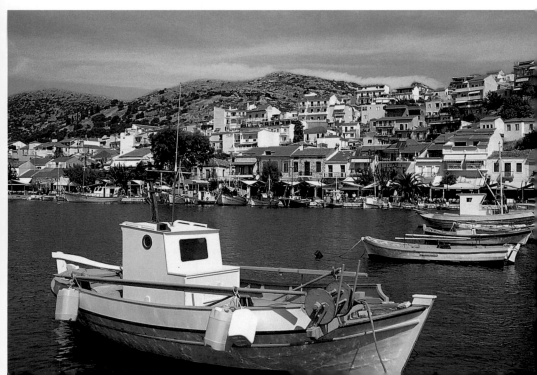

The view west from Kritinía castle, Rhodes.

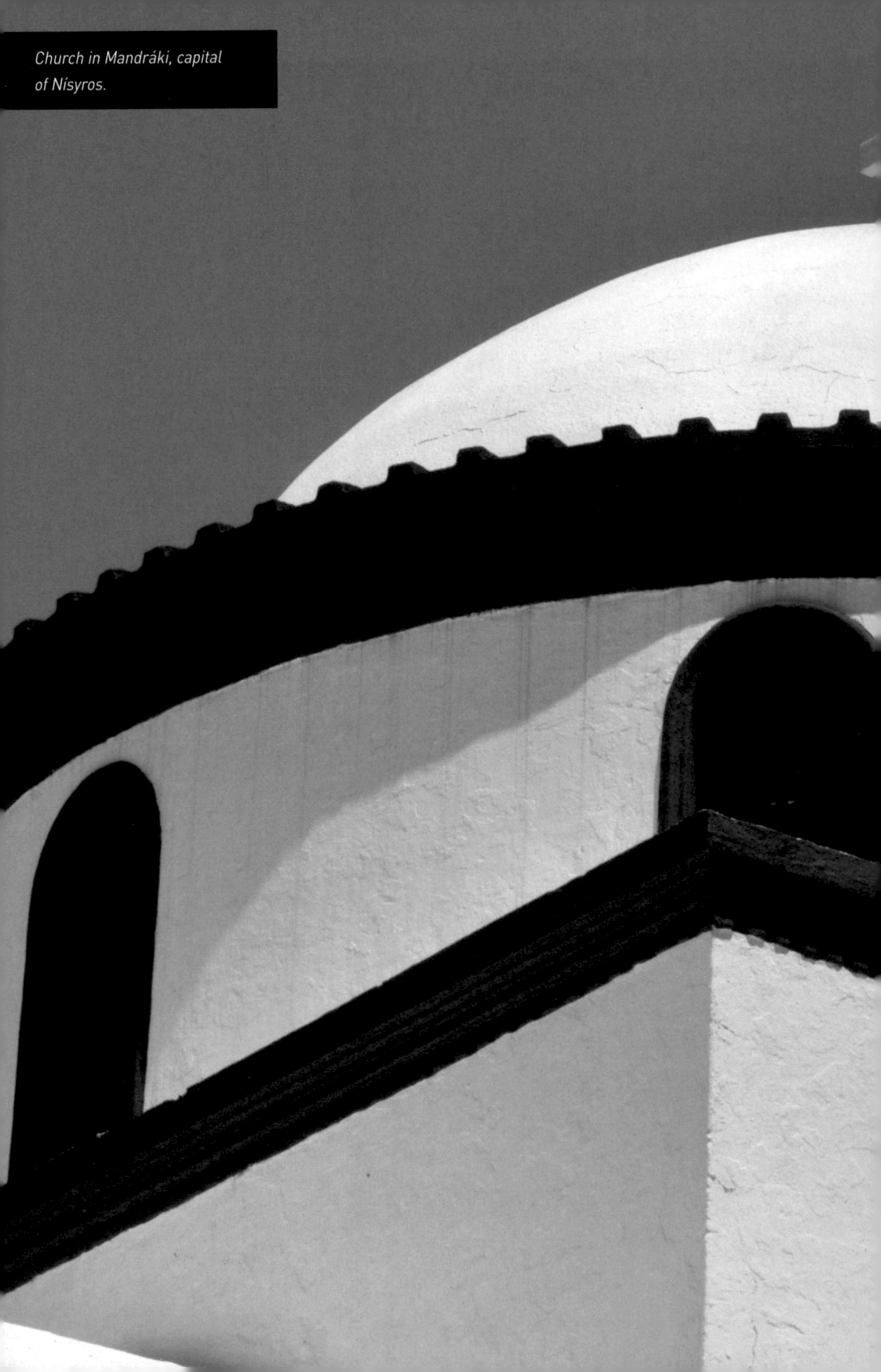

*Church in Mandráki, capital of Nísyros.*

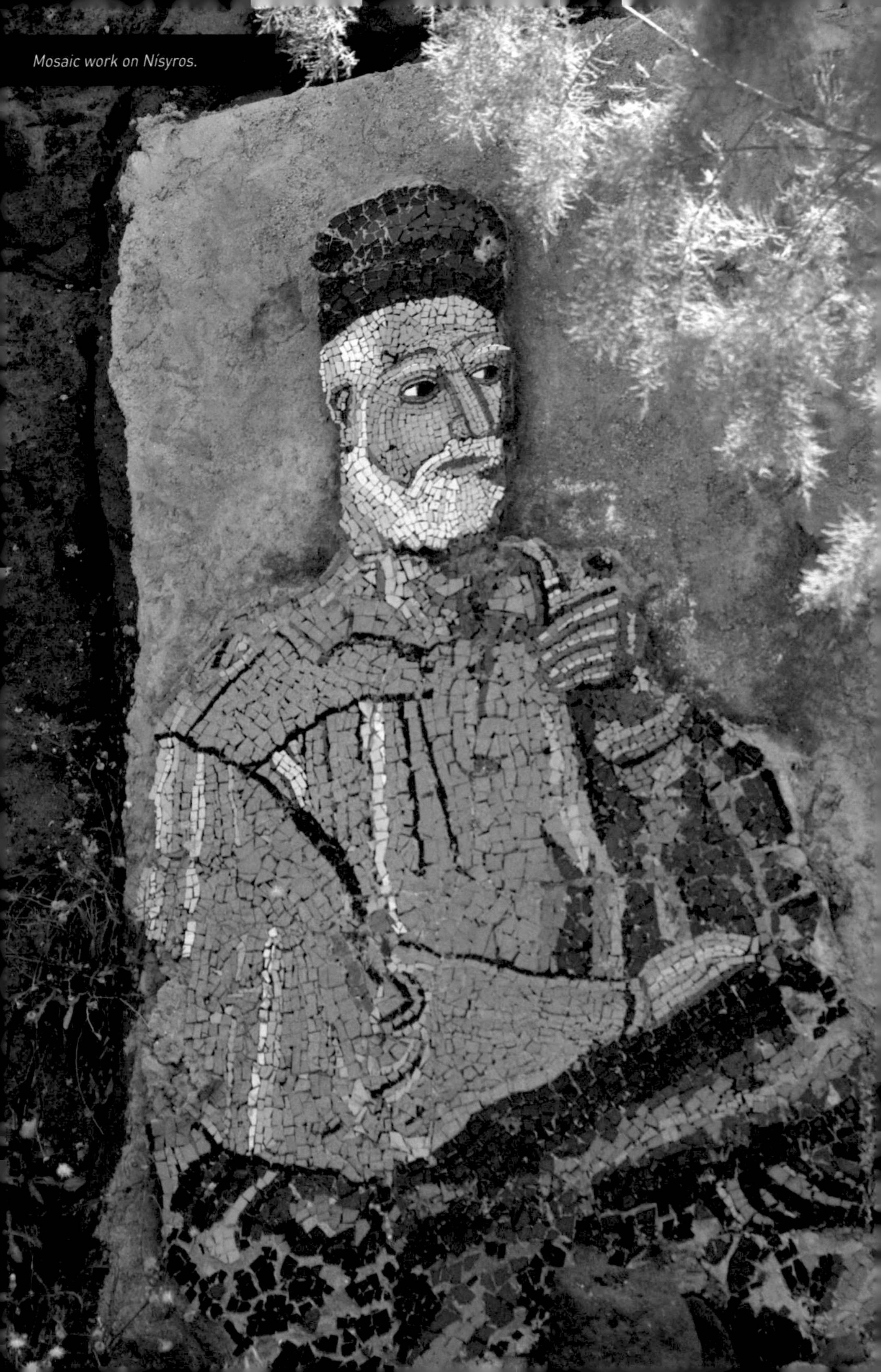
*Mosaic work on Nísyros.*

# THE DODECANESE

Rhodes, Kárpathos, Kásos, Hálki, Kastellórizo, Tílos, Sými, Nísyros, Kós, Psérimos, Astypálea, Kálymnos, Télendos, Léros, Lipsí, Pátmos, Arkí, Maráthi, Agathonísi.

*Young island-hoppers.*

The term "Dodecanese" is relatively new. When these far-flung islands were ruled by the Ottomans, they were known, incongruously, as the southern Sporades. In the early 1900s, in response to the withdrawal by the Young Turks of historic privileges granted by various sultans, 12 islands (*dódeka nisiá* in Greek) jointly protested. Their rebellion failed, but the name stuck – hence the Dodecanese (*Dodekánisos* in Greek). In fact, there have always been many more than 12 islands in this archipelago, depending on how you count: 14, 19 or (including every deserted islet) even 27 islands.

The 19 islands in these chapters are divided into three sections. Rhodes, as the capital and main local transport hub, appears separately. The collective term "Southern Dodecanese" means the islands immediately around Rhodes, most easily reached by a domestic or international flight into that island, followed by a feeder flight or ferry.

"Northern Dodecanese" islands, on the other hand, use Kós as the closest touchdown point, though some, such as holy Pátmos, are also easily reached from Sámos in the northeast Aegean. Seasonal catamarans or small *kaïkia* fill in the gaps between aircraft and conventional boats.

*Kós harbour.*

The Dodecanese were Greece's final territorial acquisition in 1948. Before that they were ruled (briefly) by the British, before which there had been a 21-month occupation by the Germans, who had succeeded the Italians upon their capitulation in late 1943. The Italians had ruled since 1912 with delusions of recreating the Roman Empire, leaving extravagant architectural follies to mark their passing. They had taken over from the Ottomans, who ousted the Knights Hospitaller of St John in 1523 and administered these islands (except for Rhodes and Kós) with benign neglect. To walk the streets of Kós or Rhodes is to witness a cultural patchwork: a minaret on one corner facing an Italian villa, across an expanse of excavated Hellenistic foundations, overshadowed by the fortifications of the crusading Knights.

# RHODES

According to the ancient Greeks, Rhodes was "more beautiful than the sun". Even today's brash resorts cannot dim the appeal of its benign climate, entrancing countryside and fascinating history.

### Main Attractions
Museum of Modern Greek Art
Lindos acropolis
Street of the Knights
Ancient Kameiros
Monólithos castle
Thárri monastery
Pigés Kallithéas

### Maps on pages
246, 252

The capital of the Dodecanese and the fourth-largest Greek island, Rhodes (Ródos) has been on the package-tour trail since the 1970s. It is one of the most cosmopolitan resorts in Greece, attracting every conceivable nationality in a seasonal repertory lasting from April to November: Italians and Spaniards in August (especially in the Old Town), Germans in spring and autumn out in the countryside, Scandinavians intent on sunshine and cheap booze during early summer, Israelis and Turks on gambling sprees, Brits and Russians seemingly all the time.

But far from the madding crowds in Rhodes Town (Old and New) and the serried ranks of umbrellas and sunloungers on the beaches, you can still find a more unspoilt island light years away from the laddish T-shirts and tawdry knick-knacks of the resorts. Frequent bus services run down both coasts from beside the "New Market", but it is worth hiring a car or jeep if you really want to explore deserted beaches, remote monasteries and castles perched above forest.

## PATCHWORK HISTORY

The legacy of ancient Greeks, crusading Knights of St John, besieging Ottomans and colonialist Italians forms a fascinating palimpsest in Rhodes Town, from castle turrets to the late

*Government House detail.*

Classical street plan. There are temple columns and Byzantine churches, mosques with minarets, plus the twin bronze deer guarding the waters of Mandráki harbour where, supposedly, the Colossus of Rhodes once stood.

This wondrous statue depicting Apollo Helios, the work of local sculptors Kharis and Lakhis, stood over 30 metres (100ft) tall. Legend made it even more impressive by describing it as standing astride the harbour entrance. But to do so it would have to have been more than 10 times its

*Wannabe ship's cat on Rhodes.*

actual size, an impossible engineering feat. Wherever it actually was, the monument stood until collapsing in an earthquake in 226 BC. The bronze was sold for scrap during the 7th century AD, carted away on camels.

Late in the Byzantine era, Rhodes was governed by the Genoese – until the Knights of St John, who had fled Jerusalem via Cyprus, captured the city in 1309, beginning a rule that lasted 213 years, under 19 Grand Masters. They substantially refortified the city, and raided Ottoman shipping. Finally, on New Year's Day 1523, Sultan Süleyman the Magnificent took Rhodes after a six-month siege that pitted 200,000 warriors against 650 knights. The Grand Master and 180 surviving brethren surrendered and, with a number of civilians, were allowed safe conduct to Malta. The Ottomans held the island for 390 years. Churches were converted to mosques, and Christians were banned from living within the city walls.

In late 1912, Italy occupied Rhodes while at war with Turkey, and embarked on a massive archaeological re-construction programme. During World War II, when Italy capitulated in 1943, the Germans took over. Rhodes was liberated by the Allies in 1945, and the Greek flag hoisted three years later when the Dodecanese became united with Greece.

These days, the island is still under siege – by tourists. Present-day **Rhodes Town ①** (Ródos) divides neatly into the various parishes of the New Town (Neohóri), settled by Greeks in Ottoman times, and the Old City. The contrast is marked: fast food, designer clothes and beaches on three sides, versus cobbled streets and a village-like feel.

## THE NEW TOWN

Here, smart shops abound, peddling designer labels at northern European prices and above despite the crisis (except during the August and February sales). Inexpensive umbrellas are big business here, and you can have any logo you like embossed on them. Sit and watch the world go by from

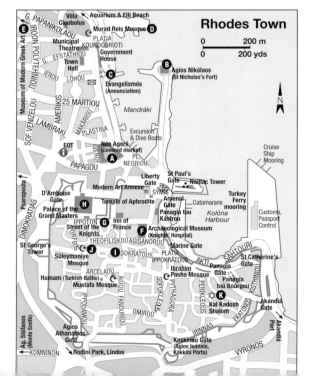

### ⊘ A GRAND PALACE

The **Palace of the Grand Masters** (summer daily 8am–8pm, winter Tue–Sun 8am–3pm) was almost completely destroyed when a munitions store in the nearby church of St John exploded in 1856, killing 800 people. During 1937–9, it was rebuilt by the Italians as a summer residence for King Victor Emmanuel and Mussolini, neither of whom ever used it. Traipse up the grandiose staircase to view ostentatious upper-floor decorations, including Hellenistic mosaics brought here from Kós. Two adjacent ground-floor galleries are devoted to ancient Rhodes and medieval, pre-Ottoman Rhodes, which, with their coverage of daily life in the Hellenistic city and the role of the Knights' outpost as a trade entrepôt respectively, are jointly the best museums on the island.

one of the expensive, touristy pavement cafés at **Mandráki** port. Marginally cheaper are the cafés inside the Italian-built **covered market Ⓐ** (Néa Agorá), whose highlight is a whimsical raised gazebo from which fish was once sold.

Excursion boats leave Mandráki quay by 9am for the island of Sými, usually calling first at Panormítis Monastery, or heading down the east coast to Líndos. But all scheduled services (except for catamarans, leaving from Kolóna) depart from Akandiá harbour, a hot 25-minute walk (or more sensibly, short if expensive taxi-ride) east.

Mandráki, guarded by the lighthouse bastion of **Agios Nikólaos Ⓑ**, is also an established port of call on the international yachting circuit, with local charters, too. Along the west quay stands a cluster of Italian-built monuments (see page 255), in its time the Foro Italico: they include the provincial administration building with its Gothic arches; the **Church of the Annunciation Ⓒ** (Evangelismós) next door, with superb 1950s frescoes by neo-Byzantine artist Photis Kontoglou; and across the way the post office, town hall and municipal (originally the Puccini) theatre, all in quick succession.

Opposite the theatre, the **Murad Reis Mosque Ⓓ** stands beside one of the island's larger Muslim graveyards. On the other side of this is the **Villa Cleobolus**, where Lawrence Durrell lived from spring 1945 to spring 1947, while working as a British-occupation civil servant. A stroll along popular **Élli beach**, past the **casino** installed in the Italian-era Albergo delle Rose, brings you to Rhodes's northernmost point, with its Italian-built **Aquarium** (daily; summer 9am–8.30pm, winter 9am–4.00pm). Immediately south, on Ekatón Hourmadiés (Hundred Date Palms) square (actually an oval), stands the **Museum of Modern Greek Art Ⓔ** (Tue–Sat 8am–3pm). Housed in the Nestorídio Mélathro, this is the most important collection of 20th-century Greek painting outside Athens or Andros. Two annexes (one in the Old Town) host worthwhile temporary exhibits; one ticket allows entry to all sites.

Inland Neohóri was once the nightlife capital of the Dodecanese, but a change in tourism patterns combined with the ongoing economic slump has cut a huge swathe through the bars – perhaps 20 remain from a 1990s zenith of 200. Surviving establishments tend to line Orfanídou and its perpendicular streets, just in from westerly, wind-buffeted **Psaroupoúla** beach.

Some 2km (1 mile) southwest of Mandráki, **Monte Smith** – more correctly, Agios Stéfanos hill – offers panoramic views over the town and sea on both sides. This was the site of Rhodes's Hellenistic acropolis, with a stadium, a heavily restored *odeion* and evocatively re-erected columns of a Temple of Apollo dating from the 3rd century BC. South of town, en route to Líndos, **Rodíni Park**, set in a canyon,

*The sublime Aphrodite Bathing wrings out her tresses in Rhodes' Archaeological Museum.*

*A loophole in the city walls.*

was the home of the ancient rhetoric school and is today a shady, cool streamside retreat with little dams, bridges and – on the clifftop just south – a large fenced reserve for the miniature Rhodian deer, *Dama dama*.

## THE OLD TOWN

The medieval walled town, a Unesco World Heritage Site, with its ramparts and 11 surviving gates, is so well preserved a visitor half expects to bump into a Knight of St John in one of the narrow cobbled streets. Most main streets follow their right-angled ancient predecessors: in the maze-like Ottoman quarters, it's easier to get lost.

Step through the northernmost **Liberty Gate** (Pylí Eleftherías) into **Platía Sýmis** to view the foundations of a Temple of Aphrodite, and the main annexe of the Modern Art Museum. Contiguous **Platía Argyrokástrou** is flanked by the Inn of the Order of Auvergne and the Knights' cathedral, **Panagía tou Kástrou**, formerly a Byzantine museum; its collection of icons

and frescoes rescued from rural chapels has been moved to the Palace of the Grand Masters.

Next stop is the 15th-century **Knights' Hospital ⓕ**, now the **Archaeological Museum** (summer daily 8am–8pm, winter Tue–Sun 8am–3pm). Among the exhibits in the Hellenistic statuary gallery is the eerily sea-eroded *Aphrodite Adioumene*, Durrell's "Marine Venus", and the more accessible *Aphrodite Bathing*, wringing out her tresses.

From the museum, the **Street of the Knights ⓖ** (Odós Ippotón) leads in medieval splendour uphill to the **Palace of the Grand Masters ⓗ** (see page 246). Italian-restored, and preserved from commercialisation, the thoroughfare houses more inns of the Knights, as their lodgings were divided by linguistic affinity. The **Inn of France**, emblazoned with the heraldry of several Grand Masters and now the French consulate, is the most imposing.

The main commercial thoroughfare is **Sokrátous ⓘ**, hosting a few

*Agios Nikólaos bastion guards Mandráki port.*

jewellers and fur shops but mostly ever-tattier tourist knick-knacks and T-shirt shops. Sokrátous links **Platía Ippokrátous** with its ornate fountain and Kastellanía (medieval "stock exchange") with the pink **Süleymaniye Mosque**  at the top of the hill, restored in 2011 but not yet open to the public. The Old Town still has a sizeable Turkish minority, using the active Ibrahim Pasha and Mustafa mosques on Plátonos and Platía Aríonos respectively, though since the Cyprus crises they deliberately keep a low profile.

Another distinguished Ottoman monument on Platía Aríonos, esteemed by Orthodox and Muslim alike, is the **hamam** (Turkish baths or Dimotiká Loutrá; closed indefinitely).

The other local minority that dwelt in the Old Town were the Jews, deported to Auschwitz by the Nazis in June 1944. Few returned, and their **synagogue Kal Kadosh Shalom** (15 April–15 Nov Sun–Fri 10am–3pm) on Simíou is essentially maintained as a memorial, although it also contains an excellent museum (www.rhodesjewishmuseum.org; Apr–Oct Sun–Fri 10am–3pm) on the former life of the community and its far-flung diaspora. Surviving **nightlife**, pitched at Greek rather than foreign tourists, comprises a half-dozen or so of high-decibel, annually changing bars on Platía Aríonos.

## THE WEST COAST

Rhodes's west coast is the damper, windier, greener side of the island, with agriculture at least on a par with tourism. Scrappy shingle beaches failed to slow hotel construction at **Ixiá** and **Triánda**, busy resorts that blend into each other and Neohóri. A road leads inland 5km (3 miles) from Triánda to the site of ancient **Ialysos** ❷ (summer daily 8am–8pm, winter Tue–Sun 8am–3pm), better known today as **Filérimos**, after the Byzantine monastery established here. Of the ancient city, only a Doric fountain and some Hellenistic temple foundations are evident. The restored Gothic **monastery**, with its vaulted chambers, early Christian

*Rhodes souvenirs.*

*Monastery icon of St Peter.*

*Archaeological Museum, Rhodes Old Town.*

mosaic floor and rampant bougainvillea, is the main attraction.

The **airport** lies between coastal Kremastí and **Paradísi** village, to whose cafés tourists often resort for solace when their homeward flights are delayed (a not uncommon occurrence).

Just past Paradísi, another inland turning leads to a famous Rhodian beauty spot, the **Petaloúdes** ❸ (Butterfly Valley; Apr–Oct daily 8am–5pm). The access road crosses the canyon about halfway along its length. Head upstream or downstream, along paths and over bridges, past the *Liquidambar orientalis* (sweetgum) trees on which Jersey tiger moths roost during summer. Black and yellow when at rest, they flash bright red wing-tops in flight. From the top of the valley, about 6km (4 miles) inland from **Soroní** on the coast road, a side road leads to the **Agios Soúlas Monastery,** whose 29–30 July festival features donkey races.

The other big tourist attraction of the west coast, 32km (20 miles) from Mandráki, is Italian-excavated **ancient**

**Kameiros** ❹ (summer daily 8am–8pm, winter Tue–Sun 8am–3pm). While no single monument stands out, it's a remarkably complete Doric townscape, without the usual later accretions. Unusually, there were no fortifications, nor an acropolis, on the gently sloping hillside.

Back on the coast again, **Skála Kamírou** (alias Kámiros Skála) is a small port with touristy fish tavernas, and afternoon ferries for the tiny island of **Hálki** opposite. **Kritinía** ❺ castle (unlocked) just overhead, one of the Knights' rural garrisons, is today a dilapidated shell but merits a visit for the views out to sea. The chapel has been consolidated in anticipation of becoming a small museum, which has yet to happen.

## THE INTERIOR AND FAR SOUTH

Inland from Skála Kamírou, sitting at the base of 1,215-metre (3,986ft) Mount Attávyros, **Embona** ❻ is the centre of the Rhodian wine industry; products of the private Alexandris

winery are considered the best. Roads looping around the base of the mountain through conifer forests to the east and west converge on the attractive village of **Siána**, famous for its honey and *soúma* – a strong, deceptively smooth grape-distillate spirit. Some 4km (2.5 miles) further, flat-roofed **Monólithos** ❼ village gives access to the eponymous **castle** (unlocked) perched on a narrow pinnacle, with a 200-metre (656ft) sheer drop all around and sweeping views west, which makes up for the fact that little remains inside. The road then continues down to the secluded **Foúrni** beaches.

Inland Rhodes is the perfect antidote to the coastal resorts, its rolling hills still partly wooded despite repeated fires started by arsonists since the late 1980s. Spared so far is densely shady **Mount Profítis Ilías** (798 metres/2,618ft), from where an old trail descends to the village of **Sálakos**, near which "Nymph" brand spring water is bottled.

Alternatively, from **Apóllona** on the mountain's south side, a paved road leads through a burnt zone, the result of a 2008 fire, to **Láerma**, and thence to the Byzantine **Thárri Monastery** ❽, reinhabited in 1990 by monks who oversaw the cleaning of its vivid 13th- to 15th-century frescoes. The road continues in round-about fashion via Profýlia and Kiotári to **Asklipió** village, where slightly later frescoes in the church of **Kímisi tís Theotókou** ❾ are in better condition, owing to the dry climate. Together these constitute the finest Byzantine art in situ on the island.

From Asklipió you return to the southeast coast at **Kiotári**, a post-1995 resort with a number of large hotels, and **Gennádi**, with vast stretches of sand-and-pebble beach. Further south, **Plimmýri** has a lovely medieval church and a sandy bay; **Prassonísi** (Leek Island) at Rhodes's southern tip is tethered by a broad, sandy causeway much favoured by windsurfers. The main island coast road loops back to Monólithos via the villages of **Kattaviá** and **Apolakkiá**, 4km (2.5 miles) north of which is the tiny Byzantine chapel of

### ⟳ Fact

Skiádi Monastery has a miraculous icon of the Panagía (Blessed Virgin) which supposedly bled when it was stabbed by a heretic in the 15th century.

*Knights' Castle at Kritinía.*

*The big rotunda at Pigés Kallithéas.*

**Agios Geórgios Várdas**, with smudged but most engaging frescoes.

Most inland villages here are moribund, with house owners living in Rhodes Town or overseas. This is especially evident in the old quarter of **Lahaniá** near Plimmýri, though the wonderful square with its taverna and pair of fountains beneath a plane tree remains traditional. From here head northwest to the fine hilltop village of **Mesanagrós**, where a 13th-century chapel hunches amidst the larger foundations of a 5th-century basilica. If you're overtaken by darkness and can't face the drive back to town, the kindly keepers at **Skiádi Monastery ⑩** just to the west may invite you to use the (gender-segregated) guest quarters.

## THE EAST COAST

The east coast, sandier and more sheltered than the west, with a warmer sea, was only developed for tourism after the 1970s, and much of it remains unspoilt. **Koskinoú** is famous for its ornate doorways and intricate pebble-mosaic courtyards. Immediately downhill, **Pigés Kallithéas ⑪** (daily summer 8am–8pm, winter 9am–3pm), a former Italian spa, is a

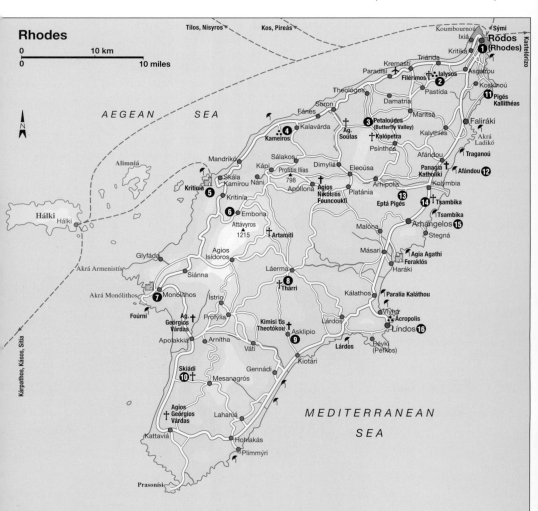

## Rhodes

0 — 10 km
0 — 10 miles

*AEGEAN SEA*

*MEDITERRANEAN SEA*

splendid orientalised Art Deco folly built by the Italians, complete with domed pavilions and palm trees. One rotunda is home to a small exhibition space and a permanent gallery on the history of the spa, which had its heyday from 1910 to 1940. Below the spa, various rock-girt beaches with supplemented sandy patches are popular, as there are no other swimming spots this close to Rhodes Town with any real character.

Wall-to-wall, multi-storey hotels pitched mainly at families characterise the north end of **Faliráki Bay**. Faliráki proper, to the south, is now but a shadow of its former youthful, boozy self since a 2003 crime spree prompted a police crackdown, and the more recent economic crisis administered the coup de grâce.

Immediately to the south looms **Cape Ladikó**, where *The Guns of Navarone*, starring Anthony Quinn, was made in 1961. Beyond the cape stretches the long, scarcely developed pebble-and-sand beach of **Afándou** ⓬. Just off the main road, peek inside **Panagía**

**Katholikí** church with its recently cleaned Byzantine frescoes.

## INLAND BEAUTY SPOT

Heading inland from the Italians' model-farm scheme at **Kolýmbia**, you reach the leafy glades of **Eptá Pigés** ⓭ (Seven Springs), one of Rhodes's most popular beauty spots. These springs feed a small reservoir dammed by the Italians to irrigate their Kolýmbia colony. If you do not suffer from claustrophobia, explore an aqueduct-tunnel leading to the little lake, or you can walk there overland, in the company of peacocks screaming in the trees.

The Greek "approach" to fertility treatment, **Tsambíka Monastery** ⓮, teeters high on the headland behind Kolýmbia, overlooking a sandy namesake beach to the south. It is believed that the Virgin, to whom the monastery is dedicated, can make women fertile. The tiny, well-restored monastic church is therefore a magnet for childless women, who come as barefoot pilgrims to revere an 11th-century icon at the 8 September festival.

*Líndos and its Knights' castle.*

*Tsambíka Monastery icons.*

**Arhángelos** , 29km (18 miles) from Rhodes Town, is the island's largest village, although its former crafts tradition is now only indicated by some pottery studios on the bypass road. Good beaches are found nearby at **Stegná** and at **Agía Agathí**, the latter reached via the little resort and pebble beach of **Haráki**, overlooked by the crumbled Knights' castle of **Feraklós**. Better than any of these, however, is the 4km (2.5-mile)-long, undeveloped beach of **Paralía Kaláthou**, beyond Haráki.

## LÍNDOS

There are regular buses to cover the 56km (35 miles) from Rhodes Town to **Líndos** , but it's more relaxing to take a boat trip and enjoy the coastal scenery. Huddled beneath yet another Knights' castle, Líndos, with its tiered, flat-roofed houses, appears initially to be the dream Greek village. But the narrow lanes of the hottest spot on Rhodes teem with day-trippers and local overnighters in high season. Medieval captains' mansions have ornate gateways and vast pebble-mosaic courtyards. Near the main square, the originally Byzantine **Panagía Church** (Mon–Sat 9am–3pm, 6.30–8pm, Sun 9am–3pm; free) preserves vivid 18th-century frescoes by Gregory of Sými. Donkeys, the Lindian taxi service, haul tourists up the steep gradient to the ancient acropolis inside the Knights' castle, with its Temple of Lindian Athena, Hellenistic stoa, and unbeatable views over 40km (25 miles) of coast.

Late into the night the village throbs to the beat of numerous bars, while by day the sand lining the northerly former port is dense with sunbathers, packed together like sardines in a can. The southern harbour, with a slightly quieter beach, is called St Paul's Bay, in honour of the Apostle who landed here in AD 58.

Líndos dates back to the Bronze Age, thanks to the only protected harbour on the island aside from Rhodes Town. With such barren surroundings, it always lived from the sea (though a spring provides ample water). In the 1960s, this then-remote spot attracted Italian, German and British painters, writers and hippie drop-outs. Past alumni include the newspaper astrologer Patric Walker (1931–95), academic and writer Germaine Greer, American humorist S.J. Perelman and various members of Pink Floyd. But now Líndos's days as an artistic colony are long over, superseded by the era of mass tourism.

Around the limestone headland, **Pévki** (Péfkos) is less frenetic than Líndos; it was originally an annexe of the latter but is now a package resort in its own right. Its beaches are small and hidden away. At **Lárdos**, 4km (2.5 miles) west, the long, gravelly beach is obvious as you approach, and is encroached upon by large hotels; **Glýstra** beach just beyond is more scenic and protected.

*Haráki resort and bay.*

# ITALIAN ARCHITECTURE IN THE DODECANESE

The Greeks understandably wanted to ignore the Italians' three-decade presence, but now recognise that their architecture had ample merit.

Thirty-one years of Italian rule in the Dodecanese left a significant architectural heritage, which has only recently begun to be appreciated. Many structures were long neglected, apparently a deliberate policy by the Greeks, who would prefer to forget the entire Italian legacy, but since the late 1990s maintenance and repair work has been undertaken. In Lakkí, on Léros in the Northern Dodecanese, buildings along the grand boulevards and landscaped squares have undergone a thorough renovation in recent years (see page 279).

These buildings are often erroneously dubbed "Art Deco"; while some, like Rhodes Aquarium and the stadium, certainly contain elements of that style, most are properly classed as Rationalist, or (on Léros) Streamline Modern. They grew out of various post-World War I European architectural, artistic and political trends, particularly Art Deco's immediate predecessor, Novecento, which originated in a movement born in Milan in 1922. The collectivist ideologies of the time were also influential, as were the paintings of Giorgio di Chirico, the Greek-Italian painter born in Vólos in 1888.

From 1924 to 1936, Italy attempted to combine Rationalist architecture and local vernacular elements, both real and semi-mythical, into a supposed generic "Mediterranean-ness". Every island got at least one specimen in this "protectorate" style, usually the police station, the post office, covered market or governor's mansion, but only on the most populous or strategic Dodecanese islands like Rhodes, Kós, Kálymnos and Léros were plans drawn up for comprehensive urban reordering.

On Rhodes, this meant the creation of a Foro Italico (administrative centre) at Mandráki. The evolving imperatives of Fascism also required a square (in Rhodes, the Piazza dell'Imperio in the Foro Italico) for large-scale assemblies. There were also structures in neo-Crusader style, such as the Cathedral of St John (now Evangelismós).

The period 1936–41 was marked by intensified Fascist ideology and increased reference to the islands' Latin heritage (the Romans and their purported successors, the Knights of St John). This entailed "purification", stripping many public buildings in Rhodes (although not in Kós, where a 1933 earthquake devastated much of the town) of orientalist ornamentation, and replacing it with poros stone (*porópetra*) cladding to match medieval structures in the Old Town. Added to this was a monumental severity and rigid symmetry – as with the theatre in Rhodes – echoing institutional buildings (especially Fascist Party headquarters) in Italy. Many Old Town buildings from the Knights' era were restored or, in the case of the Palace of the Grand Masters (see page 246), entirely rebuilt.

*St Francis of Assisi Cathedral, Rhodes.*

*The Port of Gialós, Sými.*

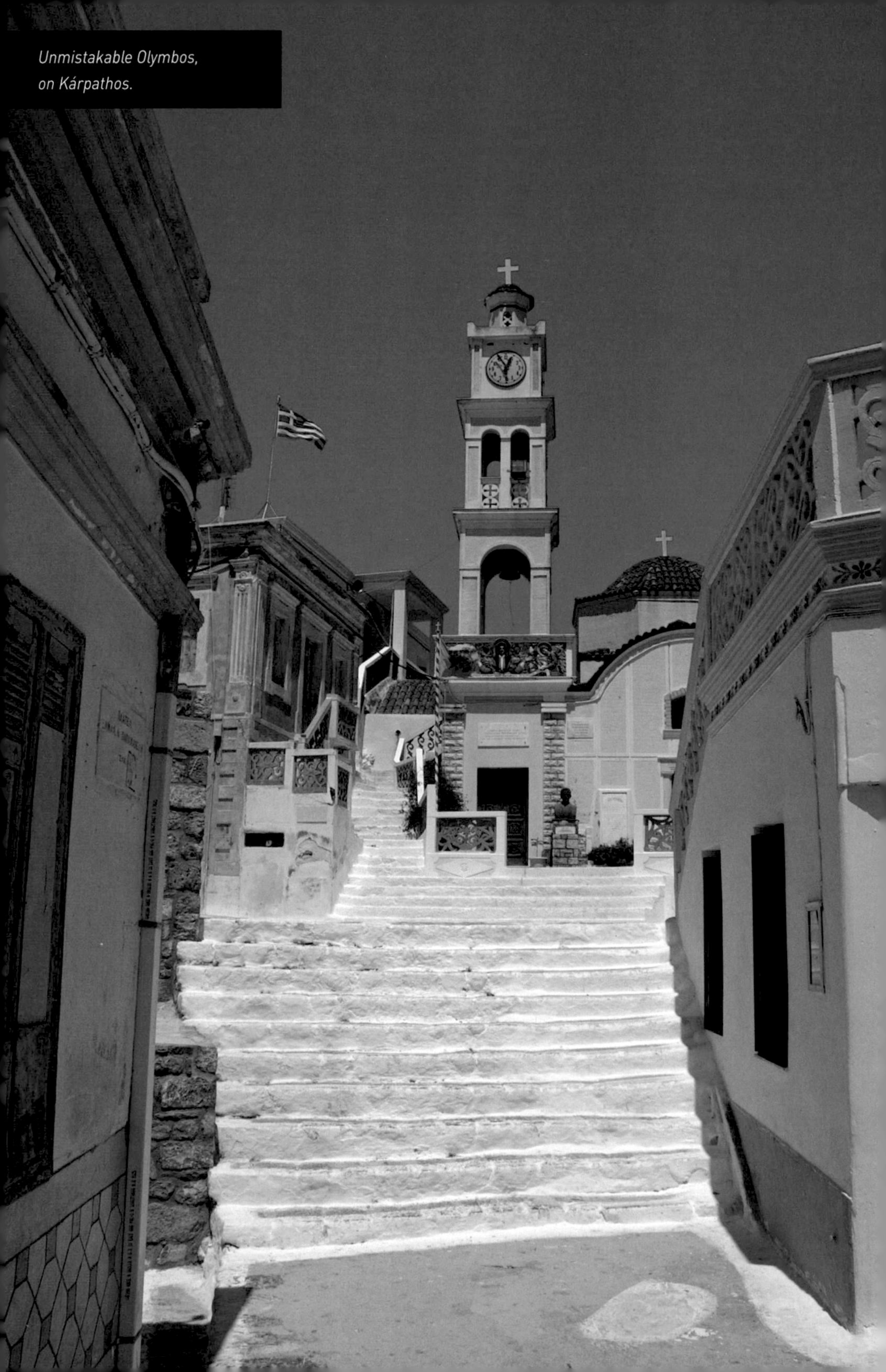

*Unmistakable Olymbos, on Kárpathos.*

# THE SOUTHERN DODECANESE

The farthest from mainland Greece, these islands, which mostly lived in the past from seafaring, have developed an idiosyncratic character, culture and architecture.

The Southern Dodecanese remain among the most tranquil and unspoilt of the islands. The islanders still cling, in places, to traditional customs and live by farming, boat-building and fishing as well as tourism.

## KÁSOS

Kásos is the southernmost and poorest Dodecanese island. Remote and barren, its plight was accentuated by a comprehensive Ottoman massacre in 1824. Before and since Kasiots took to the seas, distinguishing themselves as pilots, and helping to dig the Suez Canal. In six clustered villages on the north flank, many houses lie abandoned: summer sees a homecoming of expatriated Greek-Americans, especially for the major festivals on 17 July (Agía Marína) and 15 August (Dormition of the Virgin).

The capital, **Frý** **❶** (pronounced "Free"), is a bit shabby in parts, but it does have a few tavernas and an attractively enclosed fishing harbour, the **Boúka**, with a narrow entrance. **Emboriós**, down the coast, was the old commercial port, now silted up but still picturesque. The only conventional tourist attractions here are two caves, **Ellinokamára** and **Seláï**, beyond **Agía Marína**, the most attractive inland village.

Except at peak season when a few rental scooters or quad-bikes appear, you face long, shadeless hikes or

expensive taxi rides to get anywhere. The only half-decent beach is **Hélatros**, almost 15km (9 miles) from Frý in the southwest, via **Agios Geórgios Hadión**, one of two rural monasteries. The indolent may take boat excursions to better beaches on the offshore islets of **Makrá** (one big beach) and **Armáthia,** which has five sandy beaches.

Frý has a tiny airstrip with puddle-jumper planes to Rhodes, Kárpathos and Sitía (Crete). Fares are affordable, and a flight may be your only option when arriving or leaving in frequently

**Main Attractions**

Boúka port
Apella beach
Blue Grotto of Perastá
Emborió waterfront
Agíou Pandelímona
  Monastery
Gialós harbour
Sými frescoed churches

*A good lobster catch in Livádia, Tílos.*

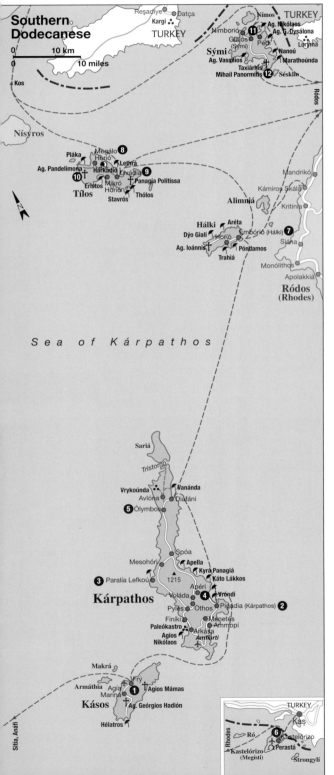

Southern
Dodecanese

0        10 km

0        10 miles

*Sea of Kárpathos*

Kárpathos

heavy seas, when ferries skip the exposed anchorage at Frý.

## KÁRPATHOS

Wild, rugged and sparsely populated, Kárpathos just edges out Kós as the second-largest Dodecanese island, marooned in crystalline sea roughly halfway between Rhodes and Crete. With vast expanses of white-sand beaches, usually underused, and craggy cloud-topped mountains soaring to 1,215 metres (3,986ft), it makes up in natural beauty for what it lacks in compelling man-made sights.

Direct seasonal flights serve Kárpathos from overseas; the alternative involves a domestic flight or ferry from Rhodes. The capital and southerly harbour of **Pigádia** ❷ (also known as Kárpathos) has undergone a tourism boom since the 1990s; in any case, the town only dates from the mid-19th century, though photos from the 1950s show an attractive townscape before the eyesore concrete blocks went up. Many families have returned wealthy from America, especially the East Coast, something which has helped fuel the building boom.

Just north of Pigádia, massively sandy **Vróndi** beach, with windsurf boards and kayaks for rent, sweeps past the 5th-century basilica of **Agía Fotiní**. Some 7km (4.5 miles) south of town is **Ammopí**, the island's longest established resort, with three coves (two sand, one pebble). Many of Kárpathos's better beaches are served by excursion boat. Among these, on the east coast, are **Kyrá Panagiá** (with the most facilities and turquoise water), or lonelier, more unspoilt **Aháta**, **Káto Lákkos** and especially **Apella,** with a 300-metre/yd-long main cove and a naturist cove a short scramble further on. Several coves in the **Amfiárti** region near the southerly airport are home to world-class windsurfing schools. **Arkása**, on the western shore, is somewhat inexplicably a resort, as the only convenient beach is 1km (0.5 miles) south at **Agios Nikólaos**; on the headland opposite are remains of the **Paleókastro**, the Mycenaean-Classical acropolis, with the mosaic-floored Byzantine church of **Agía Sofía** at the beginning of the climb. Heading north, the next substantial settlement besides the little port of **Finíki** is **Paralía Lefkoú** ❸, the main rival to Ammopí as a beach base. A remarkable topography of headlands shelters three horseshoe bays of white sand and there are plenty of places at which to stay and/or eat.

Despite the road network being mostly paved now, exploring Kárpathos can be challenging. The few filling stations are all near Pigádia, limiting the range of small scooters, and strong winds can blow two-wheelers off the road. Booking a rental car or jeep in advance for pick-up at the airport is the best solution. There are buses and pricey taxis to the less remote mountain villages like **Apéri** ❹, the elegant medieval capital, said to have the highest per capita income in Greece; **Voláda**, with a tiny Venetian citadel; and **Othos**, the highest on the island at 400 metres (1,312ft), famous for its

sweet, amber wine from vineyards on the often mist-swirled ridge above.

Although the road there has finally been completely paved, with four weekly buses, northern Kárpathos is still most easily visited via the port of **Diafáni**, served both by local *kaïkia* from Pigádia and most main-line ferries. It makes a peaceful and congenial base, except in August, with coastal walks to good beaches in either direction, but most use it as a stepping-stone to reach **Ólymbos** ❺, the island's most distinctive village, clinging to a mountainside 600 metres (1,970ft) up. Older Ólymbos houses consist of one divided room built around a central wooden pole, the "pillar of the house", to which are attached embroideries and usually a wedding portrait (and often wedding wreaths) of the owners. On a raised wooden platform behind a carved rail is rolled-up bedding, plus chests of dowry linens and festival clothes. The rest of the room is crammed with plates, lace, crochet and other souvenirs – a kitsch explosion of fairground colours – gathered

*Vrykoúnda on Karpáthos.*

by seafaring relatives. Even modern villas often have their front rooms decked out in the same way, as a shrine for family photos and icons.

Bread and biscuits are baked in several communal ovens. The flour was formerly ground by the village's several 18th-century windmills, two of which were restored as working museum pieces in the mid-1980s.

Besides the hike between Olymbos and Diafáni, there's the half-day walk via **Avlóna** hamlet to **Vrykoúnda**, where a cave-shrine of St John the Baptist is the focus for a major 29 August festival. More advanced treks from Avlóna go to Trístomo inlet or back down to Diafáni via **Vanánda** beach.

## KASTELÓRIZO

Kastelórizo's official name, Megísti, means "Biggest" – biggest, that is, of a local mini-archipelago, for this is actually one of the smallest inhabited Dodecanese islands. It's also the first point in Europe, coming from the east, and only a few nautical miles away from Kaş in Turkey, where locals go

*A fisherman lays out his nets in Livádia harbour, Tílos.*

shopping. Before 1900, Kastellórizo had a thriving town of almost 10,000, supported by its schooner fleet. The sale of the fleet to the British, World War I bombardment of French positions here by the Ottomans, and an earthquake in 1926 sent the island into terminal decline, despite its role during the 1930s as a sea-plane halt en route to the Levant.

The final nail in the coffin came in July 1944, when a fuel depot exploded, levelling more than half the port. The town had already been looted, and few chose to return after the war, when the population dropped to about 200. The US even tried to persuade Greece to cede Kastelórizo to Turkey in 1964 in exchange for limited hegemony in Cyprus. Recovery from this nadir is due in part to the return of expatriate "Kassies" from Perth and Sydney to build retirement homes, and also to the island's use as the location for the 1991 Oscar-winning film *Mediterraneo*, which prompted a wave of tourists.

This limestone island is fringed by sheer cliffs, with no beaches at all. What

remains of the red-roofed port town **Kastelórizo** ❻ is overseen by a half-ruined, red-stone Crusader castle, which is responsible for the island's Italianate name. The keep houses a small **Archae-ological Museum** (Tue–Sun 8am–11am, winter until 3pm) of local finds, including an old lighthouse lens, medieval frescoes and Byzantine pottery, while beyond in the cliff-face is Greece's only Lycian house-type tomb. The quayside mosque, dating from 1755, is now home to the **Historical Collection** (Apr–Oct Tue–Sun 11am–3pm, winter 8am–3pm), with a photo archive and ethnographic section.

Also worth seeing, a 45-minute walk from town, is the remote monastery of **Agios Geórgios tou Vounoú** with pebble-mosaic flooring and the frescoed subterranean crypt-chapel of Agios Harálambos. Get the key first from George Maltezos (tel: 6949 727789). Boats will ferry you to the satellite islet of **Ró**, topped by a Hellenistic fortress, or to the cathedral-like **Blue Grotto of Perastá** on the southwest coast which, according to local people, rivals its namesake in Capri. The cave is about 45 metres (1,47ft) long and 28 metres (92ft) high, and the rays of the morning sun create spectacular effects inside. The journey there involves a 90-minute round-trip, plus some time to swim in the deep, glowing waters. Also resident in local waters are two sea turtles, who tend to be found around Psorádia and Agios Geórgios islets or even inside the port. **Agios Geórgios**, with sun-loungers and a snack bar, makes a great day out – taxi-boats from the main port.

Kastelórizo lies 70 nautical miles from Rhodes, and ferries or catamarans make the long trip only two or three times weekly. The tiny airstrip receives almost daily flights from Rhodes, though seats can fill long in advance. The island is now an official port of entry to Greece, though ironically it's more accessible from Kaş, Turkey, which sends daily ferries (www.meisexpress.com).

## HÁLKI

Ninety minutes by boat from Skála Kamírou on Rhodes, Hálki (or Chálki) is pretty, welcoming and very popular, despite being barren, almost beachless

*Patriotic Karpáthos.*

and lacking a fresh water supply. **Emborió ❼** (Hálki), the harbour and only settlement, has numerous waterfront tavernas and abundant accommodation in its restored neoclassical mansions, though most of these are block-booked from April to October by tour companies. **Agios Nikólaos** has the highest belfry in the Dodecanese, nearly matched by a free-standing clock tower nearby.

The island's only sandy beach – artificially supplemented – is **Póndamos**, 400 metres/yds west; just overhead, **Horió** village has been deserted since the 1950s but offers spectacular views from its crumbled Knights' fortress. Tarpon Springs Boulevard, built with money from Hálki sponge fishermen who emigrated to Florida, ends at the **Monastery of Agios Ioánnis**, in the west of the island. The monastery has a huge courtyard tree and cells in which to stay the night. There are no other good roads, so pebble coves like **Aréta** and **Dýo Gialí**, on the north shore, or **Trahiá** under the castle, are reached only by boat trips or arduous hikes.

*Emborió, Hálki.*

Between Hálki and Rhodes, **Alimniá** (aka Alimiá) island has been mostly deserted since World War II, despite having good wells and excellent anchorage. The inhabitants aided the Allies under the very noses of German forces manning submarine pens here. When detected, the islanders were deported to Rhodes and Hálki as punishment, and the few returnees left again in the 1960s. With only another Knights' castle, the derelict village and seasonally grazing sheep to be seen, the island is a very occasional excursion destination from Hálki.

## TÍLOS

Tranquil Tílos has only seen significant tourism since the mid-1980s. It is home to several thousand goats but only about 500 people (the population shrinks to 100 in the winter). Though the island is bare on its limestone heights, adjacent Nísyros deposited rich lava soil in the lowlands, which with ample groundwater allows the Tiliots to farm, rather than sail as their neighbours do. Indeed, before the 1970s it was the granary of the Dodecanese, with undulating fields of wheat visible from far out to sea. The entire island, and the seas just off it, are notionally a national reserve, but other than a total local hunting ban, little has actually been done. Tílos's late, publicity-seeking mayor, Tasos Aliferis, brought the place to public attention in 2008 by officiating marriages for two Greek same-sex couples; Greek courts invalidated the rites but the couples pursued redress as far as the European Court of Human Rights, which ruled in their favour in 2013. As of late 2016, same-sex unions are recognised in Greece.

The island capital, **Megálo Horió ❽**, is slightly inland, topped by a Knights' castle that incorporates a Classical gateway and stone from the ancient acropolis. It looks south over an orchard-planted plain to red-sand **Eristos** beach, the longest on Tílos.

The harbour and main resort of **Livádia** ❾ has a long shingle beach, separated from ample accommodation and eating opportunities by a rigorously pedestrianised, flagstoned walkway. You can also walk on a good path system – assisted by an accurate map – or go by scooter to the most remote beaches, plus there's a bus service, so boat trips are only offered in summer if there are sufficient numbers (15 passengers minimum). The closest coves are **Lethrá**, **Stavrós** and **Thólos**, with the Knights' castle of Agriosykiá (one of seven on Tílos) en route. Just west of Livádia stands the ghost village of **Mikró Horió**, abandoned in the 1950s. There's another castle here, and a late-hours summer bar in a restored house.

The trans-island road passes another fort and a cave at **Harkadió**, where Pliocene midget elephant bones were found in 1971 and are now kept in a one-room museum in Megálo Horió (a new one is being built by the cave). Once past Megálo Horió, the road passes the little port of Agios Andónios and Pláka beach before ending at the 15th-century **Monastery of Agíou Pandelímona** ❿ (summer 10am–7pm, winter 10am–4pm), tucked into a spring-fed oasis-ravine. The church has a few frescoes and a fine marble floor. The big island knees-up is here, running for three days from 25 July. Almost as important is the 23 August festival at **Panagía Polítissa Monastery** near Livádia, for which special boats are laid on from Rhodes the previous day.

## SÝMI

As you approach Sými on a day-trip boat from Rhodes, flotillas of boats flee the port of **Gialós** ⓫ for remote beaches around the island. The foreign "residents" and overnighters are escaping the daily quota of trippers. Gialós, a legally protected architectural reserve, is a stunning spectacle with its tiers of pastel-coloured houses. But when the tour boats hoot their

arrival, mediocre waterside tavernas gear up to tout for business, and stalls sell imported spices and sponges, plus other knick-knacks. As soon as the trippers leave in mid-afternoon, there is more room to walk on the quay and you will get a stronger drink.

Symiots are famous as boat-builders, and a few wooden boats still take shape at the Haráni boatyards. Until it was surpassed by Kálymnos after World War II, Sými was also the sponge-diving capital of the Aegean, a role assured by an Ottoman imperial grant of monopoly in the trade. The Nazi German surrender of the Dodecanese to the Allies, which formally ended World War II in Europe, was signed in Les Katerinettes restaurant on 8 May 1945.

Built in a protected gulch and thus stiflingly hot in summer, Gialós is beautiful at night when the bay reflects the lights from the houses above. Popular with the yachting fraternity, and a discerning clientele who book the limited accommodation independently, the notably expensive "Hydra

*An excursion boat from Rhodes approaches Pédi.*

*The old stone walls of the castle overlooking Horió, Hálki.*

of the Dodecanese" has plenty of bars and tavernas scattered about. It is not, however, an island for the unfit, the elderly or the very young, who would have to manage the 357 steps of the **Kalí Stráta**, the broad stair-street climbing to the upper town of **Horió**. Follow arrows to the worthwhile local **museum** (Tue–Sun 8.30am–2.30pm; free), highlighting Byzantine and medieval Sými. Overhead is the Knights' castle, which was built on the site of – and using material from – the ancient acropolis.

The only other significant habitation is the valley of **Pédi** to the east, where flat land and a few wells allow vegetable cultivation. On the south side of the bay here, reached by a marked trail, lies the naturally sandy beach of **Agios Nikólaos**, the only one on Sými. A 2009-built yacht marina on the north shore accommodates overflow from Gialós. All Sými's other beaches are pebble; walk across the island, through the remaining juniper forest, to **Agios Vassílios** in the southwest (no facilities), or take a boat excursion

to **Agios Geórgios Dysálona**, **Nanoú** or **Marathoúnda** on the east coast – both Nanoú and Marathoúnda have good tavernas if you want to make a full day of it.

Beyond Haráni, the coastal track heads north, then west to the bay of **Nimborió**, where a Byzantine floor mosaic and catacombs can be found just inland. Other notable sacred art is found at the remote frescoed churches of **Agios Prokópios**, **Kokkimídis**, **Agía Marína Nerás** and **Megálos Sotíras**, all on or just off the main road south to the most important island monastery, **Taxiárhis Mihaíl Panormítis** ⓬.

The Archangel Michael is the patron saint of local sailors, and his feast day (8 November) brings pilgrims here from all over the Aegean. Even though the monastery was pillaged during World War II, the central church with its myriad oil lamps remains an atmospheric place, set in the middle of a giant pebble-mosaic courtyard. Things are tranquil once the tour boats have gone – it's usually the first stop coming from Rhodes.

*Looking down to Apella cove, Kárpathos.*

Windmills in Plátanos, Léros.

# THE NORTHERN DODECANESE

In a country blessed with stunning seascapes, the Northern Dodecanese have perhaps the most striking views: between Kálymnos or Nísyros and their surrounding islets, from the summits of Kós or Pátmos over half the Aegean.

From the windmills of Astypálea to the beaches and ancient ruins of Kós, the spirituality of Pátmos and the tranquillity of the tiny, sparsely inhabited islets east of Pátmos, the Northern Dodecanese have something for everyone.

## ASTYPÁLEA

Bleak, butterfly-shaped Astypálea, with about 1,400 inhabitants, is geographically closer to the Cyclades than the Dodecanese; on a clear day both Amorgós and Anáfi appear distinctly on the horizon. It belongs administratively to the Dodecanese, yet is distinctly Cycladic in architecture and culture, which is hardly surprising since it was in fact (re)settled from Mýkonos and Tínos during the 15th century.

Ferry connections are still biased towards the Cyclades and Piraeus rather than Rhodes, with which the most reliable link is by air. In peak season short-term accommodation fills up, while outsiders have renovated old houses in Hóra as summer residences. A single stretch of road linking the main resorts has been paved, taverna food has improved and an ATM has been installed, but further momentous change is unlikely.

Many visitors stay in the original, functional port of **Péra Gialós** or **Skála**, which dates from the Italian

*Nísyros landscape.*

era. Only the local ferry from Kálymnos docks here; others use the larger if inconvenient harbour at **Agios Andréas**. A long stair-street connects Skála with **Hóra** , the capital, with a line of derelict windmills trailing off to the northwest. At the pinnacle of things sits the tan-walled *kástro*, the finest example outside of the Cyclades proper, not a legacy of the Knights of St John, but a 13th-century effort of the Venetian Quirini clan. Until the late 1940s more than 300 islanders dwelt inside, but now it is abandoned, except

⊙ **Main Attractions**
Hóra, Astypálea
Mandráki, Nísyros
Brós Thermá hot springs
Climbing Mount Díkeos
Póthia architecture and
  Archaeological Museum
Agía Kiourá, Léros
Agíou Ioánnou tou
  Theológou Monastery,
  Pátmos

📍 Map on page 270

**Northern Dodecanese**

0 ——— 10 km

0 ——— 10 miles

0 ——— 5 km

0 ——— 5 miles

for two fine churches: **Evangelístria**, supported by the vaulting of the northwest entrance, and **Agios Geórgios** overlooking the sea.

Just west of Hóra's ridge, **Livádia ❷** is the island's second resort, between citrus orchards and a sandy if slightly scruffy beach. Better beaches, like nudist **Tzanáki**, and taverna-equipped, often windy **Agios Konstandínos**, lie further southeast, out on the western "wing". **Kaminákia** and **Vátses** beaches beyond can be reached by the rough onward track or on boat excursions.

The "body" of the butterfly is a long isthmus, just 100 metres/yards across at its narrowest point, by **Stenó** and **Mamoúni** beaches. **Maltezána** (officially Análipsi) to the east has become another resort, more through proximity to the airport than any intrinsic merit. Near Maltezána are the best of Astypálea's many Byzantine church-floor **mosaics**, often covered by protective gravel. A single bus plies regularly between Livádia and Maltezána; otherwise it's a single elusive taxi, or a rented motorbike or car.

## NÍSYROS

In Greek legend, Poseidon, pursuing the Titan Polyvotis, tore a rock from nearby Kós and crushed his adversary beneath it. The rock became Nísyros. The groaning of the Titan is still audible beneath the surface of the caldera in Nísyros's most impressive feature, the volcano that forms the heart of the island. Currently dormant, it was last active in 1933, and vulcanism still characterises Nísyros, from black pebbles on the shore to a thermal spa.

Once you're away from its harbour, **Mandráki ❸** proves an attractive capital. Wooden balconies hang cheerfully from tall, white houses ranged around a central communal orchard. Just off this, the well-labelled

**Archaeological Museum** (Tue–Sun 8.30am–3pm) does a gallop, over two floors, of every period of Nisyrian history, from Archaic grave goods to Roman stelae and Byzantine painted bowls. Overhead, a Knights' castle shelters the **monastery of Panagía Spilianí** (*spiliá* means cave), with an appropriately cave-like church, while to the south, the Doric citadel of **Paleókastro (unfenced)** is more impressive.

Mandráki by night is lively, with many tavernas and *kafenía* found, unusually, inland. There are few hotels, as most folk come just for the day from Kós to tour the volcano. In some establishments, you can order *soumáda*, a non-alcoholic drink now made from imported almonds. The island's green interior – from which wild almonds have sadly disappeared – is best appreciated by walking some of the remaining trail system.

The main **Stéfanos** crater, 260 metres (853ft) across, punctu-ates the nearly lifeless Lakkí pla-teau, 13km (8 miles) southeast of Mandráki. Tour buses make the trip every morning. With stout shoes, you can visit the caldera floor, braving a rotten-egg stench. Yellow sulphur crystals form around hissing steam vents while mud boils out of sight – the voice of Polyvotis. The adjacent Polyvótis crater is smaller and less visited but more dramatic. The Greek power corporation made exploratory geothermal soundings here until 1993, when it departed in the face of islander hostility – though not before destroying the 1,000-year-old *kalderími* (cobbled path or road) back down to Mandráki.

Two scenic villages perch above Lakkí: **Emborió**, almost abandoned and being bought up for restoration by outsiders, and livelier **Nikiá ❹**, with a quirky round *platía*. The Embo-riots moved down to the fishing port of **Pálli ❺** after World War II. The biggest sandy beach is 6km (4 miles) around the northeast coast, at **Pahiá Ammos**. West of Pálli, the old spa at **Loutrá** (erratic hours; bring a towel) has been restored with EU funds.

*A hike around the caldera of Nísyros's dormant volcano.*

## KÓS

The second-largest Dodecanese in population, Kós is (just) the third-largest in size after Rhodes and Kárpathos. It follows the lead of Rhodes in most things: a sea-transport hub for a gaggle of surrounding islands; a shared history, give or take a few years; a similar Knights' castle guarding the harbour, plus a skyline of palms and minarets; and an agricultural economy displaced by tourism.

However, Kós is much smaller than Rhodes, and much flatter, with only one mountain range, Díkeos, rising to 846 metres (2,776ft) in the southeast. The margin of the island is fringed by excellent beaches, which are most easily accessible by motorbike or even pedal-bike, for which cycle paths are helpfully laid out.

Kós is by no means unspoilt, and visits in midsummer, especially without a reservation, are emphatically not recommended. Yet overdevelopment has its compensations: surprisingly good restaurants scattered across the island, ample

*Kós Archaeological Museum exhibit.*

water-sports opportunities and a good infrastructure.

## KÓS TOWN

Although the Minoans colonised the site of present-day **Kós Town** ❻ during the late Bronze Age and Classical eras, the main island city-state was Astypalaia, on the far southwestern cape of Kéfalos, an ally of Rhodes in the Dorian Hexapolis. Spartan sacking during the Peloponnesian War and a subsequent earthquake (Kós is very susceptible to them, most recently in 2017) forced the population to relocate to the northern site, a process that had been completed by the mid-4th century BC. According to the geographer Strabo (c.64 BC–AD 24), the new town was a success: "She was not large but inhabited in the best way possible and to the people visiting her by sea pleasant to behold."

Yet another earthquake in 1933 devastated most of Kós Town, except for the Ottoman bazaar of Haluvaziá, but gave Italian archaeologists

### ⊘ THE ASKLEPION

The Asklepion is named after Asklepios, who lived around 1200 BC and, according to legend, was the son of Apollo and the nymph Koronis. His cult developed in Kós, and he became revered as the Greek god of healing. Shrines were built to him all over Greece, usually on a spot where there was a natural spring, and people flocked to them from all over the ancient world, hoping for cures for their ailments. The most famous of the Asklepia is this one on Kós, which housed a spa fed by two natural springs. The complex was first excavated during 1901–05 by two archaeologists, the German R Herzog and the Greek Iakovos Zaraftis. It is popularly believed that Hippocrates, after whom the medical Hippocratic oath is named, worked and taught here, but this is unlikely to be true.

a perfect excuse to excavate the ancient city comprehensively. Hence much of the town centre is an archaeological park, with the ruins of the Roman *agora*, the eastern excavation, lapping up to the 18th-century Loggia Mosque and the "Plane Tree of Hippocrates", under which the father of medicine is said to have taught. It is not really 2,500 years old, although it probably is one of the oldest trees in Europe, and now dependent on a life-support system of metal scaffolding.

The western digs offer covered mosaics and the *Xystós*, the colonnade of an indoor running track. Just south stand an over-restored *odeion*, which is sometimes used for summer performances, and the **Casa Romana** (Apr–Oct Tue–Sun 8am–8pm, Nov–Mar 8am–3pm), a restored Roman villa with floor mosaics and murals, plus good displays on everyday Roman life. The Italian-founded, 2011–16 renovated **Archaeological Museum** (hours as above) on Platía Elevtherías has a predictable Latin bias in its exhibits, although the star piece, a statue of the great healer Hippocrates, is in fact Hellenistic. Also on this square is the 18th-century **Defterdar Mosque**, still used by Kós Town's 50 or so Muslim families but not open to the public.

## AROUND THE ISLAND

Hippocrates himself (c.460–370 BC) was born and practised on Kós, but probably died shortly before the establishment of the **Asklepion** ❼ (summer Tue–Fri 8am–7.30pm, Sat–Mon 8am–2.30pm, winter daily 8.30am–2.30pm), an ancient therapeutic centre 4km (2.5 miles) southwest of town. The site is more impressive for its position overlooking the straits towards Turkey than for any surviving structures.

The masonry was thoroughly pilfered by the Knights to build the massive **Nerantziás castle** (Apr–Oct daily 8am–8pm, winter Tue–Sun 8am–3pm), which, unlike the one at Rhodes, was for strictly military purposes. It's a double fort, the smaller inner one dating from the mid-15th

*The remains of the Asklepion.*

century, and the outer circuit completed in 1514.

Between the Asklepion and Kós Town, pause at **Platáni**, roughly halfway, to eat at one of four excellent Turkish-run tavernas. As on Rhodes, most local Muslims have emigrated to Turkey since the 1960s, with about 700 remaining. There was a small Jewish community here too, wiped out with the Rhodian one in 1944, leaving behind only a marvellous Art Deco **synagogue** near Kós Town's ancient *agora*.

The road east of town dead-ends at **Brós Thermá**, enjoyable hot springs that run directly into the sea. West of town, within easy cycling distance, are the package resorts of **Tingáki** and **Marmári**, ringed by long white beaches, and less frenetic **Mastihári**, with small ferries to Kálymnos and Psérimos.

**Kardámena** ⑧ on the south coast, 25km (15 miles) from Kós Town but just 7km (4.5 miles) from the airport, is the island's cheap-and-cheerful resort, with little to recommend it aside from suggestively named bars, dance clubs,

and a long, sandy and jam-packed beach. The only cultural diversion is the Knights' castle (always open) near **Andimáhia**, a short drive away.

In the far southwest, facing Nísyros, are more scenic and sheltered **beaches**, with names like "**Sunny**" and "**Magic**", the latter arguably the best. At nearby **Agios Stéfanos**, twin 6th-century basilicas are among several early Christian monuments on the island. The Kéfalos headland beyond saw the earliest habitation of Kós: **Asprí Pétra** cave, home to Neolithic man, and Classical **Astypalaia**, birthplace of Hippocrates, of which only the little theatre remains.

The appealing villages on the wooded northern slopes of **Mount Díkeos**, collectively known as **Asfendioú** ⑨, have retained more traditional character, with whitewashed houses and attractive churches. At **Ziá**, tavernas seem more numerous than permanent inhabitants, and are especially busy at sunset and later. **Asómati's** vernacular houses are slowly being bought up and restored

*Floor mosaic inside Kós's Archaeological Museum.*

by foreigners. The surrounding juniper forest provides welcome relief from summer heat; a path from Ziá allows the ascent of **Hristós** peak on Díkeos, with a magnificent 360° view (allow three hours for the round trip in cooler weather).

On the western flank of Mount Díkeos, the Byzantines had their island capital at **Paleó Pylí** ⑩ (Old Pylí), today a jumble of ruins – except for the restored Arhángelos church, with fine 15th-century frescoes – below a castle at the head of a spring-fed canyon. Modern Pylí, 3km (2 miles) downhill, paradoxically offers something more ancient: the **Harmyleio**, a subterranean Hellenistic family tomb with 12 niches.

## KÁLYMNOS

First impressions of Kálymnos, north of Kós, are of an arid, mountainous landmass with a decidedly masculine energy in the main port town of Póthia. This is due to the former dominant industry, sponge-diving, now supplanted by tourism and commercial fishing. But the island's prior mainstay (see page 276) is in ample evidence in the home decor of huge sponges or shell-encrusted amphorae, and the souvenir shops overflowing with smaller sponges.

**Póthia** ⑪ itself (population 13,000), the third-largest town in the Dodecanese, is noisy, colourful and workaday Greek, its brightly painted houses rising in tiers up the sides of the valley flanks. Mansions and vernacular dwellings with ornate balconies and wrought-iron ornamentation (an island speciality) are particularly evident in the Evangelístria district.

The most dazzling conventional attraction is the **Archaeological Museum** (Apr–Oct Tue–Sat 8.30am–3pm). Stars of the displays from all eras include a huge Hellenistic cult statue of Asklepios, a Roman bronze of a clad woman and an unusual robed, child-sized *kouros* (most were naked). Spare time also for the **Nautical and Folklore Museum** (Mon–Sat 10am–1.30pm; Nautical section free), with fascinating photos of old Póthia and

*Rollerblading on the waterfront.*

*Kós's Castle of the Knights.*

# SPONGE-DIVING

**Sponge-diving in Kálymnos is now dying out. It has a long history, but was always hard and dangerous work.**

Kálymnos has been a sponge-fishing centre from ancient times, although a combination of fishing restrictions and marine blight have diminished the trade since the 1960s. Sponges come in various grades: the coarser ones for industry, the finer ones for cosmetic and artistic use. Although cheap artificial sponges now dominate the market, many people will still pay extra for the more resilient natural sponge.

Sponges were traditionally "cured" in two stages. First the divers trod them underfoot on the deck of the caique to "milk" them of unwanted organic matter; then they strung them together and dropped them back into the sea for a few more days of cleaning. Sponge-curing can still be observed at a few Póthia factories. Older operations have stone tubs of salt water, others bubbling vats of diluted acid which bleach the sponges. This concession to tourist tastes actually weakens the fibres. After this optional process, they are rinsed in salt water again and finally laid out to dry in the factory courtyard.

Over the years sponge-fishers developed various methods of gathering their quarry: spearing them

*The first diving apparatus or "machine" – here on display outside a taverna – revolutionised the trade.*

in shallow water; dragging a heavy blade and net along the sea-bottom so that everything – stones and seaweed as well as the odd sponge – was pulled up together; and diving – the most difficult and dangerous method.

In the old days, naked divers used to sink themselves with the heavy *skandalópetra* or "scandal stone" tied to their waists. Holding their breath, they scraped off the sponges fixed to rocks that they had spied from the surface. They could usually get two or three sponges before they had to surface for air – better divers could dive to over 10 fathoms. This was before the "machine" was introduced late in the 19th century.

The "machine" (*skáfandro* in Greek), the first diving apparatus, consisted of a rubber suit with a bronze helmet connected to a long rubber hose and a hand-powered air-pump. The diver was let out on a long cable and given enough air-hose for his final depth, where he could stay much longer, thanks to the constant air supply. Too long and too deep, as it turned out. Compressed air delivered to divers at these greater depths bubbled out of solution in their bloodstream as they rose, invariably too rapidly. The results of nitrogen embolism – known as decompression sickness or, more commonly, the "bends" – included deafness, incontinence, paralysis and, all too often, death.

By the 1950s the physiological mechanism was understood and the death and maiming halted, but too late to help hundreds of Kalymnian crewmen. Although the "machine" now seems quaintly antiquated, it was innovative enough for its time to enrich the boat captains and sponge wholesalers, who benefited from the divers' dangerous work.

Ironically, the increased efficiency in sponge-harvesting helped to wind up the industry. The Greek seabed was stripped bare, and Kalymnian boats had to sail increasingly further afield. Overexploitation of Mediterranean sponge beds was the rule even before a virus devastated them during the late 1980s. Today, sponge-divers are a rare breed: whereas in the old days, huge boats with a crew of 30 would set out in late April for six months of sponge-diving, today perhaps 10 tiny craft with 3 divers aboard each make far shorter trips.

seafarers' lives, plus poignantly primitive divers' equipment.

To the northwest loom two castles (both open all day; free): **Hrysoherías**, the Knights' stronghold, and the originally Byzantine fort of **Péra Kástro** with several open frescoed churches, standing above the medieval capital of **Horió ⑫**, still the island's second town.

The east coast is harsh and uninhabited except for the green, citrus-planted **Vathýs Valley** extending inland from a deep fjord, which comes as a surprise amid all this greyness as you round a high curve in the approach road. **Plátanos** and **Metóhi** hamlets used to live from their sweet-smelling mandarin and orange orchards, though many of these are now for sale. Yachts patronise a half-dozen tavernas at little **Rína ⑬** port, from where there are boat trips to the nearby cave of **Daskalió**, a place of Bronze-Age worship, and purportedly of refuge during the Italian era. The limestone strata are riddled with other, visitable stalactite caves. The best are **Kéfala** in the far southwest, and **Skaliá** and **Kolonóstilos** in the far north.

Most visitors stay at the beach resorts on the gentler west coast, locally referred to as **Brostá** (Forward). Local people and Greek holiday-makers gravitate towards **Kandoúni** and **Linária beaches**, although less developed **Platýs Gialós,** just north, is reckoned among the island's best. Foreign package tourists used to patronise **Melitsáhas**, **Myrtiés** (with the best beach), **Masoúri** and **Armeós**, four contiguous, heavily developed resorts now fallen on hard times. They have reinvented themselves as centres for spring and autumn rock-climbers. Kálymnos is rated one of the top five spots world-wide for the sport.

You could escape any crowds by heading north towards **Argynónda** and **Emboriós ⑭**, the end of the road 19km (12 miles) from Póthia, enjoying a mix of pebble and sand beaches, though bus service beyond Armeós is sparse. In any case, Kálymnos is just the right size to explore by scooter or on foot via the

⊘ **Fact**

Póthia has an orphanage where, until recently, Orthodox priests (the great majority of those who do not live in monasteries are married) would come to choose a bride before they were ordained. A woman without a dowry was reckoned to have little chance of finding a husband outside the Church.

*Swapping news after a service in the church forecourt, Póthia.*

surviving path network, and boat trips are also offered.

## PSÉRIMOS AND TÉLENDOS

The cheapest excursion, by daily 9.30am caique from Kálymnos, is to tiny **Psérimos** (population 35). Crowds of day-trippers from Kós flopping on **Avlákia** port's sandy beach can exceed the capacity of Avlákia's few tavernas; if you stay the night, you will find the islanders more receptive. After dark, the only sounds will be the wind rustling through calamus thickets, or the tinkle of goat bells. Alternatives to the main harbour beach – which doubles as the main street – include **Vathý**, just half an hour's walk east, or secluded **Grafiótissa** a similar distance west, 300 metres/yds of fine sand at the base of cliffs.

Seen from Myrtiés or Masoúri at dusk, the bulky islet of **Télendos** , which was split off from Kálymnos by a mid-6th-century AD earthquake, resembles a snail; others claim to see the silhouette of a petrified princess staring out to sea, jilted here by her lover. Regular caiques play from Myrtiés (daily 8am–11pm every half-hour in season).

The single waterside hamlet (permanent population 45), also named Télendos, huddles under mammoth **Mount Ráhi** (458 metres/1,502ft). Halfway up the north side of the mount, a long trek away, perches the fortified chapel of **Agios Konstandínos**. Less energetic souls content themselves with the ruined Byzantine monastery of **Agios Vassílios**, at the northern edge of the hamlet, or the Byzantine baths of **Agios Harálambos**. Télendos is more upmarket than Psérimos, and slightly less oriented for day-trippers. Most tavernas are stylish and friendly, and accommodation priced to lure custom over from the main island. Beaches vary in consistency and size; a sandy, tamarisk-shaded one stretches north of "town", while scenic **Hohlakás**, 10 minutes west, has coin-sized pebbles, as do several "pocket" coves (one naturist) beyond the sand beach.

*Télendos island, viewed from above Myrtiés.*

# LÉROS

Léros, with its half-dozen deeply indented bays, looks like a jigsaw puzzle piece gone astray. The deepest inlet, that of **Lakkí**  (now the main ferry port), sheltered an important Italian naval base from 1935 onwards, and from here was launched the submarine that torpedoed the Greek battleship *Elli* in Tínos harbour on 15 August 1940.

Today Lakkí seems bizarre, a planned town built during 1935–8 to house the staff of the Italian naval base here, and far too grand for the present population. Its Rationalist/Streamline-Modern buildings (a popular style in the 1930s, Art Deco-influenced, but more minimalist) have lately been restored, although the landscaped squares and wide boulevards remain spookily empty. The local atmosphere was long weighted by the presence of three hospitals for disabled children and mentally impaired adults, though these institutions have been mostly phased out and the facilities turned over in part to the University of the Aegean's nursing faculty.

The rest of the island is more inviting, particularly the fishing port of **Pandéli**, with its waterfront tavernas, just downhill from the capital of **Plátanos**, draped over a saddle, with a well-preserved Knights' castle containing an excellent ecclesiastical museum (the warden will give an engaging tour). South of both, **Vromólithos** has the best easily accessible and car-free beach on an island not known for good, sandy ones. In most places sharp rock reefs must be crossed when getting into the water. **Agia Marína**, beyond Plátanos, is the usual excursion boat and catamaran harbour and, like Pandéli, offers good tavernas, plus more whimsical Italian architecture.

**Alinda**, 3km (2 miles) north around the same bay, is the oldest established resort, with a long beach right next to the road – and a poignant Allied War Graves cemetery containing casualties from the five-day Battle of Léros in November 1943, when the

*Lacemaking in the shade – a local lady keeps the old crafts alive.*

*Vivid colour outlines the steps to this house.*

## ☉ OUR LADY OF CHARON

Near Lipsí's Hohlakoúra Bay, the church of Panagía tou Hárou (Our Lady of Charon) is the focus of a miracle repeated annually since 1943. The church is so named for its icon (now a copy, with the original in the town cathedral) of the Virgin cradling the crucified Christ, the only such in the Greek world. In thanks for a favour granted, a parishioner left a sprig of lilies by the icon; they duly withered, but mysteriously revived on 23 August, the Orthodox day of the Virgin's Assumption into heaven. Each year on that date the icon is processed with suitable ceremony to its old home and then back to the cathedral. Don't try travelling between local islands on this day (called Apódosi Kimíseos Theotókou in Greek). It's a major regional holiday and all ferry tickets sell out early.

### ⊘ Fact

Lipsí was the island where, in summer 2002, Alexandros Giotopoulos, the mastermind of the 17 November terrorist group, Europe's longest lasting, was finally unmasked and caught. He had been living here in a villa, under an alias, for many years; Giotopoulos and several other group members were tried on murder and bombing charges, convicted and sentenced to lengthy jail terms by late 2003.

Germans ousted an insufficiently supplied British commando force (a small underground museum at Lakkí tells the story, if not very well).

In ancient times Léros was sacred to Artemis, and on a hill next to the airport runway are knee-high remains of the goddess's "temple" – actually an ancient fort. Artemis' reputed virginity lives on in the place name **Parthéni** (*parthenos* is the Greek for virgin), the other side of the airport: an infamous concentration camp during the junta, now a scarcely more cheerful army base, as it was in Italian times. Things perk up beyond of this, with one of the island's better beaches, **Blefoútis**, plus the unusual chapel of **Agía Kiourá**, decorated by junta-era prisoners with strikingly heterodox religious murals, which the mainstream Church has always loathed – they are legally protected from further erasure.

Other bays tend not to be worth the effort spent getting there. **Goúrna**, in the west, has a long, sandy and gently shelving – but often also windy and

littered – beach. Isolated **Xirókambos** in the south refuses to face the facts of a poor beach as it struggles to be a resort; caiques from Myrtiés on Kálymnos call here in season, but be sure you have onward land transport organised.

## LIPSÍ, ARKÍ, MARÁTHI, AGATHONÍSI

The name Lipsí (aka Leipsoí) is supposed to derive from Kalypso, the nymph who held Odysseus in thrall for years. The little island (population around 700) has been transformed by tourism, real-estate development and regular ferry/catamaran services since the 1980s. The single harbour town, also called **Lipsí** ⑳, has been spruced up, accommodation has multiplied, bulldozer tracks and paved roads creep across the landscape, and scooters are made available to explore them.

An extraordinarily long shoreline esplanade links the ferry quay with the village centre, marked by the three-domed cathedral of Agios

*View of Lipsí Town.*

Ioánnis. Behind this is the main square with tavernas and an **Ecclesiastical Museum** (daily, erratic hours) with some amusing exhibits. As befits a dependency of Pátmos, older houses have their windows outlined in bright colours that change periodically. Beaches are scattered across the island. The sandiest are the town beach of **Liendoú, Platýs Gialós** in the northwest – with a seasonal taverna – and **Katsadiá**, a double bay in the south, facing Léros, again with a taverna. The most secluded are naturist pebble coves at **Monodéndri** in the east, facing scenic islets.

Lipsí appears verdant, but farming is dependent on well water; there is only one spring in the west, at Káto Kímisi. Although tractors and pumps are audible by day, the nights are given over to the sea's lapping, the crowing of errant roosters, or perhaps a snatch of music from one of three bars.

Three more remote islets north of Lipsí are far less developed and can be more quickly reached from Pátmos. The permanent population of Arkí ㉑ is just 40, and falling. There is no real village or fresh water, although a ferry dock has been built and an adjacent sandy beach created; other swimmable, pebbly coves beckon at **Limnári** and **Tiganákia**. Accommodation and tavernas are adequate in both quality, and quantity – except during mid-summer. **Maráthi** ㉒, across a channel, gets some day-trips from Pátmos and Lipsí, for the sake of its long sandy beach. It has just three permanent inhabitants, and an equal number of places to stay and eat.

**Agathonísi**, off towards Sámos (where shopping is done, children go to school and many islanders live in winter), is more of a going concern with its three hamlets and permanent population of just under 100. Connections are better too, with a catamaran service dovetailing well with appearances of the small ferry *Nisos Kalymnos*. The islet is much in the news lately as a favourite landing point for illegal immigrants (see page 56), but has a cult following

*Cats are everywhere on Pátmos.*

amongst many foreign tourists. Most of them stay at the little port of **Agios Geórgios**, with a convenient beach and several tavernas. More secluded beaches lie around the headland at **Spiliás** and **Gaïdourávlakos**, or in the far east of the island at **Póros** and **Thóli**, the latter with a Byzantine granary just inland.

## PÁTMOS

Pátmos has been inextricably linked to the Bible's Book of Revelation (Apocalypse) ever since tradition placed its authorship here, in AD 95, by John the Evangelist. The volcanic landscape, with strange rock formations and sweeping views, seems suitably apocalyptic. In 1088 the monk Hristodoulos Latrenos founded a monastery here in honour of St John the Theologian (as John the Evangelist is known in Orthodoxy), which soon became a focus of scholarship and pilgrimage. A Byzantine imperial charter gave the monks tax exemption and the right to engage in sea-trade, concessions respected by the island's later Venetian and Ottoman rulers.

Although Pátmos is no longer ruled by the monks, their presence tempers the rowdier elements found in most holiday resorts. While there is the usual quota of naturist beaches, nightlife is genteel, and the clientele upmarket (including the Aga Khan's extended family, plus various ruling or deposed royal families). Those who elect to stay here appreciate the unique, even spiritual, atmosphere that Pátmos exudes once the day-trippers and cruise-ship patrons have departed.

**Skála** ㉓ is the port and largest village, best appreciated late at night when crickets serenade and yacht-masts are illuminated against a dark sky. By day Skála loses its charm, but all island commerce, whether shops, banks or travel agencies, is based here. Buses leave regularly from the quay for the hilltop **Hóra** ㉔, but a 40-minute cobbled path short-cutting the road is maybe preferable in cool weather.

*Mosaic adorning the monastery of St John the Theologian.*

Hóra's core, protected by a massive, pirate-proof fortress and visible from a great distance, is the **Agíou Ioánnou tou Theológou Monastery** (Monastery of St John the Theologian; daily 8am–1.30pm, Tue & Sat also 4–7pm, Sun also 4–6pm). A photogenic maze of interlinked courtyards, stairways, chapels and passageways, it occupies the site of an ancient Artemis temple. The Treasury houses the most impressive monastic collection in Greece outside Mount Athos. Among priceless icons and jewellery, the prize exhibit is the edict of Emperor Alexios Komnenos granting the island to Hristodoulos.

Away from the tourist thoroughfares, Hóra is silent, its thick-walled mansions with their pebble courtyards and arcades the preserve of wealthy foreigners who snapped them up in the 1960s. From Platía Lótza in the north there is one of the finest views in the Aegean, taking in at least half a dozen islands on all but the haziest day.

Just over halfway down the path from Hóra to Skála stands the small **Apokálypsi Monastery** (same hours as main monastery), built around the grotto where John had his Revelation. A silver band on the wall marks the spot where John lay his head, while in the ceiling is a great cleft in the rock through which the divine Voice spoke. The courtyard is the usual venue for a sacred music festival in late summer.

Pátmos's remote beaches are surprisingly good, with great seascapes offshore and (usually) excellent tavernas. Buses ply between **Gríkou** resort and northerly **Kámbos**, popular with Greek families. The biggest sandy bay is exposed **Psilí Ammos** in the far south, accessible by boat trip or a half-hour walk from the road's end, and favoured by naturists. Beaches north of Skála include (in order) **Melóï**, site of the island campsite; long **Agriolivádi**; **Lingínou**, with a double cove, and popular with nudists; isolated **Livádi Geranoú** **㉕**, with an islet to swim to; and finally **Lámbi** **㉖**, which has irresistible, multicoloured volcanic pebbles.

*The Agíou Ioánnou toú Theológou Monastery.*

*Agios Nikólaos, with its lake.*

Koúles fort, Iráklio.

# CRETE

Greece's southernmost island – and the largest – is characterised by soaring mountains, a proudly independent people and unique remains of the first great European civilisation.

Crete (Kríti), claimed by many Greeks to be the most authentic island, is by far the largest. It stretches 256km (159 miles) from east to west and varies between 11 and 56km (7 and 35 miles) in width. A massive mountainous backbone dominates, with peaks stretching skywards to over 2,450 metres (8,038ft) at two points. In the north the mountains slope more gently, producing fertile plains, while in the south they often plunge precipitously into the sea. *Megalónisos* (The Great Island) is what Cretans call their home, meaning great not just in size.

Great can certainly be applied to the Minoan civilisation, the first in Europe and one with which Crete is inextricably entwined. Visitors by the thousand pour through the ruins of Minoan palace complexes, before heading towards one of the scores of excellent beaches. With three international airports, Crete cannot be classified as undiscovered, but by its scale and variety it manages to contain the crowds and to please visitors with widely divergent tastes. While a car is essential for discovering the best of the island, car hire is, unfortunately, comparatively expensive.

Most of Crete's 625,000 inhabitants live along the north coast. The mountains, honeycombed with caves, nurture a proud and ruggedly independent people – among which there is still a significant separatist movement. Crete

*Morosíni fountain.*

also has a particular musical tradition, characterised by *mantinádes* (rhyming couplet songs) and dances such as the spectacular *pentozális*. These are almost invariably accompanied by the *lýra*, the ubiquitous lap-fiddle.

For almost half the year snow lies on the highest peaks, which provide a dramatic backdrop to verdant spring meadows ablaze with flowers. This, as botanists and ornithologists know well, is *the* time to visit. The former come to see more than 130 plant species unique to the island, while the latter

**Main Attractions**

Iráklio Archaeological Museum
Ancient Knossos
Spinalónga islet
Phaistos Palace
Arkádi Monastery
Réthymno Old Town
Haniá Old Town
Kastéli Kissámou Archaeological Museum
Samariá gorge

**Maps on pages 290, 298**

are thrilled by more than 250 types of birds heading north. These migrants briefly join such rare residents as Bonelli's eagle and Eleonora's falcon. And in spring the island is redolent with sage, savory, thyme, oregano and the endemic *díktamo* (dittany).

Crete, much more than other Greek islands, is a place both for sightseeing and for spending time on the beach. Minoan ruins are the major attractions: as well as the archaeological sites, the Archaeological Museum in the capital, **Iráklio ❶**, houses a unique collection of artefacts from Europe's oldest civilisation. But there are also Greek, Roman, Ottoman and Venetian remains, and literally hundreds of Byzantine churches, many with rare and precious frescoes, usually dating from the 13th to 16th centuries. These paintings often have a distinct Cretan style, recognisable by elongated figures and attention to detail. (Many of the churches are kept locked: enquire at the nearest café for the key.) Dozens of monasteries have fallen into disuse over the years, but others still

function and have treasures as rich as their histories.

Homer's "island of 100 towns" can also be called an island of 100 beaches. Some are simply a place where a boat can be hauled ashore, but many are superb stretches of sand, often where nudity is tolerated. The bathing season – especially on the south coast facing the Libyan Sea – is long, stretching from Easter until late autumn.

## IRÁKLIO (HERAKLION)

The capital of Crete since 1971, greater Iráklio has a population of 225,000 and is the fourth-largest city in Greece. Although long exceptionally prosperous from both tourism and agriculture, the economic crisis hit here hard and early, with above-national-average unemployment and often neglected infrastructure. However, it remains a bustling, concrete-laced town, with little appeal outside of the Old Quarter.

Most tourists head for the Minoan ruins of Knossos, but this should be combined (joint ticket available) with a visit to the outstanding **Archaeological**

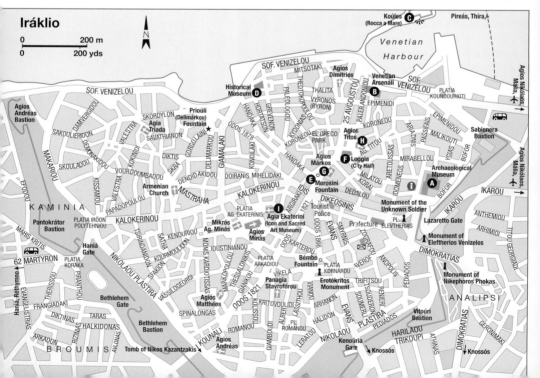

**Museum ** (Apr–Oct daily 8am–8pm, Nov–Mar Mon 11am–5pm, Tue–Sun 8am–3pm) just off focal, bustling Platía Elevtherías in order fully to comprehend the site and its contents. After a lengthy restoration, the museum finally re-opened in 2015, with all of its famous treasures – including the Malia bee pendant, the rock-crystal rhyton, the Phaistos disc, vividly painted *larnakes* and snake-goddess idols – displayed to advantage in 23 galleries.

Most of Iráklio's other major attractions date from the Venetian era, Crete's most prosperous period in historical times. Flanking the old harbour are the **Venetian Arsenáli** (covered boathouses) and the restored, nocturnally illuminated **Koúles fortress** (Apr–Oct daily 8am–sunset, Nov–Mar until 3pm), whose three reliefs of the Lion of St Mark announce its provenance. A few minutes' walk to the west of the old harbour on Sofoklí Venizélou Street, the **Historical Museum** (Apr–Oct Mon–Sat 9am–5pm, Nov–Mar until 3.30pm; www.historical-museum.gr) covers Cretan history and ethnography

from the Byzantine Empire to the present. Inside are fine icons and fresco fragments, stone relief carvings, documentation of the local Jewish, Muslim and Armenian communities, folk textiles and a re-creation of a traditional Cretan home. Models and prints show how Iráklio has developed, as does an interactive model of the medieval city. Due prominence is given to the struggle for Cretan independence and World War II resistance. Inland, **Platía Venizélou** (also known as Lion or Fountain Square) takes its popular names from the stylish 17th-century **Morosíni Fountain** and guardian marble lions. Overlooking the square is the Venetian **Loggia** (now the city hall) flanked by the churches of **Agios Márkos** and, set in its own little square, **Agios Títos**; all three have been heavily restored to repair war damage. Since 1966, when it was returned from St Mark's Basilica in Venice, the skull of St Titus, St Paul's Apostle to Crete and the island's first bishop, has been housed in Agios Títos.

Walk south through the noisy "market street", redolent with tantalising

**⊙ Tip**

The Archaeological Museum in Iráklio is best visited in the afternoon, when it is quieter. You can take a break in the garden café – but remember to retain your museum ticket for readmission.

*At the Iráklio Archaeological Museum.*

# THE ISLANDS IN FILM

**A stunning island setting does not guarantee a great film, although there have been a few memorable ones.**

Postcard-worthy beaches, stage-set ports and reliable sunshine suggest ideal cinematic locations. But luminous scenery does not equal quality; many island-shot films lack coherent plot.

Michael Cacoyannis' *The Girl in Black* (1956), followed by Jean Negulesco's *Boy on a Dolphin* (1957, with Alan Ladd and Sophia Loren) both starred Hydra, the first island on the big screen along with Crete, where the villagers of Kritsá (and Melina Mercouri) graced *He Who Must Die*, Jules Dassin's 1957 adaptation of Nikos Kazantzakis' *Christ Recrucified*. Crete and Kazantzakis, with a Mikis Theodorakis soundtrack, reappeared in Cacoyannis's *Zorba the Greek* (1964), a retelling of Níkos Kazantazákis's novel *Alexis Zorbas*, shot at Pláka and Kókkino Horió, near Haniá. Alan Bates and Anthony Quinn played the leads; the same year saw Crete again strut the boards in the hit American thriller *The Moon-Spinners*. Quinn had already starred in 1961's *The Guns of Navarone* (shot at Cape Ladikó on Rhodes – where a bay is named after Quinn – and sheer cliffs at Sými's Agios Geórgios Dyssálonas), as the Greek member of a commando team charged

*Photogenic Santoríni, made for celluloid stardom.*

with destroying an impregnable German artillery battery. Corfu (with Lefkáda) has also "starred"– in Billy Wilder's Franco-German 1978 drama *Fedora*, and (using Issos beach and Achilleion Palace, with Roger Moore as James Bond) in 1981's *For Your Eyes Only*. Moore had just played in 1979's *Escape to Athens*, a POW-breakout caper set on Rhodes, also starring Telly Savalas. Rhodes (and briefly, Sými) again figured in *Pascali's Island* (1988), based on Barry Unsworth's novel, with Ben Kingsley as an Ottoman spy and fixer. Luc Besson's *The Big Blue* (1988) was the top grossing French film of the 1980s; loosely based on the lives of two champion free-divers, it had more atmosphere than narrative. The title translates as *To Apérando Galázio* – the name of countless island bars – but the movie also put location Amorgós on the tourism map.

In the Cyclades, trashy *Summer Lovers* (1982) and *Lara Croft Tomb Raider: The Cradle of Life* (2003) both featured Santoríni, while *Shirley Valentine* (1989) showcased Mýkonos beaches and an unhappily married woman's (Pauline Collins) affair with a Greek *kamáki* (Tom Conti), the era's stereotypical (now extinct) Romeo. "She's an ex-Shirley Valentine" became universal shorthand for women staying in Greece after the romance that anchored them there ended.

The award for Worst Greek-Shot Film Ever goes to Paul Cox's *Island* (1989), set on Astypálea. Italian-produced *Mediterraneo* was filmed on Kastellórizo and won 1991's Best Foreign Film Oscar; this warmhearted portrayal of a World War II backwater did for this tiny island what *The Big Blue* had for Amorgós.

The biggest splashes have since been made by *Captain Corelli's Mandolin* (2001), shot on Kefaloniá; the virulently anti-resistance politics of Louis de Bernières's eponymous novel incensed many locals, and filming (with Nicholas Cage and Penélope Cruz) was conditional on excising controversial material; the vapid result sank without trace. No such troubles beset smash hit *Mamma Mia!* (2008), filmed on Skópelos and Skiáthos, with Meryl Streep and Pierce Brosnan. *Fugitive Pieces* (2007), Anne Michaels's best-selling Holocaust novel partly set on Zákynthos (Lésvos, Hydra and Kefaloniá in the film) was pitched as an Important Work, but proved middlebrow in the telling.

smells and jammed with people, but very touristy. Admire the Venetian Bembo Fountain and the adjacent Turkish pumphouse (now a café) at the far end before turning west towards the **Icon and Sacred Art Museum ❶** (summer Mon–Sat 9.30am–7.30pm, winter until 3.30pm), inside 15th-century Agía Ekateríni church. Stars of the collection are six icons by 16th-century master Mihaïl Damaskinos, a peer of El Greco.

You may circumambulate the 15th-century city walls which, in their day, were the most formidable in the Mediterranean. The defences stretch for nearly 4km (2.5 miles) and in parts are 29 metres (95ft) thick. En route, pause on the Martinengo bastion at the tomb of the great Irakliot author and excommunicated iconoclast Nikos Kazantzakis (1883–1957) to enjoy the views, and to consider his defiant epitaph – "I hope for nothing, I fear nothing, I am free" – reflecting his long fascination with Buddhism. Keen admirers will make for the **Kazantzakis Museum** (summer daily 9am–7pm, winter Sun 10am–3pm) in his natal village of Myrtiá (Ottoman Varvári) 24km/15 miles southeast of Iráklio. Displays illustrate his turbulent personal, literary and political life both in Greece and abroad – he spent long years effectively exiled by the Orthodox Church – with one room entirely devoted to Alexis Zorbas.

The best beaches near Iráklio are at **Ammoudára**, just west of town, and at **Tobroúk** and **Amnisós** to the east. The latter, the ancient port of **Knossos**, has the best sands and will soon be free of jet-blight once the airport moves inland in 2018.

## TO KNOSSOS AND BEYOND

Excursions from Iráklio will not only delight Minoan aficionados, but provide opportunities to savour the attractive countryside. The most famous site, of course, is the palace of **Knossos ❷**, a mere 5km (3 miles) southwest of the city centre, and easily reached on a No. 2 urban bus. (For a full exploration of the remains at Knossos, see page 310.)

At **Arhánes ❸**, 12km (8 miles) south of Knossós, an **Archaeological Museum** (Wed–Mon 8.30am–3pm; free)

*The Venetian church of Ágios Títos.*

has caused a stir with items apparently related to a human sacrifice, recovered from a Minoan temple at **Anemospiliá**, contradicting received notions of Minoan society as uniformly pacifist.

A steep climb from Arhánes leads to the summit of **Mount Gioúhtas** (811 metres/2,660ft), whose profile dominates Iráklio's horizon. At the top are a Minoan peak sanctuary, a 14th-century chapel and caves in which notionally immortal Zeus is supposedly buried.

**Týlissos ④**, 13km (8 miles) southwest of Iráklio, possesses three well-preserved small palaces, or large villas (Tue–Sun 8am–3pm), and is one of the few modern villages to retain its original pre-Hellenic name. Twenty kilometres (13 miles) further west on the same road, the elongated village of **Anógia**, where wool is spun and where many homes have looms, is a weaving and embroidery centre. Many local people still wear traditional dress on a regular basis, the men in particular looking like rebels in search of a cause. This is no stage setting: Anógia has a long tradition of resistance and revolt. The village

was razed during the rebellions of 1821 and 1866, and in 1944 the entire male population of the village was killed by German troops. It is also famous as a cradle for traditional music, with the distinguished Xylouris clan of singers and instrumentalists hailing from here.

From Anógia a side road climbs to the magnificent **Nída plateau**, from where it is a 20-minute uphill stroll to the **Idéon Andron** (Cave of Mount Ida); this was the nursery, if not the birthplace, of Zeus. Here the god was hidden and guarded by the *Kouretes*, who clashed their weapons to drown the sound of his cries, while the nymph Amalthea fed him goats' milk. Keen hikers might like to push on to the summit of **Mount Ida ⑤** (Psilorítis), at 2,456 metres (8,058ft) the highest point on Crete. The trail, part of the European E4 route, is well marked with red-and-white blazes; allow about seven hours for the round trip.

### EAST FROM IRÁKLIO

Return to Iráklio and continue eastwards along the E75 highway for 24km

*South Propylon, with its replica procession fresco, Knossós.*

### ⊘ MINOAN GLORY

The most renowned Minoan ruins – Knossos (Knossós in modern Greek), Phaistos (Festós), Mália and Káto Zákros – date from the Neo-palatial period (1700–1450 BC). Great unfortified palaces, brilliantly decorated, were built, and beautiful pottery and magnificent jewellery were produced.

The early palaces of the Proto-palatial period (1900–1700 BC), of which scant remains survive, were almost certainly destroyed by earthquakes, but it's still debatable what ended the Neo-palatial period. In the Third palatial period (1450–1200 BC) mainland Mycenaeans had supplanted the Minoans and by the Iron Age (after 1100 BC) Dorian city-states had replaced the old palaces. Surviving Minoans (the Eteo-Cretans) retired to the mountains and kept their traditions alive.

(15 miles) to the notoriously tatty resorts of **Hersónisos** ❻, **Stalída** (Stális) and **Mália** ❼. However, their beaches at least have good sand, though this does make them very popular. Hersónisos features scanty Greek and Roman remains, while close to the beach near Mália is a renowned Minoan site.

The **Malia Palace** (daily 8am–3pm), traditionally associated with King Sarpedon, brother of Minos, is contemporary with that at Knossos. The ruins are not as extensive as those at Knossos or Phaistos but, even without reconstruction, are more readily understood. The remarkable number of store rooms and workrooms, as well as the simpler style of architecture, suggests a country villa more than a palace. Excavations unearthed the Hrysólakkos (Golden Pit) from the Proto-palatial period (1900–1700 BC). The name is derived from the numerous gold artefacts found in this enormous necropolis.

From either Mália or Hersónisos, twisting mountain roads lead up to the **Lasíthi Plateau** ❽, around 840 metres (2,756ft) above sea level and 57km (36 miles) from Iráklio. This fertile upland supports potatoes, cereal crops, apples and pears, but sadly is now depopulated and neglected, with heavy spring rains in many years preventing proper cultivation. **Psyhró** in the plateau's southwest corner is home to the giant **Diktéo Andron** (Diktean Cave; daily summer 8am–8pm, winter until 3pm), supposedly the birthplace of Zeus. Nearby, **Agios Geórgios village** offers the **Cretan Folklore Museum** (Apr–Oct Mon–Sat 10am–4pm) with household, craft and agricultural exhibits.

Descend from Lasíthi via Neápoli to **Agios Nikólaos** ❾, 69km (43 miles) from Iráklio, invariably abbreviated by tourists to "Ag Nik" and once the Saint-Tropez of Crete before the current slump. This tourist paradise, overlooked by the eastern mountains, is magnificently situated on the Gulf of Mirabéllo. Here, and at neighbouring **Eloúnda** (10km/6 miles away), are some of the island's best and most expensive hotels. Unfortunately Agios Nikólaos does lack a decent beach,

*Black knitted headscarves (saríkia), pleated, baggy trousers (vrákes) and custom-made, high boots (stivánia) are the traditional male dress still worn in many parts of Crete.*

*Woven goods in Anógia.*

# A CRETAN MYTH

The story of the Minotaur is a complicated one that has survived through the centuries and is known all over the Western world.

King Minos, mythical king of Knossos, was the son of Zeus and the Phoenician princess Europa. Zeus, in the form of a bull, had seduced Europa and taken her off to Crete, where Minos and his brothers, Rhadamanthys and Sarpedon, were born. Minos spent nine years in the Diktean Cave with his father learning the arts of kingship, after which he banished his brothers and became sole ruler of Knossos.

Wishing to consolidate his power, Minos asked Poseidon for a sign of approval and the god provided a white bull from the sea to be sacrificed. However, the animal was so beautiful that Minos could not

*Vase depicting Theseus Slaying the Minotaur, c.540 BC.*

bring himself to kill it, so he sacrificed another in its place. This lack of gratitude enraged Poseidon, who made Pasiphaë, the wife of Minos, fall in love with the bull.

Daedalos, an ingenious member of the court, built a hollow model of a cow for Pasiphaë in which she could hide while the bull mounted her. The result of this union was a curious child, the half-man, half-bull Minotaur. Minos was, understandably, furious when he found out about Pasiphaë's son and, after taking advice from the Oracle at Delphi, ordered Daedalos to build a huge labyrinth under the court where the Minotaur was to live.

In the meantime the white bull had been taken to the Peloponnese by Herakles as one of his 12 tasks. There it did great damage and Minos' son, Androgeos, set out to hunt it. While out hunting, Androgeos was killed by a jealous Athenian rival. In response, Minos immediately sent his fleet to Athens and after a long war, defeated the Athenians. The Cretan king then demanded a tribute; the sacrifice of seven young men and seven maidens of Athens every year, who were to be delivered to the labyrinth to be killed by the Minotaur.

One year Theseus, son of the Athenian king Aegeus, volunteered for the sacrifice. While on Crete he met and fell in love with Ariadne, the daughter of Minos, who helped Theseus find his way through the labyrinth by providing a ball of thread that he could unravel to mark his way and prevent him getting lost. He entered the maze, killed the Minotaur with his father's sword and released the surviving captives.

Triumphant, he and Ariadne fled by sea, but the story does not have a happy ending. Theseus turned out to be a fickle lover. He soon abandoned Ariadne on Náxos, where she became the consort of the god Dionysos. Theseus was forgetful as well as fickle. He promised his father that if he survived his battle with the Minotaur he would raise a white sail on his ship as he returned home. Unfortunately, this slipped his mind, and when his father saw the ship approaching harbour with no white sail visible he assumed his beloved son was dead. Overcome with grief he drowned himself in the sea which henceforth bore his name (Aegean).

though there are some passable sands a little way southeast. Restaurants and hotels, bars and cafés cluster around Kitroplatía cove and the small so-called bottomless lake, connected to the now-disused harbour by a canal. Although it is not what most visitors come here for, the town does have a pleasant **Archaeological Museum** (shut until further notice) and a **Folk Museum** (summer Sun–Fri 9.30am–1.30pm and 5–7pm).

The nearby island of **Spinalónga**  (April–Oct daily 9am–7pm, winter by arrangement), an isolated leper colony until 1957 (the last in Europe), with a massive Venetian fortress, poignant memories and a well-restored village, is readily reached from Eloúnda or much closer Pláka by boat. The island was immortalised in Victoria Hislop's eponymous novel, and the rather better Greek bi-lingual TV series based on it – Greek tourists appear in droves.

Clinging to the hillside 11km (7 miles) from Agios Nikólaos is **Kritsá** ⓫, where Jules Dassin's *He Who Must Die* (starring Melina Merkouri) was filmed in 1956. Immediately below Kritsá stands three-aisled **Panagía Kerá church,** Crete's greatest Byzantine treasure (Tue–Sun 8.30am–3pm), its frescoes done incrementally between 1250 and 1320, and remarkable for vivid facial expressions, deep colours and rarely depicted episodes from the apocryphal gospels.

Some 2km (1.25 miles) beyond Kritsá lie the ruins of **ancient Lato** (Lató; unlocked). The pleasure here lies not so much in the fairly extensive remains of a Doric city (although they are worth seeing) but the superb views northeast towards the Gulf of Mirabéllo.

East of Agios Nikólaos, a motorway is slowly being extended to bypass some of the sites below en route to Sitía. After 19km (12 miles) on the old road, **Gourniá** ⓬ (Tue–Sun 8.30am–2.40pm) is reached. Spread over a ridge lie remains, not of another palace, but of streets and houses of a Minoan town, the best preserved on Crete. Especially in spring, when the site is covered with a riot of flowers, even those bored with old stones will appreciate the site.

*The grand stairway at Phaistos.*

*There are thousands of irrigation windmills across the Lasíthi Plateau, but none function any longer except as taverna decor, being disconnected from their water pumps.*

From highways new and old, a side road drops to the fishing port-resort of **Móhlos**, with popular tavernas and the cleanest swimming on a coast generally beset by tide- and wind-borne debris. The tiny island opposite, which can be readily reached by strong swimmers, bears the same name as the village and has scanty Minoan ruins. Well to the west lies **Psíra island,** where a Minoan port-town has been excavated – boat tours go there by arrangement.

## SITÍA AND EASTERN CRETE

**Sitía** ⑬, 70km (43 miles) from Agios Nikólaos, is a laid-back town which, to the delight of (mostly French and Italian) visitors and the chagrin of locals, has not yet hit the big time, though this may well happen soon as the local airport was substantially upgraded in 2016 and received its first international flights in 2017. Attractions include an inconspicuous Venetian fort, an **Archaeological Museum** (Tue–Sun 8am–3pm) full of finds from Zakros, a **Folklore Museum** (Mon–Sat 10am–2pm) and a decent in-town beach.

The still-active **Toploú Monastery** (Apr–Oct daily 9am–6pm, winter Fri only), its tall 16th-century Italianate bell tower beckoning like a mosque's minaret, stands in splendid isolation in the middle of nowhere, 24km (15 miles) beyond Sitía. Its greatest treasure is a minutely detailed 18th-century icon painted by Ioannis Kornaros. The monastery derived its name from a renowned artillery piece (*top* is Turkish for cannon) which formerly protected it. The monks also had other methods of protecting themselves: observe the machicolation above the monastery gate through which they poured hot oil over their assailants.

The Orthodox Church has long courted controversy by proposing to lease some of Toploú's vast landholdings for a 7,000-bed tourist complex just north on Cape Síderos, complete with golf course. This has outraged environmentalists who point out that there is very little water left for such a development in eastern Crete, however, the project is now proceeding, no doubt encouraged by the local airport upgrade.

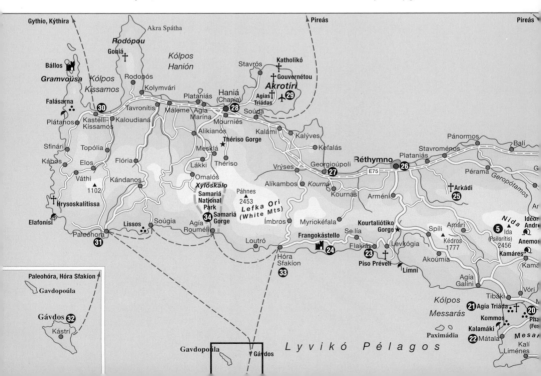

After a further 9km (6 miles), **Väï** ⓯ is renowned for its myriad palm trees and the large, sandy beach that suggests exotic tropical regions. The inedible-date palm trees *(Phoenix theophrasti)* are actually native to Crete, Amorgós, Anáfi and southwestern coastal Turkey, and were known in antiquity; the Linnaean name honours Theophrastos, the ancient botanist who described them. The beach here is usually crowded; for a quieter time, make for the mostly palm-free **Ítanos**, 2km (1.25 miles) farther north, with an ancient town adjacent.

Southwards from Väï is **Palékastro**, which made headlines during the 1990s because of the discovery of what may be the largest Minoan town yet – sadly, funds are lacking to uncover it. Nearby beaches, particularly **Hióna** and **Kvreménos** with its windsurf school, are well worth visiting.

## ZÁKROS

Some 20km (12 miles) further on you come to inland **Ano Zákros** and beach-side **Káto Zákros**, the latter adjacent to the fourth great Minoan **palace of Zákros** ⓰ (daily summer 10.30am–5.30pm, winter 8am–3pm). Hikers will prefer to make their way from upper to lower Zákros by walking through the spectacular **Ravine of the Dead**, where caves were used for Minoan burials.

The Neo-palatial period ruins at Zákros, 43km (27 miles) from Sitía, are often waterlogged, partly because Crete is tipping over longitudinally, with its eastern end sinking below and its western end rising above sea level and coastal water-tables. The main site has its customary central courtyard and royal, religious and domestic buildings and workshops radiating outwards; a spring-fed cistern still contains fresh water, inhabited by pond terrapins. Close by are the remains of a Minoan hillside town and a sheltered harbour, ideally situated for trade with the Levant and Egypt.

Unusually, the Zákros dig was originally privately funded. In 1961, prominent Greek archaeologist Nikolaos Platon was asked by the Pomerances, a New York business couple, if any Minoan sites had still to be excavated.

*Lake Voulisméni at Agios Nikólaos was once said to be bottomless, and the home of spirits. Unromantic modern surveyors have found that it is about 70 metres (230ft) deep and fed by an underground river.*

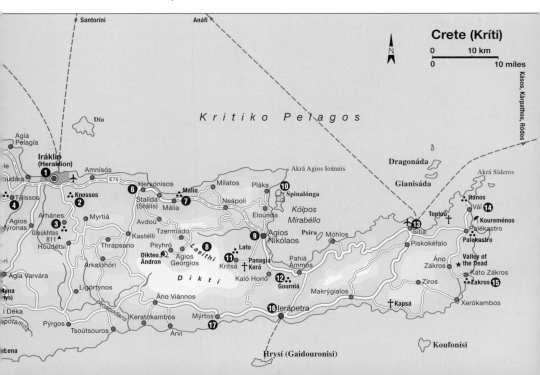

*The text of the Law Code of Gortys is written in "ox-plough" fashion, reading left to right along one line, then right to left along the next.*

*Sitía harbour.*

Yes, he told them. So what, they asked, was the problem? Money, was the reply. With that, the Pomerances underwrote the dig with no strings attached. Platon died in 1992 at the age of 83, but excavations continue.

Back at Sitía, a scenic road crosses the island's isthmus to **Ierápetra** ⑯ (35km/22 miles from Agios Nikólaos), the largest town on the south coast (and the most southerly town in all Europe). Despite a small Venetian fort (daily summer 8.30am–7.30pm; free) and a small but interesting archaeological "collection" (Tue–Sun 8am–3pm) inside a former Koranic school, it's an un-atmospheric supply point for the region's farmers, who have carpeted the coastal plain around town with plastic vegetable greenhouses. Tourists come mainly for a daytrip to **Hrysí** islet, a natural reserve with rare juniper groves and fine-sand beaches.

Fifteen kilometres (9 miles) to the west lies the pretty little beach resort of **Mýrtos** ⑰, with a villagey feel. Eastwards 24km (15 miles) from Ierápetra, past sheltered Agía Fotiá and Ahliá

coves, is the more conventional "strip" resort, and gently shelving beach, of **Makrýgialos**. From here a minor coastal road leads to the originally 14th-century **Kapsá Monastery**, built snugly into the cliffs at the entrance to a gorge. Encased in a silver casket is the skull of the monk Gerondoyannis, a 19th-century faith healer who, despite not being canonised, is a cult figure.

## SOUTH FROM IRÁKLIO

The main road south-southwest from Iráklio, over a lower point in the island's spine, goes via **Agía Varvára**, near which is the **Ómfalos** or "navel stone" supposedly marking the centre of Crete. Just beyond it you will have a breathtaking view of the **Mesará Plain**. Rich soil and a benign climate make this a cornucopia, producing a high percentage of the island's crops.

At the edge of the plain, 40km (25 miles) from Iráklio, is the almost sacred village of **Agii Déka** (Holy Ten), with its heavily restored medieval church, into which are incorporated fragments from the nearby site of Gortys (modern Górtyna). Agii Déka is renowned because in AD 250, during the persecution of the Christians under Emperor Decius, 10 men were executed here for failing to make sacrifice for the ancient gods and the health of the empire, becoming in due course among the most revered of Cretan saints.

After another 1km (0.5 miles), you reach **Gortys** ⑱ (modern Górtyna; daily summer 8am–7pm, winter until 5pm). This was the capital of the Romans who first came to Crete in the 2nd century BC, but weren't in firm possession of the island until 67 BC. Outstanding and upstanding are the Roman *odeion*, the theatre and a triple-naved basilica, although Italian excavations continue. The last is by far the best-preserved early church in Crete, built to house the tomb of Titus (Titos), Crete's first bishop, who died *c.* AD 100. However, the most renowned artefacts are some stone blocks incorporated into the *odeion*. About 2,500 years ago more than 17,000 characters were incised on these blocks to produce the Law Code of Gortys, which starkly differentiates the rights of free men and slaves.

Those in search of more ruins, or of health and good swimming, may head south to **Léndas** ⓳ (72km/45 miles from Iráklio). Nearby ancient **Lebena** was the port for Gortys, and its therapeutic springs made it a renowned healing sanctuary with an **Asklepion** (temple to Asklepios, the god of healing). Only traces of this sanctuary – notably a Hellenistic mosaic – remain. In an attempt to equal, if not emulate, the ancients, nude bathing has become popular at **Dytikós**, Léndas's best beach, 15 minutes' walk beyond the headland at the western end of the village.

**Phaistos** ⓴ (Festós), Crete's second great Minoan site, occupies a magnificent location 16km (10 miles) west of Gortys (daily summer 8am– 7pm, winter until 5pm). Most of the remains date from the Neo-palatial period, although part of the floor plan of the Proto-palatial

palace is discernible. State rooms, religious quarters, workshops, store rooms and functional plumbing can all be identified. An outstanding sight is the Grand Stairway on the west side. Nearby, again on a glorious site with views of the Libyan Sea, are the attractive Minoan ruins of **Agía Triáda** ㉑ (daily 9am–4pm), probably a summer villa.

Next, on to **Mátala** ㉒, 70km (43 miles) from Iráklio. This seaside village first gained renown when the sandstone caves in the cliffs around the small, sandy beach – actually ancient tombs – became home to substantial colonies of 1960s and 1970s hippies; Joni Mitchell stopped by too, and her song *Carey* refers explicitly to the place. Today Mátala is a mainstream resort, expensive and crowded out in season; the cave-dwellers have long since been evicted and the cliff declared an archaeological site. The main beach is still excellent, but for more seclusion walk half an hour south to "**Red Beach**", although adjacent **Kalamáki** and Kommós beaches to the north are even longer; the latter has a Minoan site (closed for excavations).

*The 16th-century Venetian fortress on Spinalónga, near Agios Nikólaos, was used as a leper colony until 1957 – the last in Europe.*

*Káto Zákros bay.*

**⊙ Fact**

The palm trees at Váï are immune to the red palm weevil, which has devastated other palm species across Greece since arriving from Africa in 2006. When attacked, these native palms excrete goo that suffocates the weevils.

The even larger south-coast resort of **Agía Galíni** lies a bit further west on the Gulf of Mesará, 70km (43 miles) from Iráklio. If Mátala proved too boisterous, then Agía Galíni with its lively nightlife will be far more so. The harbour, with a short quay and pedestrianised main street jammed with tavernas and bars, is cradled by steep slopes covered with modest hotels.

## WEST TO RÉTHYMNO

You are now in western Crete, and Réthymno province; **Plakiás ㉓**, flanked by five beaches and a spectacular mountain backdrop, lies some 40km (25 miles) from the provincial capital, and equally far from Agía Galíni via roundabout roads. The main cultural excursion from Plakiás is to **Píso Préveli Monastery** (13km/8 miles), passing en route the evocative, restored **Káto Préveli Monastery** (daily 9am–dusk), and a much-photographed arched **bridge**. Piso Préveli itself (daily 9am–dusk) has a superb position, and a courtyard fountain with the inscription "Wash your sins, not just your face."

A double bronze statue of a gun-toting monk and a Commonwealth soldier commemorates Píso Préveli's crucial role in sheltering defeated stragglers from the 1941 Battle of Crete; they were evacuated to Egypt by submarine from **Límni** beach below at the mouth of the **Kourtaliótiko Gorge**, which had a local palm forest nearly as large as that at Váï – until it caught fire in 2010. Luckily, natural regeneration is occurring.

West of Plakiás along the coast, the next resort of consequence huddles around the Venetian **castle of Frangokástello ㉔**, overlooking a good sandy beach. On 18 May 1828, 385 freedom fighters from Sfakiá and the mainland, commanded by Epirot warlord Hatzimihalis Daliannis, were killed here by a superior force of Cretan Muslims; the mysterious *drossoulítes* (dewy ones), a sunrise mirage particular to late May, are said to be their ghosts riding towards the castle.

Back in Iráklio, the oleander-lined E75 highway runs west towards Réthymno. Some, however, might

*The Fortétsa, Réthymno's medieval stronghold.*

prefer the more leisurely, picturesque but winding old road. Alternatively, leave the new road 25km (16 miles) along to arrive in **Fódele**, a small village rich in orange trees and locally made embroidery. A restored house here is spuriously claimed as the birthplace in 1541 of Domenikos Theotokopoulos, better known as El Greco. Back on the expressway, turn seawards after a further 18km (11 miles) to reach the popular resort of **Balí**, clustered around three small bays at the foot of a hill.

At **Stavroménos** or **Plataniás**, turn southeast for beautifully situated **Arkádi Monastery ㉕** (daily Apr–May & Sept–Oct 9am–7pm, June–Aug 9am–8pm, Nov 9am–5pm, Dec–Mar 9am–4pm), 80km (50 miles) from Iráklio or 25km (16 miles) before Réthymno, Crete's most sacred shrine. During November 1866, the monastery, sheltering hundreds of rebel fighters and their families, was attacked by Muslim Cretans. Rather than surrender, the abbot ordered that gunpowder stored in the now roofless room in the northwest corner of the courtyard be ignited, thus killing up to 1,000 Muslims and Orthodox. The photogenic, 16th-century rococo church facade survived, and featured prominently on the now-retired 100-drachma note.

## RÉTHYMNO

**Réthymno ㉖**, 77km (48 miles) from Iráklio, prides itself on being Crete's intellectual capital – thanks to the internationally respected university, and some native authors. Réthymno still possesses an intact Old Town with a small, extremely picturesque Venetian harbour guarded by an elegant lighthouse, though most of the medieval walls disappeared early in the 20th century. The only surviving remnant is the Porta Guora, or Great Gate, leading into Four Martyrs Square. The martyrs in question were hanged here in 1824 for apostatising from Islam back to Orthodox Christianity – a capital crime under Ottoman law.

West of the harbour looms the immense **Fortétsa** (Fortezza; daily summer 8.30am–8.30pm, winter earlier closure), said to be the largest Venetian castle ever built. The most intact, and

*Navigating the waters off the coast near Réthymno.*

*The lighthouse at Haniá, designed like a minaret, dates from 1833–40, when Crete was handed over to Egypt as a reward for helping the Turks crush the rebellious Greeks.*

*Cretan goatherds.*

most interesting, structure inside is the **Sultan Ibrahim Mosque** dating from 1647, the largest domed structure in Greece. Réthymno's other monumental attractions – the ornate, still-flowing **Rimóndi Fountain**, the Venetian **loggia** and the **Nerantzés Mosque** – a converted Venetian church – all lie between the harbour and the fortress. Spare time for the **Archaeological Museum** (Apr–Oct Tue–Sun 10am–6pm, Nov–Mar 8am–3pm), boasting a fine collection of painted clay sarcophagi, and the **Historical and Folklore Museum** (April–Oct Mon–Sat 10am–2.30pm) with a wealth of rural impedimenta.

Venetian houses with unexpected architectural delights can be found in the narrow streets linking these sights, while Ottoman features in the shape of fountains with calligraphic inscriptions and overhanging enclosed wooden balconies – the famous local *kióskia* – are evidence that Réthymno was approximately one-third Muslim before 1923.

Sun-worshippers appreciate Réthymno's wide beach, beginning immediately east of the harbour behind a palm-shaded promenade and stretching for several kilometres past the new town.

Réthymno and Haniá to the west are joined by the E75 and a less used old road. Leave either after 23km (14 miles) for **Georgioúpoli ㉗** at the mouth of the River Almyrós, a pleasant resort with a long beach; 4km (2.5 miles) inland, Crete's only freshwater lake, **Kourná**, has tavernas, idyllic swimming and pedaloes or kayaks to rent.

## HANIÁ

**Haniá ㉘** (Chania), 59km (37 miles) from Réthymno, one of the oldest continuously inhabited cities in the world, is Crete's second city and was its capital until 1971. Focus of the Old Town is the double Venetian harbour, whose broad quays are backed by characterful, colourful old buildings, their reflections shimmering in the water. The ambience is of the Levant and this is the place for the *vólta* or evening stroll.

The restored 1645-vintage **Mosque of Küçük Hasan** (Yali Tzami), by two years the oldest mosque in Crete, stands at

one end of the quay and now hosts art exhibitions; the **Fírkas Bastion** occupies the other end, next to the moderately interesting **Naval Museum** (May–Oct Mon–Sat 9am–5pm, Sun 10am–6pm, Nov–Apr daily 9am–3pm). On the bastion, in December 1913 the King of Greece officially raised the national flag for the first time on Crete. Behind the Naval Museum, inside San Salvatore church at the top of Theotokopoúlou, the well-designed **Byzantine Museum** (Tue–Sun 8am–3pm) showcases icons, jewellery, coins, a floor mosaic and fresco fragments rescued from country chapels. Both Theotokopoúlou and its perpendicular Angélou have splendid examples of domestic Venetian and Ottoman architecture.

The **Archaeological Museum** (Apr–Oct Tue–Sun 8am–8pm, Nov–Mar Tue–Sun 8am–3pm), inside a former Franciscan monastery, has a collection strongest on painted Minoan larnakes, Cretan coins with local motifs, Roman statuettes and Hellenistic mosaics. Two blocks west, on Kondyláki, **Etz Hayyim Synagogue** (May–Oct Mon–Thu 10am–6pm, Fri 10am–3pm, Nov–Apr Mon–Thu 10am–5pm, Fri 10am–3pm) is the sole reminder of Haniá's pre-World War II Jewish community of about 350; it has been lovingly restored from a wrecked state, including the *mikveh* or ritual bath, fed by a natural spring.

In the New Town, visit the lofty glass-roofed cruciform **market**, modelled on the Marseilles halles and dating from 1913, still overflowing with vegetables, fruit, fish, meat, herbs and spices, cheese and wine.

## AKROTÍRI

**Akrotíri** , a limestone peninsula stretching northeastwards from Haniá to enclose enormous, strategic **Soúda Bay**, is full of interest. First visit the hill of **Profítis Ilías**, where revolutionary Cretans gathered in 1897 to demand union with Greece. Here are the simple graves of Eleftherios Venizelos, born outside Haniá at Mourniés, and his son Sofoklis.

Other graves, 1,527 of them, are found at the immaculately maintained **Commonwealth Cemetery** near the

*Wild blooms.*

*Arkádi Monastery can lay claim to a significant past.*

### ⊘ MONASTERIES

The Akrotíri peninsula has a cluster of historic **monasteries**. The first encountered, 16km (10 miles) from Haniá, is 17th-century **Agías Triádas** (aka Zangarólon; daily 9–7pm), built in Venetian Rococo style, splendid but somewhat commercialised. A further 4km (2.5 miles) away stands **Gouvernétou**, a working monastery not welcoming to non-Orthodox. From Gouvernétou a rough 40-minute downhill scramble leads to the abandoned, enchanting and possibly enchanted **Katholikó Monastery**, concealed in a goat-patrolled ravine. Founded in about 1050, this is, if not the oldest, certainly one of the first monastic settlements on Crete.

Soúda shore, where British and Commonwealth troops killed during the 1941 Battle of Crete are buried.

Sandy **Stavrós** cove in the far northwest served as a location for *Zorba the Greek* (see also page 292).

## SOUTHWEST FROM HANIÁ

From Haniá the westward coast road passes the busy resorts of **Agía Marína** and **Plataniás** which merge imperceptibly with each other, as well as 4,465 Germans buried in the well-tended cemetery at **Máleme**.Beyond Kolymvári, one emerges at a viewpoint over the broad **bay of Kíssamos**, cradled by the peninsulas of **Gramvoúsa** and **Rodópou**, together resembling rabbit's ears on the map.

A descent to the broad coastal plain brings you to pleasant but characterless **Kastélli-Kissámos** ⑳ (42km/26 miles from Haniá), mostly visited for its ferry connection to the Peloponnese but also endowed with a superb **Archaeological Museum** (Tue–Sun 8.30am–-3pm), particularly strong on the Hellenistic and Roman town here – highlights are the mosaics upstairs

of the Four Seasons and Dionysian activities, rescued from nearby ancient villas. The closest memorable beach lies 17km (11 miles) west, via Plátanos village at **Falásarna**, with a small ancient city thrown into the bargain. Boat excursions go from Kastélli to the "Blue Lagoon" and Venetian island fortress at **Bállos**, at the tip of Gramvoúsa.

From Kaloudianá, just east of Kastéli, a good road leads south through lush countryside. There are chestnut orchards at **Élos** – where the harvest is celebrated with an October Chestnut Festival – while villages like **Topólia**, **Kefáli** and **Váthi** have lovely old chapels with 14th-century frescoes. Beyond Váthi, the route forges through a gorge to **Hrysoskalítissa** (Of the Golden Step) **Monastery** (daily 7am–sunset), 39km (25 miles) from Kastélli. The name refers to the legend that one of the 90 steps descending from the terrace appears as gold to the extremely pure at heart. Some 5km (3 miles) beyond, the road ends at **Elafonísi**, a small islet sheltering a shallow lagoon and a pale-sand beach of near-tropical beauty; it is a protected zone and thus strictly undeveloped

*Mosque of Küçük Hasan on Haniá's waterfront.*

– bring picnic food and drink – but it gets hopelessly crowded in season.

A busier road from Tavronítis, near Máleme, leads via **Kándanos**, with more frescoed late Byzantine chapels, to **Paleóhora** ㉛ (76km/47 miles from Haniá), a friendly resort with a ruined Venetian castle bracketed by a pebble beach (east) and a long sandy one (west). Boats leave at least twice weekly for the islet of **Gávdos** ㉜, Europe's southernmost point and the ultimate cult islet amongst many nationalities, increasingly developed touristically for the sake of its excellent beaches.

**Hóra Sfakíon** ㉝, 75km (47 miles) via an entirely different road from Haniá, is the "capital" of rugged Sfakiá, celebrated as the one corner of Crete that never fully submitted to Venetian, Ottoman or Nazi rule. Like Píso Préveli, it was a major evacuation point for fleeing Allied soldiers after the Battle of Crete. The current major role of this small, cliff-hanging port is as the local small-ferry terminus, with more services to Gávdos and a daily line west along the roadless coast as far as Paleóhora,

stopping en route at the tiny resorts of Loutró, Agía Roúmeli and Soúgia.

But you needn't rely on the boats – west of Hóra Sfakíon is some of the best shoreline trekking in the islands. The path threads "**Sweetwater Beach**" – the closest good one to the town – en route to **Loutró**, pleasant, although again beachless, before traversing **Agios Pávlos beach** with its Byzantine chapel on the way to Agía Rouméli(see page 308) – a long day's hike. Only the most experienced and fit hill-walkers should tackle the next tricky, two-day section to enjoyable **Soúgia**, which has a good beach, before the easy final-day section via **ancient Lissos** to Paleóhora. Lissos was known in antiquity for its Asklepion or therapeutic centre, attracting the unwell from far and wide. The Temple of Asklepios is in ruins but its mosaic floor can still be seen.

## THE SAMARIÁ GORGE

For most active, first-time visitors, however, the one "must" walk is the spectacular, five-to-six-hour traverse of the **Samariá Gorge** ㉞, at 16km (10

*Haniá harbour in the early morning light.*

miles) among the longest in Europe. The hike starts with a steep stair-path descent from **Xylóskala** at 1,200 metres (3,937ft) elevation, at the southern end of the vast **Omalós** plain, itself a 45km (28-mile) tortuous drive from Haniá. Within an hour or so of walking, the path is 600 metres (1,968ft) lower in altitude; some 7km (4.5 miles) below the start point, the hamlet of **Samariá**, abandoned in 1962, comes into view.

The going now gets tougher underfoot, albeit with less of a gradient, and involves criss-crossing the river-bed, which usually has water in it. Flash floods can occur in spring and autumn, and patrolling wardens' warnings should be heeded. The gorge progressively narrows and the walls soar straight upwards for 300 to 600 metres (985–1,970ft). Soon after passing Aféndis Hristós Chapel, the **Siderespórtes** (Iron Gates) are reached and the gorge, scarcely penetrated by sunlight here, is little more than 3.5 metres (11ft) wide.

The gorge falls within a national park strictly administered by the Haniá Forest Service, which specifically forbids a long list of activities including camping, lighting fires or making loud noises (including singing). Since its creation in 1962, the park has functioned well as a wildlife refuge. You are most unlikely to spot any *krí-krí* (wild ibex), but botanists will be delighted, while ornithologists may glimpse vultures overhead.

You emerge from the narrows at old **Agía Rouméli**, abandoned after World War II, but still face another 2km (1 mile) of hot tramping to reach its modern coastal successor. A cold beer and refreshing swim off the long sand-and-pebble beach are in order, but be aware of the time (and the seat quota) of the last boat out in either direction, or you may find yourself making an unplanned overnight stop here. If you forget the time, or if you decide you would like to overnight anyway, there are ten places to stay.

The gorge is open 1 May–31 October from dawn to about 4pm (under-15s free), subject to allowances for bad weather. After 4pm you will only be allowed into the first 2km (1 mile) from either end, and the wardens ensure that nobody camps in the gorge.

*Hung out to dry.*

The "Iron Gates", Samariá Gorge.

# THE PALACE OF KNOSSÓS

Until 1900, the Minoan civilisation was little more than a myth. Now its putative capital is one of the largest and best-restored sites in all Greece.

Some visitors to Knossos (modern Greek Knossós) find the concrete reconstructions and repainted frescoes (often extrapolated from very small existing fragments) aid comprehension. But for many, used to other, more recent, ruins that are clearly defensive or overtly religious, the site is mysterious. Can we hope to look back at fragments of a culture from 3,500 years ago and understand its imperatives and subtleties? Hiring a licensed guide – they hang about waiting for custom near the ticket booth – will make a huge difference in your experience of the palace.

In legend, Knossos was the labyrinth of King Minos, where he imprisoned the Minotaur, the human-taurine child of his wife Pasiphaë. In reality, the place was probably not a palace in the modern sense, but perhaps an administrative and economic centre, overseen by spiritual leaders.

Among the 1,300 rooms of the main palace were both the sacred and the commercial: lustral baths for holy ceremonies; storerooms for agricultural produce; workshops for metallurgy and stone-cutting. Nearby are the Royal Villa and the Little Palace.

Try to visit early or late in the day (better still, visit out of season), to avoid the worst of the substantial crowds, and to avoid being swept along by the flow. Look for the subtle architectural delights – light wells to illuminate the larger rooms; hydraulic controls providing water for drinking, bathing and flushing away sewage; drains with parabolic curves at the bends to prevent overflow.

The site is open daily Apr–Oct 8am–7pm, Nov–Mar 8am–3pm.

*Minoan fresco at the Iráklio Archaeological Museum.*

*A (replica) fresco depicting the capture of a wild bull decorates the ramparts of the north entrance, leading to the road to Knossos's harbour at Amnisos.*

*The famous double horns now sitting on the south facade were once regarded as sacred symbols, though perhaps this is an overworking of the bull motif of the site.*

*The Cup Bearers fresco.*

## Controversial restorations

In 1878 a local merchant, Minos Kalokairinos, uncovered part of Knossos, but the Muslim owners of the land prevented further excavation and even wealthy Heinrich Schliemann got entangled in unproductive negotiations for purchase.

However, once Crete gained autonomy in 1898, the way was open for archaeologist Arthur Evans to purchase the site and begin excavating. He worked here from 1900 until 1931, though by 1903 most of Knossos had been uncovered.

Evans's use of reinforced concrete to replace long-vanished timber columns, and his completely speculative upper-storey reconstructions, have received considerable criticism. Moreover, the Minoan frescoes are not only arbitrarily placed, but almost completely modern, painted from scratch by assistants Piet de Jong and the two Emile Gilliéron, father and son. Others have charged that Evans, a fairly typical Victorian chauvinist, manipulated evidence to fit his theory of the thalassocratic Minoans as prehistoric proto-British imperialists. It's also clear that both the restoration and fresco-retouching was heavily influenced by the Art Nouveau and Art Deco styles prevalent in Europe at the time.

*Wandering around Knossos – but the scale of the site is most apparent from the air: nearly 2 hectares (5 acres) of palaces ruled a population of perhaps 100,000.*

*Bull fresco at the Iráklio Archaeological Museum.*

*Sir Arthur Evans, the English archaeologist whose reconstruction of Knossos, a significant quantity of it based on conjecture, was to prove controversial.*

A cruise ship arriving at Rhodes.

# THE GREEK ISLANDS

## TRAVEL TIPS

# TRANSPORT

## GETTING THERE

### By air

Greece has good air connections with the rest of the world, being served by numerous international airlines. Direct flights to the islands generally operate from early May to late October, even into November for Rhodes and Crete.

Most scheduled airline passengers travelling to Greece make Athens's Eleftherios Venizelos Airport (www.aia.gr) their point of entry, though a number of flights (from the rest of Europe only) arrive at Thessaloníki's Makedonía Airport (www.skg-airport.gr), giving easier access to certain north Aegean islands. Scheduled flights (BA, easyJet, Ryanair, Jet2) also go much of the year to Rhodes, Crete (Iráklio or Haniá), Mýkonos, Santoríni, Kós, Skiáthos, Zákynthos, Préveza and Corfu.

Between Venizélos Airport, central Athens and Piraeus there are various connecting services. Line 3 of the metro takes you – surprisingly slowly, every half-hour – into town for €10 (€9 each for 2 people, €8 each for 3). Alternatively, take the X95 express bus (no slower than the metro) all the way to central Sýndagma Square (Platía Syndagmátos) or the X96 express bus to Piraeus port. All express buses depart from outside arrivals, with the same frequency (every 20 minutes) and the same fare (€6 at the time of writing).

A taxi from Venizélos Airport to the centre of Athens will cost €38–50 depending on time of day or night and your final destination, including airport supplement and per-bag fee. Even using the Attikí Odós (ring road) round northern Athens, or the Ymittós Peripheral,

journey time can still amount to over an hour.

Makedonía Airport is 15km (9 miles) southeast of Thessaloníki. Regular buses 78 and 78N go to the city centre (€2 coin-machine-sold tickets) and take around 35 minutes. Taxis take 20–30 minutes and cost €20.

### By sea

Most visitors entering Greece by sea do so from Italy. You can catch a boat to Greece from Venice, Ancona and Bari, but the most regular service is from Brindisi.

Daily ferry lines (less frequent in low season) connect Brindisi with the three main western ports: Corfu, Igoumenítsa and Pátra. Corfu is a 6.5-hour trip; Igoumenítsa 8 hours; and Pátra 11 to 14 hours, depending on whether you take a direct boat or one that makes a stop in Igoumenítsa. The "Superfast" ferries between Ancona and Pátra offer an efficient 22-hour crossing, as well as services from Bari and Venice.

Igoumenítsa is the ideal port of call for Paxí or Levkáda, while Pátra is best if you want to head directly to Athens or the southern Ionian islands. Regular buses connect Pátra and Athens (3-hour journey). If you plan to take your car on the boat, make reservations well in advance. Otherwise, arriving a few hours before departure time should suffice, except during peak seasons when advance booking is essential for seats or berths.

### By land

#### From Europe

The most direct overland route from northwestern Europe to Greece is a long one: 3,000km (1,900 miles) from London to Athens – a rather arduous and impractical travel option if you

are just trying to get to Greece for a brief holiday. The final approach, from Austria onward, will be via either Serbia and FYROM (Former Yugoslav Republic of Macedonia), or Romania and Bulgaria. There's not much to choose between these; the Serbian motorway network is excellent, FYROM's less so. Bulgaria has good motorways approaching Sofia, while heading onwards to the Greek frontier most of the route is now motorway standard (allow 2 hours 45min).

It is no longer possible to buy a through train ticket from the UK to Greece, and economically it never made much sense. If, as a railpass holder, you're intent on the journey, consult the ultra-useful rail-travel planning site www.seat61.com. Greece has only fitful rail links with Serbia or Bulgaria, so the most feasible route is via Italy, with a final ferry crossing as above.

### From Turkey

If you are travelling strictly overland to Greece from Asia you will pass through Istanbul and cross into Greece at the Évros River. Roads are good, and the journey from Istanbul to Thessaloníki takes approximately 15 hours; several bus companies serve the route.

Another popular option is to take one of the small boats between western Turkish ports and select Greek islands just opposite. Fares are overpriced for the distance involved, but it is undeniably convenient. The most reliable links are from Çesme to Híos (all year), Bodrum to Kos (the cheapest crossing) and Kuşadası to Sámos (no cars carried).

*Doing the donkey work in pedestrianised Hydra Town.*

## GETTING AROUND

### Public transport

#### By air

Flying to or between islands during peak season is usually, but not always, more expensive than travelling by high-speed boat or catamaran, whether you book just a seat or a cabin berth. Fares vary wildly with demand, but as an example the 50–55-minute flight between Athens and Sámos costs anywhere between €40 and €140 one-way, plus fare-dependent baggage charges.

Expect at least one of the domestically operating airlines listed in the box to vanish by the time you read this – there are too many air transport companies in Greece for the size of the market and state of the economy. The best, most current sources of discount tickets on extant Greek airlines are the local travel sites www.airtickets.gr, www.travelplanet24.com and https://gr.skyscanner.com. Foreign credit or debit cards may be viewed with some suspicion, so keep your mobile switched on when booking in case somebody wants to ring you to confirm your identity. Leave plenty of leeway in your domestic flight arrangements if you have to be back in Athens for an international flight. Island flights are often fully reserved over the summer, so book these at least a month in advance. Seats bought from a travel agency or one of the very few walk-in offices for any of the airlines listed below are subject to hefty surcharges.

#### By bus

The KTEL is a syndicate of nationwide bus companies, including the islands, whose buses are affordable and generally punctual, although on the larger islands like Crete and Lésvos frequencies can be sparse because of village depopulation. Buses on the more idiosyncratic rural routes may have a distinctly personal touch, their drivers decorating and treating the coach with great care.

Generally there is only one KTEL station per town; exceptions include Mytilíni and Iráklio (Crete), with two terminals each. On smaller islands, tickets are still sold on the bus by a

### ⊘ Useful airlines serving Greece from overseas anglophone countries

At the moment, there are only guaranteed direct services to Greece from Great Britain and Eire. Services from North America come and go – **Emirates**, **Qatari** and **American** are currently the most reliable providers from the US east coast; from Canada, Transat offers a direct link to Athens much of the year. There is no longer a non-stop service from Australia.

**Aegean Airlines** (www.aegeanair.com) Between Athens and London (Gatwick or Heathrow), Birmingham and Manchester

**British Airways** (www.ba.com) Between Athens–Heathrow, London–Skiáthos, London–Mýkonos, London–Santoríni, London–Iráklio, London–Corfu, London–Zeakynthos, London–Rhodes, London–Kos

**easyJet** (www.easyjet.com) Between various UK airports and Athens, Thessaloníki, Rhodes, Corfu, Kefaloniá, Mýkonos, Préveza (for Levkáda), Santoríni, Kos, Zákynthos, Haniá, Iráklio

**Ryanair** (www.ryanair.com) Between various UK airports, to same destinations as easyJet, but not Zákynthos, Préveza or Iráklio; also

Dublin to Athens and Haniá

**Jet2** (www.jet2com) Between various UK airports, including London Stansted, and Corfu, Iráklio, Kefaloniá, Kós, Rhodes and Zákynthos

**Qatar Air** (www.qatarairways.com) Between Athens and New York

**Emirates** (www.emirates.com) Between Athens and New York

**American Airlines** (www.americanairlines.com) Seasonally between Philadelphia and Athens

**Transat** (www.transat.com) Seasonally Toronto, Calgary, Vancouver or Montréal to Athens

conductor, but on large islands like Rhodes or Crete you must buy them in advance from ticket booths.

### Island buses

On the islands buses may be converted school buses, ultramodern coaches, or even (as on Lipsí) small mini-vans. Some drivers ricochet through mountain roads at death-defying speeds; accidents, however, are rare.

A bus of some description will usually meet arriving ferries (even if a boat is delayed) to transport passengers up the hill to the island's *hóra*, or capital. Bus stops are usually in main squares or by the waterfront in harbours, and vehicles may or may not run to schedule.

### Athens city buses and trams

Most of the regular Athens blue-and-white buses are now modern, air-conditioned vehicles, and using them is much less of an ordeal than it used to be. They are still usually overcrowded, and routes can be a mystery (placards at the stops do list the sequence of subsequent stops). However, matters are now much improved, with many stops having an electronic display showing how long until the next bus, and which number it is; once on the bus, another display, plus audible announcements, announces the next stop. Trolley buses, with an overhead pantograph, are marginally faster, and serve points of tourist interest. Most services run until nearly

midnight, a few after that on weekends.

The most useful suburban services for tourists are the orange-and-white KTEL Attica buses going from Mavromatéon 14, by Pédio toú Areos Park, to Rafína and Lávrio (alternative ferry ports for the Cyclades) and Soúnio (for the famous Temple of Poseidon there).

Ticketing can be a trap for the unwary. Plainclothes ticket inspectors will levy fines of 60 times the basic fare for travelling with the wrong ticket, an unvalidated ticket or no ticket. There are various kinds of tickets: a simple ticket (€1.40) allowing transfers within 90 minutes of first validation; a day pass valid for all urban transport methods (€4.50, good 24hr from validation) and a five-day ticket (€9). None of these are valid for journeys to/from the airport, while conversely the express-bus ticket into town from the airport is void the minute you leave that bus. Tickets are only obtainable from a dwindling network of newsagent kiosks – most can no longer be bothered to sell them – or more reliably at any metro station. Athens has a unified fare structure for all means of public transport, so that tickets are completely interchangeable.

### Athens metro and tram

The Athens metro system has halved travel times around the city and made a visible reduction in surface traffic. It runs from 5.30am–12.30am daily (Line 1

15min earlier for first/last trains), subject to strikes and staff availability. The stations themselves are palatial and squeaky-clean, with advertising placards kept to a minimum. The old ISAP line, in existence since the 1870s, has been refurbished and designated Line 1 (green on maps); it links Piraeus with Kifisiá via the city centre, but Monastiráki and Thissío stations are popular with pickpockets. Line 2 (red) links Ellinikó in the south with Anthoúpoli in the northwest of town. Line 3 (blue) joins Agía Marína with the airport at Spáta, via Monastiráki. The main junction stations are Omónia, Sýndagma and Monastiráki.

Single tickets, one-day and five-day passes as noted above can be obtained from the attended ticket windows in each station (you're encouraged to use the coin-op machines for single tickets). As on the buses, plainclothes inspectors do a roaring trade in fines levied against fare dodgers; pickpocketing is less common on lines 2 and 3.

There are also three tram lines: Sýndagma to Stádio Irínis ke Filías (SEF), SEF to Voúla and Sýndagma to Voúla. Arrivals at Pireás are strongly advised to use Line 1 just one stop to Fáliro, disembark, walk a short distance to the SEF terminal, and then continue into the centre by tram – you thus avoid passing through busy Monastiráki.

### By sea

### Ferries

Piraeus is the nerve centre of the Greek ferry network, and chances are you will pass through it at least once during your stay. In roughly diminishing order of importance, Rafína, Lávrio, Vólos, Kavála, Igoumenítsa, Agios Konstandínos, Thessaloníki, Pátra, Kyllíni and Gýthio are also useful mainland ports. In high season, especially to the Cyclades and Dodecanese, routes vary from "milk runs" on older boats stopping at five islands en route to your destination, to semi-direct ones on newer craft. It is also advisable not to purchase your ticket too far in advance: only around Easter; from mid-August to early September; and around election times do all classes of tickets actually sell out, but there are frequent changes to schedules which

*Excursion boats wait in Nísyros harbour.*

## ⊙ Ferry/catamaran/hydrofoil timetables

The best schedule resource is the website of the GTP (Greek Travel Pages), www.gtp.gr, which is fairly accurate, with updates at least every few weeks; by far the best alternative is www.openseas.gr.

Alternatively, major tourist information offices (Rhodes, Parikiá, Iráklio, etc) supply a weekly schedule, and most offices hang a timetable in a conspicuous place so that you can look up times even if the branch is closed. This should, however, not be relied on implicitly – last-minute changes are common. In general, for the most complete, impartial and up-to-date information on each port's sailings the best source is the Port Police (in Piraeus and most other ports), known as the *limenarhío*.

Be aware that when you enquire about ferries at a travel agent, they will sometimes inform you only of the lines with which they are affiliated, though this is increasingly less of a problem since most agencies now sell tickets for all local companies.

may leave you trying to get a refund if you booked early.

Personalised ticketing for all sea transport has been mandatory since 2001; it is no longer possible to purchase tickets on board, though you can upgrade your class of travel. The only exceptions are a few of the ro-ro short-haul ferries (such as Igoumenítsa–Levkímmi, Páros–Andíparos).

When you buy a ticket at Piraeus, get detailed instructions on where your boat is berthed – the quays are long and convoluted; the staff who take your ticket should also make sure you are on the right boat.

Above all, be flexible when travelling the Greek seas. Apart from schedule changes, a bad stretch of weather can keep you island-bound for as long as the wind blows above Force 7. Strikes too are often called during the summer, and usually last for a few days. Out on the islands in particular, the best way to secure accurate, up-to-the-minute information on the erratic ways of ferries is to contact the Port Authority (*limenarhío*), which monitors the movements of individual boats. Port Authority offices are usually located on the waterfront of each island's principal harbour, away from the cafés. Boats are often very late arriving – to avoid wasting time around the dock, track the real-time progress of your ferry on the live shipping map at www.marinetraffic.com.

If you are travelling by car, especially during high season, you will have to plan much further ahead because during peak season car space is sometimes booked many weeks in advance. The same applies to booking a cabin for an overnight trip during summer – and, from early August to early September, often for just a simple seat.

Gamma class – also known as *touristikí*, deck, or third – is the classic, cheap way to travel the Greek seas. Sadly, open-air deck seating is becoming a thing of the past as older boats are retired, and you may well be forced inside to take up "pullman" seats or occupy the "low class" snack bar.

### Catamarans/"high speeds"

Fleets of sleek new "high speed" *(tahyplóö)* ferries or true catamarans, made in France or Scandinavia, are slowly supplanting conventional *(symvatikó)* craft (as a stroll around the quays at Piraeus will confirm). They have some advantages over hydrofoils – they can be even faster, most of them carry lots of cars, and they are permitted to sail in wind conditions of up to Force 8, whereas "dolphins" are confined to port above Force 6.5 or so. The bad news: there may be no cabins (because they mostly finish their runs before midnight), food service often no better than on the old ferries and there are no exterior decks. The aeroplane-seating salons are ruthlessly air-conditioned and subject to a steady, unavoidable barrage of banal Greek TV on overhead monitors (even in *diakikriméni* or "distinguished" class). Cars cost roughly the same to convey as on the old-style boats, but seats are priced double. Fuel consumption on catamarans is horrendous; they only turn a profit when at least three-quarters full, and seem to spend much of their time at half-throttle – or at anchor, except in mid-summer.

Catamarans come in all shapes and sizes, from the 300-car-carrying behemoths of Hellenic Seaways in the northeast Aegean, Cyclades and central Dodecanese, to mid-sized ones plying the Argo-Saronic or between Samothráki and Alexandroúpoli, to the diminutive *Dodekanisos Express* and *Dodekanisos Pride, which* serve most of the Dodecanese islands plus Sámos, and take five cars each.

### Hydrofoils

Though catamarans are undoubtedly the wave of the future, there is still some scheduled hydrofoil service to a few islands. Like catamarans, hydrofoils are more than twice as fast as old-style ferries and about twice as expensive but, being ex-Polish and ex-Russian river craft, are not really designed for the Aegean, and prone to cancellation in bad weather conditions – their small rear sundecks will be swamped with spray in anything over Force 5.

Hydrofoils (nicknamed *iptaména delfínia* or "flying dolphins" in Greek) connect Piraeus with most of the Argo-Saronic region (Égina, Póros, Ýdra and Spétses), and Corfu with Paxí).

### Port Authority numbers

**Piraeus**, tel: 21045 11311 or 21041 47800 (recorded outgoing message in Greek only – this is also true of most busy ports).

**Vólos**, tel: 24213 53800
**Kavála**, tel: 2513 505430
**Lávrio**, tel: 22920 26859
**Rafína**, tel: 22943 21202, www.rafina port.gr

**The Ionian Islands**
**Corfu**, tel: 26610 32655
**Itháki**, tel: 26740 32909
**Kefaloniá (Argostóli)**, tel: 26710 22224
**Levkáda**, tel: 26450 92509
**Paxí**, tel: 26620 32259
**Zákynthos**, tel: 26950 28117

**The Saronic Gulf Islands**
**Aegina**, tel: 22970 22328
**Hydra**, tel: 22980 52279
**Póros**, tel: 22980 22274
**Salamína**, tel: 467 7277
**Spétses**, tel: 22980 72245

**The Cyclades**
**Andros**, tel: 22820 71213
**Íos**, tel: 22860 91264
**Kéa**, tel: 22870 21344

*Captaining a small caique.*

**Kýthnos,** tel: 22810 21290
**Mílos,** tel: 22870 22968
**Mýkonos,** tel: 22890 22218
**Náxos,** tel: 22850 22300
**Páros,** tel: 22840 21240
**Santoríni,** tel: 22860 22239
**Sérifos,** tel: 22810 51470
**Sífnos,** tel: 22840 33617
**Sýros,** tel: 22810 82690
**Tínos,** tel: 22830 22348
**The Sporades**
**Alónnisos,** tel: 24240 65595
**Skiáthos,** tel: 24270 22017
**Skópelos,** tel: 24240 22180
**Skýros,** tel: 22220 93475
**The NE Aegean Islands**
**Foúrni,** tel: 22750 51207
**Híos,** tel: 22710 44433
**Ikaría (Agios Kírykos),** tel: 22750 22207
**Ikaría (Évdilos),** tel: 22750 31007
**Lésvos (Mytilíni),** tel: 22510 24515
**Lésvos (Sígri),** tel: 22530 54433
**Límnos,** tel: 22540 22225
**Psará,** tel: 22720 61252
**Sámos (Vathý),** tel: 22730 27318
**Sámos (Karlóvassi),** tel: 22730 30888
**Sámos (Pythagório),** tel: 22730 61225
**Samothráki,** tel: 25510 41305
**Thásos (Liménas),** tel: 25930 22106
**Thásos (Prínos),** tel: 25930 71290
**The Dodecanese Islands**
**Astypálea,** tel: 22420 61208
**Hálki,** tel: 22460 45220
**Kálymnos,** tel: 22430 29304
**Kárpathos (Pigádia),** tel: 22450 22227
**Kásos,** tel: 22450 41288
**Kastelórizo,** tel: 22460 49270
**Kós,** tel: 22420 26594
**Léros (Lakkí),** tel: 22470 22334

**Nísyros,** tel: 22420 31222
**Pátmos,** tel: 22470 31231
**Rhodes,** tel: 22410 22220
**Sými,** tel: 22460 71205
**Tílos,** tel: 22460 44350
**Crete**
**Haniá,** tel: 28210 98888
**Iráklio,** tel: 2810 244956
**Kastéli-Kissámos,** tel: 28220 22024
**Réthymno,** tel: 28310 22276
**Sitía,** tel: 28430 27117

### Kaïkia and taxi-boats

Apart from slow or fast ferries, catamarans and hydrofoils, swarms of small *kaïkia* (caiques) offer seasonal excursions, pitched mostly at daytrippers. Since they are chartered by travel agencies, they are exempt from Ministry of Transport fare controls – as well as from the 30-year-old scrap-the-boat rule that is haphazardly enforced in Greece for scheduled services – and they can be very expensive if used as a one-way ticket from, say, Sámos to Pátmos.

On many islands where there are remote beaches with difficult overland access – most notably Hydra, Itháki, Sými, Hálki, Kálymnos and Pátmos – local "taxi-boats" provide a fairly pricey shuttle service. They are useful, but be aware that they usually run at set hours rather than on demand – verify return time(s) before you set out.

---

### Private transport

#### Yacht charter

Chartering a yacht is one of the more exotic ways of island-hopping in Greece. It is by no means cheap,

although hiring a boat with a group of friends may not much exceed the price of renting rooms every night for the same number of people.

Depending on your nautical qualifications and your taste for autonomy, you can either take the helm yourself or let a hired crew do so for you. There are thousands of yachts available for charter in Greece, all registered and inspected by the Ministry of the Merchant Marine. For more information, see our feature on sailing. Charter is best arranged in advance from overseas, through reputable agencies like Nautilus (www.nautilusyachting.com), Neilson (www.neilson.co.uk) and Sunsail (www.sunsail.com).

You may also find the following organisation worth consulting before chartering:
**The Hellenic Yacht Brokers' Association**
Zéa Marína, 185 36 Piraeus; tel: 210 45 33 134, www.hyba.gr

### Taxis

There are three stages to the experience of a taxi journey in Greece (especially in Athens).

First: getting a taxi. It is almost impossible at certain times of the day in Athens, and probably hardest before the early afternoon meal. When you hail a taxi, try to get in before stating your destination. The drivers are very picky and often won't let you in unless you're going in their direction. If you see an empty taxi, run for it and be aggressive – otherwise you will find that some quick Athenian has beaten you to it.

Second: the ride. Make sure the taxi meter is on "1" when you start out, and not on "2" – that's the double fare, which is only permitted from midnight to 5am, or outside designated city limits. Once inside, you may find yourself with company. Don't be alarmed. It is traditional practice for drivers to pick up two, three, even four individual passengers, provided they're going roughly in the same direction. In these cases, make a note of the meter count when you get in.

Third: navigating. You need to know exactly where you are headed. There is no equivalent requirement of London's "The Knowledge" for Athens drivers, and few even have a street atlas in the cab, though many now use GPS devices.

Fourth: paying up. If you have travelled with other passengers, make sure you aren't paying for the part of the trip that took place before you got in. You should pay the difference in meter reading between embarking and alighting, plus the minimum fare (currently €3.44). Otherwise, the meter will tell you the straight price, which may be adjusted according to the tariff that should be on a laminated placard clipped to the dashboard. There are extra charges for each piece of luggage in the boot, for leaving or entering an airport or seaport, plus bonuses around Christmas and Easter.

Some drivers will quote you the correct price, but many others will try to rip you off, especially if you're obviously a novice. If the fare you are charged is clearly above the correct price, don't hesitate to argue, in whichever language, until you get it back down to a normal and fair price. Coming out of an airport or seaport waving 50- or 100-euro notes at a driver is asking for trouble – always keep small bills and coins handy. Almost all Athens taxis are now fitted with mini-cash registers, which spit out receipts (and supposedly cut down on tax-dodging).

These rules apply more to Athens than to the islands, although it is still necessary to be pretty assertive in Thessaloníki and on Crete or Rhodes. Shared taxis, Athens-style, are not the norm in the islands, except (oddly) on Kálymnos, where they wait for passengers and only depart when full.

Various radio taxi services exist in Athens and many larger island towns. They can pick you up within a short time of your call to a central booking number, though surcharges (at least €2) apply.

## Cars

Having a car in the rural areas of the Greek islands enables you to reach a lot of otherwise inaccessible corners; however, driving a car in Athens (or any sizeable island town like Iráklio or Rhodes) is unpleasant and confusing. Tempers soon run short as signage, especially warnings of mandatory turning lanes, is practically non-existent or obscured by trees.

### Driving in Greece

All EU/EEA licences, and licences held by returning diaspora Greeks irrespective of issuing country, are honoured in Greece. Conversely, all other licences – this includes North American and Australian ones – are not valid, as many tourists from those nations attempting to hire cars have discovered to their cost. These motorists must obtain an International Driving Permit (IDP) before departure (issued by the AAA or CAA in North America on the spot for a nominal cost); the Greek Automobile and Touring Club (ELPA) no longer issues them to foreign nationals in Greece. Should Brexit proceed, UK drivers will very likely need an IDP.

With the advent of the single European market (EU), insurance Green Cards are no longer required, although check with your home insurer about the need for any supplementary premiums – many policies now include pan-European cover anyway.

Greek traffic control and signals are basically the same as in the rest of Continental Europe, although roundabouts are handled bizarrely by French or English standards – in many cases the traffic entering from the slip road, not that already in the circle, has the right of way; watch for "stop" or "yield" signs or invariably faded pavement markings.

Motorway speeds are routinely in excess of the nominal 100–120kph (62–75mph) limits, and drivers overtake with abandon, often on the verge side. On other island roads, posted limits are typically 70–90kph (40–55mph). A red light is often considered not so much an obligation as a suggestion, and oncoming drivers flashing lights at you on one-lane roads means the opposite of what it does in the UK. Here, it means: "I'm coming through" (although often it can mean "Watch out, police control ahead"). Typical local tricks include barging out of side roads without looking, or ambling down the middle of the road straddling the divider line, so drive defensively – particularly in August, when Athenians return to their natal islands and apply urban driving habits to back-country roads.

Greece has a mandatory seatbelt law (€350 fine for non-observance, plus €80 for the driver if the passenger wasn't buckled up), and children under 10 are not allowed to sit in the front seat. It is an offence to drive without your licence on your person (another €350 fine). Run a red light? That will be €700; drink-driving penalties are even more draconian. Every car must also carry a first-aid kit, reflective warning triangle and 3-litre fire extinguisher (although hire companies tend to skimp on this). Police checkpoints at major (and minor) junctions are frequent, and in addition to the above offences you can be penalised for not having evidence of insurance, paid road tax or registration papers in/on the vehicle. If it's clear you've no fixed residence in Greece, your license may be confiscated and held to ransom at the nearest police station pending payment of the fine (within 10 working days, 50 percent discount on the above quoted fees).

Super and normal unleaded petrol, as well as diesel, are readily available throughout Greece, although filling up after dark can be tricky. Most garages close around 8pm and, although a rota system operates in larger towns, it is often

### ⊙ Car hire (rental)

Hiring a car in Greece is not always as cheap as you might hope, owing to demand, high insurance premiums and import duties. Prices – from €18 to €40 per day – vary according to the type of car, season and length of rental and should include CDW (collision damage waiver) and VAT at 24 percent. Payment can, and often must, be made with a major credit card. A full home-country driving licence (for EU/EEA residents) or an International Driving Permit (for all others) is required and you must be at least 21 years old.

From overseas, you can book a car in advance through international aggregator websites such as www.comparecarrentals.co.uk, www.carrentals.co.uk, www.autoeurope.com, www.auto-europe.co.uk and www.rentalcargroup.com. Only if you're a member of some corporate or other affinity group are you likely to get as good a deal (or better) directly through the websites of major rental chains like Hertz, Avis or Budget.

*It's preferable to wear a helmet.*

difficult to ascertain which station is open. Credit cards are widely accepted, but always ask first – card-swiping machines can be mysteriously "broken".

Parking in the larger island towns is uniformly a nightmare; even assuming you find a convenient space, residents-only schemes and pay-and-display systems are the norm. Sometimes tickets are sold from kiosks, sometimes from a machine, sometimes you can pay by mobile. When in doubt about a spot, don't park there – fines are typically €70 and upwards.

### Road maps

Gone are the days when visitors had to suffer with mendacious or comical maps that seemed based more on wishful thinking (especially projected but unbuilt roads) than the facts on the ground. There are now two commercial Greek companies producing largely accurate maps of the country: Terrain (www.terrain maps.gr) and Anavasi (www.anavasi. gr). They can be found country-wide, in tourist-shop racks and better bookshop chains like Newsstand. Anavasi (the best by far for Crete, and many other islands) has its own convenient shop in central Athens at Voulís 32, selling some Terrain products as well. Orama is one ubiquitous map publisher whose products are worth avoiding.

### Motorcycles, quad-bikes and bicycles

On most Greek islands you will find agencies that hire small motorcycles, various types of scooters, 50cc and above, and even mountain bikes. These give you the freedom to wander where you will, and weekly rates are reasonable.

For any bike of 50cc or over, both helmets and a motorcycle driving licence are theoretically required, and increasingly these rules are

> ### ☉ Breakdowns
>
> The Greek Automobile Association (ELPA) offers a breakdown service for motorists, which is free to AA/RAC members (on production of their membership cards). Phone 10400 for assistance nationwide. Some car-hire companies have agreements instead with competitors Hellas Service (dial 1057), Interamerican (dial 1158) or Express Service (dial 1154), but these call centres can be slow to dispatch aid. Preferably, ring a local garage number, especially if this is what the hire company instructs you to do.

enforced. The UK P-type license for scooter-learners is *not* honoured in Greece. The ill-fitting helmets offered are a bit of a joke, but if you refuse them you may have to sign a waiver absolving the dealer of criminal/civil liability – and police checkpoints can be zealous, levying stiff fines (€175 after discount) on locals and visitors alike. Having only a car license while driving a scooter will get you another, steeper fine. Many rental agencies now refuse to give out scooters to folk without the requisite license, steering them to quad bikes instead – which accounts for their sudden popularity. They are unstable on turns (thus helmets are supplied for riding them too) but given the two-wheeler license law you may not have another choice.

Before you set off, make sure the bike – of whichever sort – works by taking it for a test spin down the street. Brakes in particular are often mis-set, lights may need new fuses or bulbs and spark-plugs get fouled. Otherwise, you may get stuck with a lemon, and be held responsible for its malfunctioning when you return it. Reputable agencies often furnish you with a phone number for a breakdown pick-up service, or will come retrieve you themselves.

Above all, don't take unnecessary chances, like riding two on a bike designed for one. More than one holiday in Greece has been ruined by a serious scooter accident – hospital casualty wards are wearily familiar with "road rash". It is strongly suggested that where possible you stick to traditional scooters of 50–100cc displacement, with skinny, large-radius ("number 16"), well-treaded tyres. The new, predominant generation of automatic, button-start *mihanákia/papákia* (as they're called in Greek slang), with their sexy front fairings and tiny, fat, no-tread tyres, may look the business but they are unstable and unsafe once off level asphalt. In particular, if you hit a gravel-strewn curve on one of these you will go for a spill, and at the very least lose most of the skin on your palms and knees. In any case, consider buying a pair of biker's gloves – they can be had for around €20. You may feel hot and stupid wearing them in summer, but you'll feel even more stupid with your hands wrapped in gauze for the balance of your holiday.

## A

### Accommodation

#### How to choose

There is a broad range of accommodation in Greece; consult the companion Walking Eye app for a sample of different categories across the country. On the islands the most affordable lodging are private rented rooms (*enikiazómena domátia*), which are increasingly self-catering studios (if only just a mini-kitchen in the corner) or full-on apartments (*diamerísmata*).

When accommodation-hunting on the spot, local public or private tourist offices can be of help if no rooms are on offer when you disembark. The best system is booking a room a few days (or, in summer, weeks) in advance.

#### Hotel categories

The Greek authorities have five categories for hotels, with a star system ranging from one-star (basic) to five-star (deluxe). Although stars are supposed to be an accurate reflection of the hotel's quality, a swimming pool or tennis court could rate an establishment as 4-star or 3-star even though in other respects it has indifferent facilities. Also, room numbers can limit a hotel's maximum rating, so you may encounter 14-room two-star hotels superior to a nearby 50-room three-star.

The following general principles apply, however: two-to-five-star hotels all have private bathrooms, and most 1-star hotels do as well. Four- or five-star hotels must have a bar and at least one restaurant, while offering a choice of breakfasts. Two- or three-star should provide a basic buffet breakfast – "enhanced continental" is the rule;

rented rooms do not offer breakfast unless they also have a snack-bar license.

Multi-starred hotels will have some or all of these facilities: a swimming pool, fitness centre, sauna, hamam and/or full spa, "private" beach, conference hall and other businessperson's amenities, entertainment programmes for children, 24-hour desk attendance, and "tamed" taxi service. Almost all hotels now offer in-room or lobby wi-fi (often charged extra). Multi-starred hotels generally stock premium bath sundries in small bottles which you are expected to take home (in modest quantities); Korres and Apivita are the two top brands, respectively. Bedding should be orthopaedic and/or natural fibre.

#### Traditional settlements and restoration inns

Traditional settlements (*paradosiakí ikismí*) have been officially protected as such, with modern constructions banned by law. Buildings in these villages were variably restored as inns under Tourism Ministry initiative during the 1970s and 1980s, though all are now privatised. Since then, private renovators have opened other, generally higher-quality, inns, rescuing older buildings at risk on numerous islands. Restoration inns exist in the following locations, with many featured in the companion app:

**Hydra Town** (several sponge-magnates' mansions, done up as hotels)
**Ía, Fíra and Imerovígli**, Santoríni (interlinked skaptá – dug out – houses in the cliff face)
**Ermoúpoli**, Sýros (many Belle Epoque mansions converted to hotels)
**Mestá**, Híos (several houses, as suites/apartments)

**Avgónyma** and **Volissós**, Híos (entire houses, or apartments within)
**Kámbos** region, Híos (a few restored mansions)
**Psará island** (a restored prison)
**Rhodes Old Town** (high-quality, expensive, restoration inns in medieval structures)
**Haniá,** Crete (restoration inns around the Old Harbour)
**Réthymno**, Crete (restoration inns in old-town Venetian buildings)
**Crete** (converted farm or pastoral buildings across the island)
**Gialós** and **Horió**, Sými (old houses divided into apartments)
**Emborió**, Hálki (houses divided into apartments)
**Corfu** (restored olive mills or manor houses in remote locations)

#### Mountain refuges and monasteries

The only mountain refuge in the Greek islands is the popular, well-run Kallérgi hut in Crete's White Mountains, near the Gorge of Samariá (elevation 1,680 metres/5,512ft; www.kallergi.co).

The *xenónes* (guest lodges) of monasteries or convents are intended for Orthodox pilgrims. The only ones in the islands at all used to hosting the heterodox are Skiádi in southern Rhodes and Agíou Ioánni Prodrómou on Hálki. Doors close at sunset and a donation may be expected.

#### Camping

Organised campsites in the islands are limited to Santoríni, Sífnos, Sýros, Páros, Náxos, Íos, Lésvos and Pátmos.

### Admission charges

Most archaeological sites and museums, public or private, have admission charges varying from €2 for minor affairs up to €20 for five-star attractions like the Parthenon, though €12 is about tops for the islands (eg Lindos acropolis or Knossos). Occasionally (as in Athens, Iráklio and Rhodes) you can get a joint ticket covering 2–4 sites and museums at an advantageous price. From November to March, most state-run sites give free admission to EU nationals on Sunday; Monday or Tuesday are typical closure days. Students with valid ID get one-third to one-half off entry fees, as do certified teachers, archaeology students and people aged 60 or over. On August full moon evenings, sometimes in July or September too, major archaeological sites like the Parthenon, Lindos or Sámos's Heraion have free admission for all until about 1.30am – magical. Ask locally, as not all sites participate in this programme.

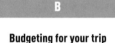

### Budgeting for your trip

Greece is no longer by any stretch of the imagination an inexpensive country. Travelling as one of a couple in high season, you should allow a minimum of €35 for a share of accommodation (budget €45–55 each in the biggest cities and name resorts), €15–20 for your half of a sit-down meal, €6–12 daily for site/museum admissions, and €13–17 for your share of the cheapest, smallest rental car – before petrol costs, which luckily have fallen since 2015. As elsewhere, most things are more expensive for people travelling alone; single

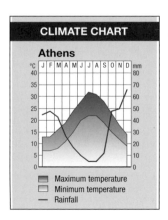

accommodation often costs almost as much as double occupancy.

### Business travellers

Business travellers are well catered for; even modest hotels have some sort of "business person's corner" with a computer and printer, as well as Wi-fi signal for devices (in the common areas if not in all the rooms). Fancier hotels tend to have conference/event rooms as well as lounges suitable for semi-formal meetings.

### Children

Children are adored in Greece, and many families are still highly superstitious about their welfare – don't be surprised to see toddlers with amulets pinned to their clothes to ward off the evil eye. So expect your own kids to attract attention. Children are given quite a bit of leeway in Greece and treated very indulgently. They are allowed to stay up late and are routinely taken out to eat in tavernas.

### Climate

In general, the north coast of each island is subject to more summertime gales and cooler temperatures than the protected south coast; be sure to check on a map exactly where a holiday resort is before making a final booking. Many travellers underestimate the differences in climate between individual island chains.

The green, cool Ionian islands, for instance, are prone to rainy spells from mid-September through to the start of June. By contrast, Rhodes and Crete's southern coast can offer swimming for the hardy as late as mid-December. If planning to visit any of the islands from mid-September through to the end of April, a good rule to follow is this: the further south the island is geographically, the better the sunshine rate will be.

On the whole, islands are ill-equipped for visitors during the winter months. Heating can be basic or non-existent, boats are infrequent, tinned food may be all that

is available on the smallest islands and amenities are scarce. The tourist season is officially "over" in late October, although it extends into November on Rhodes and Crete, but ends mid-September on northern islands like Thásos or Límnos.

Late spring (late Apr–end June) and autumn (Sept–Oct) are the best times to visit. During these periods, you will find mild to warm temperatures, sunny days and fewer tourists. Throughout July and August, Greece is at its hottest and stickiest, and most crowded. Yet millions of tourists seem to prefer the heat and the company.

### What to wear

If you visit Greece during summer, you should bring lightweight, cotton clothing. Add a pullover or shell jacket to this and you will be prepared for the occasional cool night breezes, or conditions on open boat decks. Lightweight shoes and sandals are ideal in the summer, but you will also need a pair of comfortable walking shoes that have already been broken in. If you plan to do any rigorous hiking on the islands bring sturdy, over-the-ankle boots with a good tread; leather will be more comfortable in summer temperatures than high-tech synthetic materials. If you visit Greece during winter, which can be surprisingly cold, bring the same kind of clothes you would wear during spring in the northern part of the United States or Central Europe. At any time of year, bring one change of smart-casual clothing – multi-star hotels enforce dress codes at dinner.

### Crime and safety

Sadly, Greece is no longer the crime-free haven of yesteryear. Locking cars and houses is now the norm everywhere, even in the deep countryside where people used to leave a set of keys dangling from the front door.

Central Athens in particular has become hazardous at times. Cars with valuables exposed (or even not) are routinely broken into in such neighbourhoods as Exárhia, Gázi and Keramikós; the thieves, often drug addicts, will steal almost anything irrespective of value, even raggedy items of clothing.

Organised gangs of pickpockets and bag-snatchers frequent

*Cold frappés with an unobstructed sea view.*

the metro lines and stations most popular with tourists, in particular Line 3 from the airport, Line 1 from Piraeus, Monastiráki plus Sýndagma stations, and the X95 bus-stop area at Sýndagma. They usually work in teams, and may be plausibly well dressed. If you are surrounded and pushed up against the carriage wall, or forced to squeeze past them to retrieve your luggage from the rack in the airport-route cars, your wallet or other valuables are about to be (or have just been) lifted. Your cards will be used to obtain cash advances within minutes at exchange booths that are in cahoots with the thieves. Nothing substantive is being done about the problem other than recorded announcements in the cars telling you to be aware.

Young single females should be alert to the possibility of drugged drinks as a prelude to rape attempts in popular, rowdy beach resorts. Be suspicious of men who offer to bring you cocktails, whose preparation you cannot witness. The perpetrators, it must be said, are as (or more) likely to be other foreigners as Greeks. Use common sense when arranging rides afterwards back to your accommodation.

Because of heightened security considerations it is unwise to leave luggage unattended anywhere except in a hotel lobby, under the gaze of the desk staff. However, belongings inadvertently left behind in a café will still usually be put aside for you to collect.

## Cultural events

The economic crisis has reduced the scope and length (if not the existence) of many events, but there's still an appreciable calendar between late spring and autumn. Below are the most likely survivors, with a long track record behind them. Sadly, few have properly maintained – or even any – websites; the best strategy is to enquire if you're there at the time, rather than make a special trip.

**Early August Kióni** Music Festival on the island of Itháki (Ithaca).

**Mid-August** Varkaróla Festival, Paleokastrítsa, Corfu.

**Mid-June–late Sept** Ippokrateia Festival, Kós. Various events all around the island.

**Late July–mid-September** Sými Festival; mixed classical and Greek pop performances, culminating in film showings.

**July–September** Iráklio Festival – concerts, theatre, opera and dance by world-class acts.

**August, 3rd Week** Levkáda International Folklore Festival, with overseas groups.

**End August–Early September** Sacred music festival on Pátmos.

**July–September** Paxos International Music Festival; world, jazz and classical, with Greek and international artists.

## Religious festivals

(* denotes that this is also a legal holiday, with everything closed.)

**1 January\*** *Feast of Agios Vasílios* (St Basil).

**6 January\*** *Agia Theofánia, Tá Fóta/ Epiphany*: Blessing of the waters – at any island, youths dive for the honour of retrieving a crucifix cast into the port by the local bishop or priest.

**February–March** Carnival season for three weeks before Lent: all over Greece. Some islands with celebrations of special interest are Zákynthos, Corfu, Híos (Mestá, Olýmbi), Lésvos (Agiásos), Agía Anna (Évvia), Kefaloniá, Kárpathos, Iráklio, Réthymno and (best of all) Skýros. Depending on the place, expect masqueing, obscene songs, floats, pranks, food-fights and people rapping each other on the head with squeaky plastic hammers.

*Tsiknopémpti* or **"Roast-Smell" Thursday** The last day, 59 days before Easter, on which the devout may consume meat. All grill-type tavernas are booked up days in advance for a final binge.

**"Clean" Monday\*** Beginning of the fast for Lent – last day of cheese-eating, 11 days after *Tsiknopémpti*. Picnics in the countryside and kite-flying, all over Greece.

**25 March\*** *Evangelismós/Feast of the Annunciation/National Day*: military parades in all main towns, pilgrimage to Tínos.

**Easter Weekend\*** *Good Friday, Holy Saturday* and *Easter Sunday* are celebrated throughout Greece. The date usually, but not always, precedes or follows Western Easter by one to five weeks, but they can coincide, as they did in 2011, 2014 and 2017; for the exact date in any given year, consult http://5ko.free.fr/en/easter.php.

**23 April** *Feast of St George*: celebrated especially in Kalíópi (Límnos), Asigonía (near Haniá) and Pylí (Kós). If Easter occurs later, George is honoured on Easter Monday.

**1 May\*** *Workers' Day*: picnics in the countryside all over Greece; also usually demonstrations by disaffected labour in larger towns.

**May/June** *Agion Pnévma/Pentecost Monday\**, 50 days after Easter. The resulting three-day weekend (*triímero*) is the excuse for the first proper excursion to the holiday islands and the start of the "season".

**17 July\*** *Agía Marína*. A big festival in rural areas, as she is (in one aspect) a major protector of crops. In many parts of Greece, especially where refugee communities from the Black Sea are to be found, it's considered bad luck to swim on this day as the saint in a malevolent guise always claims a drowning victim.

**19–20 July** *Profítis Ilías/Prophet Elijah*. Almost every island has at least one summit in his honour, where there will be gathering, feasting and music (if only from cranked-up car sound systems) outside the saint's chapel or monastery.

**6 August\*** *Metamórfosi toú Sotíros/ Transfiguration of the Saviour*. Mega food-fight with flour, squid ink, etc on Hálki; big commemoration in Pythagório, Sámos, where Christ is said to have aided the victorious Greek fleet in the 1824 battle of the Mykáli Straits on that day.

**15 August\*** *Kímisi tís Theotókou/ Dormition of the Virgin*: festivals all over the islands, especially Páros, Agiásos and Ólymbos (Kárpathos). Major pilgrimage to Tínos. In Orthodox theology, the "Assumption" into Heaven takes place eight days later, on 23 August, also celebrated in some spots.

**29 August** *Apotomí Kefáliskefálisis toú Prodrómou/Beheading of John the Baptist*. Pilgrimage festivals at Vrykoúnda on Kárpathos, and the remote Agíou Ioánnou monasteries on Crete's Rodópou peninsula, and in western Kos.

**8 September** *Génnisis tís Panagías/ Birth of the Virgin*. The second-biggest Marian festival after 15 August; notable observances at Tsambíkas Monastery on Rhodes, where childless women crawl up the steps on hands and knees in supplication for conception, and on Spétses, where the day is also the anniversary of a naval victory over the Ottomans in 1822.

**23–24 September** *Agios Ioánnis Theológos/St John the Divine*. Special celebrations outside Nikiá, Nísyros and on Pátmos at the saint's monastery, with special liturgies.

**26 October** *Agios Dimítrios/St Demetrios*. The name-day of possibly a fifth of the male population, and traditionally the first day new wine was ready to drink.

**28 October\*** *Ohi (No) Day*: anniversary of Greek leader Metaxas's supposed one-word response to Italy's ultimatum in 1940, prior to Greece's unexpected defeat of the Italian invasion force. Military parades and patriotic speeches in major cities.

**8 November** *Tón Taxiarhón Mihaïl ke Gavriïl/Archangels Michael and Gabriel*. Of the many rites at churches and monasteries

dedicated to them, the grandest are at Panormítis on Sými – effectively extending that island's tourist season until then – and at the monastery outside Mandamádos, Lésvos.

**4 & 6 December** The saint's days respectively of Varvára (Barbara) and Nikólaos (Nicholas), with seaside chapels and bigger churches of the latter *en fête. Ta Varvaraníkola*, as the three successive days are known, quite reliably marks the start of winter, with the first biting cold and heavy rainfall.

**Christmas season** All over Greece. In a dwindling number of places, children sing *kálenda* (carols) from door to door for a small gratuity; mostly nowadays an excuse for Western-style commercialism and an outbreak of plastic inflatable Santas on chimneys, balcony railings, etc. Both 25 December and 26 December are legal holidays; the latter is not "Boxing Day" as in Britain, but *Sýnaxis tís Panagías*, the "Gathering of the Virgin's Entourage".

**31 December** *Paramoní tis Protohroniás/New Year's Eve*. Many Greeks play cards for money on this occasion, and cut the *vasilópitta* pie with its lucky coin hidden in it. Special celebration in the town of Híos.

## Customs regulations

### Currency restrictions

Imported cash sums of more than €10,000 or its equivalent should be declared on entry. UK readers should watch for changes to this threshold in the event of Brexit.

### Duty-free goods

For travellers arriving from non-EU countries, allowances for duty-free goods brought into Greece are:

**Tobacco** 200 cigarettes, or 100 cigarillos, or 50 cigars, or 250g of tobacco.

**Alcohol** 1 litre of spirits or liqueurs over 22 percent volume, or 2 litres of fortified, sparkling or still wine.

**Perfume** 60cc of perfume, plus 250cc of eau de toilette.

Non-EU residents can claim back Value Added Tax on any items costing over €120, provided they export the item within 90 days of purchase. Tax-free forms are available at a very few tourist shops and department stores. Keep the receipt and form. Make your claim

at the customs area of the air- or sea-port when departing.

### Duty-paid goods

There are no official limitations to the amount of duty-paid goods that can be moved between EU states. However, cigarettes and most spirits are still slightly cheaper in Greece than in Britain and Ireland, so don't stuff your luggage with such articles.

If you buy goods in Greece for which you pay tax, there are no restrictions on the amounts you can take home (until Brexit). EU law has set "guidance levels", however, as follows:

**Tobacco** 3,200 cigarettes, or 400 cigarillos, or 200 cigars or 3kg of tobacco.

**Spirits** 10 litres

**Fortified wine/wine** 90 litres

**Beer** 110 litres

If you exceed these amounts you must be able to prove the goods are for personal use.

### Importing cars

EU-registered cars are no longer stamped into your passport on entry to the country (if you arrive by ferry, keep the tickets as these are considered proof of date of entry). They can circulate freely for up to six months, and are exempt from road tax as long as this has been paid in the home country – however, you are not allowed to sell the vehicle. Non-EU/EEA nationals will find that a bizarre litany of rules apply to importing cars, chief among them that you must re-export the car when you depart, or have it sealed by Customs in an off-road facility of your choosing.

Cars detected circulating after the initial six-month period without valid road tax are liable to immediate seizure by undercover agents of the "Economic Crimes" corps, and are auctioned off if an enormous import duty is not paid.

### Disabled travellers

Despite nudging from the EU, Greece has some way to go before becoming fully compliant with regulations on facilities for disabled people.

Athens, with lifts in the metro, "kneeling" buses on many routes, recorded announcements and visual displays of upcoming stops on the metro plus all buses or trams, and ramps (when not blocked by illegally parked cars) at kerbsides, is furthest ahead. The new Thessaloníki metro should also be EU-compliant regarding facilities for disabled people.

Elsewhere, amenities can be poor – there are few or no sound pips for the sight-impaired at pedestrian crossings, and it is common to see the wheelchair-bound tooling down the middle of the asphalt rather than risking the obstacle course of a typical pedestrian pavement.

As of 2018, all hotels must have at least one disabled-friendly room with wide doors and safety handles in the bath, as well as ramps for wheelchair access to common areas. Expect compliance to be laggardly.

## E

### Eating out

#### What to eat

There is considerable regional variety in Greek cuisine and sadly, there's also considerable variety in quality.

Vegetarians are not well catered for; most main courses will include fish, meat or meat bouillon. Your best bet is combining a selection of *mezédes* (little plates of food and dips, hot or cold), many of which are vegetarian or dairy-based.

#### Where to eat

Eating establishments have much the same profile throughout the islands.

### ⊘ Austerity dining

The ritual of families and friends patronising tavernas twice a week is now suspended, thanks to hard times. Most Greeks, not just students nursing one coffee all evening, have had to learn to be careful with money. It is still considered an honour to snaffle the bill and pay for everyone, but long gone are the days when diners would order more starters towards the end of the meal, destined never to be touched, just to impress.

However, the classical taverna is by no means the only establishment. You will also find the *estiatório*, the traditional urban restaurant, which ranges from an *(ino)magirío* or tradesman's lunch-hour hangout, with ready-cooked *(magirevtá)* food and bulk wine, up to pricey linen-tablecloth places with bow-tied staff.

The *psistariá* is a barbecue restaurant specialising in lamb and pork chops, or chicken on a spit; a *psarotavérna* specialises in fish and shellfish; while *gyrádiko* and *souvlatzídiko* stalls purvey *gýros* and *souvláki* respectively, sometimes to a sit-down trade, garnished with salads.

Popular among the intelligentsia are *koultouriárika* restaurants, Greek nouvelle cuisine based on updated traditional recipes; and *mezedopolía* (or *tsipourádika* in northern islands, *rakádika* on Crete), where the local tipple accompanies *mezédes*.

Some tavernas, especially in non-touristy areas, may not have menus out (though they must keep one somewhere for consultation), in which case it's wise to establish the price of at least the most expensive main courses.

#### When to eat

Greeks take lunch between 2pm and 3.30pm. The evening meal, between 9pm and 11.30pm, can either be another full meal, or an assortment of *mezédes*. A usual breakfast in Greece is merely a pastry and coffee. However, wonderful *píttes* (turnovers) are available from bakeries.

#### Fish and seafood

Seafood is generally expensive, except for frozen squid and fried tiddlers. Scaly fish usually lie in an iced tray for you to choose from, and your dish is priced by weight (less often by the portion). It is prudent to watch the (uncleaned) fish being weighed, and reiterate the price you are quoted, as "fingers on the scales" and later misunderstandings are not unknown. There is also lots of farmed and frozen seafood (often marked on menus only with a "k" or "kat.", for *katapsygméno*, or just an asterisk) lying in ambush for the inexperienced.

#### Alcoholic drinks

Bottled wine at a tavern will cost €12–35 depending on quality and

where you are; bulk wine (*hýma*) runs €6–12. *Oúzo*, *soúma* or *tsípouro* comes usually in 200ml karafákia, starting from €6.50; on Crete, local *rakí* is much cheaper.

#### Coffee, chocolate and tea

Whole arabica beans suitable for cafetière or percolator coffee are making steady inroads among locals and tourists fed up with the ubiquitous "Nescafé", the generic term for any instant coffee. The formula sold in Greece is stronger than that made for Anglo-Saxon markets, and the most palatable use for it is in *frappé*, iced instant coffee whipped up in a shaker, and an entirely Greek innovation despite its French name. *Gallikós* ("French"), percolated coffee, is synonymous with *fíltrou* (filtered). Espresso and cappuccino are ubiquitous, though not always expertly made. *Freddoccino*, another resourceful Greek invention, is a cold double cappuccino for the summer months.

*Ellenikós kafés* is Greek coffee, made from fine-ground robusta beans, boiled and served with the grounds in the cup – the same style as across the Balkans and Middle East. A large cup is a *diplós*. Sugar (lots of it for Greeks) is added at the preparation stage. For those who like it without, *skétos* ("plain") is the magic word. If you like some sugar, ask for *métrios*; if you want it syrupy, say *varý glykós*.

Chocolate drinks (*tsokoláta*) can be very good indeed, served cold (maybe with ice cream) or hot according to season.

Tea (*tsái*) is the ragged stepsister of the hot-drinks triad. Quality bulk or bagged tea, whether green or black, is sold in speciality shops, but you'll usually have to make do with teabags of obscure Ceylonese or Madagascan vintage, served either with milk or with lemon.

Herbal teas are easy to find in shops, and at more traditional *kafenía*. *Hamomíli* is camomile tea, while *alisfakiá* (sage tea) is found on many of the Dodecanese and Cyclades.

### Embassies and consulates

#### Foreign embassies in Athens

All embassies are open from Monday to Friday only, usually from 8am until 2pm, except for their own national holidays (as well as, usually, Greek ones).

**Australia** Corner Kifissías and Alexándras avenues, Level 6, Thon Building, Ambelókipi; tel: 210 87 04 000, www.greece.embassy.gov.au/athn/home.html

**Canada** Gennadíou 4, Kolonáki, (Evangelismós metro); tel: 210 72 73 400, www.canadainternational.gc.ca/greece%2Dgrece/

**Ireland** Vassiléos Konstandínou 7 (by National Gardens); tel: 210 72 32 771, www.dfa.ie/irish-embassy/greece/#

**South Africa** Kifissías 60, Maroússi; tel: 210 61 06 645.

**UK** Ploutárhou 1, Kolonáki (Evangelismós metro); tel: 210 72 72 600, https://www.gov.uk/government/world/organisations/british-embassy-athens

**Consulates:** Corfu, 1st floor Mantzarou 18, Kérkyra Town; tel 26610 23457 or 26610 30055

Crete, Candia Tower, 5th Floor, Thalitá 17, Platía Agíou Dimitríou, Iráklio; tel 2810 224012

**US** Vasilísis Sofías 91, Ambelókipi (Mégaro Mousikís metro); tel: 210 72 12 951, https://gr.usembassy.gov

## Emergencies

The following numbers work country wide:

**Police:** 100
**Ambulance:** 166
**Fire brigade, urban:** 199
**Forest fire reporting:** 191

For less urgent medical problems, hotel staff will give you details of the nearest hospital or English-speaking doctor.

## Entry requirements

Citizens of EU nations and EEA countries have unlimited visitation rights to Greece. With a valid passport, citizens of the US, Canada, Australia and New Zealand can stay in the country for up to 90 days (cumulative) within any 180-day period, with no visa necessary. Over-stayers are fined very heavily on exit, to the tune of several hundred euros. To stay longer, you must obtain a permit from the nearest Aliens' Bureau or foreigners' division of the local police station; however, this is lately proving nearly impossible (and very expensive) to do. Citizens of all non-EU/EEA countries should contact the nearest Greek embassy or consulate about current visa and permitted length-of-stay requirements. Arrangements for UK nationals in the event of Brexit are uncertain at the time of writing.

## Etiquette

The Greeks are at heart a very traditional nation, protective of their families and traditions. So to avoid giving offence it is essential to follow their codes of conduct.

Local people rarely drink to excess, so drunken and/or lewd behaviour is treated with at best bewilderment, at worse severe distaste (or criminal prosecution, as many young louts on Rhodes, Zákynthos, Corfu and Crete have learnt to their cost).

Nude bathing is legal at only a few beaches (such as on the island of Mýkonos), but it is deeply offensive to many Greeks. Even topless sunbathing is sometimes frowned upon, so watch out for signs forbidding it on beaches. The main rules of thumb are these: if it is a secluded beach and/or a beach that has become a commonly accepted locale for nude bathing, you probably won't offend anyone; also don't skinny-dip within view of any shoreline chapel. Despite assorted scandals and embarrassing espousal of retrograde issues in recent years, the Greek Orthodox Church still commands residual respect in Greece (more in the countryside), so keep any unfavourable comments about the clergy or even Greek civil servants to yourself.

Greek authorities take the unauthorised use of drugs very seriously indeed; this is not the country in which to carry cannabis, let alone anything stronger.

## Dress codes

The Greeks will not expect you, as a tourist, to dress as they do, but scuffed shoes or ripped jeans (except in alternative clubs) can be considered offensive by Greek elders.

In certain places and regions, you will encounter explicit requirements or conventions concerning the way you dress. To enter a church, men must wear long trousers or shorts covering the knees, and women dresses with sleeves. Often skirts or wraps will be provided at the entrance if you do not have them. Not complying with this code will be taken as insulting irreverence.

Some specific areas have their own dress codes. On Mýkonos, for example, male and female tourists alike will shock no one by wearing shorts or a swimsuit in most public places. But dressing in this way would be severely alienating in a mountain village in Crete, or in any other area that is less accustomed to tourists. And while shorts may be uniform male summer apparel at island resorts, when visiting Athens you will notice that *nobody* wears shorts in town, even in roasting temperatures. The best approach is to observe what other people are wearing and dress accordingly.

In general, both Greeks and tourists dine in casual dress. You will only need formal dress if you plan to go to fancy establishments, casinos, formal affairs and so on.

## Health and medical care

There are few serious diseases in Greece, apart from those that you can contract in the rest of Europe or the United States. Citizens of the US, Canada and the EU do not need any vaccinations to enter the country.

The most common health problems encountered by tourists involve too much sun, too much alcohol or sensitivity to unaccustomed food. Drink plenty of water, as dehydration can be a problem in the heat.

### Drinking water

People carrying a large plastic bottle of mineral water is a common sight in Greece, but it is not the best way of keeping hydrated, as sunlight releases toxic chemicals from the plastic into the water, and the spent bottles contribute enormously to Greece's litter problem. Buy a sturdy, porcelain-lined canteen and fill it from the cool-water supply of bars and restaurants you've patronised; nobody will begrudge you this. Although unfiltered tap water is generally safe to drink, it may be brackish, and having a private water supply is much handier. On the larger islands, certain springs are particularly esteemed by the locals – queues of cars, and people with jerry-cans, tip you off. If you do want bottled water, it can be bought almost anywhere that sells food, even in beach cafés and tavernas, though more conventionally at kiosks and minimarkets. A large bottle should not cost more than about 80 euro-cents, often less.

### Drugs and medicines

Greek pharmacies stock most over-the-counter drugs, and pharmacists are well trained. The Greeks themselves are enthusiastic hypochondriacs and potion-poppers, so all manner of homeopathic or herbal remedies and premium-ingredient dietary supplements are available (expensively). Many formulas that would be obtainable only on prescription elsewhere are freely obtainable in Greece – though you may have to try half a dozen pharmacies before finding stock, especially on the smaller islands.

Essential drugs, often made locally under licence, are price-controlled, with nearly uniform rates all over the country, but discretional or imported sundries can be expensive. Ideally, pack a supply of your favourite remedies to last the trip.

### Medical treatment

For minor ailments your best port of call is a pharmacy. Greek chemists usually speak good English and are well trained and helpful, and pharmacies stock a good range of medicines (including contraceptives) as well as bandages and dressings for minor wounds.

Certain pharmacies are open outside of normal shop hours and at weekends, on a rotating basis. You can find out which are open by consulting the bilingual (Greek/English) card posted in pharmacy windows or doors. In big cities, and major tourist resorts such as Crete or Rhodes, one or two pharmacies will be open 24 hours a day.

There are English-speaking GPs in all the bigger towns and resorts, and their rates are usually reasonable. Ask your hotel or the tourist office for details.

Treatment for broken bones and similar mishaps is given free of charge in the state-run Greek hospitals – go straight to the casualty/emergency ward (*epígon peristatiká* in Greek). If an EU/EEA resident, bring your European Health Insurance Card, obtainable (until at least 2019) in the UK online at www.gov.uk/european-health-insurance-card. Be aware that holders of such cards are only entitled to free treatment in the casualty ward, and at the few still-functioning *agrotiká iatría* (remote rural clinics). If you make the mistake of attending a hospital's outpatient clinic, you'll pay full whack for everything at private rates, and charges are eye-watering. For more serious problems you should have private medical insurance. If you have a serious injury or illness, you are better off travelling home for treatment if you can. Greek public hospitals lag behind Northern Europe and the US in both hygiene and standard of care; locals bring food and bedding when visiting sick relatives, and must bribe nurses and doctors for anything beyond the bare minimum in care. All these conditions have been severely exacerbated by the ongoing crisis, with health-care provision very hard hit.

### Animal hazards

Nearly half the stray dogs in rural areas carry echinococcosis (treatable by surgery only) or kala-azar disease (leishmaniasis), a protozoan blood disease spread by sandfleas. So beware of befriending importunate pooches.

Mosquitoes can be a nuisance in some areas of Greece, but topical repellents are readily available in pharmacies. For safeguarding rooms, accommodation proprietors often supply a plug-in electric pad, which vaporises smokeless, odourless rectangular tablets. If you see them by the bed, it's a good bet they will be needed; refills can be found in any supermarket. Some lodgings now hang mosquito nets over beds. With global climate change and the spread of the Asian tiger mosquito, isolated cases of dengue and West Nile fever have occurred in Greece.

On the islands, poisonous baby pit vipers and scorpions are a problem in spring and summer. They will not strike you unless disturbed, but do not put your hands or feet in places (such as holes in drystone walls) that you haven't checked first. When swimming in the sea, beware of jellyfish, whose sting is not toxic but can cause swelling and hurt for days. A good over-the-counter remedy for this is Fenistil gel.

When the grape harvest is underway (August–October), many islands are plagued by large wasps. Some are so aggressive that they harass swimmers out at sea. The stings are excruciating; again Fenistil helps.

At rocky shorelines, it is worth wearing plastic or trekking sandals to avoid sea urchins (those little black underwater pincushions that can embed their very sharp, tiny and brittle spines into unwary feet). A local Greek remedy is to douse the wound with olive oil and then gently massage the foot until the spines pop out, but this rarely works unless you're willing to perform minor surgery with pen-knife and sewing needle – which should be done, as spine fragments tend to go septic.

### Insurance

The benefits of medical insurance coverage for private treatment are noted above. You will have to pay for private treatment up front, so keep receipts for any treatment or medicines you pay for to make a claim. If you plan to hire a motor scooter in Greece, or engage in any adventure sport, make sure your travel insurance policy covers such activities and note the official license requirements for scooter hire.

### Internet

Greece has become thoroughly "wired" in recent years, with bars, cafés, hotels (sometimes only the common areas) and even many tavernas offering a Wi-fi signal. Much of the time it is free, or free for the price of a coffee, drink or meal, but usually password protected. Speeds are apt to be moderate rather than blistering – especially in rural areas. With the prevalence of smart phones, tablet devices and laptops, internet cafés per se are effectively extinct. Hotel internet charges can be ruinous so avoid using the service until you know the charges.

## L

### Left luggage

**Hotels** Most hotels in Greece will store locked suitcases for up to a week if you want to make any short excursions. This is usually a free service, provided you've stayed a night or two, but the hotel will accept no responsibility in the highly unlikely event of theft.

**Commercial offices** On the islands there are left-luggage offices in many harbour towns. For a small charge space, can be hired by the hour, day, week or longer. Although contents will probably be safe, take small valuables with you.

### LGBTQ travellers

Greek society has long been ambivalent about the LGBTQ community, at least outside the predictable arenas of the arts, theatre and music industry. The age of consent for all sexual acts is 15, and bisexual activity is not uncommon among younger men, but few same-sex couples (male or female) will express affection in public. Mýkonos, the exception to this, is famous as a gay mecca, and Skála Eresoú on Lésvos (where the poetess Sappho was born) serves the same role for lesbians. Most larger islands have at least one partly gay naturist beach. But elsewhere in Greece single-sex couples are liable to be regarded as odd, although usually as welcome as any other tourists. If discreet, you will attract no attention asking for a double room and will find most people tolerant.

## M

### Media

#### Print and web-based media

Many kiosks throughout Athens and major island resorts receive British newspapers, either late the same afternoon or sometime the next day. The English online edition (www.ekathimerini.com) of centre-right Greek newspaper *Kathimerini* is the best source of Greek news, albeit heavily abridged from the parent publication. The bilingual site http://greece.greekreporter.com/category/greek-news/ is also well worth a look.

*Greek newspapers – your best bet for English-language news is online.*

### Radio and TV

Ellinikí Radiofonía is the Greek state-owned radio, divided into three different "programmes"; the Déftero Prógramma (Second Channel, FM 102.9–103.7 plus regional frequencies, or via web at http://webradio.ert.gr/deftero/) broadcasts quality Greek music. Try also the excellent private station Kanali 1, out of Piraeus (FM 90.4), or there is a plethora of private stations broadcast locally from just about every island or provincial town, no matter how tiny. The BBC can be listened to live through iPlayer.

There are three state-owned and operated television channels (ET1, ET2 and ET3); several private television channels (Antenna, Net, Mega, Star, Skaï – the best, www.skai.gr/player/tvlive/; no relation to Rupert Murdoch's Sky – and Alpha) also operate. Often they transmit foreign films and programmes with Greek subtitles rather than being dubbed. Several cable and satellite channels, including Sky and CNN, are also available in the better hotels.

### Money

The Greek currency is the euro (*evró* in Greek), which comes in coins of 1, 2, 5, 10, 20 and 50 cents (*leptá*), plus 1 and 2 euro, as well as notes of 5, 10, 20, 50, 100, 200 and 500 euros (the last two denominations are rarely seen, and the ECB has ceased printing 500s). The 200- and 100-euro notes are the most likely to be counterfeit and thus may be treated with extreme suspicion.

All banks and most hotels buy foreign currency at the official rate of exchange fixed by the Bank of Greece. Exchange rates fluctuate almost daily; for the current rate, check www.xe.com.

Travellers' cheques are now well and truly obsolete; take instead a prepaid cash-card which can be used in any ATM. Travel agencies are no longer allowed to change foreign currency; on the largest islands, visit the Bank of Greece, which gives surprisingly good rates for banknotes with no commission levied.

### Credit/debit cards

Many of the better-established hotels, restaurants and shops accept major credit cards, as do all airline and ferry-company websites, plus the domestic Greek travel websites www.airtickets.gr and www.travelplanet24.com. Many travel agencies and websites, however, will add a surcharge (typically 3%) to credit-card purchases of tickets. The average low-star hotel or taverna does not, however, take cards, or only accepts details as a booking deposit, so enquire before ordering if that is how you intend to pay. Visa Debit, Visa, Mastercard and American Express are accepted by the numerous autoteller machines (ATMs); Visa Electron may not be. Most debit and all credit cards, however, charge a surcharge to do so, the latter's can often amount to over five percent of the transaction value, so debit cards are usually the best option to avoid high charges. This caveat aside, you will find that this is the most convenient and least expensive way of getting funds, and most machines operate around the clock.

## O

### Opening hours

All banks are open 8am–2.30pm Monday to Thursday, and 8am–2pm on Friday. But since ATMs are now ubiquitous – even the smaller islands will have at least one – few travellers see the inside of a bank nowadays.

The schedule for business and shop hours is more complicated, varying according to the type of business and the day of the week. The main thing to remember is that shops generally open at 8.30 or 9am and close on Monday, Wednesday and Saturday at 2.30pm. On Tuesday, Thursday and Friday most businesses close at 2pm and reopen in the afternoon from 5pm to 8.30pm (winter), 5.30 or 6pm to 9pm (summer).

Supermarkets, both large and small, are the only shops guaranteed to be open all day (Mon–Fri 8am–9pm, Sat 8am–8pm). Especially on resort islands, there will be at least one open short hours on Sunday too (typically 10am–4pm).

In our Places sections, we give the full range of opening hours for museums and archaeological sites. Be aware, however, that the last permitted admission is always at least 15, and sometimes 30, minutes before the stated closing time.

### "Greek time"

Beware Greek schedules. You will soon learn that schedules are very flexible in Greece (both in business and personal affairs). To avoid disappointment, allow ample time when shopping and doing business. That way, you may also enter into the Greek spirit of negotiation, in which a good chat can be as important as the matter of business itself.

Although shops and businesses generally operate during the hours indicated above, there is no real guarantee that when you want to book a ferry or buy a gift, the relevant office or shop will actually be open.

Siesta (*mikró ýpno* in Greek) is observed throughout Greece, and even in Athens the majority of people retire behind closed doors between the hours of 2.45pm and 5.30pm. Shops and businesses also close, and it is usually impossible to get much done until late afternoon or early evening. To avoid frustration and disappointment, shop and book things between 10am and 1pm Monday to Friday.

Since 1994 Athens and the largest towns have experimented with "continual" *(synéhies)* hours during the winter to bring the country more in line with the EU, but this seems to

be discretionary rather than obligatory, with some stores observing the hours and others adhering to traditional schedules. So far it has not caught on across the rest of the country.

Tourist shops throughout the country usually trade well into the evening during summer. But butchers and fishmongers are not allowed to open on summer evenings (although a few disregard the law), and pharmacies (except for those on rota duty) are never open in the evenings or on Saturday morning.

## Photography

Although Greece is a photographer's paradise, taking photographs at will is not recommended. Cameras are permitted in museums (except for certain exhibits), but to be used without tripod or flash. Watch out for signs showing a bellows camera with a red "X" through it, and do not point your camera at anything in or near airports – most of which double as military bases.

### Postal services

Most local post offices are open weekdays from 7.30am until 2pm. However, the main post offices in central Athens (on Eólou near Omónia Square and on Sýndagma Square at the corner of Mitropóleos Street) are open longer hours on weekdays, as well as having short schedules on Saturday. Rhodes Neohóri post office also has evening and Saturday morning hours.

Postal rates are subject to periodic change; currently a postcard or lightweight letter costs 90 eurocents to any overseas destination. For large letters or parcels, see www.elta.gr/en-us/calculatepostage. aspx. Stamps are available from the post office or from authorised stationers and hotels, which may charge a 10–15 percent commission. Outbound speeds are reasonable – as little as three days to northern Europe, a week or so to North America.

If you want to send a parcel from Greece, do not wrap it until a post office clerk has inspected it, unless it is going to another EU country, in

which case you can present it sealed. Major post offices sell various sizes of cardboard boxes in which you can pack your material, as well as twine, but you should bring your own tape and scissors.

Letters from abroad can be sent Post Restante to any post office, which will hold it for a month. Take your passport or other convincing ID when you go to pick up mail.

## Religious services

Most major towns and island resort areas with significant foreign patronage or a large expat community – most notably Rhodes, Sámos, Corfu, Náxos, Crete and Santoríni – have at least one church dedicated to the Catholic, Anglican or other Protestant (eg Swedish Lutheran) rites, or an agreement for part-time use of an Orthodox premises. There are effectively functioning Catholic parishes on Rhodes, Crete, Corfu, Sýros and Tínos, where foreigners are welcome, plus the busy Armenian Apostolic church of Sourp Garabed in Iráklio, Crete. Etz Hayyim synagogue in Haniá, Crete, also welcomes foreign worshippers. Placards posted on the churches themselves, or handouts at the local tourist office, give current information on service schedules (which may be anything from once a month to two or three times weekly).

## Student travellers

In addition to museum and archaeological site discounts, students and under-26s, with the appropriate documentation, are eligible for discounted fares and youth passes on some shipping lines, including those operating to and from Italy.

## Telephones

Greece has one of the highest per-capita mobile-phone usage rates in the world, and a mobile is an essential fashion accessory for any self-respecting Greek, as well as a means of communication. Foreign mobile owners are well catered for, with thorough coverage and, as of 2017, abolition of roaming charges for UK- or EU-based services. On all islands within sight of Turkey or Albania, be wary of your mobile being "kidnapped" by the networks of those non-EU countries, especially at points (eg Corfu, Ikaría, Híos, Kastellórizo) where the Greek signal is much weaker. Manually select a Greek network if necessary, to avoid being hit by an outrageous call bill (typically £1.50/min plus VAT) upon return home.

North American users will have to bring a tri-band phone for use in Greece. If you're staying for any amount of time, North Americans or Australians will find it better to buy a pay-as-you-go SIM card from one of the three Greek providers (Vodafone, CosmOTE, Wind). As an anti-terrorism strategy to keep you from using your phone to set off bombs remotely, you will have to register your identity (and the device) upon purchase.

Calls from hotel rooms typically have a minimum 200–300 percent surcharge on top of the standard rates – to be avoided for anything other than brief local calls.

For overseas calls outside of the EU, you can avoid the truly outrageous local landline rates by buying a code-card, where you scratch to reveal a 12-digit code, then ring an 807-prefixed number to enter said code, then the number you want. It may all sound a bit of a hassle, but savings can amount to about 70 percent. If you have a laptop, bring a Skype headset along to take advantage of Wi-fi zones for calling abroad. Smaller device owners can use FaceTime or make calls via WhatsApp or Facebook.

### Time zone

Greece is two hours ahead of GMT and, like the rest of Europe, observes Daylight Saving Time from 3am on the last Sunday in March until 3am on the last Sunday in October.

### Tipping

Menu prices at most cafés, *meze-dopolía* and *tavernas* include a service charge, but it is still customary to leave an extra 5–10 percent on the table for the waiting staff. Taxi drivers are not tipped per se but may "round up" fares to the nearest half-euro. Hotel porters should be given a euro or so per bag.

### Toilets

Public conveniences, often subterranean ones in parks or plazas, or perched on a harbour jetty, are of variable cleanliness and rarely have paper. Most people just buy a drink in a café and use their facilities. In busy areas, some cafés post signs reading "Toilets for customers only". Elsewhere, establishments are a bit more lenient about those caught short just popping in.

### Tourist information

#### Tourist offices

If you would like tourist information about Greece during your trip, visit the nearest Greek National Tourist Organisation – GNTO, or EOT in Greek. They provide information on public transport, as well as leaflets and details about sites and museums. There are several regional GNTO offices on the islands. The information booth in Athens can be found at the base of Dionysíou Areopagítou, at the edge of the Pláka district.

On many of the islands there are municipal tourist information centres open from June to September. These are usually prominently sited near the centre of the main town, and provide all the local information you might need. Some can even help with finding accommodation.

#### Tourist police

The Greek Tourist Police are a branch of the local police, found in many large island towns; on the most heavily visited ones, for example Rhodes, they have a separate premises. Each tourist policeman should speak at least one foreign language well. They should be your first port of call in the event of a serious incident involving rogue hoteliers or restauranteurs, and should also be consulted if you are the victim of a serious crime such as assault or robbery, if the regular police seem to be uninterested.

### Greek National Tourist Organisation offices overseas

**Worldwide:** Greek National Tourism Organisation, www.visitgreece.gr

**UK and Ireland:** Great Portland House, 4 Great Portland Street, 5th Floor East, London W1W 8QJ; tel: (020) 7495 9300.

**US & Canada:** 800 3rd Avenue, 23rd Floor, New York, NY 10022; tel: (212) 421-5777.

### Tour operators

Mass-market bucket-and-spade holidays are easy to find on the web. Otherwise, here are a few suggestions for quality packages and bespoke itineraries on the islands:

**GIC the Villa Collection**
UK Tel 020 8232 9780
www.gicthevillacollection.com
Excellent portfolio of luxury villas in the Ionian Islands (except Zakynthos), Crete, Sámos and the Sporades.

**Hellenic Adventures**
USA Tel: 1-800 851 6349
www.hellenicadventures.com
A less usual Híos, Lésvos and Límnos itinerary, plus a more popular Mýkonos, Rhodes and Santoríni tour.

**Hidden Greece**
UK Tel: 020 8758 4707
www.hidden-greece.co.uk
Tailor-made specialists to many small, overlooked islands like Psérimos or Irakliá.

**Insight Guides**
www.insightguides.com/holidays
Offers holidays to numerous destinations around the globe, including the Greek islands. You can book trips, transfers and a range of exciting experiences through our local experts, from Crete and the Cyclades to a romantic Greek Island-Hopping Honeymoon itinerary.

**Simpson Travel**
UK Tel: 020 3627 2996
www.simpsontravel.com
Premium villas on all the Ionian Islands (particularly the stunning Rou Estate on Corfu), Skópelos and Crete.

**Sunvil**
UK Tel: 020 8758 4758
www.sunvil.co.uk
Top-quality hotels and apartments, especially strong in the Sporades,

Ionian Islands, Límnos, Sámos, Cyclades and Dodecanese.

**Travel à la Carte**
UK tel: 020 7286 9255
www.travelalacarte.co.uk
Villas and apartments on Kefaloniá, Levkáda, Meganísi, Paxí, Itháki, Corfu and Sými.

**Villa Plus**
Tel: 01727 836686
www.villaplus.com
The main provider of villas in north-eastern Corfu, from Aharávi to Nissáki inclusive.

### Tours by sea

**Peter Sommer Travels**
UK Tel: 01600 888220
www.petersommer.com
Upscale, academic-led, small group tours with a focus on archaeology, both on land or by small schooner, taking in Crete, the Dodecanese and certain Cyclades during spring or autumn.

**Swimtrek**
UK Tel: 01273 739713 US Tel: 1-877 455-SWIM
www.swimtrek.com
For avid swimmers, who get to swim 5km (3 miles) daily between select Cyclades, Sporades, Ionians and around Crete.

### Walking holidays

**Exodus**
UK Tel: 020 3811 4578
www.exodus.co.uk
Walking tour of Páros, Santoríni and Náxos, or just on Évvia.

**Jonathan's Tours**
France Tel: 00 33 5 62 33 87 90
www.jonathanstours.com
Itineraries, often bespoke, on Crete and Ándros, with an ultra-experienced, certified mountain guide.

**Ramblers' Walking Holidays**
Tel: 01707 331133
www.ramblersholidays.co.uk
Interesting itineraries on Tínos and Ándros; Sífnos and Mílos; Hydra and Póros.

### Wildlife tours on Crete, Sámos and Lésvos

**The Travelling Naturalist**
UK Tel: 01305 267994
www.naturalist.co.uk

**Naturetrek**
UK Tel: 01962 733051
www.naturetrek.co.uk

### Writing workshops/holistic holidays

**Astra**
US Tel: (303) 321-5403

www.astragreece.com

**Skyros Centre**
UK Tel: 01983 865566
www.skyros.com

**Yoga Plus**
UK Tel: 07931 203114
www.yogaplus.co.uk

### Websites

Greek weather forecasts are available at:
www.meteo.gr
http://poseidon.hcmr.gr
Windsurfers in particular should consult the Greek pages of:
www.windguru.cz
Reviews and sales of books on all aspects of Greece can be found at:
www.hellenicbookservice.com
Buying ferry tickets online and don't just want individual company sites?
www.goferry.gr
For reliable destination information and links have a look at:
www.greecetravel.com
The Ministry of Culture site has impressive coverage of state-run museums, archaeological sites and remote monuments on:
www.odysseus.culture.gr
All the Greek reptiles and amphibians (surprisingly compelling) are at:
www.herpetofauna.gr
All the naturist beaches – which usually happen to be the best ones – are on:
http://barefoot.info/greekgde.html

---

## W

### What to bring

#### Adaptors

220–240V AC is the standard household electric current throughout Greece. Shavers and hairdryers from North America that are not dual-voltage should be left at home in favour of versatile travel models – they can be bought in Greece if necessary. Otherwise, buy a small transformer before you leave home. Greek plugs are either the standard round, two-pin Type C European

#### ⊙ Weights and measures

Greece is completely metric. The only exception is that land is measured and sold by the *strémma* (1,000 sq metres/10,764 sq ft).

continental type, or the slightly heftier Type F Schuko, different from those in North America and the UK; plug adaptors for American appliances are easy to find in Greece, three-to-two-pin adaptors for UK appliances much less so, so these are best purchased before departure in the UK.

#### Sun protection

A hat, sunscreen and sunglasses are essential for protection from the midday sun, but if you fail to bring them, sunscreens of up to SPF50 are widely available in pharmacies and cosmetics shops, and sun-hats and sunglasses can be found everywhere.

#### Toiletries

Most international brands are widely available, except on the smallest islands. Feminine hygiene products are more likely to be sold in supermarkets than in pharmacies.

#### Torch/flashlight

Pack one, as walking home from island tavernas can be tricky if there's no moon. If you forget, Maglites or similar are widely sold.

#### Universal plug

Greek basins often aren't equipped with plugs, so if you want water in your sink a universal plug is essential.

### Women travellers

Lone female visitors may very occasionally be targeted for attention by predatory Greek males, especially around beach bars and late-night clubs, but in general machismo is no longer any more a problem than elsewhere in southern Europe. Inexorable changes in Greek culture mean that Greek women have much more sexual freedom than previously, especially in the cities, so foreign tourists are no longer such a novelty. There is now little controversy about Greek women spending time with their male counterparts, up to and including cohabiting before (or instead of) marriage.

However, in remote areas, many Greeks are still highly traditional and may find it hard to understand why you are travelling alone. You may not feel comfortable in all-male drinking cafés.

# LANGUAGE

## THE GREEK LANGUAGE

Modern demotic Greek is the outcome of gradual evolution undergone by the Greek language since the classical period (5th–4th centuries BC). The language is still relatively close to ancient Greek: it uses the same alphabet and some of the same vocabulary, though the grammar – other than the retention of three genders – is considerably streamlined and is less complicated. Many people speak English, some very well, but even just a few words in their native language will always be appreciated.

### Pronunciation tips

Most of the sounds of Greek are reasonably straightforward to pronounce for English-speakers. There are only six vowel sounds: *a, e, i, o, u* and *y* are consistently pronounced as shown in the table below. The letter *s* is usually pronounced "s", but as "z" before an *m* or *g*. The sound represented here as *th* is always pronounced as in "thin", not "that"; the first sound in "that" is represented by *d*.

The only difficult sounds are *h*, which is pronounced like the "ch" in Scottish "loch" (we render this as *kh* after "s" so that you don't generate "sh"), and *g* before *a* or *o*, which has no equivalent in English – it's somewhere between the "y" in "yet" and the "g" in "get".

The position of the stress in words is of critical importance, as homonyms abound, and Greeks will often fail to understand you if you don't stress the right syllable (compare *psýllos*, "flea" with *psilós*, "tall"). In this guide, stress is marked by a simple accent mark ( ´ ) except for single-syllable words which are, however, still stressed. Greek uses the diaresis ( ¨ ) over

vowels, which may or may not have the primary stress as well, to mark them off as the second letter of a dipthong.

Greek word order is flexible, so you may often hear phrases in a different order from the one in which they are given here. Like the French, the Greeks use the plural of the second person when addressing someone politely.

We have used the polite (formal) form throughout this language section, except where an expression is specified as "informal".

## COMMUNICATION

**Good morning** *kaliméra*
**Good evening** *kalispéra*
**Good night** *kaliníhta*
**Hello/Goodbye** *giásas* (informal:) *giásou*
**Pleased to meet you** *hárika polý*
**Yes** *ne*
**No** *óhi*
**Thank you** *evharistó*
**You're welcome** *parakaló*
**Please** *parakaló*

*Political banner in Mytilini, Lesvos.*

**Okay/All right** *endáxi*
**Excuse me (to get attention)** *Me synhoríte*
**Excuse me (to ask someone to get out of the way)** *sygnómi*
**How are you?** *Ti kánete?* (informal:) *Ti kánis?*
**Fine, and you?** *Kalá, ke esís?* (informal:) *Kalá, ke esí?*
**Cheers/Our health!** *Yiámas!* (when drinking)
**Could you help me?** *Boríte na me voithísete?*
**Can you show me...** *Boríte na mou díxete...*
**I want...** *Thélo...*
**I don't know** *Den xéro*
**I don't understand** *Den katálava*
**Do you speak English?** *Miláte angliká?*
**Can you please speak more slowly?** *Parakaló, miláte pió sigá*
**Please say that again** *Parakaló, xanapésteto*
**Please write it down for me** *Na mou to grápste, parakaló*
**Here** *edó*
**There** *ekí*
**What?** *ti?*
**When?** *póte?*
**Why?** *giatí?*

**Where?** *pou?*
**How?** *pos?*

## TELEPHONE CALLS

**the telephone** *to tiléfono*
**phone card** *tilekárta*
**May I use the phone please?** *Boró na tilefoníso, parakaló?*
**Hello (on the phone)** *Embrós/Légete*
**My name is...** *Légome...*
**Could I speak to...** *Boró na milíso me...*
**Wait a moment** *Periménete mía stigmí*
**I didn't hear** *Den ákousa*

## IN THE HOTEL

**Do you have a vacant room?** *Éhete domátio?*
**I've booked a room** *Ého kratísi éna domátio*
**I'd like...** *Tha íthela...*

### ⊙ Numbers

**1** *énas/mía/éna* (masc/fem/neut)
**2** *dýo*
**3** *tris/tría*
**4** *tésseres/téssera*
**5** *pénde*
**6** *éxi*
**7** *eftá*
**8** *októ*
**9** *ennéa*
**10** *déka*
**11** *éndeka*
**12** *dódeka*
**13** *dekatrís/dekatría*
**14** *dekatésseres/dekatéssera*
**15** *dekapénde*
**16** *dekaéxi*
**17** *dekaeftá*
**18** *dekaoktó*
**19** *dekaennéa*
**20** *íkosi*
**30** *triánda*
**40** *saránda*
**50** *penínda*
**60** *exínda*
**70** *evdomínda*
**80** *ogdónda*
**90** *enenínda*
**100** *ekató*
**200** *dyakósia*
**300** *trakósies/trakósa*
**400** *tetrakósies/tetrakósa*
**500** *pendakósa*
**1,000** *hílies/hília*
**2,000** *dýo hiliádes*
**1 million** *éna ekatomírio*

*Street sign.*

**a single/double room** *éna monóklino/díklino*
**double bed** *dipló kreváti*
**a room with a bathtub/shower** *éna domátio me baniéra/dous*
**One night** *éna vrádi*
**Two nights** *dýo vradiá*
**How much do you charge?** *Póso hreónete?*
**It's expensive** *Íne akrivó*
**Do you have a room with a sea view?** *Éhete domátio me théa pros ti thálassa?*
**Is there a balcony?** *Éhi balkóni?*
**Is the room heated/air-conditioned?** *Éhi thérmansi/klimatismó to domátio?*
**Is breakfast included?** *Mazí me to proinó?*
**Can I see the room please?** *Boró na do to domátio, parakaló?*
**The room is too...** *To domátio íne polý...*
**hot/cold/small** *zestó/krýo/mikró*
**It's too noisy** *Éhi polý thóryvo*
**Could you show me another room, please?** *Boríte na mou díxete éna állo domátio, parakaló?*
**I'll take it** *Tha to páro*
**Can I have the bill, please?** *Na mou kánete to logariasmó, parakaló?*
**dining room** *trapezaría*
**key** *klidí*
**towel** *petséta*
**sheet** *sendóni*
**blanket** *kouvérta*
**pillow** *maxilári*
**soap** *sapoúni*
**hot water** *zestó neró*
**toilet paper** *hartí ygías*

## AT A BAR OR CAFÉ

**bar/café** *bar/kafenío* (or *kafetéria*)
**patisserie** *zaharoplastío*

**I'd like...** *Tha íthela...*
**a coffee** *éna kafé*
**Greek coffee** *ellinikó kafé*
**filter coffee** *gallikó kafé/kafé fíltro*
**instant coffee** *neskafé* (or *nes*)
**espresso** *espréso*
**cappuccino** *kapoutsíno*
**iced cappucino** *freddocino*
**white (with milk)** *me gála*
**black (without milk)** *horís gála*
**with sugar** *me záhari*
**without sugar** *horís záhari*
**a cup of tea** *éna tsáï*
**tea with lemon** *éna tsái me lemóni*
**orange/lemon soda** *mía portokaláda/lemonáda*
**fresh orange juice** *éna frésko hymó portokáli*
**a glass/bottle of water** *éna potíri/boukáli neró*
**with ice cubes** *me pagáki*
**an ouzo/brandy** *éna oúzo/koniák*
**a beer (draught)** *mía býra (varelísio )*
**an ice-cream** *éna pagotó*
**a pastry, cake** *mía pásta*
**oriental pastries** *baklavá/kataifi*

## IN A RESTAURANT

**Have you got a table for...** *Éhete trapézi giá...*
**There are (four) of us** *Ímaste (tésseres)*
**I'm a vegetarian** *Íme hortofágos*
**Can we see the menu?** *Boroúme na doúme ton katálogo?*
**We would like to order** *Théloume na parangíloume*
**Have you got (bulk) wine by the carafe?** *Éhete krasí hýma?*
**a litre/half-litre** *éna kiló/misó kilo*
**of white/red/rosé wine** *áspro/kókkino/rozé krasí*
**Would you like anything else?** *Thélete típot' állo?*

**No, thank you** *Óhi, evharistó*
**glass** *potíri*
**knife/fork/spoon** *mahéri/piroúni/ koutáli*
**plate** *piáto*
**napkin** *hartopetséta*
**Where is the toilet?** *Pou íne i toualétta?*
**The bill, please** *To logariasmó, parakaló*

## FOOD

### Mezédes/Orektiká

*taramosaláta* **fish-roe dip**
*tzatzíki* **yoghurt-garlic-cucumber dip**
*melitzanosaláta* **aubergine purée**
*loukánika* **sausages**
*tyropitákia* **cheese pies (small)**
*gávros marinátos* **marinated anchovy fillets**
*eliés* **olives**
*dolmádes, giaprákia* **vine leaves stuffed with rice**
*kopanistí* **tangy fermented cheese dip**
*saganáki* **fried cheese**
*tyrokafterí* **soft cheese seasoned with hot peppers**
*fáva* **puréed yellow split peas**
*piperiés florínis* **red sweet pickled peppers**

### Meat dishes

*kréas* **any meat**

*arní* **lamb**
*hirinó* **pork**
*kotópoulo* **chicken**
*moskhári* **veal, beef**
*psitó* **roast or grilled**
*sto foúrno* **roast**
*sta kárvouna* **grilled**
*soúvlas* **on the spit**
*souvláki* **brochettes on skewers**
*kokinistó* **stewed in tomato sauce**
*krasáto* **stewed in wine sauce**
*lemonáto* **stewed in lemon sauce**
*avgolémono* **egg-lemon sauce**
*tiganitó* **fried**
*kapnistó* **smoked**
*brizóla* **(pork or veal) chop**
*païdákia* **lamb chops**
*sykóti* **liver**
*sykotákia* **small liver chunks, chicken or lamb**
*kymás* **mince**
*biftéki (gemistó)* **small burger (cheese-stuffed)**
*keftédes, keftedákia* **small meatballs**
*soutzoukákia* **rissoles baked in red sauce**
*giouvarlákia* **mince-and-rice balls in egg-lemon sauce**
*makarónia* **spaghetti**
*piláfi* **rice**
*me kymá* **with minced meat**
*me sáltsa* **with tomato sauce**
*pastítsio* **macaroni "pie" with minced meat**
*gýros me pítta* **doner kebab**

### Seafood

*frésko* **fresh**
*katapsygméno* **frozen**

*psári* **fish**
*ostrakoidí* **shellfish**
*glóssa* **sole**
*xifías* **swordfish**
*galéos* **small shark**
*koliós* **mackerel**
*barboúnia* **red mullet**
*sardélles* **sardines**
*gávros* **fresh anchovy**
*marídes* **picarel**
*mýdia* **mussels**
*strídia* **oysters**
*kydónia* **cockles**
*kalamarákia* **small squid**
*thrápsala* **large deep-water squid**
*soupiés* **cuttlefish**
*htapódi* **octopus**
*garídes* **prawns**
*astakós* **lobster**

### Vegetables

*angináres* **artichokes**
*arakádes, pizélia* **peas**
*domátes* **tomatoes**
*fakés* **brown lentils**
*fasólia/fasoláda* **stewed white beans**
*fasolákia (fréska)* **green (runner) beans**
*hórta* **various greens, wild/ cultivated**
*karóta* **carrot**
*kolokythákia* **courgettes**
*kounoupídi* **cauliflower**
*koukiá* **broad beans**
*kremmýdi* **onion**
*frésko kremmýdi* **spring onion**
*láhano* **cabbage**
*maroúli* **lettuce**
*melitzánes* **aubergines**

## ⊙ Our transliteration system

In Greece, most town and village names on road signs, as well as most street names, are written in Greek and the Roman alphabets. There's no universally accepted system of transliteration into Roman, and in any case the Greek authorities are gradually replacing old signs with new ones that use a slightly different system. This means you will have to get used to seeing different spellings of the same place on maps, signs and in this book.

To the right is the transliteration scheme we have used in this book: beside each Greek letter or pair of letters is the Roman letter(s) we have used. Next to that is a rough approximation of the sound in an English word.

|  | |  |  |
|---|---|---|---|
| Α | Α | a | far |
| Β | Β | v | vote |
| Γ | Γ | g/y | got *except before "e" or "i", when it is nearer to y*acht, *but rougher* |
| Δ | Δ | d | then |
| Ε | Ε | e | egg |
| Ζ | Ζ | z | zoo |
| Η | Η | i | ski |
| Θ | θ | th | thin |
| Ι | Ι | i | ski |
| Κ | Κ | k | kiss |
| Λ | Λ | l | long |
| Μ | Μ | m | man |
| Ν | Ν | n | no |
| Ξ | Ξ | x | taxi |
| Ο | Ο | o | road |
| Π | Π | p | pen |
| Ρ | Ρ | r | room |
| Σ | Σ/Σ | s | set *or* charisma |

|  | |  |  |
|---|---|---|---|
| Τ | Τ | t | tea |
| Υ | Υ | y | mildly |
| Φ | Φ | f | fish |
| Χ | Χ | h | loch |
| Ψ | Ψ | ps | maps |
| Ω | Ω | o | road |
| ΑΙ | ΑΙ | (ai) e | hay |
| ΑΥ | ΑΥ | (au) av/af | have/raffle |
| ΕΙ | ΕΙ | (ei) i | ski |
| ΕΥ | ΕΥ | (eu) ev/ef | ever/left |
| ΟΙ | ΟΙ | (oi) i | ski |
| ΟΥ | ΟΥ | (ou) ou | tourist |
| ΓΓ | ΓΓ | (gg) ng | long |
| ΓΚ | ΓΚ | (gk) ng | long |
| ΓΞ | ΓΞ | (gx) nx | anxious |
| ΜΠ | ΜΠ | (mp) b | beg |
| | | *or* mb | limber |
| ΝΤ | ΝΤ | (nt) d | dog |
| | | *or* nd | under |
| ΤΖ | ΤΖ | (tz) tz | fads |

## ⊙ Emergencies

**Help!** *Voíthia!*
**Stop!** *Stamatíste!*
**I've had an accident** *Íha éna atíhima*
**Call a doctor** *Fonáxte éna giatró*
**Call an ambulance** *Fonáxte éna asthenofóro*
**Call the police** *Fonáxte tin astynomía*
**Call the fire brigade** *Fonáxte tous pyrosvéstes*
**Where's the nearest hospital?** *Pou íne to pio kondinó nosokomío?*
**I would like to report a theft** *Égine mia klopí*

---

*pantzária* **beetroots**
*patátes (tiganités/sto foúrno)* **potatoes (fried/roasted)**
*radíkia* **chicory leaves**
*revýthia* **chickpeas, garbanzos**
*skórdo* **garlic**
*spanáki* **spinach**
*spanakópitta* **spinach pie**
*vlíta* **notchweed, amaranth greens**
*gígandes* **stewed butter beans**
*domátes gemistés* **stuffed tomatoes**
*piperiés gemistés* **stuffed peppers**
*saláta* **salad**
*domatosaláta* **tomato salad**
*angourodomáta* **tomato and cucumber salad**
*horiátiki* **Greek "peasant" salad**

### Fruit

*míla* **apples**
*verýkoka* **apricots**
*banánes* **bananas**
*kerásia* **cherries**
*sýka* **figs**
*stafýlia* **grapes**
*lemónia* **lemons**
*pepónia* **melons**
*portokália* **oranges**
*rodákina* **peaches**
*ahládia* **pears**
*fráoules* **strawberries**
*karpoúzi* **watermelon**

### Basic foods

*psomí* **bread**
*aláti* **salt**
*pipéri* **pepper**
*ládi* **oil**
*xýdi* **vinegar**
*moustárda* **mustard**
*voútyro* **butter**
*tyrí* **cheese**
*avgá (tiganitá)* **(fried) eggs**
*omelétta* **omelette**

*marmeláda* **jam, marmelade**
*rýzi* **rice**
*giaoúrti* **yoghurt**
*méli* **honey**
*záhari* **sugar**

### Desserts

*galaktoboúriko* **custard pastry**
*karydópitta* **walnut pie**
*halvás* **semolina-based dry confection**
*katlitsoúnia* **sweet-soft-cheese-and-cinnamon-filled turnover**
*ravaní* **semolina and syrup cake**

### ALCOHOLIC DRINKS

*býra* **beer**
*krasí* **wine**
*áspro* **white wine**
*kokkinélli, rozé* **rosé wine**
*mávro* **red wine**
*me to kiló* **wine by the kilo**
*hýma* **bulk, from the barrel**
*(aerioúho) neró* **(sparkling, fizzy) water**
*retsína* **resin-flavoured wine**
*oúzo* **aniseed-flavoured grape-pressing distillate**
*rakí, tsikoudiá* **Cretan distilled spirit from vintage crushings, unflavoured**
*tsípouro* **Sporades/north Aegean version of *rakí***
*soúma* **Rhodes/Sámos version of *rakí***

### SIGHTSEEING

**information** *plirofories*
**open/closed** *anihtó/klistó*
**Is it possible to see...** *Boroúme na dhoúme...*
**the church/archaeological site?** *tin eklisía/ta arhéa?*
**Where can I find the custodian/key?** *Pou boró na vro to fýlaka/klidí?*

### AT THE SHOPS

**shop** *magazí/katástima*
**What time do you open/close?** *Ti óra anígete/klínete?*
**Are you being served?** *Exiperitíste?*
**What would you like?** *Oríste/ti thélete?*
**I'm just looking** *Aplós kitázo*
**How much is it?** *Póso kostízi?*
**Do you take credit/debit cards?** *Éhete mihánima POS?*
**I'd like...** *Tha íthela...*

**this one** *aftó*
**that one** *ekíno*
**Have you got...?** *Éhete...?*
**size (for clothes)** *número*
**Can I try it on?** *Boró na to dokimáso?*
**It's too expensive** *Íne polý akrivó*
**Don't you have anything cheaper?** *Den éhete típota pió ftinó?*
**Please write it down for me** *To gráfete parakaló?*
**It's too small/ big** *Mou pái pára polý mikró/megálo*
**No thank you, I don't like it** *Óhi evharistó, den m'arési*
**I'll take it** *Tha to páro*
**I don't want it** *Den to thélo*
**This is faulty; can I have a replacement?** *Avtó éhi éna elátoma; boró na to aláxo?*
**Can I have a refund?** *Boró na páro píso ta leftá?*
**a kilo** *éna kiló*
**half a kilo** *misó kilo*
**a quarter (kilo)** *éna tétarto*
**two kilos** *dýo kilá*
**100 grams** *ekató grammária*
**200 grams** *diakósia grammária*
**more** *perisótero*
**less** *ligótero*
**a little** *lígo*
**very little** *polý lígo*
**with/without** *mazí me/horís*
**That's enough** *ftáni*
**That's all** *tipot'álo*

### TRAVELLING

**airport** *aerodrómio*
**boarding card** *kárta epivívasis*
**boat** *plío/karávi*
**bus** *leoforío*
**bus station** *stathmós leoforíon*
**bus stop** *stási*
**catamaran** *katamarán*
**coach** *púlman*
**ferry** *feribót*
**first/second class** *próti/défteri thési*
**flight** *ptísi*
**hydrofoil** *iptámeno delfíni*
**motorway** *ethnikí odós*
**port** *limáni*
**return ticket** *isitírio me epistrofí*
**single ticket** *apló isitírio*
**taxi** *taxí*

### PUBLIC TRANSPORT

**Can you help me, please?** *Boríte na me voithísete, parakaló?*
**Where can I buy tickets?** *Pou na kópso isitírio?*
**At the counter** *sto tamío*
**Does it stop at...?** *Káni stási sto...?*

You need to change at... *Tha prépi n'aláxete sto...*

When is the next bus/ferry/catamaran to...? *Póte févgi to leoforío/feribót/katamarán gia...?*

How long does the journey take? *Pósi óra káni to taxídi?*

What time will we arrive? *Ti óra tha ftásoume?*

How much is the fare? *Póso stihízi to isitírio?*

Next stop please *Káne tin ypómeni stási, parakaló*

Can you tell me where to get off? *Tha mou píte pou na katévo?*

Should I get off here? *Edó na katévo?*

## AT THE AIRPORT

I'd like to book a seat to... *Tha íthela na kratíso mia thési gia...*

When is the next flight to... *Póte íne i epómeni ptísi giá...*

Are there any seats available? *Ypárhoun thésis?*

Can I take this in my carry-on? *Boró na to páro avtó sti hiraposkeví?*

My suitcase didn't arrive *Den éftase i valítsa mou*

The flight has been delayed *I ptísi éhi kathistérisi*

The flight has been cancelled *I ptísi mateóthike*

## DIRECTIONS

right/left *dexiá/aristerá*

Take the first/second right *Párte ton próto/déftero drómo dexiá*

Turn right/left *Strípste dexiá/aristerá*

Go straight on *Tha páte ísia/efthía*

after the traffic lights *metá ta fanária*

Is it near/far away? *Íne kondá/makriá?*

How far is it? *Póso makriá íne?*

It's five minutes' walk *Íne pénde leptá me ta pódia*

It's 10 minutes by car *Íne déka leptá me avtokínito*

100 metres *ekató métra*

opposite/next to *apénandi/dípla*

crossroads *dhiastávrosi*

forking *dífhala*

Where is/are...? *Pou íne...?*

Where can I find... *Pou boró na vro...*

a petrol station? *éna venzinádiko?*

an ATM *éna avtómato?*

a hotel? *éna xenodohío?*

How do I get there? *Pos na páo ekí?*

Can you show me where I am on the map? *Boríte na mou díxete sto hárti pou íme?*

Am I on the right road for... *Gia... kalá páo?*

No, you're on the wrong road *Óhi, pírate láthos drómo*

## ON THE ROAD

Where can I hire a car? *Pou boró na nikiázo avtokínito?*

What is it insured for? *Ti asfália éhi?*

By what time must I return it? *Méhri ti óra prépi na to epistrépso?*

driving licence *díploma*

petrol *venzíni*

unleaded *amólyvdi*

oil *ládi*

Fill it up *Óso pérni*

My car has broken down *Éhi páthi vlávi to avtokinitó mou*

I've had an accident *Íha éna atíhima*

Can you check...? *Boríte na elénhete...?*

the brakes *ta fréna*

the clutch *to ambrayáz*

the engine *i mihaní*

the exhaust *i exátmisi*

the fanbelt *o imándas*

the gearbox *i tahýtites*

the headlights *ta fanária*

the radiator *to psygío*

the spark plugs *ta buzí*

the tyre(s) *ta lástiha*

## TIMES AND DATES

(in the) morning *to proí*

afternoon *to apógevma*

evening *to vrádi*

(at) night *(ti) nýhta*

yesterday *htes*

today *símera*

tomorrow *ávrio*

now *tóra*

early *norís*

late *argá*

a minute *éna leptó*

five/ten *pénde/déka*

minutes *leptá*

an hour *mia óra*

half an hour *misí óra*

a quarter of an hour *éna tétarto*

at one/two (o'clock) *sti mia/stis dýo (i óra)*

a day *mia méra*

a week *mia evdomáda*

(on) Monday *(ti) deftéra*

(on) Tuesday *(tin) tríti*

(on) Wednesday *(tin) tetárti*

(on) Thursday *(tin) pémpti*

(on) Friday *(tin) paraskeví*

(on) Saturday *(to) sávato*

(on) Sunday *(tin) kyriakí*

## HEALTH

Is there a chemist nearby? *Ypárhi éna farmakío edó kondá?*

Where is the duty chemist? *Pou íne to farmakío tis vardiás?*

Which chemist is open all night? *Pio farmakío dianikterévi?*

I don't feel well *Den esthánome kalá*

I'm ill *Íme árostos* (feminine *árosti*)

He/she's ill *Íne árostos/árosti*

Where does it hurt? *Pou ponái?*

It hurts here *Ponái edó*

I suffer from... *Pásko apo...*

Diabetes *diavítis*

Asthma *ásthma*

Arthritis *arthrítida*

I have a... *Ého...*

headache *ponokéfalo*

sore throat *ponólemo*

stomach ache *kilíopono*

Have you got something for travel sickness? *Éhete típota gia ti navtía?*

It's not serious *Den íne sovaró*

Do I need a prescription? *Hriázete syndagí?*

It bit me (of an animal) *Me dángose*

It stung me *Me kéntrise*

bee *mélisa*

wasp *sfíka*

It bit me (a mosquito, fly, gnat) *Me tsímpise*

mosquito *kounoúpi*

gnat *sknípa*

fly *míga*

sticking plaster *lefkoplástis*

diarrhoea pills *hápia gia ti diária*

### ⊙ Notices

ΤΟΥΑΛΕΤΕΣ **toilets**

ΑΝΔΡΩΝ **gentlemen**

ΓΥΝΑΙΚΩΝ **ladies**

ΑΝΟΙΚΤΟ **open**

ΚΛΕΙΣΤΟ **closed**

ΕΙΣΟΔΟΣ **entrance**

ΕΞΟΔΟΣ **exit**

ΑΠΑΓΟΡΕΥΤΑΙ ΕΙΣΟΔΟΣ **no entry**

ΕΙΣΙΤΗΡΙΑ **tickets**

ΑΠΑΓΟΡΕΥΤΑΙ ΤΟ ΚΑΠΝΙΣΜΑ **no smoking**

ΠΛΗΡΟΦΟΡΙΕΣ **information**

ΠΡΟΣΟΧΗ **caution**

ΚΙΝΔΥΝΟΣ **danger**

ΑΡΓΑ **slow**

ΔΗΜΟΣΙΑ ΕΡΓΑ **road works**

ΠΑΡΚΙΝΓ **parking**

ΧΩΡΟΣ ΣΤΑΘΜΕΥΣΕΩΣ **car park**

ΑΠΑΓΟΡΕΥΤΑΙ Η ΣΤΑΘΜΕΥΣΗ **no parking**

ΤΑΞΙ **taxi**

ΤΡΑΠΕΖΑ **bank**

ΤΗΛΕΦΩΝΟ **telephone**

ΕΚΤΟΣ ΛΕΙΤΟΥΡΓΙΑΣ **out of order**

Books go in and out of print, or change imprints, with such rapidity of late that publishers are not listed here except for websites of obscure Greek presses. For most books, a web search with the author and title should suffice to dredge up its current incarnation (which these days may be a Kindle or print-on-demand edition only, or a used copy for a few pennies).

**FURTHER READING**

## ANCIENT HISTORY AND CULTURE

Burkert, Walter **Greek Religion: Archaic and Classical**. Excellent overview of the gods and goddesses, their attributes, worship and the meaning of major festivals.

Cartledge, Paul **Cambridge Illustrated History of Ancient Greece**. Large, illustrated volume by a distinguished contemporary classicist. Also, his **The Spartans: The World of the Warrior-Heroes of Ancient Greece** reassesses this much-maligned city-state, secretive and a source of outsider speculation even in its own time.

Finley, M.I. **The World of Odysseus**. Reissued 1954 standard on just how well (or not) the Homeric sagas are borne out by archaeological facts.

Gere, Cathy **Knossos and the Prophets of Modernism**. Puts the digs at Knossos in the cultural context of their time, documenting the reciprocal effects of contemporary art and Minoan aesthetics as reconstructed by Evans's assistants, and the "blurry boundary between restorations, reconstructions, replicas and fakes".

Grimal, Pierre, ed. **Dictionary of Classical Mythology**. Still considered tops among a handful of available alphabetical gazetteers.

Hornblower, Simon **The Greek World, 479–323 BC**. The eventful period from the end of the Persian Wars to Alexander's demise; the standard university text.

Lefkowitz, Mary **Greek Gods, Human Lives: What We Can Learn from Myths**. Rather than being frivolous, immoral or irrelevant, ancient religion and its myths, in their bleak indifference of the gods to human suffering, are rated as more "grown up" than the later creeds of salvation and comfort.

Macgillivray, J. Alexander **Minotaur: Sir Arthur Evans and the Archaeology of the Minoan Myth**. Excellent demolition job by an archaeologist, on how Evans manipulated the evidence at Knossos to fit his powerful Victorian-era prejudices.

## BYZANTINE HISTORY AND CULTURE

Norwich, John Julius **Byzantium** (3 vols): **The Early Centuries, The Apogee** and **The Decline**. The most readable and masterful popular history, by a noted Byzantinologist; also available as one massive volume, **A Short History of Byzantium**.

Rice, David Talbot **Art of the Byzantine Era**. Shows how Byzantine sacred craftsmanship extended from the Caucasus into northern Italy, in a variety of media.

Runciman, Steven **The Fall of Constantinople, 1453**. Still the definitive study of an event which continues to exercise modern Greek minds. His **Byzantine Style and Civilization** covers art, culture and monuments.

Ware, Archbishop Kallistos **The Orthodox Church**. Good introduction to what was, until recently, the *de jure* state religion of Greece.

## ANTHROPOLOGY AND CULTURE

Bent, James Theodore **Aegean Islands: The Cyclades, or Life Among the Insular Greeks**. Originally published in 1881 and reissued regularly since, this remains an authoritative source on pre-tourism island customs and folklore, based on several months' winter travel.

Clark, Bruce **Twice a Stranger: How Mass Expulsion Forged Modern Greece and Turkey**. The background to the 1923 population exchanges, and how both countries are still digesting the experience three generations later. Readable and compassionate, especially the encounters with elderly survivors of the experience.

Danforth, Loring H. and Tsiaras, Alexander **The Death Rituals of Rural Greece.** Riveting, annotated photo essay on Greek funeral customs.

Du Boulay, Juliet **Portrait of a Greek Mountain Village**. Ambéli, a mountain village in northern Évvia, as it was in the mid-1960s. A sequel, **Cosmos, Life, and Liturgy in a Greek Orthodox Village**, explores how the Church underpins the interior lives of the villagers.

Kenna, Margaret E. **Greek Island Life: Fieldwork on Anafi**. Her 1966–7 doctoral research, reflected in her notebooks and letters home, when pre-tourism culture still survived.

Kulukundis, Elias **The Feasts of Memory: Stories of a Greek Family.** A journey back through time and genealogy by a diaspora Greek two generations removed from Kásos, poorest of the Dodecanese. A 2003 re-release, with an extra chapter, of his 1967 classic **Journey to a Greek Island**.

Llewellyn Smith, Michael **The Great Island: A Study of Crete**. Before he was a known historian (and twice ambassador to Greece), a young Llewellyn Smith wrote this, with good analysis of folk traditions and in particular Cretan song.

Papalas, Anthony J **Rebels and Radicals: Icaria 1600–2000**. The lowdown on that most peculiar of mid-Aegean islands, delving into its Ottoman past, American diaspora links, unexpected Communist affiliations and recent touristic development.

Sutton, David **Memories Cast in Stone: The Relevance of the Past in Everyday Life**. 1990s ethnology of Kálymnos, where tenacious "traditional" practices such as dynamite-throwing *panigýria* and dowry-collecting confront the new, pan-EU realities.

Tomkinson, John L. **Festive Greece: A Calendar of Traditions** (Kindle Edition only). Gazetter with lots of photos, of all the most observed feast days of the Church – and the often pagan *panigýria* accompanying them.

## CUISINE AND WINE

Dalby, Andrew *Siren Feasts*. Analysis of classical and Byzantine texts shows how little Greek food has changed in three millennia.

Davidson, Alan *Mediterranean Seafood*. 1972 classic, re-issued in 2002 and 2012, that's still the standard reference, guaranteed to end every argument as to just what that fish is on your taverna plate. Complete with recipes.

Kochilas, Diane *The Food and Wine of Greece: More Than 250 Classic and Modern Dishes from the Mainland and Islands*. As it says, by the doyenne of Greek cookery writers, long resident on Ikaría. She has several other titles too.

Lazarakis, Konstantinos *The Wines of Greece*. An overview of Greece's major recognised wine-producing regions, in a revised 2018 edition.

## MODERN HISTORY

David Brewer, *Greece: the Hidden Centuries*. Greeks under Ottoman and Venetian rule, from the fall of Constantinople until the 1820s insurrection. Refreshingly revisionist work on the period, uniformly dismissed in standard (and nationalist) narratives as a new dark ages but here put in proper perspective, with many sacred cows slain along the clearly written way.

Clark, Alan *The Fall of Crete*. Breezy military history by the late, maverick English politician; good on the battles, and more critical of the command than you'd expect.

Clogg, Richard *A Concise History of Greece*. Clear, lively account of Greece from Byzantine times to 2012, with helpful maps and well-captioned artwork. The best single-volume summary; last updated in 2014.

Koliopoulos, John and Thanos Veremis *Greece, the Modern Sequel: From 1831 to the Present*. Thematic and psycho-history of the independent nation, tracing trends, first principles and setbacks.

Potts, Jim *The Ionian Islands and Epirus*. And erudite ramble through

all these islands, touching on history, popular culture and their vital relation to the mainland opposite.

Seligman, Adrian *War in the Islands*. Collected oral histories of the caique flotillas organised to raid the Axis-held Aegean islands. Detailed maps and period photos liven up the service jargon.

Woodouse, C.M. *Modern Greece: A Short History*. Spans the period from early Byzantium to the early 1980s. His *The Struggle for Greece, 1941–1949* is the best overview of that turbulent decade, and has aged well despite the brief 1990s opening of Soviet archives.

## MODERN GREEK LITERATURE

Beaton, Roderick *An Introduction to Modern Greek*. Readable survey of Greek literature since independence. *A Century of Greek Poetry, 1900–2000*. Well produced bilingual volume, with some lesser-known surprises alongside the big names.

Cavafy, C.P. *Collected Poems*, trans. by Edmund Keeley and Philip Sherrard or *The Complete Poems of Cavafy*, translated by Rae Dalven. Long reckoned the "standard" versions in English; 2007 translations by Evangelos Sachperoglou and Stratis Haviaras will also appeal but don't break radically new ground.

Elytis, Odysseas *Collected Poems*, *The Axion Esti*, *Selected Poems* and *Eros, Eros, Eros*. Pretty much the complete works of the Nobel laureate, in translation by George Savidis, Edmund Keeley and Olga Broumas.

Hatziyannidis, Vangelis *Four Walls*. Hatziyannidis's abiding obsessions – confinement, blackmail, abrupt disappearances – get an airing in his creepy debut novel, set on an unspecified east Aegean isle, where a reclusive landowner takes in a fugitive woman who convinces him to revive his father's honey trade – with unexpected consequences.

Kazantzakis, Nikos. Nobel laureate, woolly Marxist/Buddhist and voluntary exile, his books bear out the old maxim that classics are praised but unread. Whether in convoluted, untranslatable Greek or wooden English, Kazantzakis can be hard going. *Zorba the Greek* (*The Life and Culture of Alexis Zorbas*, in the original) is a surprisingly dark and nihilistic work, worlds

away from the two-dimensionality of the film; *The Last Temptation of Christ*, also filmed, provoked riots by Orthodox fanatics in 1989; *Report to Greco* explores his Cretanness; while *Christ Recrucified* (*The Greek Passion*) encompasses the Easter drama within Christian-Muslim dynamics on Crete.

Ladas, Alexis *Falconera* (Lycabettus Press, Athens, www.lycabettus.com). Ripping good yarn, with plenty of Boy's Own action (but some convincingly well-written un-Boy's Own sex), fictionalising in part of a daring raid to interfere with Germany resupply of Crete by the British-supported Greek Raiding Schooner Flotilla, in which the author served.

Markaris, Petros *The Late-Night News* (as *Deadline in Athens*, in US), *Che Committed Suicide*. The first (1995) and third (2003) volumes of the pitch-perfect Inspector Costas Haritos series, the only ones easily available in English, revealing a grittier Greece few visitors see behind the souvláki-and-syrtáki stereotypes. Hooked? There's also *Zone Defence* (2011), again starring Inspector Haritos. You'll get a truer picture of the country from these often eerily prophetic detective thrillers than from a whole shelf of history/anthropology texts or often poor foreign correspondent reports.

Myrivilis, Stratis; trans. Peter Bien. Two novels set during the 1920s on Lésvos, Myrivilis's homeland: *The Mermaid Madonna* and *The Schoolmistress with the Golden Eyes*. The cheap-and-nasty, heavily abridged paperback editions of these are worth avoiding in favour of the original 1950s full-length hardbacks, readily available online.

Papadiamantis, Alexandros; trans. Peter Levi *The Murderess*. Landmark social-realist novel, set on Skiáthos at the turn of the 19th/20th centuries.

Seferis, George; trans. Edmund Keeley *Collected Poems 1924–1955*, *Complete Poems*. The former has Greek-English texts on facing pages, preferable to the so-called "complete" works of Greece's other Nobel literary laureate.

Strani-Potts, Maria *The Cat of Portovecchio: Corfu Tales*. Specifically, the thinly disguised working-class district of Mandoúki during the decade after World War – with a cat as a unifying thread.

## FOREIGN WRITERS ON THE ISLANDS

Carroll, Michael *An Island in Greece: On the Shores of Skopelos*. That island, plus surrounding ones, through a young boat-bum's eyes in the 1960s; essentially adopted by a leading local family, he still lives there.

De Bernières, Louis *Captain Corelli's Mandolin*. Heart-rending tragicomedy set on occupied Kefalloniá during World War II which despite dubious politics has acquired cult status.

Fowles, John *The Magus*. Bestseller, inspired by Fowles's spell teaching on Spétses during the 1950s, of post-adolescent manipulation, conspiracy and cock-teasing (the usual Fowles obsessions).

Green, Peter *The Laughter of Aphrodite*. Historical novel by a distinguished classicist successfully recreates Sappho of ancient Mytilene and her milieu.

Jinkinson, Roger *Tales from a Greek Island* and *More Tales from a Greek Island*. Stories long and short set in and around Diafáni, Kárpathos, where Jinkinson lives much of the year. Poignant, blackly funny, even revisionist about World War II heroics.

Manus, Willard *This Way to Paradise: Dancing on the Tables* (www.lycabettus.com). American expatriate's affectionate summing-up of 35-plus years living in Líndos, from its innocence to its corruption. Wonderful anecdotes of the hippie days, and walk-on parts for the famous and infamous.

Miller, Henry *The Colossus of Maroussi*. Miller takes to Corfu, the Argolid, Athens and Crete of 1939 with the enthusiasm of a first-timer in Greece; deserted archaeological sites and larger-than-life personalities.

Stone, Tom *The Summer of My Greek Taverna*. Set in a thinly disguised Kámbos of early-1980s Pátmos, this is a poignant cautionary tale for all who've ever fantasised about leasing a taverna (or buying a property) in the islands.

Travis, William *Bus Stop Symi*. Chronicles three years' residence there in the pre-tourism 1960s; fairly insightful, though resented on the island for its artistic licence.

Unsworth, Barry *Pascali's Island*. Late-Ottoman Rhodes seen through the eyes of Basil Pascali, hapless spy and fixer.

Waller, John *Greek Walls, An Odyssey in Corfu* and *Corfu Sunset, Avrio Never Comes*. Good-natured, optimistic expats-build-and-then-renovate-a-house sagas stretching over five decades, from undiscovered island of 1966 to the new century. His more recent *Walking the Corfu Trail: With Friends, Flowers and Food* is exactly that.

Wheeler, Sarah *Evvia: Travels on an Undiscovered Island*. A five-month ramble through Évvia in the early 1990s, juxtaposing historical/cultural musings with adventures on the ground.

## ARCHAEOLOGICAL AND HIKING GUIDES

Burn, A. R. and Mary *The Living Past of Greece*. Worth toting around for the sake of lively text and clear plans; covers most major sites from Minoan to medieval.

Hetherington, Paul *The Greek Islands: Guide to the Byzantine and Medieval Buildings and Their Art*. As it says, though there are some astonishing omissions of stellar monuments like Rhodes's painted churches in favour of the obscure.

Wilson, Loraine *High Mountains of Crete*. Almost 100 walks and treks, mostly in the White Mountains but also mounts Psilorítis and Díkti, described by the most experienced foreign guide.

## BOTANICAL FIELD GUIDES

Baumann, Helmut *Greek Wildflowers and Plant Lore in Ancient Greece*. As the title says; lots of interesting ethnobotanical trivia, useful photos.

Fielding, John and Nicholas Turland *Flowers of Crete* Massive, expensive volume with 1,900 colour plates of the Cretan flora, much of which is found on neighbouring islands.

Huxley, Anthony, and William Taylor *Flowers of Greece and the Aegean*. The only volume dedicated to both islands and mainland, with good photos, though taxonomy is now a bit obsolete.

### ☉ Send Us Your Thoughts

We do our best to ensure the information in our books is as accurate and up-to-date as possible. The books are updated on a regular basis using local contacts, who painstakingly add, amend and correct as required. However, some details (such as telephone numbers and opening times) are liable to change, and we are ultimately reliant on our readers to put us in the picture.

We welcome your feedback, especially your experience of using the book "on the road". Maybe you came across a great bar or new attraction we missed.

We will acknowledge all contributions, and we'll offer an Insight Guide to the best letters received.

Please write to us at:
**Insight Guides**
**PO Box 7910**
**London SE1 1WE**

Or email us at:
**hello@insightguides.com**

# CREDITS

## PHOTO CREDITS

## COVER CREDITS

## INSIGHT GUIDE CREDITS

**Distribution**
**UK, Ireland and Europe**
Apa Publications (UK) Ltd;
sales@insightguides.com
**United States and Canada**
Ingram Publisher Services;
ips@ingramcontent.com
**Australia and New Zealand**
Woodslane; info@woodslane.com.au
**Southeast Asia**
Apa Publications (SN) Pte;
singaporeoffice@insightguides.com
**Worldwide**
Apa Publications (UK) Ltd;
sales@insightguides.com
**Special Sales, Content Licensing and CoPublishing**
Insight Guides can be purchased in bulk quantities at discounted prices. We can create special editions, personalised jackets and corporate imprints tailored to your needs. sales@insightguides.com
www.insightguides.biz

**Printed in China by CTPS**

**Editor:** Helen Fanthorpe
**Author:** Marc Dubin
**Head of Production:** Rebeka Davies
**Update Production:** Apa Digital
**Picture Editor:** Tom Smyth
**Cartography:** original cartography Berndtson & Berndtson, updated by Carte

First Edition 1990
Sixth Edition 2018

### CONTRIBUTORS

This new edition of *Insight Guide: The Greek Islands* was commissioned and copyedited by **Helen Fanthorpe**. It has been thoroughly updated by **Marc Dubin** – a well-travelled resident of Sámos and London.

### ABOUT INSIGHT GUIDES

**Insight Guides** have more than 45 years' experience of publishing high-quality, visual travel guides. We produce 400 full-colour titles, in both print and digital form, covering more than 200 destinations across the globe, in a variety of formats to meet your different needs.

**Insight Guides** are written by local authors, whose expertise is evident in the extensive historical and cultural background features. Each destination is carefully researched by regional experts to ensure our guides provide the very latest information. All the reviews in **Insight Guides** are independent; we strive to maintain an impartial view. Our reviews are carefully selected to guide you to the best places to eat, go out and shop, so you can be confident that when we say a place is special, we really mean it.

**Legend**

**City maps**

| | |
|---|---|
| | Freeway/Highway/Motorway |
| | Divided Highway |
| | Main Roads |
| | Minor Roads |
| | Pedestrian Roads |
| | Steps |
| | Footpath |
| | Railway |
| | Funicular Railway |
| | Cable Car |
| | Tunnel |
| | City Wall |
| | Important Building |
| | Built Up Area |
| | Other Land |
| | Transport Hub |
| | Park |
| | Pedestrian Area |
| | Bus Station |
| | Tourist Information |
| | Main Post Office |
| | Cathedral/Church |
| | Mosque |
| | Synagogue |
| | Statue/Monument |
| | Beach |
| | Airport |

**Regional maps**

| | |
|---|---|
| | Freeway/Highway/Motorway (with junction) |
| | Freeway/Highway/Motorway (under construction) |
| | Divided Highway |
| | Main Road |
| | Secondary Road |
| | Minor Road |
| | Track |
| | Footpath |
| | International Boundary |
| | State/Province Boundary |
| | National Park/Reserve |
| | Marine Park |
| | Ferry Route |
| | Marshland/Swamp |
| | Glacier        Salt Lake |
| | Airport/Airfield |
| | Ancient Site |
| | Border Control |
| | Cable Car |
| | Castle/Castle Ruins |
| | Cave |
| | Chateau/Stately Home |
| | Church/Church Ruins |
| | Crater |
| | Lighthouse |
| | Mountain Peak |
| | Place of Interest |
| | Viewpoint |

# INDEX

# INSIGHT ⊙ GUIDES

# OFF THE SHELF

Since 1970, **INSIGHT GUIDES** has provided a unique perspective on the world's best travel destinations by using specially commissioned photography and illuminating text written by local authors.

Whether you're planning a city break, a walking tour or the journey of a lifetime, our superb range of guidebooks and phrasebooks will inspire you to discover more about your chosen destination.

## INSIGHT GUIDES

offer a unique combination of stunning photos, absorbing narrative and detailed maps, providing all the inspiration and information you need.

## PHRASEBOOKS & DICTIONARIES

help users to feel at home, when away. Pocket-sized with a free app to download, they go where you do.

## CITY GUIDES

pack hundreds of great photos into a smaller format with detailed practical information, so you can navigate the world's top cities with confidence.

## EXPLORE GUIDES

feature easy-to-follow walks and itineraries in the world's most exciting destinations, with our choice of the best places to eat and drink along the way.

## POCKET GUIDES

combine concise information on where to go and what to do in a handy compact format, ideal on the ground. Includes a full-colour, fold-out map.

## EXPERIENCE GUIDES

feature offbeat perspectives and secret gems for experienced travellers, with a collection of over 100 ideas for a memorable stay in a city.

## www.insightguides.com

# The Greek Islands:
## main ferry routes

0        50 km

0        50 miles